Mike Dash read history at the University of Cambridge. He is the author of five previous books, including *Thug* – also published by Granta Books – and the bestsellers *Tulipomania* and *Batavia's Graveyard*. He lives in London with his wife and daughter. For further information and exclusive new material, see www.mikedash.com

'[An] engaging and meticulously researched true-crime story' *Guardian*

'*Satan's Circus* allows you to enter a long-gone world which shows that today's perceived disintegration of society's values and its moral fibre actually began decades ago . . . a fascinating tale and one that would lend itself superbly to the cinema screen' *Scotland on Sunday*

'If the story that Mike Dash tells in *Satan's Circus* sometimes seems like a chapter from *Gangs of New York*, that's because it is . . . This is a true-crime thriller – it gives you a murder . . . a probably wrongful execution, a large cast of gamblers, gangsters, crooked cops and often crookeder lawyers, politicians and journalists – but it is also a portrait of the end of an era' *Daily Telegraph*

'This is the story of the only cop to have been executed for murder – and it's a real toe curler . . . It's a fascinating tale into which Dash weaves many disparate elements . . . an exciting combination of political and social history as well as a salutary moral tale of the evils of greed and corruption' *Tribune*

'*Satan's Circus* is a thrilling, atmospheric story peopled with outlandish characters, but it also conveys a profound understanding of how New York's criminals, policemen and politicians conspired on a systematic basis' *Sunday Express*

SATAN'S CIRCUS

Murder, Vice, Police Corruption and
New York's Trial of the Century

MIKE DASH

GRANTA

Granta Publications, 12 Addison Avenue, London W11 4QR

First published in Great Britain by Granta Books, 2008
This paperback edition published 2009

A CIP catalogue record for this book is
available from the British Library.

1 3 5 7 9 10 8 6 4 2

ISBN 978-1-84708-064-6

Printed and bound in Great Britain by
CPI Bookmarque, Croydon

CONTENTS

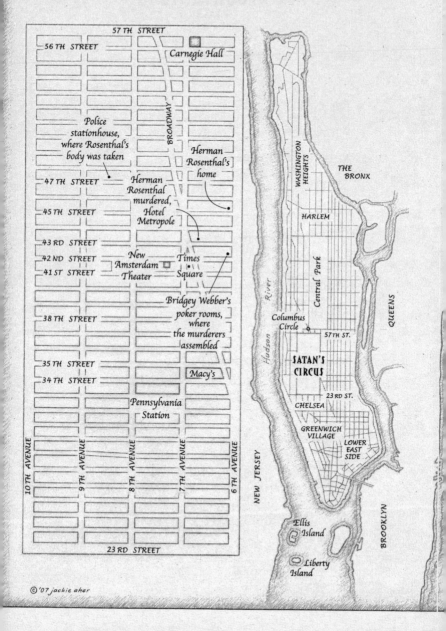

SATAN'S CIRCUS in New York City, 1890-1912

57 TH STREET

56 TH STREET

Carnegie Hall

BROADWAY

Police
stationhouse,
where Rosenthal's
body was taken

Herman
Rosenthal's
home

47 TH STREET

Herman
Rosenthal
murdered,
Hotel
Metropole

45 TH STREET

43 RD STREET

42 ND STREET

New
Amsterdam
Theater

Times
Square

41 ST STREET

Bridgey Webber's
poker rooms,
where
the murderers
assembled

38 TH STREET

35 TH STREET

34 TH STREET

Macy's

Pennsylvania
Station

10 TH AVENUE

9 TH AVENUE

8 TH AVENUE

7 TH AVENUE

6 TH AVENUE

23 RD STREET

© '07 jackie aher

NEW JERSEY

Hudson River

WASHINGTON HEIGHTS

THE BRONX

HARLEM

Central Park

Columbus
Circle

57 TH ST.

SATAN'S
CIRCUS

23 RD ST.

CHELSEA

GREENWICH
VILLAGE

LOWER
EAST
SIDE

QUEENS

Ellis
Island

Liberty
Island

BROOKLYN

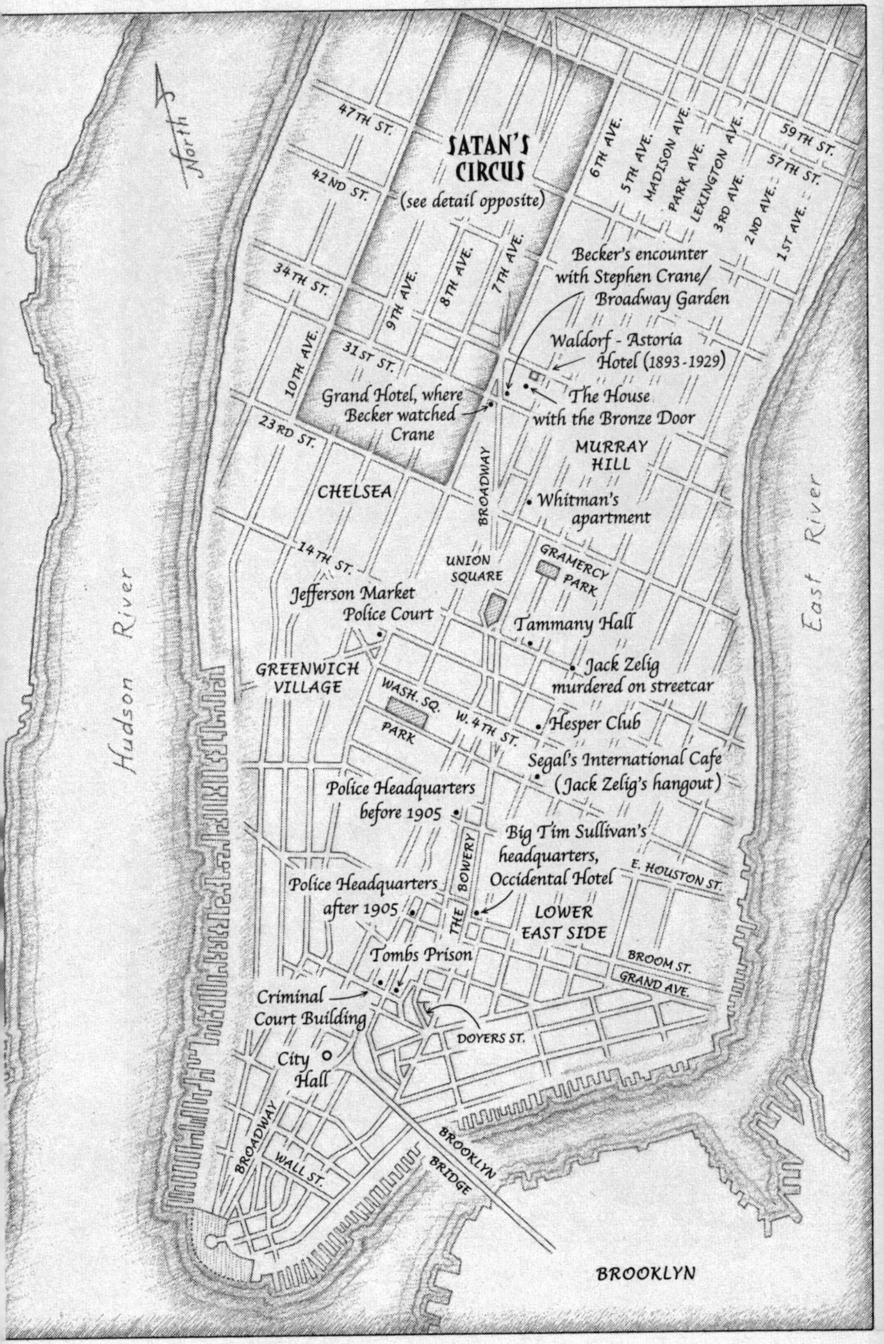

North
47TH ST.
42ND ST.
34TH ST.
31ST ST.
23RD ST.
14TH ST.
59TH ST.
57TH ST.
SATAN'S CIRCUS
(see detail opposite)
6TH AVE.
5TH AVE.
MADISON AVE.
PARK AVE.
LEXINGTON AVE.
3RD AVE.
2ND AVE.
1ST AVE.
10TH AVE.
9TH AVE.
8TH AVE.
7TH AVE.
Becker's encounter with Stephen Crane/ Broadway Garden
Waldorf - Astoria Hotel (1893-1929)
Grand Hotel, where Becker watched Crane
The House with the Bronze Door
MURRAY HILL
BROADWAY
CHELSEA
Whitman's apartment
Hudson River
East River
UNION SQUARE
GRAMERCY PARK
Jefferson Market Police Court
Tammany Hall
GREENWICH VILLAGE
Jack Zelig murdered on streetcar
WASH. SQ. PARK
W. 4TH ST.
Hesper Club
Segal's International Cafe (Jack Zelig's hangout)
Police Headquarters before 1905
Big Tim Sullivan's headquarters, Occidental Hotel
THE BOWERY
E. HOUSTON ST.
Police Headquarters after 1905
LOWER EAST SIDE
Tombs Prison
BROOM ST.
GRAND AVE.
Criminal Court Building
DOYERS ST.
City Hall
BROADWAY
WALL ST.
BROOKLYN BRIDGE
BROOKLYN

Herman Rosenthal

Charles Becker

Charles and Helen Becker

Big Tim Sullivan

Charles Whitman *(Library of Congress)*

Jack Rose *(Library of Congress)*

Jack Zelig

John Goff *(Library of Congress)*

PREFACE

NEARLY 5 MILLION men and women have served the United States as police officers.

Only one has been executed for murder.

This is the story of Charles Becker—a New York police lieutenant widely reviled in the first decades of the last century as "the crookedest cop who ever stood behind a shield"—and of the raucous, gaudy city that made him. It is also the story of the precinct that Becker's career so frequently returned him to: Satan's Circus, in midtown Manhattan, then both New York's entertainment district and the heart of its vice trade.

The cast of characters is extraordinary. Aside from Becker himself—who was able, brave, intelligent, and yet utterly corrupt—the book tells of "Big Tim" Sullivan, an election-rigging vice lord who stole hundreds of thousands of dollars from ordinary New Yorkers, yet was borne to his funeral through a crowd of more than 20,000 weeping citizens; of Jack Zelig, the beloved gangster; and of John Goff, a onetime terrorist turned sadistic hanging judge. Elsewhere in its pages you will meet "Gyp the Blood," a back-snapping thug and uselessly incompetent murderer; the sinister "Bald Jack" Rose, his entirely hairless procurer; and Bill Devery, the hulking, shrewd police chief who ran his city as one vast racket and used the money he extorted from Manhattan's brothels to found the New York Yankees.

Since even a novelist would hesitate to invent such characters, I want to make it clear that nothing of what follows is fiction. *Satan's Circus* is closely based on contemporary sources—legal documents, newspapers, and an archive of detailed reports filed by the most prolific private detective of the day—which make it possible to reconstruct the events of a century ago in remarkable detail. Nor are any of the conversations I have included in the book invented; each one was either recalled, word for word, by one of the participants or noted down by a reporter. In the handful of places where I have speculated on the thoughts and motives of individuals, I have acknowledged that fact in the text or in the notes.

Mike Dash
London
April 2, 2006

"I've been living on chuck steak for a long time. Now I'm going to get me a little of the tenderloin."

CAPTAIN ALEXANDER "CLUBBER" WILLIAMS
CELEBRATES HIS APPOINTMENT TO POLICE NEW YORK'S THEATER,
GAMBLING, AND PROSTITUTION DISTRICT—
"THE RICHEST GRAFTING TERRITORY IN THE CITY"

CHAPTER 1

WIDE-OPEN

BROADWAY GARDEN WAS DEBAUCHED. To think of the place as just another New York saloon was perverse; the Garden bore about as much resemblance to one of the sagging, smoke-stained taverns squatting on street corners downtown as a diamond did to a paste bauble. Combining the attractions of a bar, restaurant, dance hall, and vaudeville show, it was bigger and busier than half a dozen low dives rolled into one.

The Garden owed much of its popularity to its superb location. It stood near the corner of Broadway and West Thirty-first Street, in the heart of New York's entertainment district, and Broadway itself—the busiest, most brightly lit thoroughfare in the world—swept a living tide of likely customers past its doors at all hours of the day and night. Even some time after midnight on a Tuesday morning, one of the quietest evenings of the week, the Garden was all jostle and hubbub, loud music and light: the sort of place that filled readily with fashionable drunks, young couples flirting their way through clandestine assignations, and single men with darting eyes who called in when the theaters closed in the hope of making the acquaintance of a chorus girl.

On this particular evening—it was some way past midnight on September 16, 1896—a young man, rather smartly dressed in a jacket, waistcoat, and straw hat, was dawdling at a table in the Garden's restaurant. He was in his middle twenties and not especially attractive: pale and thin, of average height, and sporting a poorly nourished mustache that quite failed to impose itself on a face dominated by a large nose and larger teeth. His long, tawny hair had been greased, parted in

1

the middle and then plastered down across his forehead. Occasionally, as he leaned forward, a few strands would break free and dangle limply across one eye until they were pressed back into place.

Sharing the young man's table, and sitting directly opposite him, were two much better-looking women. These girls were even younger than their host, perhaps eighteen or twenty years old, and they were fashionably clad in thick, embroidered silk, their waists tightly nipped with stays and their neatly made-up faces half hidden beneath elaborate hats. They called themselves actresses, but they were really nothing more than dancing girls, high kickers from a nearby show. They had drunk enough over the last few hours to feel pleasantly relaxed, and now they chattered happily, giggling as they told tales of their experiences. Their companion, listening attentively, scrawled notes down on a paper pad.

Skulking unobtrusively some twenty yards away, a second man observed this scene with interest. He was a good deal taller and much stronger than the first, but less extravagantly dressed. He was doing his best to remain inconspicuous. His vantage point, the lobby of Broadway's Grand Hotel, was well suited to this purpose; it was crowded and less well lit than the street outside, and by pressing himself flat against a wall the man could keep a close eye on the Garden with little chance of being seen himself. He had done this sort of thing often enough to learn patience, and after a while he was grimly pleased to note that a third young woman had walked up to the table in the restaurant. The newcomer was even more striking than the chorus girls: exceptionally beautiful, her pretty, mobile face framed by a mass of startling dark red curls. She was wearing a simple shirtwaist—a fitted blouse with mannish collar and cuffs—that neatly displayed her figure, and she slid into the seat beside the man with greasy hair. He greeted her enthusiastically.

Now the watcher knew that he was right. He pulled out a pocket-watch and checked the time. It was approaching 2:00 A.M.

The watching man did not have long to wait. The little group around the table broke up only a few minutes later, when one of the dancers rose to leave and the young man in the straw hat offered to escort her to a streetcar stop about a hundred yards away. The other two girls loitered on the nearest corner, waiting for him. When their companion returned, he seemed lost in thought, head down, eyes fixed on the sidewalk, and only half aware of a pair of late-night revelers lurching down the road ahead of him. These men reeled up to the redhead and the chorus girl and passed them rather close; perhaps a few words were exchanged.

At once a loud commotion snapped the young man from his reverie. The tall figure of the watcher from the Grand Hotel had materialized behind the girls and seized both by their wrists, his fingers gripping them so fiercely that they had no hope of escape. They screamed out in surprise and fear, twisting desperately to see who had accosted them, but their captor would not release his hold. After a few seconds of struggle, the redhead's imprisoned arm went limp, her shoulders slumped, and she burst into tears—"the wildest and most hysterical sobbing," her male companion thought, that he had ever heard.

The girl's captor stared down at her, and his wide mouth cracked into a grin. He relaxed his grip but kept hold of her wrist. To the young man who had sat with her in the Garden—hurrying now toward her over the road—he seemed "picturesque as a wolf," his face a study in triumph.

The wolf fixed both girls with his gaze. "Come to the station house," he said. "You are under arrest for soliciting two men."

His name was Charley Becker, and he was a New York City cop.

Becker was not much older than the women he was arresting—he had only just turned twenty-six—and was an unusual policeman. Most Manhattan patrolmen of the day were stocky, street-smart Irishmen in their thirties or early forties: brave when called upon, perhaps, but swaggering, casually brutal, and all too frequently corrupt. Men of this sort, with ten or more years' service on the streets, were princes of the city. Left to patrol their beats largely unsupervised, they became intimately familiar with the local tavern keepers, street vendors, and crooks, and few were above pocketing a dollar here and there for over-looking harmless violations, nor accepting a pint of beer and a free meal from saloons that remained open after closing time. Becker, in contrast, came from a German family, which made him "Dutch" in the police parlance of the day and an exotic rarity in a force still then more than two-thirds Irish. Standing six feet two inches in his socks, he towered over most of his contemporaries. In a department all too often officered by men of few brains and less imagination, he was also markedly intelligent.

Charley Becker's ancestry, cleverness, and height all set him apart from other New York policemen. But it was his inexperience that most clearly marked out the young patrolman within the precinct. With fewer than three years' service to his name, Becker was scarcely more than a rookie: a policeman who retained some of the traits of a civilian and had yet to master all the finer details of his job. Still, months pounding a beat on the streets of Manhattan, weeks of after-hours plainclothes duty in New York's Nineteenth Precinct, and long nights swapping stories with colleagues in the nearby station house had begun to teach harsh truths about the city. Now Becker's police career had reached a fork familiar to every officer. He could try to be an honest and upstanding cop, stick strictly to the rules, and stay untainted by corruption. Or—more likely and far easier—he could yield to the temptations of the entertainment district.

Already Becker's views were being colored by experience. Respectable women, he had learned, did not wander through the theater district after midnight. Men who paid for the company of girls in fancy bars such as Broadway Garden wanted something in return. And beauties like the little redhead in his grasp did not consort with plainer, older men for the mere pleasure of their company. "Any woman," he believed, "who talks to a man late at night on the street is a prostitute."

Elsewhere in the United States—indeed elsewhere in New York—Becker's comment might have seemed outrageous. But not in midtown Manhattan. The grid of streets of which the Garden was a part had long been notorious throughout the city, and at midnight, by the cold glare of a thousand arc lights, the sidewalks swarmed with touts hawking the services the neighborhood was famous for: late-night drinking, gambling, and sex. It was a simple matter, in the early-morning hours, to find a gaming "hell" offering high-stakes card games, to drink oneself into a stupor in one of the hundreds of blind tigers (as unlicensed drinking dens were known), or to visit a brothel that sold girls as young as twelve for a dollar a time. Shocked clergy-men called the place "Satan's Circus," and denounced it from their pulpits. For everyone else it was the Tenderloin: the most glamorous, notorious square mile on earth.*

Officer Becker had grown in confidence working undercover in Manhattan. In his time on the force, he had learned how to keep his bosses sweet, how to control the local toughs without bothering his desk sergeant too much (lavish use of the nightstick was prescribed for this), and, above all, the importance of maintaining a steady stream of arrests. Promotion came more readily to men whose records demon-strated energy, and—in Satan's Circus after dark—there were many opportunities to bulge the file. Prostitutes, in particular (as the police-man well knew), were easy prey. They invariably give themselves away "by some indescribable wearing of the sealskin saque or the jaunty hat"; better yet, their clients rarely wanted trouble, and the girls mostly thought of an arrest as a hazard of the job. In the course of his midnight patrols on Broadway, Becker had skulked and watched

---

*Satan's Circus housed a greater concentration of prostitutes than any equivalent area in the country: A dozen brothels clustered along West Thirty-first Street alone, and as many as 5,000 girls plied their trade within the narrow confines of the district as a whole. Various streets developed specialties of their own. The French Madame's, and other dance halls on Sixth Avenue, offered the cancan and (in private booths) explicit sexual exhibitions called circuses. "Soubrette Row," as West Thirty-ninth was known, was famed for prostitutes who "resort to unnatural practices [fellatio], and as a result the other girls will not associate or eat with them." Meanwhile, up on West Fortieth Street, some of Manhattan's more ambitious streetwalkers brazenly sought customers among the worshippers who attended the Reverend Adam Clayton Powell's church, prompting the outraged preacher to complain that "harlots would stand across the streets on Sun-day evenings in unbuttoned dresses, soliciting men as they left our service."

plenty of ordinary-looking men pick up pretty part-time prostitutes in the Garden. Now, with not one but two girls in his grasp, he was relishing the prospect of an easy arrest.

The redhead and the chorus girl were proving awkward, it was true. Both women bitterly proclaimed their innocence, denied soliciting, and insisted they had said nothing to the passing revelers. To make matters worse, their male companion had not made himself scarce, as the policeman had probably expected. Instead here he was, hurrying over to insist that he, too, had witnessed nothing of the sort. A few months or years before, a younger Becker might well have believed them. Now, though, he had become implacable. He was about to march his prisoners off when the imprisoned chorus girl turned and, in sheer desperation, gestured to her new acquaintance. "Well, he's my husband!" she cried out.

Thrown for a second by the dancer's lie, Patrolman Becker turned toward the lank-haired man. The girl's claim seemed obviously preposterous, but he dared not simply dismiss it. It was dangerously unheard of for an ordinary patrolman to detain a married lady and her husband. Any mistake could be embarrassing and costly.

In the barely perceptible pause that followed, the man from the Garden made up his mind to lie. "Yes," he stated firmly. "I am."

Probably the policeman doubted him. But he had experience enough to know that there was nothing to be gained by arguing with a gentleman. He dropped the chorus girl's arm, releasing her. "Still," he added, "I have got this other one."

"Why arrest her either?" the young man demanded.

By now Becker had had enough. "Say," he snarled back, turning, "do you know this woman?"

There was such an unmistakable hint of menace in the policeman's voice that the girls' companion felt it wisest not to lie again. "I know nothing at all about her," he confessed. Becker flashed him a tight smile. "Well," he said, "she is a common prostitute, and I am arresting her for soliciting those two men. If you people don't want to get pinched, too, you had better not be seen with her."

And, tightening his grip around the redhead's wrist, the policeman turned smartly away and marched off toward the station house.

They formed a peculiar crocodile: Becker in the lead, dragging his prisoner behind him, and trailed at a distance of a yard or two by the agitated chorus girl and her by-now-cowed companion.

The Nineteenth Precinct building was only a block away, and Becker hurried up the steps to the front door, pushing the girl in before him. He propelled his prisoner to a high writing desk positioned just inside the entrance and presented her to the policeman sitting there, Desk Sergeant McDermott.

There can be no doubt that both officers recognized the girl. Her name was Ruby Young, though within the borders of Satan's Circus she was generally known by her more glamorous alias, Dora Clark. Young was an interesting case, at twenty far more attractive than the ordinary run of prostitutes, and better-spoken, too—a girl, one contemporary observed, who seemed "obviously above the level of her kind." This, together with her pretty face and figure, enabled her to snare clients of the highest class. She had recently enjoyed assignations with a wealthy businessman living at the Waldorf-Astoria hotel, perhaps the grandest such establishment in the city.

All this suggests that Young was still new to her trade and had not yet embarked upon the inevitable drift of fresh-faced novice prostitutes, who began their careers on the streets near Broadway and ended them, a few years later, on the waterfront. Still, for all her looks, Ruby had yet to find herself a rich patron or secure the comfortable arrangement with a rich man that might have taken her off the streets. She had been detained for soliciting in Satan's Circus three times within the last four weeks and was now well known at the station house. McDermott took one look at her and gestured with a thumb. "Take her back," he said, and the girl was escorted to the cells.

Young's friend, the high-kicking actress, had trailed her to the precinct house in the hope of interceding on her behalf. But the sergeant's short, brutal dismissal of the redhead left her incapable of further protest. It remained to the lank-haired man in the straw hat to ask McDermott if he could at least send a few things down to Young to help make her more comfortable. The man also gave the desk sergeant a statement of the night's events, seen from his own perspective. He appeared angry and defiant and might, he added, even make a statement in the girl's defense when she was brought before the city magistrate.

McDermott looked down thoughtfully from his high stool. "Well," the sergeant said, "that may all be true. I don't defend the officer. I do not say that he was right or that he was wrong. But I give you the plain advice of a man who has been behind this desk for years and knows how these things go, and I advise you simply to stay at home. If you monkey with this case, you are pretty sure to come out with mud all over your face."

The would-be witness mulled this over. "I suppose so," he replied. "I haven't a doubt of it. But I don't see how I can, in honesty, stay away from court in the morning."

"Well," McDermott snapped in some impatience, "do it anyhow." But what he was thinking was, "I have seen you somewhere before. I know you vaguely. *I recognize your face.*"

In fact, most educated people in New York had seen the young man's face. He was newly famous, the author of a book that everyone who cared for literary fashion had devoured, lionized in the way that only the very latest writers can be, and certainly so well known that what seemed at first a small affair threatened to turn into a scandal. Charles Becker, who did not list reading among his pleasures, was one of the few people in Satan's Circus who would not have recognized the distinctive features of his adversary and at least paused to consider whether it was worth the risk of tangling with him.

The man's name was Stephen Crane, and he was widely acclaimed as one of the finest writers in America. "Bohemian in the best sense," according to the *New York Journal*, and by some way the most celebrated of Manhattan's literary men-about-town, Crane—in the New York of 1896—possessed renown equal to that enjoyed by any politician or famous sportsman. The author, still only twenty-four, had been welcomed into the grandest mansions on Fifth Avenue and become acquainted with many of the city's leading public servants, among them the commissioners of police. His doings were followed with interest in the daily papers. Should he choose to appear before the New York magistrates, testifying on behalf of a mere streetwalker, it would cause an undoubted sensation.

It was not, in fact, unusual for Crane to be found slumming in Satan's Circus. True, his shining reputation rested on his Civil War novel *The Red Badge of Courage*, a frank account of the fear experienced by a soldier during his first taste of battle, which had enjoyed a stunning and complete success when it appeared in 1895. But Crane's real interests lay elsewhere. His first book had been a sympathetic portrait of a New York prostitute, so bold and avant-garde that it had failed to find a publisher. His next was an equally unsparing analysis of alcoholism. His newspaper articles—the tremendous acclaim accorded to *The Red Badge* ensured that editors were keen to hire him—concerned themselves chiefly with the lives of New York's most impoverished citizens, and as if that were not enough to shock the more genteel of his admirers, the fashionable young writer chose to live not in a well-heeled part of town but on a disreputable stretch of Sixth Avenue, where the poor were not simply a hobby; they were his neighbors. Crane's fascination with the lives of bums, drug addicts, and prostitutes set him apart from almost all of his contemporaries, and though his articles sold papers, even the editors who commissioned him privately thought his pieces "queer." Before long, the writer was dressing as a tramp to write an account of life in a downtown flophouse, and lining up half the night with beggars in a blizzard for a handout of food.

Crane's most recent foray into Satan's Circus had been his most controversial yet. Returning from a trip out west, the novelist had turned in a highly informative article on New York's numerous opium dens, going so far as to smoke the drug himself in order to inform his readers of its principal effects. His employer, William Randolph Hearst's *New York Journal*, was sufficiently encouraged by the ensuing furor to commission yet another selection of pieces. This time (the newspaper proudly announced) Crane's canvas would be broader: nothing less than "a series on life in New York." But the author was not ready to abandon his old stomping grounds just yet. "He chose," the *Journal* added in trumpeting the serial, "the police courts as his first subject."

It was for this reason that Stephen Crane had begun the morning of September 14, 1896, at one of Manhattan's busiest courts and spent the day examining the array of petty criminals and prostitutes, picked up by the police in the course of the previous evening, who were hauled one after another before an unsmiling magistrate. He was a talented observer, and the sheer mechanics of the process obsessed him—not least, he wrote, "the kaleidoscopic view of the characters who passed rapidly before the judicial gaze." But there was still much Crane felt he did not understand. He needed to see how the men and women who had come before the bench lived their lives away from the court. It was vital, he concluded, to "study these victims of injustice in their own haunts."

That decision explained Crane's appearance at Broadway Garden the next evening, his choice of dinner companions, and the enthusiasm with which he had made the acquaintance of Ruby Young. It also explained the writer's perverse willingness to offer testimony on Young's behalf the next day. A starring role before the magistrates, even as a witness, would certainly add interest to a newspaper account. But even the impetuous Crane had to acknowledge that there was a good deal of truth in what Sergeant McDermott had told him. Associating with a prostitute was scandalous in any circumstance. Appearing in court to defend one could scarcely fail to stain his reputation.

In his published account of events at Broadway Garden, certainly, Crane was careful to attribute only the noblest of motives to himself. He was, he implied, so chivalrous that Young's profession was a mere irrelevance; the simple fact that a woman had been badly treated by a bullying policeman overrode consideration of her station. These protestations of nobility won over most of his admirers and were, inevitably, broadcast by the *Journal*, which stood squarely behind its man. But—as Sergeant McDermott had predicted—the youthful novelist's true role in the Ruby Young affair struck other men as questionable. Staider newspapers than Hearst's found Crane's willingness to consort with prostitutes discreditable, no matter what his reasons, and several concluded that the writer's motives were not as pure as he implied. Crane, the *Boston Traveler* went so far as to observe, had probably entered the entertainment district "on a genuine 'lark' and, when his companion was apprehended, invented the tale about searching for book material. That is the way it looks to a cold and unprejudiced world." There were others who openly suspected that, far from being a victim of an overzealous cop, Crane had engineered the whole affair in order to provide himself with dramatic copy for an article and—not incidentally—the means with which to criticize a police force he believed to be oppressive and whose men he mistrusted and despised. In this interpretation Patrolman Becker, and not Ruby Young, was the true victim of entrapment.

"The policeman flatly lied," Crane protested in the *Journal*. But even among the writer's friends there were many who thought that he should never have become involved in such a grubby fracas. "Go home," a fellow reporter advised him as he left the Nineteenth Precinct building. "Your own participation in the affair doesn't look very respectable. Go home."

Ruby Young was arraigned the next day.

Jefferson Market Police Court, where Becker's prisoner was brought shortly before noon, was a scowling Gothic monstrosity that loomed over a corner on Tenth Street and Sixth Avenue, its ornate redbrick facade making it look more like a place of worship than a court of law. "The windows," Crane wrote in his own description of the place,

were high and saintly, of the shape that is found in churches. From time to time a policeman at the door spoke sharply to some incoming person. "Take your hat off!" He displayed in his voice the horror of a priest when the sanctity of the chapel is defied or forgotten.

The Market's magistrates processed an endless parade of drunks, streetwalkers, delinquent saloonkeepers, and petty thieves with mechanical efficiency, devoting just a few minutes to each case. Most of the infractions they dealt with were minor and were punished with small fines. The more persistent offenders might receive sentences of a few days in the cells.

By the time Young was called to the bar, the courthouse was crowded, as it was every day, with a throng of clerks, policemen, witnesses, and gawking spectators, many of whom had turned attendance at the Market into a sort of hobby. The latter were, Crane had once noted with a frisson of disgust, mere parasites who wore "an air of being in wait for a cry of anguish, some loud painful protestation that would bring the proper thrill to their jaded, world-weary nerves." When, at the end of an earlier hearing, a young servant girl was sent to jail for theft and let out a howl of anguish, "the loungers, many of them, underwent a spasmodic movement as if they had been knived."

In ordinary circumstances Young's hearing would soon have been over. Women picked up for soliciting in Satan's Circus had almost no chance of mounting a defense, and the word of a policeman was always preferred to theirs. Still, Ruby had done what she could with her appearance. Despite her long night in the cells, the auburn hair that made her so recognizable had been pinned up and artfully arranged, and although she had slept in the clothes she had worn the previous night, one of the reporters in the courthouse wrote that she "certainly did not look dissipated and was very neatly and prettily dressed." The girl sobbed violently, and not entirely for effect, as she was led forward, and stood before Magistrate Robert C. Cornell "flushed and downcast" while a charge of soliciting was read against her.

Becker gave his evidence first. Clad now in his patrolman's uniform, with its thick blue jacket and large shiny buttons fastened up to the neck, he seemed a much more imposing figure than he had in plainclothes hours earlier. He was strongly built, with a bulky body that was mostly muscle, large hands, broad shoulders, and an impressive chest. A billy club and a service-issue Colt revolver protruded from his belt, and he carried his tall white helmet tucked under one arm.

As he came striding into court, Becker looked like a policeman, too. He had a broad, regular face, with brown eyes set a little wide, and was, one reporter noted, "dark in hair and skin. His nose is big and straight, jutting out uncompromisingly over a long upper lip, a mouth like the cut of a knife, and a chin that sticks out squarely at the end of a jaw that looks like a granite block." The whole effect was set off by a thick, bristling mustache of the sort then favored by members of the force. Becker kept his neatly trimmed, so that it did not droop down around the corners of his mouth as the mustaches worn by older officers generally did, and his hair was short and closely cropped. His military bearing and impressive looks struck many of the spectators in the court, and though his speech and manner were evidently less assured—"he talks like a man who might have had an education in the public school," another reporter sneered—he delivered his statement in a clipped and practiced tone that brooked little argument.

"What have you got to say to this charge, young woman?" Cornell asked the girl when he was done.

Ruby had listened to Becker's account with slowly mounting anger. Now she attempted to defend herself. "The charge is false," she wailed through squalls of tears. The girl denied emphatically that she had talked to any man outside Broadway Garden; Becker, she swore, could not possibly have seen anything inappropriate. The patrolman had invented the charge because he had a grudge against her.

Allegations of police corruption of this sort were heard each day at the police court, and just as frequently dismissed; they were, after all, almost the only defense open to women caught touting for business on the streets. But the story that Ruby Young now told was so unexpected that it raised a shout of laughter in the room.

"The charge is founded," the girl explained, "upon the desire of this policeman to assist a couple of brother officers in gratifying a spite they have against me." Becker, Young continued, her voice hardening in indignation, had charged her with soliciting as a result of an incident that had occurred about a month earlier, when a certain Patrolman Rosenberg—also of the Nineteenth Precinct, and like Becker in plainclothes—had accosted her at midnight. The girl, misled by the shadows and the policeman's swarthy skin, had made a fatal mistake: thinking that Rosenberg was a black man trying to pick her up, she had abused him and chased him off. "I told him to go about his business," she added to suppressed amusement, "adding that I wanted nothing to do with negroes." Rosenberg, incensed, detained her on the spot, and when the story had emerged at the courthouse the next day, the patrolman was so humiliated by the titters running round the court that he had sworn revenge and told Ruby that he would henceforth arrest her on sight. The girl had been locked up each time she had set foot in Satan's Circus since.

Young's story gave even Magistrate Cornell pause. "Is there any doubt in this case, Officer?" he queried, turning back to Becker.

The policeman kept his head. "None at all," he returned airily. "She is an old hand and always lies about it."

Cornell returned his gaze to the girl standing at the bar and pondered for a moment. "You do not deny you frequent the Tenderloin, do you?" he inquired.

Ruby started to reply, then hesitated. "There would be no use in making such a denial," she murmured at last.

That settled matters for Cornell. No respectable woman, after all, would be found walking through the vice district alone, and he was about to issue Young with a fine when there was a sudden commotion on the public benches. Magistrate, court officers, and spectators all swung around to find the source of the disturbance. "The interruption," the *New York Sun*'s reporter noted, "came from a slender young man of medium height with tawny hair parted in the middle and falling in great masses over his temples." He had jumped to his feet and was attempting to identify himself. Stephen Crane had kept his promise to attend the hearing.

Crane had arrived in court several hours earlier, avoiding any fuss. He had kept his peace while he heard the evidence against his casual acquaintance. Now that he could see that Young was adjudged guilty, though, he could no longer remain silent. "Just a word, Your Honor," the writer called to Magistrate Cornell. "I know this girl to be innocent." In the shocked silence that followed, Ruby (Crane himself would write) "in uncomprehending wonder gazed at him. She could hardly understand how it was that he dared to defend her."

Cornell, who knew the writer slightly, gestured his assent, and Crane rattled off a hurried, nervous summary of events at Broadway Garden, insisting that he had kept the redhead constantly in sight as he left the premises—a dubious proposition, as it happened, since he had certainly turned his back on her in order to take her friend the chorus girl to her streetcar stop. But the novelist's name and fame lent added weight to his testimony, and so cast doubt on Becker's word. The statement was certainly enough for Magistrate Cornell. He ordered that Ruby be discharged forthwith.

"But, Your Honor," Young stammered as she stepped down, "I will be arrested on sight the next time I show my face in the precinct."

"I will look out for that," Cornell assured her. Perhaps fearing that the magistrate would change his mind, the girl hurried from the court, vanishing into the lunchtime crowds that rushed along Tenth Street. Crane followed after her more slowly, a magnet for the dozen court reporters who surrounded him on the steps outside.

"I well knew I was risking a reputation that I have worked hard to build," the writer told them all with calculated modesty.

> But she was a woman and unjustly accused, and I did what was my duty as a man. I realized that if [I] should stand tamely by, in such a case, our wives and sisters would be at the mercy of any ruffian who disgraces the uniform. . . . The arrest was an outrage, and I'd do the same thing again if I had to, even if I lost any little reputation I may have and strived to get. If the girl will have the officer prosecuted for perjury, I will gladly support her.

The reporters wrote down this whole speech, scribbling away in shorthand to transcribe it all. As they did so, a tall man jogged down the steps behind Crane's back, twisting to glare at the triumphant novelist as he passed. It was Charley Becker, angry and humiliated, leaving the courthouse with his sworn testimony ignored and his honor cast in doubt. The patrolman shot a second glance at Crane as he went past: a look of malevolence and hatred. Perhaps fortunately, his accuser failed to notice it.

Becker gave his side of the story later that same day to a reporter from the *Journal* who tracked him down on his usual beat, patrolling Broadway between Thirty-fifth and Thirty-ninth streets. Predictably enough, it differed considerably from Stephen Crane's.

"I arrested the woman because of what I, myself, saw," the policeman said. "If Mr. Crane says I took her away from a party of persons with whom she was conversing, he is mistaken. To do such a thing would be simply suicidal for a man in my position. I am in this business not for glory, but to earn my living honestly. I wish to retain my position and, if possible, to get ahead."

It was only half the truth, of course. If Becker had not despised Ruby Young before he arrested her—and, given her charges against Rosenberg and the well-known clannishness of the police, he probably had—he had good reason to do so now. The next time he encountered the girl along his beat, at three in the morning on October 4, he walked up behind her, seized her by the throat, kicked her, and threw her to the ground. A crowd of passersby intervened before he could inflict real damage. A few days later, the little redhead was attacked again, this time by another prostitute. Ruby's assailant, a handsome-looking, hard-faced Irish girl known throughout the Tenderloin as "Big Chicago May," struck her a fierce blow on the head, and "a lively fight ensued." May, it would emerge, was a close friend of Becker's.

Such continued ill treatment proved counterproductive, for it merely steeled Young's resolve. As New York slid toward bitter autumn, she thought with increasing frequency of Crane, of how he had stepped forward to defend her at Jefferson Market, and of the promise he had made outside the court: "If the girl will have the officer prosecuted for perjury, I will gladly support her." As it happened, the novelist himself had decided not to press charges of his own against the police and had also rebuffed an invitation from Chief Peter Conlin, the ranking officer of the department, to give a longer statement regarding the whole affair. Probably Crane's sudden reticence owed something to the warnings he was now receiving from the Nineteenth Precinct, not least the suggestion that he himself could well face prosecution for immoral living if he continued to pursue his case. But Ruby had little left to lose. Three weeks after the incident at Broadway Garden, she went into the police headquarters on Mulberry Street and pressed formal charges against Becker and a second officer from the same precinct, alleging that both men had been consistently harassing her.

The incident had now blown up into a serious affair. Charges of this sort could be answered only at a "police trial": a formal hearing before one of the city's four police commissioners at which both parties would be represented by attorneys. Such trials were not uncommon at the time; there were an average of more than 1,000 of them in New York each year after 1889, this at a time when there were only 4,000 or so men on the whole force. But they were not to be taken lightly. Officers found guilty of serious misconduct could lose their jobs, and fines and suspensions were commonplace.

Becker was in trouble, and he knew it. The policeman was sufficiently concerned to have the date of his hearing put back twice, to allow more time for the gathering of evidence. He also found the money to hire a shrewd, experienced attorney by the name of Louis Grant. But his final preparation was perhaps the most significant. On the afternoon his trial was scheduled to begin—October 15, 1896—Officer Becker rallied the support of colleagues from the West Thirtieth Street station, and when he made his way down Mulberry Street to the hearing, he did so in the company of a bodyguard. Callow patrolman though he was, Becker entered the headquarters building surrounded by a phalanx of policemen made up of every member of his precinct not on duty at the time.

Police trials seldom lasted longer than an hour or two, but this would prove to be the longest in the department's history. Becker and his adversaries, Young and Crane, reported to police headquarters at 3:00 P.M. as asked. Commissioner Frederick Grant* kept them waiting while he handled other business, and the proceedings did not get under way until after ten in the evening. Despite the lateness of the hour, however, Grant declared his intention to complete the trial that night. Crane canceled a supper engagement, dined off a brought-in sandwich and a bottle of beer, and was finally called to give evidence at 1:00 A.M. The proceedings did not draw to a close until 2:40 A.M.

Much of that time was taken up by a parade of twenty or so men and women from Satan's Circus who testified for Becker. Lawyer Grant had corralled a throng of cabdrivers and prostitutes to support his client's story—just the sort of people, cynical reporters observed, who depended heavily on the goodwill of the local beat policeman for their living. These witnesses gave similar accounts, some insisting that they had seen Young and her friend the chorus girl touting for business on the street corner, others confirming that the redhead worked regularly as a prostitute.

The testimony with the greatest potential to damage Young came from the girl's new enemy, the intimidating Chicago May. "A huge blonde whose diamond earrings seem as big as hickory nuts," May earnestly testified that Ruby had promised her $25 to give false evidence against Becker. The patrolman, Young had told her, "must be broken." When he had been, she would take a ship to Europe.

Chicago May's undoubted lies had less impact than they might have thanks largely to Young's lawyer, David Neuberger. His vigorous cross-examination destroyed what little credibility the Irish street-walker had:

> "What's your occupation?" Mr. Neuberger asked this woman, whose blushes are not visible.
> "I'm a typewriter," she replied.
> "On what machine do you typewrite?"

---

*He was the eldest son of former president Ulysses S. Grant, and no relation of Becker's lawyer.

She did not know.

"Name one typewriting machine."

She could not.

"Did you earn those diamonds with your wages as a type-writer?"

Still, Neuberger did not have things entirely his own way. Lawyer Grant landed his share of stiff blows, most of them on Stephen Crane. The men of the Nineteenth Precinct had evidently used the weeks before the trial to dig for evidence discreditable to the novelist, and Becker's counsel marshaled the facts relentlessly. Was it not true, Grant began, that Crane actually derived most of his income from the immoral earnings of prostitutes? The author denied it. Well, the attorney went on, had he not recently shared a house on West Twenty-second Street with several unmarried women? "I refuse to answer," Crane muttered in response to this suggestion, "because it would tend to degrade me."

Scenting blood, Grant went on to describe the detritus the police had uncovered in a search of the writer's apartment. An opium kit—lamp, needle, pipe, and scraper—had been discovered among his possessions. The lawyer tried hard to get Crane to confess that he had used it, and though the witness argued convincingly that the layout was merely a souvenir brought home from his newspaper investigations, he was forced to admit that he had lived for six weeks that summer with a woman who was not his wife. To straitlaced New Yorkers of the time, such an admission was shocking enough. What made it worse was the revelation that the couple had taken a room in a brothel where the girls were well known for robbing their clients. Thoroughly angered and ashamed, Crane nonetheless refused to name the girl he had shared the place with. "On what ground?" an exultant Grant demanded. "Because it would tend to degrade me," the writer mumbled once again.

Nearly an hour of this examination ended with Crane utterly humiliated. "So thick and fast did Lawyer Grant fire the red-hot questions at the witness," one reporter in the courtroom noted, "that he finally put his hands up to his face as if to prevent them burning into his brain." At that moment the young writer recognized the wisdom of Sergeant McDermott's warning. He did indeed have mud all over him.

Of course, the *Journal*, Crane's own paper, exploded in an editorial, the whole interrogation was typical of the excesses of New York's police, "part of a deliberate and despicable scheme of intimidation by which any voluntary witness in a trial for police outrage may become a victim." But that scarcely mattered when, inevitably, Crane's revelations supplied the headlines the next day, which was what Becker had wanted. The real issues of the trial—Ruby Young's veracity and the patrolman's supposed brutality—were obscured and forgotten. By the time Commissioner Grant retired to consider his judgment, none of the principal players in the drama retained much credibility as a witness.

In these circumstances the verdict was a formality; Becker was acquitted. The consequences for his accusers were equally predictable. Ruby Young continued to be harassed by the men of the Nineteenth Precinct whenever she dared set foot in Satan's Circus. And Stephen Crane discovered that the Manhattan police, when roused, made formidable enemies. For the rest of his short life—he died in 1900 at the age of only twenty-nine—the novelist prudently remained well beyond the grasp of the NYPD. He left town almost immediately to report on the insurgency in Cuba and was scarcely ever seen in New York again. On the one occasion that he did return, in 1898, Crane was recognized in a theater lobby by a patrolman who instantly attempted to arrest him.

As for Charley Becker, who left court surrounded once again by a guard of brother officers, he had learned a good deal about the power of his badge. Three years of unblemished service had been put at risk, and he owed his triumph solely to the support of his colleagues. Becker was still new enough to the uniform to remember his own days as a civilian. But something had changed inside him since that night at Broadway Garden. He was a policeman's policeman now.

CHAPTER 2

KING OF THE BOWERY

CHARLEY BECKER WAS NOT a native New Yorker. He had been born, in July 1870, on a farm some eighty miles from Manhattan and grew up in what was one of the poorest districts of upstate New York. His upbringing was harsh: The Becker farm was isolated, the land barren, the living uncertain, the family itself austerely religious. He was the youngest child in a family of ten, born to a father who died when Charley was only four years old. He appears to have shown no sign, in his youth, of hating life in the tiny, closed community where he grew up—a place that offered few real opportunities and little to look forward to except a life of backbreaking work. But he left home at the first opportunity, aged only twenty, and headed straight for the city. For Becker, New York offered the temptations and rewards that his birthplace never could.

Becker was a third-generation American. His grandfather, Heinrich Becker—born in Hesse-Kassel, in the western reaches of Germany, at the tail end of the eighteenth century—was a wood turner. His father, Conrad—also born in Germany—was a farmer who wrested a living from a parcel of land in a desolate spot in the western reaches of Sullivan County, on the border between New York State and Pennsylvania. Even in 1870 the district was still frontier country: barely settled, scarcely tamed. There was only one real town, Callicoon Depot on the Delaware River: a ramshackle settlement, with a population of fewer than six hundred, so unprepossessing that even a local writer promoting the place as a summer residence for city folk admitted that it had "no claim to beauty." The hinterland, meanwhile, consisted largely of impenetrable forest, filled with panthers and deer and dotted here and there with tiny settlements so small that they were scarcely even hamlets.

Callicoon had its advantages, of course: The air was clear, the water pure, and the little town nestled in the foothills of the Catskills, shielded from the worst of the winter winds. But it was notorious, in equal measure, for the poverty of its soil. The Becker farm, two miles south of the tiny village of Callicoon Center, stood—the first historian of the district noted—"in the woods beyond the bounds of civilization," and after paying for his land, Heinrich had "but little, if anything, left except his wife and children." Foul weather reduced the family to near starvation on several occasions; wild animals devoured their crops; and when a harvest was brought in, the only means of transporting it to market was on the elder Becker's back, "a journey which required three days for its performance. There was no road better than a trail through the woods, which was made visible only by marked trees."

It was not until the 1870s—by which time Conrad Becker had six sons to help him on the land—that the farm became at last productive. A sliver of road, snaking through the forest, now ran the seven miles to town, and the Depot had in turn been linked to New York by rail. Even after Charley's birth, however, his father and grandfather were both forced to work occasionally as carpenters in order to earn money. "No one," the future policeman wrote of his childhood home, "can do more than make a base living on it, and a poor one at that."

The sheer effort required to extract a living from the Beckers' impoverished plot is eloquently illustrated by the fact that not one of Conrad's sons remained at home to take over the farm. The three eldest of the Becker boys—Franklin, Howard, and Paul—abandoned Callicoon for California, and of them only Paul ever returned. The roguish fourth son, Jackson, fled soon afterward, preferring (as a member of his family recalls) a rootless existence spent "variously as a broker, a searcher for gold, an osteopath or probably a chiropractor, and a con man." The fifth, John, left home around 1888, seduced by the lures and snares of New York City.

Charley himself thus came to manhood in a home where there were few male influences. His father died, aged fifty-two, in 1877. His octogenarian grandfather followed five years later. And of his numerous brothers, only John was close enough in age to be a friend. Brought up by a widowed mother, the pet of several older and unmarried sisters, Charley experienced a relatively solitary childhood. Neighbors remembered him as an able, decent child who worked hard and never seemed to get into trouble. According to Baltazer Hauser, who owned a farm adjoining the Becker property for sixty years, "Charles Becker was one of the most honest and best boys I ever knew." Another local resident had similar memories. "Becker's people were the very best of neighbors," recalled Philip Huff, the son of a local lumberman, "and Charley Becker was an honest and very bright boy. I never knew him to do anything wrong or get into trouble of any kind."

Only one of Becker's early acquaintances, indeed, had a bad word to say of him. "There was," Hauser confessed, "only one thing about him that could be criticized; that was that he was headstrong. He would always do the right thing or quit." It was this mulishness, perhaps, that prompted the boy to leave the village as soon as he turned twenty. His brother John—a year his senior—was planning to join New York's police department, and it may be that his encouraging reports persuaded Charley to take his chances in Manhattan. In the autumn of 1890, Becker packed a bag and hitched a lift to Callicoon Depot. From there the great metropolis was just a train ride away.

The New York, Ontario and Western Railway took the best part of three hours to clack and rattle Becker into the heart of the city. For much of the journey, the engine threaded through the same wooded, unspoiled countryside in which the farm boy had grown up. But as the little steam train with its smoke-smeared carriages began to puff its way along the Hudson River, the view through its grimy windows changed. Farms, woodland, and open spaces receded from view, to be replaced by a seemingly endless parade of houses and apartment buildings, offices, saloons, factories, warehouses, and wharves, sprawling out to the horizon in all directions. For a boy brought up in a village of perhaps two hundred people, it must have been an overwhelming sight. And these were simply the outskirts of the greater conurbation to the south: New York.

It was already possibly the greatest city on the planet. London was bigger, Paris and Vienna more cultured. But no rival could match Gotham for vigor or the sheer pace of its growth. Seen from the perspective of just over a century, the New York of 1890 still seems in most respects quite modern. True, the first subway was still fourteen years away, Grand Central Station would not be completed for more than two decades, and—in the absence of refrigeration—elections could still be won and lost over the cost of ice.* The city's tallest building was Trinity Church, at 284 feet, and its most ambitious office tower soared a mere eleven stories. But New York was changing with astonishing rapidity. Steel-frame construction and the safety elevator—the twin inventions that made skyscrapers practicable—were about to add a third dimension to the city. Downtown Manhattan's unique steam heating mains had been laid in 1881, the Brooklyn Bridge was completed in 1883, department stores had begun springing up along Sixth Avenue, and the cat's cradles of telephone wires festooning the streets announced the introduction of modern communications.

The electric light, meanwhile—introduced to New York in 1880—had transformed the old gaslit thoroughfares, and cable cars and elevated railways made their appearance almost simultaneously.

---

*In April 1900, the American Ice Company (which had muscled its way to an effective monopoly over the supply of ice to the city) announced that it was doubling its prices from 30 cents to 60 cents per hundred pounds. This put its product—the only effective preservative of milk, medicines, and numerous foods—beyond the reach of many poor New Yorkers and would certainly have led to a sharp increase in infant mortality, food poisoning, and general discomfort had not an enormous public outcry forced a reversal of the decision. In the course of the subsequent inquiry into how American Ice had secured exclusive rights to unload its product at city piers, it was revealed that New York's $15,000-a-year mayor, Robert Van Wyck, owned—and had apparently not paid for—$680,000 worth of ice-trust stock. The resultant scandal was generally agreed to have cost the Democrats the municipal elections of 1901.

The former, which traveled along tracks at street level and were powered by endless steel belts, had severe drawbacks, among them lethal momentum. ("Once a motorman gripped the cable," one critic of the system explained, "his streetcar was jerked along at thirty miles per hour, far faster than horses. Speed couldn't be varied at corners, so cars whipped passengers around spots like Dead Man's Curve at Union Square, gongs clanging wildly.") The latter, a product of the Rapid Transit Act of 1875, proved more successful and soon took the place of the city's old-fashioned horse-drawn trams, at least on routes running north and south through Manhattan. By 1890, El lines ran along—or rather over—Second, Third, Sixth, and Ninth avenues, their trains puffing their way from stop to stop at twelve miles per hour and linking hitherto-distant suburbs such as the Bronx to the great shopping and entertainment districts downtown. Overhead tracks girdled the boroughs of Manhattan and Brooklyn with long lines of fragile-looking iron pillars that plunged the streets beneath them into shadow, and the trains themselves spewed out noise and ash as they chugged along, their progress marked by clouds of soot that swirled briefly over the heads of passing New Yorkers before settling like grimy snow upon the pavements. With the lines complete, it became possible to leave home in Washington Heights, in the far north of the city, and reach Wall Street in less than an hour.

Industry flourished in the crowded city. Manhattan was a center of the tobacco, print, and textile trades, the last of which employed as many as 80,000 workers—most of them in sweatshops of the nastiest and most exploitative kind—and shipping from all over the world crowded into New York's magnificent harbor, bringing cargoes of raw materials for factories, coal for power, and labor, in the form of boatloads of immigrants. By the time the American Tobacco Company opened its new offices there in 1890, Manhattan was already home to eighty of the United States' hundred largest companies and could claim to be the country's economic hub.

The New York that Charley Becker found when he first came to the city was, in short, not merely an impossible dream for the millions of new Americans who arrived by sea but a pungent lure to the out-of-towners who rolled in by rail, the city that offered everyone everything:

> Wall Street supplied the country with capital. Ellis Island channeled its labor. Fifth Avenue set its social trends. Broadway (along with Times Square* and Coney Island) entertained it. Its City Hall, as befitted an unofficial Capitol, welcomed heroes and heroines with keys and parades and naval flotillas, and paid farewell respects to national leaders by organizing processions along Manhattan's black-draped streets. New York, moreover, was the nation's premier source for news and opinion; like a magnet, it attracted those seeking cosmopolitan freedom; and as the biggest city of the biggest state it exercised extraordinary influence in national politics.

The product of a century of rapid change was clear to see. In 1800 the northern edges of New York fell roughly along Houston Street, no more than two miles from the southern tip of Manhattan. By 1890 the city had swollen to engulf the entire island, twelve miles long and two miles wide, and spilled onto the mainland to the east. Not every inch of ground was covered yet; rickety shantytowns and even grubby little farms still survived in the shadow of the fashionable Dakota Apartments, just completed on the Upper West Side, and streets in several outlying districts, laid out in anticipation of future construction, remained for the time being nearly empty, with only a building or two dotted along their lengths. Yet the speed with which New York had grown still amazed outsiders. The city's population had risen from less than 75,000 in 1800 to 1.6 million nine decades later; that of the neighboring borough of Brooklyn from a mere 4,000 to 800,000. When the British novelist Arnold Bennett visited the Bronx a short while later, he was shown around "an area where five years previously there had been six families, and where there are now over two thousand."

---

*In 1890—and until 1904—known as Longacre Square.

This was a polyglot society. In the last years of the nineteenth century, New York was home to men and women from more than fifty nations: a city of immigrants, still growing at the rate of 20,000 new citizens a month. "Every four years," it was observed, "New York adds to itself a town the size of Boston," and by 1898—when the five boroughs of Manhattan, Brooklyn, Queens, the Bronx, and Staten Island combined to form a single vast metropolis—it was already the largest Jewish city, the largest Italian city, and one of the two or three largest German cities on earth.

New York was, in consequence, a city of neighborhoods, more so even than it is today. Wealthy Germans lived out in the suburbs, in Williamsburg and Bushwick, and poorer ones in "Kleindeutschland," the blocks that lay east of Bowery—itself an earthy mile-long paradise for "tourists, sailors, slummers and others in search of a good time," packed with saloons, theaters, and dance halls. Italians gravitated toward "Little Italy" or Greenwich Village, Jewish families to the Lower East Side or the districts north and east of Central Park, blacks still mostly to the "African Tenderloin" on the Upper West Side, the Chinese to a densely crowded district just to the north of City Hall.

But it was wealth, more even than race or class, that determined the patterns of New York life. The richest and most eminent citizens lived, as they had done for years, in the center of Manhattan, along Fifth Avenue and Madison. They formed a self-selecting social elite consisting principally of families whose prominence extended back a century, together with a leavening of new money in the form of Vanderbilts and other robber barons. The truly wealthy lived in mansions amounting sometimes to châteaus and were fiercely conformist, devoting themselves to business and to play. Only a handful dirtied their hands by dabbling in politics; when Theodore Roosevelt, who had been born a New Yorker, resolved to turn his hand to public service, he did so with the greatest hesitation, and as late as 1900—just before his election as vice president—still hardly thought of himself as a statesman at all. Politics were, indeed, rarely discussed in polite society. "Topics tolerated in other homes were banished," one writer on the social scene explained. "Food, wine, horses, yachts, cotillions and marriages were the only acceptable subjects."

The rest of New York's people lived less privileged existences. To the north and south of Central Park dwelled the professional classes, who made up perhaps a third of the city's population and led mostly law-abiding lives: managers, brokers, bookkeepers, small businessmen, and clerks who worked hard, labored to improve themselves, and yearned for respectability. To the east and to the west—strung literally and metaphorically along the edges of Manhattan—the working classes eked out livings of a more precarious sort. Poor, itinerant, and mostly recent immigrants, they lived crammed by the tens of thousands into dingy, dangerous tenements that lined both sides of almost every street and stretched below Fourteenth Street into portions of the city where the overcrowding was worse even than in Bombay—524 souls per acre in 1890, a figure that continued to rise until it topped 700 a decade later and was equivalent to half a million inhabitants per square mile.

This was life lived on the borders of endurance, on wages that seldom amounted to more than a few dollars a day. A single tenement measuring 25 feet by 100 and built six stories tall (the maximum height permitted by the city's zoning laws) would be divided into twenty-four minuscule apartments, with one toilet shared by thirty people. The front room of a typical two-room residence did duty as a kitchen, dining room, living room, and bedroom, and though some were well lit and ventilated, most were not. There were no gardens and no playgrounds; children's games were played on rooftops or in the streets. Women hung out of windows or gathered on the steps to gossip, but most maintained a certain distance from even their closest neighbors, if only because pride forbade them from confessing the extent of their misery when times were bad. According to Owen Kildare, a New York reporter who had grown up in one of the city's poorest districts, apartment doors would be opened not merely for ventilation but to demonstrate to neighbors that food was being cooked within. When money was tight, the doors stayed closed and "there [was] no feast, just the tea and the bread and scheming how to explain this unwelcome fact to the neighbors."

For all this, even life in the Manhattan slums represented an advance on what millions of new Americans had known in Europe. The better places actually appeared palatial to those more used to life in rural Ireland or the ghettos of czarist Russia. "We rented an apartment in a workers' district," recalled Leon Trotsky in his memoirs, "and furnished it on the instalment plan. That apartment, at $18 a month, was equipped with all sorts of conveniences that we Europeans were quite unused to: electric lights, gas cooking range, bath, telephone, elevator, and even a chute for garbage."

Charley Becker, when he first came to New York in 1890, probably arrived in the city with little more money than most dwellers in the city's tenements; a few tens of dollars were probably all that he could save, or even borrow from a family that was hardly wealthy. But he enjoyed considerable advantages over the majority of immigrants. He was an American citizen, had no dependents, and could have gone back to his village easily enough. In John Becker, moreover, he had his own guide to life in Manhattan—one who knew how to rent a place to live and get a job.

Becker's first task would have been to find lodgings. Virtually all unmarried New Yorkers of the period took a room in a boardinghouse or found a tenement family to take them in. ("Two-thirds of New York boards," the saying went, "and three-thirds takes in boarders.") Where he stayed remains unknown, though it was surely not one of the city's casual lodging houses, which catered solely to the poor.* Becker's first home in Manhattan was probably one of the small, family-owned boardinghouses that proliferated in the city and were generally run by working-class women who needed extra income in order to supplement their husbands' uncertain wages. Although often

---

*These, the muckraking journalist Jacob Riis recorded, varied from relatively salubrious twenty-five-cent properties, where "guests" could at least expect their own bed, flimsily partitioned, down through fifteen-cent dives, where the residents slept four deep on filthy bunks, to ten-cent properties, where "the locker for the sleeper's clothes disappears. There is no longer need of it. The tramp limit is reached, and there is nothing to lock up, save, on general principle, the lodger."

disappointingly threadbare and uncomfortable, boardinghouses of this sort provided meals, did their guests' laundry, and offered a mending service. And in return for their few dollars a week (at least according to the gossip of the day), young, good-looking male guests such as Becker could hope to enjoy more personal attention from the landlady or her daughters, the operation of a guesthouse being regarded as a useful way of meeting likely husbands.

Finding work in a city as crowded and as hard-edged as New York was a good deal more difficult than finding a room, but Becker secured a position as a clerk working at Cowperthwait's, a renowned furniture store on Chatham Square. It was a decent job; clerking was white-collar work, rarely well paid but infinitely more respectable than manual labor. The hours clerks worked were good by the standards of the time—generally from 7:30 in the morning until 4:00 P.M., which meant that they could visit a bar or watch a baseball game before returning home to supper. And the prospects were, if scarcely dazzling, at least acceptable: perhaps a supervisory position in a decade or so, and eventually a senior clerkship bringing with it a salary of $1,200 a year.

For Becker, nonetheless, life at Cowperthwait's seems to have held little appeal. He resigned his position at the store less than a year after leaving Callicoon, perhaps because he found the job too tedious or fell out with a superior. But it is probably no coincidence that Charley's departure from Chatham Square coincided more or less exactly with John Becker's appointment as a New York policeman. Perhaps the elder brother's reports of life in uniform were enough to persuade the younger man to join him. It seems clear enough, in any case, that Becker began preparing himself for a police career within a few months of arriving in New York. Between 1891 and 1893, the brawny young man took work as a baker's assistant, a door-to-door clothing salesman, and as a bouncer in a German beer garden off the Bowery. All these were necessary preparations for an application to the force.

To most casual observers, the idea that an ambitious would-be policeman might benefit from two years of casual employment, concluding with a spell spent pitching drunks out of a bar, seems utterly absurd. Only a few years later, a position as a saloon bouncer—an occasionally dangerous job associated, in New York dives such as John McGurk's notorious Suicide Hall,* with numerous disreputable practices—would have been enough to disbar a man from a career with the police. It was not even an attractive line of work. A job in the liquor industry, in the 1890s, meant laboring long hours for low pay at a time when even an experienced bartender took home little more than $500 a year. But one thing could be said of the saloons along the Bowery where Becker guarded doors: They were the best possible places to attract the notice and the patronage of the politicians who controlled New York's police.

Bartenders and saloonkeepers had played a vital part in the running of the city for more than a century. They were helped on their way by a sharp decline in the number of patricians and respectable businessmen willing to take a hand in local government—as early as 1850, it was said that the best way to break up a political meeting was to burst into the council chamber yelling, "Your saloon's on fire!"— and tended to be natural leaders: gregarious, well connected, and on good terms with everyone from the local bigwigs to the beat policeman. Many served informally as "locality mayors," an important but amorphous role bestowed on neighborhood fixers who "had the ear of the ward heeler, the district boss and the precinct chief, and could get erring sons out of jail, arrange for permits and variances to fly easily through the machine, and could take on spokesman tasks, as with the press, for the neighborhood at large." Their saloons made ideal meeting places and were used for decades as makeshift political

---

*Situated on the Bowery, Suicide Hall swarmed with prostitutes and had earned its name from the frequency with which despairing girls downed drafts of carbolic acid or flung themselves from its balconies to their deaths on the dance floor below; as word of their deadly proclivities spread, the place become a gruesome sort of tourist attraction, and it was said that McGurk's lurid business cards circulated among sailors in every major seaport in the world. The Hall's bouncers, led by a fearsome former gangster known as "Eat 'Em Up Jack" McManus, specialized in ejecting obstreperous customers who had complained of being cheated by the place's infamous headwaiter, "Short Change" Charley— a man regarded as the master of the art of proffering change in three-cent pieces in place of dimes.

headquarters and as hangouts for the street gangs that were all too often loosely allied with one political party or another. The most powerful had the sort of political pull known at the time as "positively gravitational." "Silver Dollar" Smith, a saloonkeeper and pimp who got his name from the gimmick of setting a thousand silver dollars in the concrete floor of his saloon, liked to boast that he more or less ran the Essex Market Court House from his premises across the road. And Barney Rourke, a highly influential figure in the Third Election District, was so important to the politicians of the day that when President Chester Arthur visited New York and Rourke sent a message regretting that he was too busy to go uptown that day, Arthur made his way into the slums instead, and their meeting was held in the back room of Rourke's saloon.

Seen from this perspective, Becker's choice of employment makes sudden sense. The casual jobs he took in bakeries and selling door-to-door offered the chance to save the money he would need. And work as a bouncer gave him the opportunity to meet the sort of men who could readily secure a coveted nomination to the New York Police Department, not to mention daily opportunities to impress them with his physical prowess. By swapping a position in the back room of a furniture store for one in front of a Bowery saloon, Becker—guided no doubt by his brother—made sure that he would be seen in all the right places by all the right men. More than that, he put himself in the perfect place to get a Manhattan education: a detailed understanding of how the city really worked.

For much of the nineteenth century, America's principal towns were ruled by great political machines.

Chicago, Kansas City, Philadelphia, Boston, Cincinnati, and, of course, New York each developed organizations capable of delivering votes to pliant officials, and each found itself in thrall to the powerful local "bosses" who evolved to control them. The machines were, for the most part, incorporeal, unofficial, and unorthodox, and they flourished best in fast-changing immigrant societies, in which many voters had no long-standing allegiance to the politicians who vied for their support. They worked primarily by the manipulation of patronage, exchanging jobs and other favors for votes, and soon grew into powerful organizations. The machines employed violence and coercion to achieve their aims—the most obvious of which were securing wealth and power for those who ran them—and continued to do so well into the early years of the twentieth century. But their leaders understood that not even the grossest election frauds could keep a genuinely unpopular administration in office. Holding on to power meant keeping popular support—and that was best achieved by tackling problems that county and local governments otherwise ignored. By the time that Charley Becker arrived in New York, it was widely recognized that the simplest way for voters in America's great cities to solve problems with the collection of rubbish, arrange for potholes to be fixed, obtain coal if short of money, and even find work when unemployed, was to solicit the help of a machine politician. The machines offered what amounted to a social safety net in cities where being poor, homeless, or jobless might otherwise have been intolerable—all in return for support at the polls.

Machine politics had come into existence at the tail end of the eighteenth century, and reached its apogee after the Civil War. In New York its earliest manifestations can be traced to the 1780s, and by the end of the nineteenth century several competing machines coexisted in the city. But one of these stood out among the rest, famous and notorious in equal measure, and known not merely in Manhattan but around the globe. This was the Democrat political club based in a large, square brownstone on East Fourteenth Street, just off Union Square: a building known to its members as the Wigwam and to an incredulous world as Tammany Hall.

The Society of St. Tammany, to give the organization its proper name, was founded in 1786 and named after a Native American chief. It was controlled by thirteen senior officials known as "sachems," but much of the machine's real power rested in the hands of its district captains. Each captain took responsibility for an election ward, and each was expected to maintain his own organization, supervising the activities of the dozens of ambitious and hardworking minor politicians who managed Tammany's affairs along single streets or in a handful of city blocks. Over the years, as the society grew larger, it penetrated deep into the fabric of New York, particularly in the immigrant quarters south of Fourteenth Street. Even the poorest and most marginal inhabitants of a well-run district knew their block leader by sight, and the strong roots that the society thus developed throughout Manhattan secured it power.

It took the best part of a century to build the Tammany machine. As early as the 1840s, it became infamous for promoting cronyism, corruption, and lawlessness on a heroic scale. But the Hall only really came of age a decade later, during the mayoralty of wily Fernando Wood, a long-time member of the Wigwam who perfected election fraud on a wide scale, harnessing the power of Manhattan's violent street gangs in the Democratic cause and deploying their members to threaten and coerce voters, intimidate officials, and even steal the ballot boxes in exchange for virtual freedom from arrest. At much the same time, Tammany's numerous appointees to the City Council perfected the practice of colluding in order to hand New York's business to favored contractors. Corrupt councilmen would lease out the city's property to allies at knock-down rates or arrange for heavily padded quotes to be accepted, then split the difference between the bid price and the real one with their partners. The members of this council got so many things done so crookedly that they became known as the "Forty Thieves."

Wood's malign genius provided Tammany with the tools it needed to remain in power. But it was one of his successors, William Tweed, who really epitomized the excesses of the Democrat machine. Under Tweed—a remarkable figure, larger than life, who stood six feet tall and weighed three hundred pounds—small-time crooks became suddenly untouchable, and friends of the Wigwam were granted governmental sinecures. The comedian "Oofty-Goofty" Phillips was made clerk to the water board; a criminal by the name of Jim "Maneater" Cusick became a court clerk.

Such placemen made possible the staggering corruption and graft that turned Tweed into a wealthy man. Under the boss's rule, New York spent $10,000 on a $75 batch of pencils, another $171,000 on tables and chairs worth only $4,000, and $3.5 million on "repairs" to the brand-new Criminal Courts Building behind City Hall that had already cost twice what the United States had paid for the whole state of Alaska. By the time of his eventual exposure, in 1873, it was calculated that the total stolen by Tweed and his cronies had exceeded $50 million.* Of this, no more than $800,000 was ever recovered.

Tweed's disgrace changed Tammany forever, for the Hall survived only by reinventing itself. The old boss's crude and blatant methods were abandoned, and Tammany took to painting itself as a reforming organization. It helped that Tweed's successor, the felicitously named "Honest John" Kelly, had spent the last few years in Europe and so bore no responsibility for the phenomenal boondoggles that had shocked New York. But as Tammany recovered its confidence under Honest John's calming leadership, it also began exploring better ways of making money.

Outright fraud involving padded contracts went out of fashion; it was simply too risky now to steal the people's taxes in this way. Instead the Hall sought other sources of income. The sale of jobs continued and indeed was regularized. The machine also raked in vast sums by auctioning off franchises to run city utilities, notably the elevated railways. Increasingly, substantial contributions to Tammany's campaign funds also came from assessments levied on New York's vice trade, which was milked unmercifully for years. Kelly's greatest triumph, though, was to reach an accommodation with his political enemies, who controlled many of Manhattan's uptown wards. During his years in office, Tammany made several concessions to the rival Custom House machine, which boosted the Republican cause in much the same way that Tammany promoted the Democrats. Slivers of patronage granted to the Custom House further minimized the prospect of exposure.

The Hall's relationship with crime was regularized and brought to a high state of efficiency by Kelly's successor, Richard Croker. It was no coincidence that the new boss was a former street brawler and

---

*Equivalent to $780 million today, some 80 percent of which was split among only five men.

petty gangster who had once been tried for murder. Croker, who ran Tammany from 1886 until 1902—and thus had charge of the machine when Becker arrived in New York—was a far more genuinely menacing figure than the affable Boss Tweed. He was utterly ruthless, almost entirely self-interested, and victory in three successive elections made him virtually untouchable.

Still, Tammany was far from an entirely malign influence, even at the apogee of Croker's power. A good deal of effort was poured into programs for better schooling and social relief, which immeasurably improved the Hall's standing in the densely populated wards downtown. The machine also became ever more intimately concerned with the affairs of immigrants. "There is," the boss himself boasted to the British journalist W. T. Stead, whom he met on a transatlantic liner,

> no such organization for taking hold of the untrained friendless man and converting him into a citizen. Who else would do it if we would not? Think of the hundreds of thousands of foreigners dumped in our city. They are too old to go to school. . . . They are alone, ignorant strangers, a prey to all manner of anarchical and wild notions. . . . Tammany looks after them for the sake of their votes, grafts them upon the Republic, makes citizens of them in short; and although you may not like our motives or our methods, what other agency is there by which so long a row could be hoed so quickly or so well?

If there was one ward boss who embodied the best and the worst of Tammany Hall, who was admired as much as he was feared, who was generous with his time and money and yet remained engaged in almost every kind of vice, that man was "Big Tim" Sullivan.

The tallest, best-proportioned, nicest-looking, most beloved district leader that New York ever produced, Sullivan ruled like a king over a ward that encompassed Charley Becker's first workplaces as well as most of the heaving slums south of Fourteenth Street. His district ran from the Bowery east to the tenements of the Lower East Side and had been organized so competently that it became the greatest Democratic stronghold in the city. Tim always knew every detail of his prospects intimately. In the run-up to one election early in his career, he discovered that there were three die-hard Republicans living in one part of his ward, and he reported back to Croker accordingly. When the ballots were counted and the district's vote was found to stand 395 to 4 in favor of the Democrats, Sullivan was outraged. "They got one more vote than I expected," he told the boss. "But I'll find that feller."

Tim had been born, in 1863, on Greenwich Street, in the heart of Manhattan's most noisome slum. His father died when the boy was only four, and his mother remarried a violent alcoholic. The family lived miserably in a crowded wooden tenement, taking in boarders to survive, and it is scarcely surprising, in such circumstances, that the future politician received little formal schooling. Tim took part-time jobs from the age of seven, at first working as a bootblack with a stand in the local police station house—a fine spot from which to learn the realities of life downtown. Soon afterward he began hawking newspapers, progressing eventually to a position as a sort of wholesaler and organizer of younger boys. A natural leader, Sullivan did what he could to help the desperate, starving, and sometimes parentless children who looked up to him. Owen Kildare—who was orphaned in infancy and thrown onto the streets, aged seven, when his foster mother acquired a lover—recalled that when he first ventured timidly down Theater Alley, where the newsboys gathered, it was the adolescent Sullivan who approached him, advanced him a nickel as working capital, and "taught me a few tricks of the trade and advised me to invest my five pennies in just one, the best selling paper of the period."

At eighteen, Sullivan went to work for a newspaper distributor, a job that considerably broadened his horizons. On occasion he found himself required to go as far uptown as Central Park, this at a time when some slum dwellers lived out their entire lives without ever going north of Fourteenth Street. By now Tim stood over six feet tall, and his height and "round handsome face, bright smile and piercing blue eyes" made him physically imposing, an important asset for aspiring politicians of the day.

Big Tim was an archetypal ward boss. He surrounded himself with men he could rely on—mostly members of his extended family; his principal aides were his brothers Paddy and Dennis,* his half brother Larry Mulligan, and cousins named Florrie, Christy, and "Little Tim"—and operated not from one of the newfangled Democratic club-houses then springing up throughout the city but in the old style, dispensing help and patronage from a chain of dubious saloons. One of his earliest establishments was the headquarters of the Whyos, at the time Manhattan's most notoriously violent street gang and a useful group to have on one's side come election time. When he finally became respectable, Tim moved out of his saloons and into a suite at the Occidental Hotel on the Bowery: a grand four-story structure, popular with actors and noted for the vast erotic fresco, depicting Diana bathing with a group of nymphs, that adorned the ceiling of its bar.

Big Tim's most celebrated trait was his generosity. He was known to rise at dawn to lead gangs of the unemployed uptown to find laboring jobs on public works, and he served a vast annual Christmas dinner to as many as 5,000 Bowery bums, on one occasion spending $7,000 to set out a spread comprising 10,000 pounds of turkey together with hams, stuffing, potatoes, 500 loaves of bread, 5,000 pies, 200 gallons of coffee, and a hundred kegs of beer. In the summer months, he organized elaborate clambakes in Harlem River Park. These daylong celebrations served a twofold purpose, cementing the Sullivan clan's reputation among the tenement poor while providing Big Tim and his cronies with an excuse to shake down businessmen and saloonkeepers along the Bowery—each of whom was expected to buy sheaves of five-dollar tickets.

All in all, there was—as Alvin Harlow, the Bowery chronicler, observed—"never a more perplexing admixture of good and evil in one human character than in that of Timothy D. Sullivan." Tim's friends were loyal to him for life, and he was certainly capable of extending genuine kindness to men who could do him no conceivable good. Once, observing that an elevator attendant he'd met in Albany had

---

*Popularly known, thanks to a face that had received some severe blows in fights, as "Flat-Nose Dinny."

never been to a "grand occasion" in his life, Tim spent $3,000 on a banquet for the man, with assemblymen and judges as guests, and a favorite dispensation was to grant a loyal supporter the right to organize a benefit in his own favor. These functions generally took the form of balls—"rackets," they were called, because of the noise they generated. With Sullivan around, the recipients of this signal honor never had trouble selling tickets, and "Commodore Dutch," a young Bowery bum employed to watch the goings-on in Tim's saloons, at one time cleared $2,000 a year from the "Annual Party, Affair, Soirée & Gala Naval Ball of the Original Commodore Dutch Association." Yet this was the same Sullivan who was reported, on oath before a committee of the state assembly, to have personally beaten up opposition voters on election day, who loudly announced that if a Republican opponent dared to send in student volunteers to watch the polls, "I will say now that there won't be enough ambulances in New York to carry them away," and whose most vocal supporters were once described by the *New York Herald* as "bullet-headed, short haired, small eyed, smooth shaven, and crafty looking, with heavy, vicious features, which speak of dissipation and brutality, ready to fight at a moment's notice."

Of course, the licensed excesses of the Sullivan clan, and the violence unleashed by their supporters, would scarcely have been possible had New York possessed an independent, vigorous police. But if Charley Becker learned one thing from the months he spent standing at the door of a Bowery saloon observing all the comings and goings on that famous street, it was that the city's thousands of patrolmen were far from independent. Manipulating polls could be done only with the tacit agreement of the local precinct captains and the studied negligence, if not the active connivance, of hundreds of beat policemen. Collecting graft from the gambling houses, brothels, and late-opening saloons, and guaranteeing their proprietors the right to run unmolested, also required control of the police.

It was New York's tragedy that its police department had long been vulnerable to such manipulation. The city had a lengthy history, extending back at least a century, of shameless exploitation of the police. Thousands of men had won promotion as a result of their zealousness in carrying out orders from the machines; many ordinary officers, perhaps even the majority, saw themselves as acolytes of a political party first and as patrolmen a distant second. And if Becker wished to join their ranks, his first step was to acknowledge this truth.

Becoming a policeman, in the early 1890s, was largely a matter of connections. A prospective recruit knew someone who knew a district leader, or perhaps he came to the attention of a ward activist while working in the beer halls of the Bowery. At that point, soundings would be taken and loyalties assessed. Then, if all was well, the man received an introduction to one of New York's police commissioners.

In theory, potential new recruits could also apply to the department through a committee called the Civil Service Board. The board was highly respectable—it was an independent and upstanding body, a product of the reform movement of the 1880s that was committed to appointing men on merit. But its application process was rigorous. In one three-year period, its members considered 815 applications from would-be recruits, referred a mere 229 of these candidates to police surgeons for a physical examination, and eventually offered jobs to 135. The four commissioners, meanwhile, accepted 856 requests for nominations and granted 778. Men applying to the Civil Service Board, in other words, had a one-in-eight chance of getting onto the force. Men who had the support of a commissioner got their appointments through in nine cases out of every ten.

The explanation for this spectacular discrepancy was simple: The commissioners took bribes. This was hardly surprising; they were part of the political establishment so comprehensively tainted by Tammany Hall, and a product of the mutually advantageous accommodation between the Democrats and their rival Republicans that had plunged the city into a morass of corruption. For $250 to $300 per man in Becker's day (half to a quarter of a full year's pay), recruits of the approved political persuasions were shepherded gently through the NYPD's appointment process. And—since the number of men anxious to join the police always exceeded the number of vacancies—the commissioners had little trouble in ensuring that their candidates met the broad requirements of the force, which included stipulations that applicants stand at least five feet seven inches tall and weigh at least 130 pounds. But favored men got special treatment. Tammany Hall paid a tutor to "cram" loyal Democratic candidates for the not-too-tricky entrance tests, and there were cases of men who failed the physical examination being sent back to the surgeons time and again until—sometimes at their fifth or sixth appearance—the doctors finally passed men with incurable infirmities such as poor eyesight, acute rheumatism, or curvature of the spine. Occasionally, when a recruit was a renowned partisan of one faction or the other, even greater allowances were made. A single felony conviction was supposed to bar a man from ever joining the police, for instance. In practice, however, a number of New York patrolmen had convictions for burglary or theft.

The advantages of this system were obvious, not least to the commissioners themselves. New York got policemen who had lived in the city long enough to be politically connected and thus knew their districts well. And—at an average of three hundred new recruits every twelve months—each member of the four-man Police Board received tax-free bribes amounting to $22,000 a year, a sum large enough to be a temptation to even the most affluent among them. So lucrative was the post of commissioner, in fact, that the men who held it could afford occasional indulgences. Favored political candidates might receive their nominations free of charge. Particularly outstanding recruits were also sometimes ushered in without request for payment. New York's famous "Broadway Squad"—a body of policemen assigned to patrol the most fashionable stretches of the celebrated street, made up entirely of handsome, physically imposing men—got several of its best recruits this way. Since the chief purpose of the squad was to keep pickpockets and sneak thieves away from respectable citizens, escort well-to-do ladies across the street, and in general reassure New York's upper classes that the city was properly policed (thus, hopefully, blinding them to excesses elsewhere), such apparent indulgences were no doubt considered investments.

Charles Becker's police patron was one of the four commissioners sitting in 1893: a well-known New York merchant by the name of John F. McClave. McClave, who was in his fifties, first joined the board in 1884. He was one of two Republicans who shared power with a pair of Tammany Democrats. He was also thoroughly corrupt—a failing unsurprising in a man of previously modest means who found himself exposed to considerable temptation. As a police commissioner, treasurer of the Board of Police, a trustee of the Police Pension Fund, and a member of the committee on repairs and supplies, McClave saw numerous opportunities to channel funds into his own accounts. He took them.

How Becker made McClave's acquaintance is not known. Ordinarily the would-be policeman would have been recommended to him by a district political leader, or perhaps been befriended by one of Manhattan's "buffs": businessmen who made it their job to help the police, expecting favors in return. The most influential of these men—they were usually middle-ranking politicians such as aldermen, state senators, or assemblymen—protected and assisted individual patrolmen and even controlled, to some extent, promotions to the higher ranks. Whatever the truth, McClave's willingness to promote Becker's career implies two things: that the Callicoon farm boy had Republican leanings, which would have made him a comparative oddity in a police department still dominated by Tammany, and that Becker had no scruples about paying for his job rather than taking the more honorable but risky course of applying through the Civil Service Board.

In this, of course, the novice patrolman was no different from most of the men then serving with the police department, and the truth was that his physical attributes alone would have made him an impressive candidate in any era. Whether or not Becker really needed McClave's support to obtain an appointment, however, the commissioner at least ensured that his young protégé made swift progress with his application. Becker parted with the $300 he had saved in the autumn of 1892, a little more than a year after his older brother joined the force. Thanks no doubt to McClave, his case received favorable consideration. His appointment was confirmed that November. By Christmas the new recruit was in training. And by the beginning of February 1894, he was in uniform.

CHAPTER 3

GRAFT

IT WAS SHORTLY AFTER midnight in the rattletrap old station house on West Twentieth Street. Up on the second floor, in the great barracks of a dormitory, the men of the police reserve slumped facedown on their bedbug-ridden mattresses. The patrolmen slept in unwashed flannel underwear, their damp outer clothing slung on lines along the sweating walls. It was still winter, and both windows had been battened firmly down; the air in the room was stale and rank, and in the center of the floor a squat, potbellied stove blazed heat in all directions, adding the stink of burning coal to the powerful aromas of tobacco, bodies, and beer.

Fresh out of training school, the raw recruit inched through the fug, groping his way from bed to bed until he reached his locker. It was the farthest from the window, naturally, and the iron bed frame next to it had been moved into the room that afternoon. Doing his best not to disturb the men sleeping beside him, the young patrolman perched upon his lumpy mattress and bent to untie his laces. As he did so, the bed collapsed beneath him with a crash and a great shout of laughter filled the room. It was not a friendly sound.

Reassembling a gimmicked bed frame in the dark was tricky work, and it took the young man quite a while to do it. As he slipped and sweated on a floor slick with tobacco juice and rat droppings, the men closest to him began to talk among themselves. The veterans' accents were all Irish, and they were making no attempt to keep their voices down. It seemed they wanted to be overheard.

"Say, Mac, do you think the big Dutchman can take it?"

"I very much doubt it, Paddy."

"Have you got the rope, Jim?"

"Sure thing, Pat, and the handcuffs, too."

"Hey, Bill, where's the tar pot?"

"It's okay, Paddy, Barney the Brute is looking after that. He's got it on the stove downstairs."

"Say, John, have you got the tape?"

"Sure, and the paint pots, too. What color are you going to use, green or yellow?"

"Oh, I think we'll use the yellow. He's Dutch anyway."

At last the voices stilled and turned to raucous snores. The temperature in the stifling room rose higher, and the rasps of slumbering patrolmen began to mingle once again with the distant yells of drunks in the cells far below. Miserably, in the darkness, the rookie stretched out on his reassembled bed. At that moment he wished that he had stayed at home.

Not 1894 but 1900. Not the recollections of Charley Becker but those of another newly qualified policeman, named Cornelius Willemse. Yet Willemse's vivid memories of the hazing he endured ring true for any year during the 1890s. Initiation into New York's police was protracted, often physically arduous, and—as Willemse himself observed—"especially strong if your speech had no touch of the welcome brogue and your nationality didn't happen to indicate a pure strain from the Emerald Isle, and not too far north at that." Becker's own earliest experiences almost certainly resembled those described by his near contemporary: practical jokes, then whispered threats—to heighten the tension—and finally, a week or so later, a midnight encounter with a squad of veterans:

One night I woke up and discovered I was tied to the bed. The room was semi-dark and the gang was around me with their raincoats up to their eyes, and helmets on; they looked like so many medieval warrior ghosts. They pulled my bed out into the middle of the room under the little gas jet, shoved the other beds back against the wall, and began the evening's entertainment—for everybody but me.

Police initiation rituals, Willemse added, followed a pattern. Newly qualified officers were generally painted green, the Irish veterans' favorite color, first. After that, their tormentors would produce rolls of adhesive tape, plaster thick strips of it over the rookie's body, and forcibly depilate him. Sometimes a recruit was tarred. The climax to the ceremony was a solemn oath, taken by all new men, never to reveal department secrets.

Rituals of this sort had emerged, probably, fifty years earlier, and some may have been older still. There had, after all, been police in Manhattan for as long as there had been a city: a night watch at first (commanded, as late as 1798, by the mayor in person) and then a force of part-time patrolmen, often muscular carters by profession, led for more than half a century by a powerfully built high constable named Jacob Hays. By the early 1840s, though, the septuagenarian Hays— who still patrolled the lower reaches of the city armed with no more than a gold-tipped staff, immutably clad in a black suit and stovepipe hat—had been overwhelmed by a city that had grown to 300,000 people and was increasingly menaced by violent street gangs. Prominent New Yorkers now compared their watch unfavorably to the larger, better organized, more disciplined police forces springing up in Europe. In 1845, when Hays retired, the watch system was dissolved and replaced at last with a New York Police Department.

The newfangled NYPD was given all the resources that policemen needed, including mounted patrols and a detective department. But it took time, even then, to make the force effective. Most of its officers were drawn from the same small pool of volunteers who had formed the watch; little effort was made to test recruits, law was taught sketchily at best, and there was no formal weapons training of any sort. Standards were lax in other ways as well: European visitors were shocked to see New York policemen puffing on cigars and spitting out tobacco juice, and patrolmen did not even wear uniforms until the 1850s, years after they were introduced elsewhere. As late as 1893, the department remained perennially undermanned and underfunded.

To take only one example, communication between the headquarters building on Mulberry Street and outlying precincts still took place by telegraph, not telephone, and messages came down the wire letter by letter, to be announced by a system of ringing bells that had been the last word in modernity when introduced four decades earlier. Orders to policemen on the beat had to be conveyed via messengers. "In this respect," one despairing police commissioner complained, "New York City, the metropolis of the nation, is far behind many cities of the third, fourth and even fifth class in this country."

There were bright spots in the department's record, certainly. The Detective Bureau, for many years under the sway of the formidable Inspector Thomas Byrnes, was widely praised and often effective, and by the 1890s even ordinary patrolmen were beginning to take some pride in their professionalism. Older, more experienced officers with families to support banded together to form the influential Patrolmen's Benevolent Association—a union in all but name, devoted to improving conditions, salaries, and prospects. Men of this sort were almost always more committed to police work than their younger, brasher colleagues, and they formed a counterbalance to the domination of the force by the political machines.

By Charley Becker's day, in short, New York's police stood at something of a crossroads. The NYPD appeared—at least to out-of-towners—to be much like any other police force in the United States or Europe. Its men were uniformed, trained, armed, and highly visible. Order was, in general, maintained; the courts were full; the jails were full; sensational cases were resolved. Byrnes and his detectives often appeared in the press, their chief boasting of his achievements in preventing crime and catching criminals. Yet the department's fatal entanglement in New York politics remained an enduring blot upon its record. The great majority of its men owed their jobs to the patronage of well-connected local politicians, and an officer's loyalty to his bosses was brutally enforced. In the early days of the department, each man's appointment had been renewable annually, and men who angered influential politicians, or merely failed to demonstrate a willingness to follow orders, were speedily dismissed. Even now, half a century later,

New York patrolmen still lived in terror of upsetting their superiors, with all that that implied for the performance of their jobs. No one who came into contact with the police could remain unaware of their dark depths for long, and every man who joined the force had to make his own accommodation with the temptations available. Charley Becker, when he donned the uniform in 1893, made his mind up early on and stuck to it. The decision that he made shaped the remainder of his life.

Corruption remained endemic in New York. True, Tammany's worst excesses now lay in the past. The theft of millions from the public purse, as practiced by Boss Tweed, had proved too blatant even for the Hall and far too unpopular with voters, too, which was why Honest John Kelly had preferred to raise cash from public utilities instead. Under Croker, though, even these extortions had been deemed dangerously high-profile. Between 1886, when the new boss seized power, and 1894, when Becker began to patrol the city streets, Tammany instead made millions from vice.

The system was pervasive and effective. No brothel or gambling house could operate without paying monthly tribute for protection; no saloon could stay open late unless it made appropriate "contributions" in return. Best of all, extortion of this sort roused little protest. Taxpayers' money remained safe and the powerful shareholders of large corporations unoutraged. Even those who actually ran Manhattan's vice saw such excesses as inevitable. Long custom had (as Police Commissioner William McAdoo observed a few years later)

> made the keepers of disorderly and gambling houses not only willing but eager to pay the money. As a matter of fact, the manager of a disorderly house, whether man or woman, does not feel any sense of security unless some one representing the police authorities has received money. These men and women will withhold their money from the landlord and pay their "protection rent" [in preference]. . . . A corrupt police captain doesn't have to force payments. They will thrust money upon him and those under him. These men and women feel that when they pay their money they are going to be protected.

The only protests of note came from religious leaders and reform groups, which campaigned largely ineffectually against the triple evils of gambling, drunkenness, and the "white slave trade." Such protests, when confined to church, were routinely ignored, and even complaints to the district attorney's office were simply brushed aside; what proof, some Tammany placeman would inquire, was there of any wrongdoing? Since ministers and upper-class reformers ("mugwumps," as they were derisively known) shuddered at the prospect of actually soiling their hands in the vice districts, evidence of the sort required to go to court was generally not forthcoming.

Every few years protests would rise to a crescendo, often in the wake of some especially dramatic crime. As recently as 1892, the Reverend Charles Parkhurst—whose attention had been drawn to New York's lowlife by a murder in a saloon the preceding Christmas Eve—had become so outraged by the casual arrogance of the then district attorney in dismissing his complaints that he had donned a disguise, hired a detective, and set off on an extended tour of downtown dives and brothels. Parkhurst had returned some weeks later to deliver several detailed sermons on Manhattan vice, creating such a citywide furor that Tammany had closed down half a dozen brothels in response.*

---

*Parkhurst's adventures—heavily covered by the press—shocked and amused New York in equal measure. The magnificently bearded minister had been accosted in the first saloon he entered by a teenage girl demanding, "Hey, whiskers, going to ball me off?" and then propositioned by more than fifty whores along one block of Bleecker Street— all of them touting for business within the hearing of a beat patrolman. Later Parkhurst visited a "tight house" (where all the girls wore tights) and called in at Hattie Adams's celebrated bordello on West Twenty-seventh Street, where he was treated to a cancan exhibition that climaxed with one Amazonian blonde kicking away a derby hat held six feet off the floor. It was not until his detective introduced him to the Golden Rule Pleasure Club, a specialist brothel operated by a madam known as "Scotch Anne," that Parkhurst flinched. The house, down in Greenwich Village, was located in a darkened basement divided into flimsy wooden cubicles and inhabited by heavily made-up men in women's clothing who chattered away in artful falsettos and gave each other female names. The minister, bemused by this outlandish sight, had to be taken to one side and told that the denizens were male prostitutes. At this even Parkhurst turned and fled, calling, "Why, I wouldn't stay in that house for all the money in the world!"

Ordinarily, however, politicians and police let things be. The NYPD's precinct captains knew that action on their part would be highly unpopular, not merely with the bosses of the political machines but also with the tens of thousands of ordinary New Yorkers who patronized the vice districts. It was simpler and much more lucrative to control and license sin. Madams and gamblers paid for appropriate protection. The police collected the money, kept a portion for themselves, and channeled the rest upward to City Hall.

It was easy for Tammany and its allies at the Custom House to control this system. So long as the machines retained the power to appoint policemen, they could ensure that those who joined the force were partisans who would accept the status quo. And with loyalists in senior positions and allies on the Board of Commissioners, corrupt politicians could break any policeman who annoyed them, having him fined, suspended, fired, or even jailed.

Cooperation with New York's machines was guaranteed in still-more-sinister ways. The senior officers who arranged the collection of payments—and benefited directly from doing so—were kept in line by the simple expedient of being made to pay so heavily for promotion to the most lucrative posts that they had to graft in order to recover their investments. By 1893, when Becker joined the force, the assessment to be promoted from patrolman was $500, men paid as much as $4,000 to become sergeants, and a captaincy routinely cost $12,000— sums that no man could afford himself. Prospective candidates were generally forced to borrow funds from obliging politicians, and the handful who refused to pay found promotion denied to them. One sergeant, who had an excellent record and had excelled in his exams, twice rose to the head of the list of men qualified to become captains. Twice he refused to pay the requisite bribe to the commissioners; twice they ensured he was passed over. Each failure resulted in the man's name being returned to the foot of the sergeants' list, and the third time he reached the top, he capitulated and agreed to pay. On this occasion (thanks, he was told, to competition from another candidate, but perhaps simply to reinforce the lesson) the sum demanded of him was $15,000.

Over time the corruption of the city became an open secret. During his first years on the force, Becker—like every newly qualified policeman—would have seen examples of abuse of power all around him. Even New York's most lauded officer, Inspector (by now Superintendent) Byrnes did not bother to investigate robberies unless the victim offered a substantial reward, and, despite never having earned more than $5,000 a year, had built up savings totaling $600,000 by the time of his retirement. Byrnes claimed to have amassed this fortune with the help of tips passed to him by friendly Wall Street brokers, but at least part of it was the product of more serious corruption, for while chief of the Detective Bureau he had developed ties with most of New York's burglars and pickpockets. Crooks were permitted to operate, within carefully defined territories, on condition that they handed back the proceeds of certain robberies on demand, and it was these comfortable arrangements, rather than any special competence as a thief taker, that enabled Byrnes to recover and—with a flourish—return the purses, watches, and silver filched from the Fifth Avenue elite.

Byrnes was admittedly a special case: an officer so celebrated that he stood head and shoulders above every other policeman in the city. But there were plenty of other veterans around to show each batch of new recruits how things were done in Manhattan. The most notorious among them, certainly, was Inspector Alexander Williams, a man reputed to have engaged in an average of one fight a day throughout his years on patrol. Williams, who earned the nickname "Clubber" for the enthusiasm with which he wielded his nightstick,* became so widely known throughout the city that tourists stopped to gawk when he passed on the street. By 1887, after twenty-one years on the force, he had been the subject of 358 formal complaints, but his clout with New York's politicians was such that although fined 224 times, he had never suffered serious punishment. A few years later, when Williams's brutal career was at last subjected to detailed scrutiny, it was discovered

---

* "There is more law in a policeman's nightstick," Clubber liked to say, "than in a decision of the Supreme Court."

that many of the records relating to charges against him were mysteriously missing and that others had lain on file for years without being proceeded with.

Nor was Inspector Williams the lone example of a tough and well-connected cop made good. The larger-than-life figure of Captain William S. Devery was if anything even more beloved by New York's newspaper reporters, who liked to tease him for his habit of beginning sentences by saying, "Touchin' on and appertainin' to." A cigar-chomping Irishman, almost illiterate but shrewd, Devery liked to manage his men not from an office but from a spot on the corner of Twenty-eighth Street and Ninth Avenue. The magnificently mustached "Big Bill" sat there every night from nine in the evening until 2:00 or 3:00 A.M., clever eyes gleaming in his fleshy face as he received reports from policemen, bail bondsmen, gamblers, dive owners, and assorted criminals. It was common knowledge that the captain had banked a fortune by extending his protection to all manner of illegal businesses, and his fat fingers were thrust deep into several other pies as well. It was Devery who enforced his good friend Tim Sullivan's lucrative monopoly on the arrangement of prizefights in Manhattan.

The amoral Captain Devery, more so even than Clubber Williams, set a significant example to the young policemen of the 1890s. He differed from his peers in being more or less openly corrupt, and yet somehow he still survived every attempt to unseat him. For editors such as Lincoln Steffens of the *Commercial Advertiser,* he was a "magnificent villain, always good for a scandal and some laughs at the same time—as a character, as a work of art, he was a masterpiece." By the middle of the decade, indeed, Devery had developed his robust sense of humor into a weapon, for as Steffens conceded, "Not only I myself—every reporter I ever assigned to roast the man came back smiling, and put the smile into his report." But in truth much of what Big Bill did was no laughing matter—not least because, taking over the Eleventh Precinct on the Bowery, he proceeded to rake in graft so blatantly that he was finally indicted for extortion. Devery's pull within Tammany Hall was so formidable, however, that he was acquitted on a technicality, had his badge restored to him by the Supreme Court, and was made chief of police in 1898. This, one authority on the New York of the period observes, "was a title he tainted so thoroughly that it was abolished after his resignation in 1901."

Devery's survival, in the face of repeated attempts to secure his dismissal, could hardly fail to send a message to all ranks of the force. Corrupt officers with the right connections—his repeated triumphs over his enemies implied—had nothing to fear from the law. And the ruthless use that Big Bill made of departmental procedure was another education in itself. Policemen who protested his excesses found themselves exiled to some remote, semirural precinct well away from both their families and the graft—being "sent to Goatville," they called it, a terrifying prospect. When the new chief of police fell out with a Captain Herlihy, he had his enemy transferred to Kingsbridge, in the farthest reaches of the Bronx, and "gave him two and a half hours to take up his duties here—no mean feat considering the transportation available at the time. If Herlihy had not made it, Devery was prepared to bring charges [against him] for being absent from duty."

It was impossible to serve on a force commanded by the likes of Bill Devery without thinking at least a little about the tests and the temptations of police work. Most officers in the early 1890s drew the inevitable conclusion that the graft was time-honored and that those who chose to sample it were unlikely to be punished. Honest men who wanted a career learned not to protest too much. And Patrolman Charley Becker, who lacked neither connections nor ambition, observed, with crystal clarity, the rewards available to the police of New York.

Life for a newly qualified patrolman could be hard nonetheless. Training was still rudimentary (recruits in 1893 received no more than a month at a school of instruction, learning 250 general orders, 700 police rules, and the basics of criminal law, first aid, and the Manhattan sanitary code), and thousands of New York policemen devoted their lives to routine work that offered scant excitement: long hours of

patrolling nighttime streets, rattling padlocks, and standing firm on
street corners in a howling gale. Working conditions, even in the
heart of the city, remained abysmal. Half the precinct houses in the
city were so unsanitary that they would be condemned a few years
later, the police commissioner of the day complaining that each of his
men was forced to work in

> the vilest of surroundings, in constant discomfort, and at the
> risk of his health. Under such circumstances, he has little
> incentive to read anything but sensational newspapers, and to
> swap stories and gossip about the department. The bad police-
> man gets the chance here to contaminate the good one, and
> the whole arrangement makes for demoralization and hope-
> lessness on the part of the rank and file.

Conditions on the streets were scarcely better. In winter, men summoned from reserve were expected to charge out of their overheated
rooms straight into temperatures that plunged well below freezing. In
summer, streets and stations alike stank of rotting garbage. And, to
make matters worse, the police worked longer hours than almost anybody in Manhattan—an average of nearly seventeen in every twenty-
four, patrols of up to twelve hours' duration being followed every other
day by an equal period spent "in reserve." These brutal working practices were a consequence of the "two-platoon system," a compulsory
rotation that called—in the name of efficiency—for half the entire
force to be available for duty at any given time. Schedules were
arranged in such a way that no policeman could hope for more than
four hours' sleep while on reserve. Nor was it uncommon for the men
to be on their feet for much of their reserve periods, attending court
and responding to all sorts of emergencies. Even a writer friendly to
the police conceded, as early as 1885, that the system appeared to have
been "devised to get all the duty out of a Patrolman that his system will
stand."

Officers drained by their long hours developed ways of coping.
Men on night patrol might spend as much time searching for a quiet

spot where they could get some rest as they did policing the streets. "Cooping," as it was known, had been honed into a fine art by several generations of policemen, for each precinct maintained a number of roundsmen, veterans whose job it was to check the men on the beat to see that they were at their posts. Some roundsmen remembered their days on patrol well enough to wink at the occasional indulgence; others were tougher, making it their habit to double back after checking on a man to make certain he had not vanished straight into the nearest saloon. Most feared of all were the "shoo flies"—roundsmen in plainclothes sent in from headquarters to shake up the comfortable arrangements that frequently developed between the officers of a precinct. Shoo flies were assessed according to the number of "didos" (disciplinary complaints) that each wrote up, and—as Cornelius Willemse recalled—"they did their jobs uncomfortably well."

The poor working conditions endured by the police might have been palatable had the men been well paid. Superficially at least, they seemed to be: The starting pay for a first-year patrolman was $800, higher than almost any other working-class salary of the time. But rookie officers such as Becker—already impoverished by the bribes they'd had to pay to join the force—soon discovered that they were required to buy not only their own uniforms and guns, at a cost of well over $300 a man, but also their precinct-house beds and bedlinens: demands that put a further heavy strain on a patrolman's wallet. Then there were the mandatory levies to the Patrolmen's Benevolent Association, irregular political campaign "assessments" of $10 a man and more, and annual fund-raisers, organized by both Tammany and the Custom House, to which their partisans were expected to contribute. Many policemen resented the requirement to purchase tickets to some politician's clambake, but open opposition to the system was suicidal. "The first couple of years were always the most expensive to be a cop," concluded Willemse, looking back. "Moneylenders made fortunes off youngsters who were forced to pay for years and years before they got their affairs straightened out. You wonder why policemen go into restaurants and don't pay for their meals? How can they afford to?"

Short of cash but long on opportunities, few New York patrolmen were entirely clean. It was simply unrealistic to expect the police to pay for their appointments to the force and do their duty in a city that was corrupt from top to bottom, repay the politicians who did them favors, enforce the terms of the graft, and take home their own indifferent pay without seizing the chance to earn a little extra for themselves. A scattering of officers remained famous for their rectitude—men such as Captains Harkins and Gallagher, who quietly donated most of their wages to the poor, and "Honest Dan" Costigan, who cleaned up Chinatown, turning down thousands of dollars' worth of bribes in the process. The fact remains, however, that Costigan's incorruptibility was sufficiently unusual to earn him a nickname, and the pressures on a recruit's paycheck made most happy to accept the odd gratuity. An apple exacted from a street vendor whose cart stuck out an inch or two onto the pavement, a pint of beer served free by a saloon found open after closing time: few thought such "gifts" really wrong. "Cops," Willemse wrote with careful understatement,

> pick up an extra dollar now and then, to be sure, but they usually spend it as fast as they get it. I was no exception to this rule. I'm not trying to pose as a saint or a reformer, or one who was shocked by anything I saw. If I found an open door on post, or picked up a man for safe keeping while helplessly drunk, found a lost child or warned a man of a violation before taking action, and they felt like slipping me a few bucks, I took it and my conscience didn't bother me then, nor does it now. Of course there are cops who have never taken a dollar, at least I've heard about them, but I never saw one.

The line that most policemen of the nineties drew was not the largely unrealistic one between absolute honesty and outright corruption but that which divided "honest" from "dishonest" graft. Few officers spurned honest graft, which—from a beat patrolman's point of view—consisted of reward money that should not have been accepted or cash proffered by shopkeepers in exchange for overlooking harmless violations. Some men working in Satan's Circus used the same term to cover "gambling donations," the dollars paid by gamblers to hire off-duty men to guard their premises. Dishonest or "dirty" graft was everything else: protection money and the proceeds of extortion. Only a minority of New York's beat policemen (albeit a significant minority) crossed this line and involved themselves in genuinely criminal activity.

The real point, as the Brooklyn judge William Gaynor* once conceded, was that such abuses remain private. New York's police, in Gaynor's view, existed to "preserve outward order and decency" in the city. It would be asking too much to expect them to be inwardly decent as well, and even the city's handful of honest policemen believed that corruption in the department was far too deeply ingrained to be eradicated. Superintendent Byrnes himself cautioned one prominent police commissioner against attempting to reform the force: "It will break you," the great detective warned. "You will yield. You are but human."

Despite the manifold discomforts of life on the beat, Patrolman Becker's own police career got off to a promising start. For whatever reason—his size, his looks, his brother's help, perhaps Commissioner McClave's—the young policeman's early postings were all prestigious ones. There would be no years in the wilds of north Manhattan for him; instead Becker began his service with eighteen months in the Second Precinct, where he served with the "Dock Rats," a special squad assigned to the quays and wharfs around the harbor. After that, in the spring of 1895, he transferred to Satan's Circus. A few weeks on the beat in the city's most lucrative precinct ended with his assignment to plainclothes, quite a coup for so young an officer.

There can be no doubt that Becker was, at the very least, exposed to considerable temptation during the formative years of his career. The Manhattan waterfront may have been in steep decline by the early 1890s; the superior port facilities of Brooklyn and New Jersey had seen

---

*Mayor of New York from to 1909 to 1913.

to that. But the Dock Rats still had ample opportunity to filch from cargoes on the wharves, and even the most honest among them routinely picked up extra cash from steamship companies who used them as additional security whenever the great liners docked. For those willing to graft, there were plenty of river pirates and thieves ready to pay officers to look the other way, and such opportunities were multiplied later, in Satan's Circus, where even the lowliest policeman expected— at the very least—to receive free meals and beer from the local saloons and fleshier favors from the brothels on his beat.

Patrolman Becker's first brushes with the underworld seem to have dated to his posting to Satan's Circus. He had not been in the district long before he made the acquaintance of May Sharpe, the brassy prostitute who figured so memorably in the Stephen Crane affair. According to the memoirs Sharpe compiled years later, she and Becker became friends in 1895, when the patrolman was twenty-five years old and the glamorous May a mere nineteen. Within a short time, acquaintance ripened into a business relationship. There were obvious advantages, for Chicago May, in having a beat policeman in her pocket. The benefits to Becker were financial, and perhaps physical as well.

May Sharpe was an ambitious and successful criminal, able to pay well for protection. An Irish girl who had run away from home aged only thirteen, absconding with her parents' life savings of £60, May wound up in New York in 1894. By then she was already displaying the talents that would turn her into one of the most notorious crooks of the era. Though working primarily as a streetwalker, she branched out into the more lucrative fields of robbery and blackmail, stealing from clients who were mostly too drunk or too embarrassed to complain, and working hand in hand with the city's "creep" and "panel" joints—brothels whose rooms were equipped with secret entrances through which skinny men would crawl, while a client was noisily occupied, to steal the contents of his wallet. At around the same time, May became renowned throughout Satan's Circus as the "Queen of the Badger Game," a form of extortion that involved girls threatening well-off customers with exposure, either to their wives or, in the case of unmarried men, to their business partners or perhaps in the form of a suit for breach of promise of marriage. In almost every case, middle-class clients would discreetly settle for a handsome sum in order to preserve their reputations. Abe Hummel, the junior partner in the notorious law firm of Howe & Hummel,* and famous in his day as probably the most crooked lawyer in the city, made his fortune bro-kering deals of this sort.

By the time she first encountered Becker, May's activities already extended to theft, and it was here that her new friend was of most value to her. Sharpe had a well-developed taste for jewels—"she invented the system," a contemporary reporter noted, "of taking men into halls and there, burying her face in their chests, she bit the stones out of their scarf pins and went blithely on her way"—and around 1896 she stole a large consignment of jewelry from a traveling sales-man whom she had laid low with some knockout drops. The robbery took place on Becker's beat, and he agreed to shield May from her pursuers in exchange for a valuable stolen ring. This was no small matter, for the value of the consignment was such that the girl was eventually forced to flee as far as New Haven, Connecticut, to escape pursuit. Becker did his bit by concealing her in a rented room on Fifty-third Street and then hiding her for several days in the apart-ment of a drug addict by the name of Pauline Washbourne, who was conveniently smitten with him.

---

*At its peak this legendarily corrupt practice received fat retainers from virtually every thief, gangster, brothel keeper, and abortionist in the city. All seventy-four madams rounded up during a purity drive in 1884 named Howe & Hummel as counsel, and at one time the firm represented 23 of the 25 prisoners awaiting trial for murder in New York's Tombs prison and had an undeclared interest in the twenty-fourth. William F. Howe—a trial lawyer with a shady past, noted for his corpulence, diamond jewelry, and florid style—handled the criminal work. His partner, Hummel, a rake-thin, runtish genius (he stood less than five feet tall), specialized in civil cases and was widely cele-brated for his skill in spotting loopholes in the law. Hummel once found an error in pro-cedure that led to the release of 240 of the 300 prisoners on Blackwell's Island; on another occasion the partners invoked a technicality that, had it been allowed, would have set free every prisoner then awaiting trial, or recently convicted, of first-degree murder in the entire state. The firm flourished until 1907 from offices opposite the new police headquarters on Centre Street. Its cable address was LENIENT.

Becker's first fleeting appearance in the New York press, which came in the midst of one of the city's periodic drives to clean up the liquor industry, similarly suggests a man coming to terms with a pervasive climate of corruption. Midway through August 1895, a patrolman named McConnell appeared in court to testify that Augustus Elder's bar on Fifty-second Street had been trading on a Sunday, when all saloons should have been closed. Becker took the stand as a rebuttal witness, stating on oath that he had checked the same establishment's doors and locks and found that it had been completely empty. It was not uncommon in those days for ward bosses to protect a friendly tavern owner by countering dangerous testimony in this manner; what was unusual was the unhappy outcome of the case. Officer Becker's testimony was not believed, and Elder was convicted for his breaches of the excise law. The saloonkeeper went to prison for thirty days; no action, unsurprisingly, was taken against Becker for his perjury.

Charley Becker presumably was paid, in cash or kind, for providing assistance in such matters. His favorite graft, nonetheless, was detaining women in the Tenderloin for soliciting. The scant handful of records that survive from these early years show that, even before the Crane affair, he had been involved in at least one case in which a girl had been unlawfully detained. A few months later, in February 1897, the young patrolman inadvertently became embroiled in another fracas after arresting a woman who had asked him directions to the subway. She turned out to be "a respectable New Jersey matron" and had to be released the next morning, with apologies.

Many, if not all, of these arrests were suspect. It was common practice in the 1890s for patrolmen to stop girls on the street, arrest them for solicitation, and have them locked up at the nearest station house. Their release would be secured by a bail bondsman, who used funds provided by the girl's pimp or madam or obtained from her family. The original charge would then be quietly dropped on the understanding that the bail money was forfeit, and the cash split among the arresting officer, his precinct captain, and the bondsman. Dirty graft of this sort was endemic throughout the Tenderloin; the prostitutes, who were losing money while in prison, were happy to post bail, and their procurers accepted the practice as a form of tax. It was only when a greedy officer detained an innocent woman—as Becker contrived to do on these occasions—that the system ever came to light.

Of course, Patrolman Becker did his share of ordinary police work, too. There were long hours spent walking the beat, days and nights in tedious reserve, and the occasional excitement. On one occasion the rookie policeman was waylaid in a lonely stairwell and robbed by two women armed with guns. On another, less than a week after arresting Ruby Young, Becker found himself involved in the pursuit of three burglars whom he saw emerging from a Broadway cigar store at dawn. He gave chase; one man escaped, Becker brought the second down with a blow to the head from his nightstick,* and the third man was shot and killed by another beat policeman.

Once again Becker found himself in the papers, but on this occasion he was praised for acting bravely and correctly. The burglars—in the police account, at least—had been given several chances to stop; both Becker and his colleague, Officer Carey, were said to have discharged warning shots into the air before opening fire in earnest; and at least one press report noted that the criminals were armed and ready to shoot back. The incident made the front pages of the New York papers, and Becker was formally commended for his actions by Police Commissioner Grant. Not until sometime later did it emerge that the dead man was no burglar but an innocent plumber's mate by the name of John Fay, who had walked into the path of Carey's bullets. Becker was lucky once again; the shooting was accepted as an accident, and no action was taken against the two patrolmen.

---

*Police nightsticks were formidable things. Twenty-six inches long, an inch and three-quarters thick, and made of locustwood—light but strong—they could easily kill if brought down hard enough on a man's head. "All you got to do," Lincoln Steffens was informed by one veteran officer, "is to tap the extremities, head or feet, so as to send a current through the spine. . . . It's the funniest sight in the world to see the effect of a proper lick with the stick on a man's two feet. I remember the first time I got one just right. That bum rose, stiff as a stick; he didn't bend a knee or move an arm. He just rose up, running. . . . It was beautiful."

In the 1890s, nonetheless, Charley Becker was not the sort of policeman often singled out for praise. He seemed content to be a patrolman of the old school, modeling himself, apparently consciously, on the club-swinging cops who had formed the backbone of the NYPD a decade earlier. Becker seems to have had no compunction in taking his nightstick to New York's citizens even when they posed him little threat. In the spring of 1897, he was charged with beating up a teenage boy in the lobby of a Tenderloin theater; once again the case went nowhere.

The way in which a policeman comported himself on the street could have important consequences for his career. An officer who stuck to the rules and resisted temptation might find himself adopted by an eager mugwump, anxious to hold him up as an example; one newly qualified patrolman by the name of Bourke, who bravely shut down the dance hall operated by a celebrated fixer known as "King" Callahan,* found himself promoted to the rank of roundsman by a reformist police commissioner. Patrolman Becker's handiness with a nightstick attracted the attention of much darker elements; his mentor in the later 1890s was none other than Clubber Williams, who for all his faults had a deserved reputation for displaying paternal interest in rookie officers. Exactly what persuaded Clubber to take the young Becker in hand is not known; possibly it was politics, for both men were Republicans. Whatever the reason, the two officers formed a friendship that endured for many years.

Becker's eagerness to accept Clubber's friendship is perhaps more surprising. A few years earlier, certainly, a man with Williams's pull could have been nothing but good news for a young patrolman's career. By the time the two men met, however, the old inspector was a mere shadow of his former self. Denounced for brutality, openly suspected of corruption, and intimately associated with the Tenderloin, Williams had been paraded before the widest-ranging commission of inquiry into corruption that New York had ever known. The revelations that

---

*A famous place, noted in the middle 1890s as "every slummer's first stop," where pickpockets operated en masse and the singing waiters included a young Al Jolson.

ensued forced Tammany to find new ways of doing business in Satan's Circus, helped to shape Becker's career—and changed the city's view of its police forever.

The Senate Committee Appointed to Investigate the Police Department of the City of New York—the Lexow Committee, as it was familiarly known, after the state senator who chaired it—began its deliberations early in February 1894. It was not the first commission set up to tackle Manhattan corruption: An earlier inquiry into the policing of the city had reported as long ago as 1840; another had sat in 1875; and a third (led by none other than Theodore Roosevelt), in 1884. Each committee had found vice flourishing in the city, and each concluded that New York's police abetted it. Firm evidence of wrong-doing, admittedly, was scanty, and none of the commissions produced credible witnesses who could describe the inner workings of the system. Even so, accumulated testimony demonstrated that some senior officers had been pocketing $10,000 a year from graft as early as 1839.

The failure of a whole succession of inquiries to yield results was easy to explain: Witnesses were simply too frightened of the police to talk. Men who had been subpoenaed to give testimony proffered feeble excuses to explain their nonappearance or proved to have frustratingly hazy memories of dates, places, and amounts. Public opinion was mollified with a handful of trials, but reformers were left with little to show from any of the three investigations. A few dozen policemen—mostly juniors—lost their jobs. A single corrupt judge was fired. But the precinct captains and the ward bosses who between them ran the system were unscathed. No man well enough acquainted with the system to hurt it ever gave detailed evidence.

The Lexow inquiry, though, was different. For one thing, it had far more clout than any of its predecessors. The new commission was the creature of Thomas Platt, the powerful Republican boss of the Custom House, who had fallen out disastrously with Tammany's Boss Croker after three successive Democratic election triumphs had upset the comfortable accommodation between the parties in New York. Gorged on victory, the Hall no longer saw the need to channel patronage to its traditional opponents and had begun to withhold the city offices on which Platt depended to secure the loyalty of his partisans. There was little Platt could do to hurt Tammany in staunchly Democratic Manhattan. But a Republican majority in the state assembly at Albany offered him the chance to seek revenge. It was there that Platt engineered the appointment of Senator Lexow and his committee.

Platt's aim, in setting up this new commission of inquiry, was not to end New York rackets; they had the potential to enrich his political machine just as they enriched the Democrats. The boss merely wanted to force Croker to restore the old division of the city's graft. The plan, it seems, was to let Lexow and his colleagues loose on a few junior placemen, create a stir in the New York press, scare the Hall into concessions, and then shut the commission down. The scheme would probably have worked had not a rump of mugwumps in the state assembly not contrived to maneuver several independent lawyers onto the committee. By the summer of 1894, Lexow's commission had turned into a real crusade against police corruption—one that would run for the best part of a year, produce more than 10,500 printed pages of evidence, and examine nearly 680 witnesses.

The man chiefly responsible for this state of affairs was an irascible Irishman named John Goff, the attorney chosen by the mugwumps as chief counsel. A thin-skinned, self-educated lawyer of limited ability—he was ignorant of great swaths of the law and dependent more on his undoubted ability to read character than on learning of any sort—Goff was an outlandish character. He had in his younger days been an active member of the revolutionary Clan na Gael, a terrorist group dedicated to the violent overthrow of British rule in Ireland.* Now, two decades later, he still possessed "the square features and craggy nose of a brawler," but the addition of a snow-white beard had left him looking like a patriarch from Genesis. No one who actually encountered Goff,

---

*In 1874–76, Goff had been one of the organizers of the renowned *Catalpa* expedition, in which a New Bedford whaler had sailed halfway around the world to rescue six convicted Irish rebels from a penal colony in western Australia. The venture, popularly known as Goff's Irish Rescue Party, had been successful, severely humiliating the British government of the day.

however, could be deceived by his benign appearance for long. The Irish attorney was infamous for his hot temper, and those unfortunate enough to be subjected to his interrogations visibly withered under the gaze of piercing blue eyes glittering dangerously from beneath a pair of shaggy eyebrows.

It took even John Goff some time, but by the summer of 1894, helped by two young lawyers named Frank Moss and William Travers Jerome, the fearsome prosecutor had begun to secure truly damning testimony of police corruption. Goff's first victim was none other than Commissioner McClave, whose account books proved to contain details of numerous suspicious payments. In one eight-month period, the Lexow panel heard, the commissioner had banked well over $20,000, each deposit coinciding to within a few days with the appointment of a new precinct captain. Nor was the testimony that Goff teased out of ordinary New York storekeepers any less revealing. One woman, a recent immigrant who operated a tiny cigar shop, swore under oath that she had been arrested as a prostitute and seen her children packed off to an asylum when she refused to pay her beat policeman the necessary bribe.

For a while the police themselves resisted even Goff's attempts to make them talk; the strategy of scornful silence had always served them well before. But the Lexow Committee's lawyers were more persistent than their predecessors. When a famous precinct captain—a longtime partisan of Tammany—found himself sentenced to three and a half years in prison for accepting the gift of a six-dollar basket of fruit, several of those scheduled to follow him onto the witness stand hastily rethought their positions.

The man who finally exposed the New York graft was Captain Max Schmittberger, a tall, handsome man who had once been a member of the Broadway Squad. Schmittberger was an unusual policeman in several ways. He was such a strapping model of a cop that he had been excused the usual initiation fee when he joined the force in 1874; the Tammany block leaders who found him working in a bakery thought he would look good in decorative posts. And, being German, he felt less bound by the Irish oaths of allegiance and secrecy that he, like every other patrolman, had been made to swear. Schmittberger also had a large family and was most reluctant to go to prison. Charged in October 1894 with accepting a $500 gratuity from a steamship company, he agreed to tell Goff everything.

Captain Schmittberger's evidence was nothing short of a sensation. For the first time, a serving policeman openly discussed the intricacies of police corruption in Manhattan, setting out in detail how the system worked. What really shocked the New Yorkers who read his testimony was how well refined and how pervasive graft in the vice districts had become: Every dollar collected by a precinct captain, Schmittberger explained, was split, with 20 percent going to the officer who collected it (usually the "ward man," the precinct detective), 25 percent to his superiors, and the remainder to the precinct captain. Having unbuttoned thus far, Schmittberger went on to implicate Tammany Hall itself in the operation of the system. It was he who explained that the transfer of captains from one precinct to another—far from reducing the chances of corruption—actually fueled the system, since each time a new man arrived in a post, all the brothels, gambling dens, and dubious saloons that operated in his district would be expected to pay a further "initiation fee," generally amounting to $500 each. Similar payments were exacted whenever a shady business of this sort changed hands or a successful gambler or madam expanded into new premises. It also cost $500 to reopen a brothel or gaming "hell" after a raid.

By the time that Captain Max was through, the Lexow investigation had acquired a new momentum. There was no longer any doubt that there would be changes in New York. Nor was it now possible for even the most senior officers in the department to escape Goff's clutches. The Lexow Committee spent a good deal of time listening to Alexander Williams, whose extraordinary career was mercilessly dissected over several days. Although, even as an inspector, Clubber had earned a salary of no more than a few thousand dollars a year, it transpired that he had somehow accumulated a house on East Tenth Street; a seventeen-room mansion in Cos Cob, Connecticut; a small steam yacht; and a jetty, extending 160 yards out to sea, that had cost him $39,000 to build. The wealth required to purchase all these assets, Goff alleged, came from $15-a-month protection payments made by more than six hundred lottery shops, not to mention contributions from uncounted numbers of gambling dens, whorehouses, and pool-rooms. Clubber also had a financial interest in a New York hotel and in Hollywood Whisky, a rotgut brand that bartenders in his district were well advised to stock.

There was a limit, of course, to what even John Goff could prove. Williams brazened it out—he had, he shrugged, made some lucky real-estate investments years earlier in northern Japan—and Superin-tendent Byrnes, who followed him onto the stand, stuck firmly to the claim that his own fortune was the product of stock-market specula-tion. Neither man was charged with any wrongdoing, and for all Goff's efforts only a handful of their colleagues were ever tried for corruption. But both Williams and Byrnes felt it expedient to resign soon afterward, and overall the impact of the Lexow hearings was immense. Virtually every facet of police corruption lay exposed, and the extent of Manhattan's graft had been laid out in such minute detail that even Bill Devery, confronted with Goff's evidence, confessed: "I've got to hand it to you, feller. Honest, I had no idea it was so good until I saw it all set out in black and white."

It was scarcely surprising, then, given the blizzard of hostile newspa-per reporting that accompanied these hearings, that Tammany lost the municipal elections of 1894. Even cynical New Yorkers had been shocked at the sheer extent of John Goff's revelations, not least by the clear proof that bribes paid by the brothels of Satan's Circus went straight into the coffers of the Hall. The incoming reformist mayor lost no time in appointing four new police commissioners to replace McClave and his disgraced associates, and one of them—the bump-tious, passionate, and able Theodore Roosevelt—soon made himself famous for a well-publicized campaign to rid the department of cor-ruption. Even Roosevelt, however—all fizzing energy and courage—found it impossible not merely to reform the police but to banish vice itself. The future president's short tenure at police headquarters (he lasted barely eighteen months on Mulberry Street) made the daunting scale of the task facing reformers in New York clearer than ever.

Roosevelt's first months in charge of the New York Police Department, admittedly, saw him attain fresh heights of popularity. The commissioner began by announcing that he would save the city's taxpayers $1,200 a year by dismissing the two elderly aides who had served his predecessor and replacing them with a "girl secretary" named Minnie Kelly—a raven-haired beauty in a tight corset whose appearance at headquarters provided New York's newspaper reporters with reams of copy. The old system of purchase was halted; henceforth men wishing to join the police were required to meet stringent physical requirements and had to undergo a series of exams. Some attempt was even made to tidy up headquarters itself, a cluttered, cramped, and stuffy building (most of the windows had been nailed shut years earlier) long ago stained a mustard yellow color by the New York soot. Still more widely acclaimed was a drive, which the commissioner led in person, to keep patrolmen on the beat after midnight.* Even the more enlightened of Tammany's supporters admitted that such reforms were overdue.

It was one thing, though, to court newspaper publicity by humiliating negligent officers, and quite another to retain the support of voters while actually obeying the law. Roosevelt's popularity soon plummeted when he ordered his men to enforce the city's liquor legislation, drafted by upstate Republicans: rural conservatives, religious radicals, and Prohibitionists who hated alcohol. Closure of Manhattan's thousands of taverns and bars after midnight and on Sundays enraged the city's drinking men—not least Jews, whose religion forbade them to visit saloons on Saturdays, and shift workers, who were glad of the chance to get a drink in the middle of the night. To make

---

*The results of this campaign were certainly intriguing. On his first nocturnal excursion down Third Avenue, Roosevelt stumbled over one beat policeman slumped asleep in a butter tub in the middle of the pavement, his snores loud enough to be heard across the street. Another was found engaging a prostitute, and half a dozen others were mysteriously absent from their posts. Only a single cop was patrolling his beat in accordance with the regulations, and seven malefactors were hauled into headquarters the next morning to explain themselves.

matters worse, Roosevelt had chosen to begin the campaign in June 1895, the warmest summer month for years, and by Sunday, July 21— the hottest day of the year so far—the whole city was in turmoil. Some half a million New Yorkers streamed out of Manhattan, heading for Long Island or New Jersey, where liquor was still openly available; saloonkeepers defied Roosevelt's orders, standing outside their premises to personally vet those invited to enter through side doors; and as many as eight bars out of every ten opened in some shape or form.

The excise-law fiasco was a disaster for the forces of reform. Roosevelt's mailbag began to feature death threats and letter bombs, and by autumn thousands of voters who had once supported the mugwumps had been driven back into the Tammany fold. The Hall, indeed, won the next city election even more convincingly than the reformers had managed to do at the height of the Lexow hearings, and when all the results were in, thousands of men and women danced through the streets of Satan's Circus singing endless choruses of the Tammany campaign slogan:

> *Well, well, well!*
> *Reform has gone to hell!**

Mugwumps, it became clear, could never hope to hold power in New York for long. Voters might despise corruption, and even hate the Tammany machine, but neither could they abide strict enforcement of the law. "The people may not always like us," Boss Croker complacently observed, "but they can never stomach reform. . . . Tammany is not a wave, but the sea itself."

And yet—despite everything—things did change after a fashion. Tammany's power was never again quite so absolute as it had been between

---

*The reformers did not give up even then, of course. Dr. Parkhurst in particular fought on almost until his death in 1933, at the advanced age of 91. The old thunderer's departure was an unusual one; Parkhurst fell from the roof of his summer residence while sleepwalking.

1890 and 1893, and not even Croker dared to be quite so obvious, so unfeeling, as he had been. The loss of an election, however promptly it had been redeemed, came as a shock to Democrats who could remember nothing but repeated victories, and the readiness of Manhattan's electorate to vote in a reform administration if they were pushed too far was duly noted. When it did return to power, Tammany preferred to be considerably more discreet in its handling of graft and corruption, and considerably more distant from crime and criminals. The sachems of the Hall learned the lessons of Lexow well, and the cleverest among them—including Croker's fast-rising deputy, a brilliant but taciturn young ward leader named Charles Murphy—realized that a close association with the police damaged their reputation. Murphy favored raising money from clean graft wherever possible and frowned heavily on any direct links between his deputies and their old allies, the precinct captains. He also recognized that Tammany had to stand for something other than self-aggrandizement, and he offered his support to a rising generation of far more active politicians—men such as Al Smith and Robert F. Wagner, who supported beneficial social legislation and would eventually become public servants of considerable accomplishment. These reforms, it is true, failed at first to convince a skeptical electorate that the Hall had really changed, and in the wake of Tammany mayor Van Wyck's disgraceful involvement in the Ice Trust scandal, a reformer named Seth Low won the mayoral election of 1901. But Murphy persisted nonetheless, and when he finally succeeded the far more rough and ready Croker in the wake of Low's victory, these policies became official.

So far as the Hall, the press, and the general public were concerned, intimate ties between politicians and the police thus became history. But this did not mean that grafting in Manhattan ceased. Freed at last from their political overlords, the New York police simply began to keep the wages of corruption for themselves. Boss Murphy's strategy became the making of Bill Devery, who seized on the chance to centralize what had been a diffuse, indeed a headless, system. New York became even more outrageously wide open. The city was systematically apportioned: Brothels catering to men of consequence and influence were designated "headquarters houses," and precinct captains were ordered not to touch them. Gambling was also revolutionized. Hitherto, gaming-house proprietors had received what amounted to a license from a district boss and paid protection money to their precinct captain. Under Devery—and for years afterward—gambling "contributions" were channeled directly to a handful of Tammany sachems, led by Big Tim Sullivan, and to a small group of policemen.

Devery's scheme meant, in principle, that graft now flowed directly to him, and it had the side effect of seriously reducing the amount of cash paid out to ordinary patrolmen. A revealing story, often told by the police of the time, related that when one beat policeman was brought before the chief to answer charges of grafting, Devery pounded his fist on his desk and roared, "That's got to stop! If there's any graftin' to be done, I'll do it—leave it to me. What I want to know is, have you noticed any stray grafts runnin' around loose that I have overlooked?" The general result was a system of corruption that was simpler to control and much less easy to buck. But since the graft available to ordinary patrolmen rapidly dried up, it also had the unintended benefit of making many ordinary policemen more honest, however unwillingly.

Charles Becker was one of those who changed his ways in consequence. By 1900 there had been no civilian complaints concerning his behavior for years. No formal charges had been brought against him since the summer of 1897, and he had apparently decided that the best way to get ahead in the post-Lexow police department was to keep quiet and work hard.

He was no longer concerned only for himself, in any case. Becker was an attractive man—"Handsome Charley," his colleagues called him, in testament to his height and to the deep dimple that creased his left cheek when he smiled—and in the indulgent and promiscuous Manhattan of the nineties there were thousands of women for whom a good-looking young police officer appeared a very worthwhile catch. Becker took full advantage of this situation and enjoyed a number of affairs, one of them with Pauline Washbourne, the smitten young drug addict in whose apartment he had once stashed jewels stolen by

Chicago May. Soon he was proposing marriage to Mary Mahoney, a girl whom he had quite possibly met at home in Callicoon, since she had relations in the nearby town of Jeffersonville.

The couple was married in downtown Manhattan in February 1895, but there was no honeymoon. The new Mrs. Becker "caught cold" on her wedding night and was ordered to bed. Ten days later her illness was diagnosed as tuberculosis ("hasty consumption," it was termed), a generally fatal affliction in that era. Mary languished for some time, seeking treatment both from doctors in New York and, when that had no effect, at a new sanatorium run by the eminent specialist Dr. Harold Loomis up in the Catskills. But her various treatments were to no avail, and on October 15 she died.

Perhaps Becker was callous; perhaps there had simply been no opportunity for real intimacy. In any event, the prospect of returning to a single life in the boardinghouses of Manhattan seems to have held no appeal, and he wasted little time in finding a second wife. The patrolman's new bride was a Canadian girl, Letitia Stenson, who came from the town of Kingston, Ontario. Becker and Letitia had met each other before Mary's death, and they became engaged soon afterward. They married three years later, in April 1898, and appear to have been moderately happy for a while. Their only child, a son—named Howard Paul after two of Charley's elder brothers—was born in December 1899.

Becker's spare time was, nonetheless, spent apart from his wife. He followed sports: boxing, principally, and baseball a little, though in truth the performance of New York's baseball teams during the 1890s left a good deal to be desired. He liked to hunt and fish for trout, and he loved horses, a passion that was probably a legacy of his youth. When the opportunity arose, he went driving in Central Park. The remainder of his off-duty hours were at least partly devoted to activities that might help his career. At some point, probably not long after his enlistment in the police, he became a Freemason, like so many other members of the force.*

---

*Becker's lodge was the Polar Star, 245, F&AM, of New York.

The notion of Charley Becker as a Mason would have surprised few who knew him well. He had always been an ambitious man, and by 1900 he was growing more ambitious still. He was ambitious because he now had a family and the responsibility to care for and provide for a wife and child. He was ambitious because he saw that many of his colleagues in the police department could not match his own intelligence, and he believed that he deserved promotion. And he was also ambitious because he now understood New York.

There was a good deal to be said for life as a patrolman. It was a secure job, which carried with it prospects of a pension, and one that Becker actively enjoyed; unlike a number of his colleagues, who felt uneasy with authority, he actually *liked* being a policeman. But without access to graft, it was not well paid. For Becker, maddeningly, real money was something other people had. He could see it as he stumped up and down his beat in Satan's Circus; he could feel it being made. Above all, he knew the people making it.

CHAPTER 4

STUSS

THE BUILDING AT 33 West Thirty-third Street, close to the
Waldorf-Astoria hotel on the fringes of the vice district, did not
attract attention from most passersby. The premises themselves
were well built and substantial, as befitted such an elegant address, but
then so were many similarly solid properties in the heart of fashionable
Manhattan. The casual observer, noting muted signs of wealth and
taste in the exterior, might suppose the place was home to a banker
from some Wall Street institution.

Upon close inspection, nonetheless, the house seemed definitely
odd. It attracted, for one thing, far too many callers to be a simple private dwelling, and many of these visitors appeared at the unsocial hour
of midnight, sometimes later. It was more than a little queer that all of
them were male and sumptuously attired, and that many were decidedly familiar to even casual readers of the New York press. And it was
stranger still that a uniformed policeman stood on guard outside the
front door every evening, tipping his hat to the best-dressed callers as
they swept past him up the steps.

It was only when an observer's gaze fell upon the door itself that
the purpose of the building was revealed. The entrance to number
33 looked nothing like those that adorned everyday Manhattan
homes, with their knockers, bells, and polished wood. It was, for one
thing, made entirely out of metal several inches thick—wrought iron
so heavy that it took a husky doorman all his strength to push it to and

fro—and it hung within a massive iron frame, so stoutly built and strong that it reminded people passing of the entrance to a bank vault. This impression was amply reinforced by the numerous bolts and locks that studded the door—far more than ordinary security could possibly require. And when the iron barrier swung open, affording glimpses of the entrance hall, an even stranger sight appeared: A second doorway, still more strongly armored than the first, barred the way into the interior. It, too, was of metal, this time a lavishly decorated bronze; once, long ago, it had hung across a portal in the Doge's Palace at Venice. The purpose of this second door was not entirely decorative. Whenever it was shut and barred, unwanted visitors gaining entry to the property would find themselves trapped within its narrow vestibule. At the very least, the time required to force an entry would give the building's occupants a head start to make good their escape—via a rear exit, over the roofs, or through one of two tunnels leading to adjacent properties with which the building was supplied. Seeing the bronze door hanging, tightly closed and defiant, within the entrance hall of number 33, any knowledgeable New Yorker would have instantly identified the building as a gambling "hell"—a private and illegal business whose prime purpose, after making money, was to ensure complete discretion to its well-heeled clientele.

The House with the Bronze Door was indeed a famous gaming club: perhaps the richest and most opulent in all Manhattan, an island rich in such amenities. The property had first opened back in 1891 and proceeded to run largely unmolested for a dozen years, a phenomenal achievement. When called upon at last, however, the metal doors did prove their worth, resisting the attentions of policemen armed with blowtorches for the better part of half an hour while the house's staff took their equipment and their customers to safety through their secret passages.

The sums that had been invested to turn the House with the Bronze Door into one of the finest establishments in New York were colossal. The syndicate that owned the club had hired Stanford White—then perhaps the best-known architect in the United

States*—to gut and remodel the interior, then spent a further half a million on furnishings. White had toured through Europe and Asia purchasing antiques, spending $20,000 on the bronze door alone. While still in Venice, he had hired a team of ten master carvers and packed them off to Manhattan, where they spent two years working on a single ornamental banister.

Nor was the rest of the interior neglected. According to the *New York Sun*,

> The large reception room at the back of the street floor is of gold, and the floor is covered with red velvet carpet. . . . On the walls are oil paintings which cost a fortune. On the floors were the finest examples of the art of the great rug-makers of the East. The floors were of hard wood, the work of experts. The ceilings were frescoed as only the homes of the rich could be. On the second floor is the large roulette wheel room. It is arched, with the ceiling covered with paintings. On this floor is a bath with a marble reclining slab and other apparatus which is said to have cost the owners $2,000.
>
> Fair play and courtesy were the keynotes of the place. The house had the reputation of integrity and honesty. The word of the player was always accepted without question. With admission to the house went the privilege of indulging in all the good things which the place afforded. A visitor was the guest of the house and was treated accordingly. At midnight a buffet lunch was served for guests. Between times wines, brandies, and cigars which cost a dollar apiece were there for those who wanted them. It has been estimated that at least $25,000 a year was spent in providing refreshments and food for visitors of the house.

---

*Aside from scandalizing New Yorkers with the nude statue of Diana that he erected atop the three-hundred-foot tower (modeled on the Giralda at Seville) that soared over the second Madison Square Garden, White later became the victim in a celebrated society murder. He was shot dead by his mistress's cuckolded husband while watching a performance of *Mam'zelle Champagne*.

The expenditure of the best part of a million dollars would have alarmed most ordinary investors. But Frank Farrell, the master gambler who was the House's principal backer, had a solid grasp of economics. The sums wagered, and lost, within his club's gorgeous interior were consistently enormous; around 1900, it was estimated that as much as $50,000 changed hands there every night, thanks at least in part to limits that were high and also elastic. The sheer variety of attractions on the premises helped; in addition to roulette, baccarat, pinochle, and poker, there was a dice game known as Klondike, too, and sundry other forms of betting. The biggest single sum ever won in the House was said to be a staggering $165,000, which must imply that larger sums by far were lost. Certainly the player who carried off $210,000 after two consecutive winning nights at the House gambled away all of that money over the ensuing weeks and lost a further $80,000 into the bargain.

It was the sheer profitability of the House with the Bronze Door that gave the place its true importance. The House was not—could not have been—in the least way typical of the ordinary gaming establishments of the city, and it had, in fact, no more than a handful of true competitors anywhere in the world. But neither was it a mere curiosity. Frank Farrell may not have been the only gambler to realize that his gentlemanly clientele made up a negligible proportion of the betting men of New York, nor even that when hundreds of thousands of clerks, laborers, and other sporting types made penny wagers on the horses or on cards, their bets—contemptible in isolation—totaled a sum in excess of the largest staked within the House. He was, however, the only man to draw the logical conclusion that money won from genteel customers could be profitably reinvested in a much rougher class of premises. Farrell's rivals—men such as Richard Canfield, owner of the elegant Saratoga Club and perhaps the best-known gambler of the nineteenth century—had parlayed their precarious respectability into grudging acceptance by high society. Farrell, less bothered by the social whirl, cared less what his clients thought of him. He took the vast profits earned by the House with the Bronze

Door and used them to open up a chain of seedy betting shops, called poolrooms, throughout the city and its suburbs. Within a few years, he controlled 250 such establishments, taking millions of small bets on racing, fights, and baseball games and swelling his profits to an almost inconceivable extent. So rich, indeed, did Farrell become that by 1903 he was able to throw away $18,000 in what many thought to be a suicidal wager: the purchase of a franchise to play in baseball's American League and the establishment of a brand-new New York ball club to rival not merely the celebrated Giants but Brooklyn's Robins, too. Farrell should perhaps have listened to his critics; he and his partner, Bill Devery (whose close association with the gambler in this venture no doubt explained how the House with the Bronze Door ran so freely for so long), lost money on their team in all but one of the years that they controlled the franchise. But the fact that Farrell had cash to lavish on so quixotic a gamble as the useless, struggling New York Yankees showed just how much could be made from low-class gambling in the city.

During the wide-open years that followed Tammany's return to power in 1897, hundreds of minor entrepreneurs followed Frank Farrell's lead. By 1900 there were well over a thousand poolrooms and card rooms in Manhattan, far outnumbering the two dozen or so substantial gambling palaces and the two hundred lesser gaming clubs scattered through the borough. Many of these places—particularly the poolrooms, which, handling racing and sports betting, required telegraph equipment and other expensive fittings—were fortified nearly as strongly as the House with the Bronze Door, a fact William McAdoo, the new police commissioner, discovered after taking office. The typical poolroom, McAdoo wrote, was a considerable enterprise, employing ten men and playing host to as many as two hundred or three hundred gamblers at a time. Such places were often concealed in lofts where,

> once rented, a partition is put up, dividing the room into
> two unequal parts. Often there is no door whatsoever in

the partition, only a small hole that would trouble a fat pigeon to go through. Behind the partition are the human spiders themselves, principals or agents of the big octopus. About one o'clock in the day . . . the wretched army of unfortunate and desperate gamblers, after having passed through several outer guards and two or three doors stronger and thicker than those of some safes, gather in this dingy, ill ventilated, smoke-poisoned room; for in order not to make things too public the windows are generally blinded, and the average gambler pays little attention to what he is breathing, fevered as he is by the devil of chance. . . . In many pool rooms, to make sure the victim cannot escape by any possible means with his money, there are various games played in the large outer room before opening time and after the races are over. The main thing that the victims want to know is the names of the horses, the jockeys and the betting odds as established at the race track. An attendant pastes lightly on the wall a sheet called the "dope-sheet" which gives this news. The poor, foolish crowd casts their eyes on this and the jabber and chatter about horses goes up.

Those who preferred to gamble on something more immediate were also well catered for in Manhattan. Numerous poker rooms flourished in the slums. Blackjack was gaining in stature, too, and roulette was—thought McAdoo—more popular than any other game of chance. Neither of these games, nonetheless, came close to being the favorite pastime of New York's gamblers. That honor went to the now-forgotten game of faro, originally a French invention, which had first appeared in Louisiana sometime before 1800. Faro had grown in stature throughout the nineteenth century, eventually spawning a faster, simpler variant known as stuss. The game was easy enough to grasp: Players gathered around an elaborately printed table, known as a layout, and wagered against the house by betting on the order of cards drawn from a dealing case. But, as in roulette, the variety and complexity of the wagers allowed could be bewildering, and even experienced players found it difficult to master the ever-shifting odds.* Faro's real attraction lay in its reputation for offering gamblers a better chance of winning than any other game of cards; the margin in the house's favor, while difficult to calculate, was generally reckoned to be little more than 1.5 percent. "An almost conclusive argument," one player observed in 1900, "for the theory that the percentage at honest faro is virtually non-existent is the fact that the canny management of Monte Carlo has never permitted the game to be played at that celebrated resort."

"Honest faro" was, however, seldom found in the United States. Crooked layouts were especially common in Satan's Circus, where the game became—in the words of one early historian of gambling—"the medium of the first extensive cheating at cards ever seen in the United States, and the rock upon which was reared the wolf-traps of the nineteenth century." Trimmed and sanded cards and rigged dealing boxes were readily available and openly advertised as "advantage tools" in the trade press of the day. By manipulating concealed springs and sliding plates, skilled dealers, known as "mechanics," could make cards appear as and when they wanted them, and they were paid accordingly. The potential for cheating was even greater in stuss, a game in which the cards were shuffled only after bets were made.

There were indeed almost endless opportunities for canny hucksters to rook the city's gamblers. Crooked play was ubiquitous throughout the New York of the day, and if a scant few low establishments were honest, the vast majority were bent in varying degrees. Manhattan supported so many card sharps and con men that by 1910 the fraternity had acquired its own unofficial meeting place: a hangout known as the Stag

---

*The game of faro was played thus: The first card drawn from a dealing box was regarded as dead. Thereafter cards were pulled out two at a time, the first in each pair being the bank's and the second the players'. If a gambler bet on, say, the dealing of a four, and a four was drawn on the bank's turn, he lost. If the card emerged on the player's turn, he won. If two fours were drawn together, bets were split. The game's influence can be gauged from the number of faro terms that found their way into everyday English. Players tracked the cards that had been dealt by "keeping tabs," and they "broke even" when they bet a card to win and lose an equal number of times; other preferred "stringing along," a method for betting on twenty-one different groups of cards simultaneously.

Café, run by a gambler named Louis Harris who (under the alias of "Dan the Dude") became another friend of Becker's. Horse races were rigged, either in the traditional way (involving the bribing of jockeys or the doping of their mounts) or via increasingly elaborate scams involving manipulation of the posting of results. Roulette wheels were often weighted to give the house an extra edge, and lottery draws were fixed. But the most common fraud by far involved the marking of playing cards. It was not hard to obtain specially printed packs that enabled a skilled sharp to know exactly what was being dealt or to doctor a deck with a custom-made "poker ring," worn as normal on the finger of one hand and equipped with a tiny concealed needle with which to prick the surface of a card. In these ways thousands of poor men (and a few women) were relieved of their wages every week.

It was largely thanks to endemic cheating that gambling ranked ahead of every other form of vice in terms of the profits it produced. Some notion of the sums taken by gaming clubs and poolrooms in Manhattan was given by the *New York Times*, which in 1900 trumpeted the results of an investigation of the city's vice. According to the *Times'* calculations, the owners of the city's largest clubs paid as much as $12,000 a year for protection; their lesser competitors were required to part with nearly $2,000; poolrooms stayed open in exchange for $300 a month and crap games for $150. The total handed over to the police amounted to some $3 million a year, the paper added: taxes that were "as fixed as the laws of the Medes and Persians" and which could easily amount to 20 or 30 percent of a house's turnover.* Yet men such as Frank Farrell prospered in the face of such demands. Gambling—more profitable than the liquor trade, more respectable than pimping, better protected, certainly, than both—was the safest way to make a fortune in Satan's Circus. Several thousand men earned their livings from it at the turn of the century. Among them were some of the rawest characters in the city—and a handful of the richest.

---

*Richard Canfield, according to another estimate, paid $1,000 a month—in cash, across a table at Delmonico's—to ensure that his premises received protection, plus between 15 and 25 percent of his profits.

* * *

The man who made more from gambling than anyone else was almost certainly Big Tim Sullivan. By 1907, when he was forty-four years old, Sullivan had emerged as Tammany's most important conduit to New York vice, with interests that had expanded from the mere handful of saloons he had owned in the 1880s to encompass a nationwide circuit of vaudeville theaters, several dozen nickelodeons, a variety of clubs and bars, numerous gambling establishments, and—practically certainly—income from a good number of brothels.

Tim had always been careful not to say exactly how he made his money, although he vehemently denied involvement in the "white slave trade," as prostitution was generally known. "Nobody who knows me well," the Tammany man had declared in 1901,

> will believe that I would take a penny from any woman, much less from the poor creatures who are more to be pitied than any other human beings on earth. I'd be afraid to take a cent from a poor woman of the streets for fear my mother would see it. I'd a good deal rather break into a bank and rob the safe. That would be a more manly and decent way of getting money.

Sullivan's denials were probably true insofar as they went; no conclusive evidence ever did emerge to prove that the Tammany leader profited directly from prostitution. But it was commonly accepted that Tim's agents and subordinates on the Lower East Side did arrange protection for brothels and more or less certain that Sullivan himself contracted syphilis, probably from a liaison with a prostitute, during the first decade of the new century. Nevertheless, the Sullivan clan's sensitivity to the least hint of involvement with white slavery was so acute that a cousin, the diminutive and saturnine "Little Tim" Sullivan, was sent to lead an ostentatious drive against downtown bordellos in the winter of 1901, throwing furniture out into the streets and roughing up the local pimps. All this made it altogether simpler for Sullivan himself to focus his energies on gambling, and he began investing heavily in such ventures.

Big Tim was himself a committed gambler, who wagered, mostly unsuccessfully, on fights and horses and, during a brief spell in Congress, from 1902 to 1904, became the poker and pinochle champion of the House of Representatives. But the Tammany man's own businesses catered resolutely to the working class. Though Sullivan was influential enough to be gifted memberships to many of the city's plushest gaming clubs, he was seldom seen in any of them, preferring to devote his time to more working-class pursuits. In the late 1890s, Tim took a hand in horse racing, helping to organize the Metropolitan Jockey Club and supplying most of the funds needed to open a new racetrack on Long Island. Closer to home, he also arranged protection for dozens of small poolrooms, stuss houses, and lotteries in Manhattan and became a patron of several "private social clubs," where gamblers and politicians mixed to make book and raise funds for the Wigwam.

The most lucrative of Sullivan's interests were operated in partnership with the Considine family, represented in New York by the brothers Jim and George, who shared Big Tim's interest in boxing (George was for a while the manager of the famous heavyweight Jim Corbett). But Tim also operated on his own behalf, for example by helping to found the Hesper Club, an influential Second Avenue clubhouse, popular with gambling types, where frequent poker parties were held and a small casino operated. Sullivan played little active part in the running of the club, which was founded in 1899. But his influence was obvious to anyone who glanced inside the entrance, where a letter from the big Irishman hung in an honored spot within a golden frame. "Should it be possible," Tim's note assured its readers, "for me at any time to serve any of the members I will gladly do so. A simple word from you will command me."

The Hesper flourished for a dozen years, becoming a meeting place for a generation of New York fixers and aspiring politicians, and Sullivan's prominent interest in the place was widely remarked upon. Very few of the Irishman's casual acquaintances, on the other hand, understood the central role that Big Tim played in regulating gaming through all five boroughs of the city. According to the *Times*, Sullivan devoted a good deal of his energies to heading a secret "gambling commission," consisting of four members, which not only collected and shared out the millions raised in protection money, but in effect licensed all the betting premises that operated in the city. Tim's committee, the paper charged, met weekly in an apartment just off Broadway and consisted of "a commissioner, who is at the head of one of the city departments, two state senators, and the dictator of the pool room syndicate of this city." It required little knowledge of local politics to identify three of these men as Sullivan, Frank Farrell, and State Senator McLaughlan, the last representing the interests of the Democrats of Brooklyn. As for the mysterious "head of one of the city departments," only the most naïve of the *Times'* readers could have failed to recognize a reference to Bill Devery, then still chief of police. The brilliance of Tim's system would have been immediately apparent to any reader who guessed the men's identities. Between them the four members of Sullivan's committee controlled the police, Manhattan politics, and the State Gambling Commission. The scheme was airtight.

Sullivan never formally admitted that this secret "commission" existed. But the indications are that it did, and that it was not a recent innovation. As early as 1880, New York's gamblers had organized an informal association to channel the payment of protection money, a wise move that had resulted in a boom in gaming in the city. By 1900, apparently, the commission had reached a high state of efficiency. According to the *Times'* evidence,

> the money is not only apportioned at these conferences, but licenses to run gambling houses are virtually issued there. . . . Not a gambling house is running in this city to-day that is not known to this board, and not a place is running that does not pay a tax to this board. Its system is as complete as any branch of city government. There are no leaks, and no unauthorized places can run for twenty-four hours without "putting up" or shutting up.

Licenses to operate, the paper added, cost $300, a sum paid to the local precinct captain, who retained it in exchange for collecting monthly payments. Thereafter, however, the vast majority of the protection money gathered from across the city—at least 80 percent— was passed up to the members of the commission itself.

Sullivan and his gambling commission were thus hugely influential in New York. They in effect regulated the livelihoods of every gambler in the city: something that the owners of gaming clubs and petty card sharps more or less openly acknowledged in their periodic complaints that the syndicate was licensing far too many premises and thus diluting the profits available to those already in business. The commission also operated as a sort of professional association, hearing complaints from aggrieved parties, issuing judgments, and above all ensuring the continuing smooth running of the industry—notably by ensuring that the premises it licensed maintained reasonable discretion. Gamblers who ran afoul of the authorities or of their fellows might be issued with warnings or paid to get out of town for a few weeks or months while things cooled down.

The appearance of Sullivan's group—whether or not it was quite as all-powerful as the *Times* asked its readers to believe—made it possible for wealthy gamblers to flourish more or less free from the attentions of the police. By 1907 there were more than a dozen eminent gaming lords active in the city, every one of them—like Frank Farrell and Sullivan's business partners, the Considine brothers—well connected politically. Not all were partisans of Tammany; Sam Paul, whose main business was running cheap stuss houses south of Fourteenth Street, was a noted Republican fixer connected to Boss Platt and the Custom House brigade. Some of these men (Paul was a good example) had once been minor gangsters; they had obtained a concession to run a club as reward for some service rendered and so clawed their way into a rough respectability. Others—generally the most successful of their breed— were lifelong gamblers themselves who had turned their knowledge of betting into a business. Men of this sort took good care to assure themselves of firm political support and often ran a wide variety of businesses, from bookmaking through gaming clubs and loansharking.

In New York in the first years of the new century, the most eminent gambler of the latter type was Arnold Rothstein. A gifted young

East Sider with a marked ability to hustle pool, Rothstein—like Charles Becker—was a third-generation American gone bad. He had been born into a virtuous, hardworking family: His grandparents had fled the anti-Jewish pogroms convulsing Russia in the 1850s; his father was a respected businessman so renowned for Solomonic judgments that he was known as "Abe the Just"; his brother had trained to be a rabbi. But Rothstein rebelled, shocking his devout parents by leaving school to lounge around in bars and poolrooms. The boy had talent nonetheless, and the mathematical brain of the instinctive oddsmaker; by 1900, when he was eighteen, he was already running his own card games. In a few years, he had made sufficient money to branch out by lending some to other gamblers, at rates that rose as high as 48 percent. Rothstein advanced these loans from a large wad of cash that he always carried on his person; after a run of luck, his funds might total well over $10,000. Fellow gamblers began calling him "The Big Bankroll."

In person Rothstein struck most observers as average and unremarkable, possessing the useful ability to fade unnoticed into the background of any scene. He was of no more than average height and had an expressionless round face, dark hair, and the ghostly pallor of a man who worked mostly by night. Perhaps thanks to this avoidance of sun, he retained his boyish aspect into adulthood, always seeming, one acquaintance noted, "as if he never had to worry about razors." Rothstein was not without vanity, at one point paying to have all his teeth removed and replaced by a set of dentures so dazzling that "they made many professional beauties jealous." But twitting the Bankroll on his ordinary looks was hardly sensible. Rothstein could be steely and unyielding, and so obdurate that he would hang around in cold doorways for hours, waiting for the chance to waylay those who owed him cash. He had few friends and apparently no interests outside his work. "He lived only for money," one New York journalist recalled years later. "He even liked the feel of it. He wasn't right even with himself. For every friend, he had a thousand enemies."

An obsession with dollars and cents was not, of course, unusual in the sort of circles that the Bankroll moved in. But Rothstein was no ordinary gambler. He was more ambitious than most of his contemporaries and made it his business to be politically connected. His principal acquaintance, unsurprisingly, was Big Tim Sullivan, with whom he had engineered a meeting, in the 1890s, by hanging around Tim's cousin Florrie's pool hall. The young Rothstein had made himself useful, running errands, doing favors; a decade later, thanks in part to Sullivan's patronage, he emerged as a leading figure in Satan's Circus. Even this, though, was not sufficient for him. He continued to intrigue, sitting for long hours in a booth at a local restaurant, receiving supplicants and doing deals. Before long he was firmly established as a kingpin, a court of appeal, and a lender of last resort. "Arnold Rothstein was chiefly a busybody," one man who knew the gambler summarized things just after Rothstein's death,

> with a passion for dabbling in the affairs of others. He was also a fixer, a go-between, not merely between law-breakers and politicians, but between one type of racketeer and another. Because he measured his success in these roles by only one yardstick, money, he was always on the make. It follows that I may have placed his penchant for making money first, but this was a trait he shared with many. As a fixer, as a go-between, he stood alone.

The Big Bankroll took his new position as a gambling lord seriously. His aim was to avoid disruptions to the smooth running of his many business interests, and he worked hard to keep the peace in Satan's Circus, arranging payoffs and soothing ruffled feathers; most of all he stamped out trouble and suppressed dissent. Rothstein's most distinctive characteristic, in short, was that he thought of other people's business as his own, insofar as the success of his own wide-ranging schemes required political calm and a minimum of unwelcome publicity.

It was in this capacity that Rothstein would stumble into Becker's story. And the man who would drag him there was yet another gambler—one a good deal less able than Rothstein and much less savvy than Big Tim. His name was Herman Rosenthal, and in the summer of 1900 he was in trouble.

The problem, Herman sniffed, lay with his wife.

In the early months of the new century, Rosenthal was twenty-five years old and still anonymous: yet another ambitious East Sider making his way in an overcrowded city. Unlike both Becker and Rothstein, he was a first-generation immigrant, having stepped ashore in New York at the age of five. Herman's family had come from Estonia, though there were also relatives in Germany. He had enjoyed an unremarkable childhood in the densely populated tenements of the Lower East Side, joined a modest street gang, and left school and home on the same day, aged fourteen. In his youth Rosenthal was a decent fighter, fast on his feet, and he knew his way around the streets. Having already earned a little money working as a newsboy, selling papers at one end of Brooklyn Bridge, he found work as a runner for a poolroom, carrying messages and recording bets for the place's clients.

Work as a runner brought in little money—barely enough for a boy without a home to live on. But Herman's prospects improved considerably when he met and married Dora Gilbert in 1897. He was by then in his early twenties; his wife was a few years older and pretty, if scarcely beautiful: a small, dark-haired woman who had been brought up in the tenements like her husband and whose morals were sufficiently elastic to make her useful to her spouse in unusual ways. Dora provided Herman with the comforts of home, of course—cooked meals, clean clothes, if not yet children. But, more than that, she was for the next two years the couple's principal source of income. At a time when Rosenthal's own earnings remained uncertain, his wife sold favors to provide for them. She worked as a prostitute after her marriage, and her husband was her pimp.

The Rosenthals had first gone into business around 1898, at a time when—for all the efforts of the Reverend Parkhurst—"sporting men" (the contemporary euphemism for sexually active middle- and upper-class males) could take their pick from more than 250 brothels in

Satan's Circus alone.* Many of these establishments advertised widely to attract customers; it was common for gentlemen arriving at the best hotels to find elegantly engraved invitations awaiting them, requesting the pleasure of their company at some high-class house. Less wealthy clients hunted through coded advertisements in newspapers in search of places touting "magnetic treatments," "manicures," or the ubiquitous "French lessons." Herman, who lacked the resources to advertise, adopted a less sophisticated and more direct approach: He took to loitering in the lobby of the Metropolitan Opera House, waiting for a performance to finish, and then touted for business among the opera's well-heeled patrons. Potential clients would follow him around the corner to an apartment on West Fortieth Street, where they were greeted by Mrs. Rosenthal and the two girls she employed. Herman stood guard and collected payment.

As Rosenthal and his wife discovered, there was plenty of business, even in the lowest brothels. It was widely accepted at this time that men of all classes were prey to a morbid degree of lust that no genteel, well-brought-up wife could be expected to satisfy. It was, in consequence, thought understandable—even acceptable—for men to frequent brothels, and there were even those who regarded the habit as admirable, since it spared girlfriends and fiancées from the perils of seduction and decent wives from submitting to practices they found objectionable. There were a million unmarried men in Manhattan, and tens of thousands of others who were dissatisfied, for whatever reason,

---

*The sex trade was, indeed, the reason the district had developed as it had. The first whorehouses in Satan's Circus, which had opened not long after the appearance of the big theaters and concert halls nearby, had drawn such raucous crowds that they quickly drove the old inhabitants of the area north. Landlords unable to attract middle-class tenants were thus forced to choose between "dividing their properties into multiple-family dwellings for working-class tenants, or lease to agents who in turn rented to prostitutes and madams who could afford high rents," as one historian of prostitution explains. Bordellos were the more profitable option, and before long, dozens had sprung up between Carnegie Hall and the Waldorf-Astoria hotel, sometimes twenty to a block. These were, of course, relatively high-class operations, and the sex available in Satan's Circus was generally more sophisticated than that sold, say, down on the East Side.

with the sexual possibilities available at home. In these circumstances bordellos of all kinds thrived.

For a couple such as the Rosenthals, located in the heart of Manhattan, the heavy costs of working in Satan's Circus were offset by the advantages. There was, for instance, business to be done with tourists. Sporting men were known to travel to New York from all over the country in order to sample the fleshy delights of Manhattan, where a sexual smorgasbord of possibilities scarcely dreamed of in their hometowns lay waiting to be sampled. According to Nell Kimball, a renowned madam from sinful New Orleans, even the working girls of the Deep South

> sat around in their underwear or wrappers, drank beer, joshed a lot in country talk, felt at home with the simple horny guests that came to them with dusty shoes and derbys. There was a morality about those places that mirrored the words of the whores and their guests. They were . . . doing it mostly the straight and traditional American way, as they had been raised. Frenching was talked and joked about, but rarely asked for or offered. The Italian Way, entry through the rear, was kind of a joke carried over from farm boys experimenting on themselves and with each other, considered a sign of depraved city sinning. Memories of Bible lessons and hellfire from their country churches was still there in the middle class whorehouse . . . The idea of flogging for fun, or being stomped on by high heels . . . was like spitting on the flag.

Kimball's views were evidently shared by the more sophisticated of her clients. As one indignant American traveler, with experience of brothels all around the world, complained, "I consider the quality of sex [generally available in the United States] to constitute an indictment against the American man's taste and degree of civilization. . . . Foreign whores somehow manage to feign an attitude that leads you to believe, at least for the moment of intercourse, that you have their attention and that they are interested in seeing you and having a pleasant time . . . they always seem just a little surprised when you give them money."

There were no such problems in Satan's Circus, and it is likely that Dora Rosenthal and her girls offered the broad menu of services demanded by well-traveled clients. But that was not in itself enough to guarantee the success of an establishment bled white by demands for graft from the police and Tammany. Pimps and madams had to consider carefully the productivity of the women working for them, and it was here that Herman—with his complicated relations with the staff—apparently experienced difficulty.

Some New York whores worked at an amazing pace; according to the accounts book of one fifty-cent bordello, its most productive girl copulated with forty-nine men in one day, a total made possible by the fact that she kept the sort of hours that would have shamed a sweatshop worker. Others labored in short, intense bursts at the rate of a dollar or two for between ten and fifteen minutes of their time. The record for the fastest turnover of clients seems to have belonged to the whore who contrived to have intercourse with fifty-eight men in one three-hour period, and the houses fortunate enough to employ girls of this type could turn profits of $1,500 a month or more. But Herman, procuring for only a few hours every evening, and quite possibly unable to demand such selflessness from his spouse, never made this sort of money. The couple managed no more than a modest living— and as Rosenthal's wife grew older and plumper, the price that she commanded fell. Business difficulties, and perhaps the strange, skewed character of the relationship, took their toll, and soon the couple separated. Shortly thereafter, Dora divorced her husband and went off to open a boardinghouse, leaving Herman in effect without a job.

By 1900, then, Rosenthal was busy casting about for other ways to make money. He promoted a few fights, but with such moderate success that a return to the world of gambling began to seem a safer option. The former pimp was, however, now too old and too grand to work as a runner, and in any case he had grown accustomed to living in a certain style. Herman knew he would be better off as the owner of some gambling concession, but he also recognized that he could not operate without protection. He turned, as if by instinct, to Tim Sullivan.

Big Tim, as things turned out, liked the idea. Rosenthal's antecedents must have helped; the Irishman was known to have a soft spot for former newsboys, and over the years he helped many old friends from the streets to set themselves up in business. If the stories that went around New York a few years later are to be relied on, Sullivan may have gotten to know Herman as early as the mid-1890s, when the young would-be gambler—like his near contemporary Arnold Rothstein—hung out at his saloons, earning nickels running errands. But there were other, better, reasons for Sullivan's interest in Rosenthal as well. Like many Tammany politicians, Tim had great respect for the abilities and intellect of the young Jewish men who frequented his saloons and clubhouses. He liked to keep some "smart Jew boys" around him, and—perhaps because their generally superior education made them numerate—often set them up as bookmakers or as the managers of stuss houses. "Gambling," he always pointed out, "takes brains."

Sullivan and Rosenthal, one New York journalist recalled, "hit it off at once" when Herman renewed their acquaintance in 1900 or so, and before long, Big Tim had "made a special pet" of the aspiring gambler. In the course of the next decade, the Irishman would repeatedly advance Rosenthal funds, investing in various business ventures. No doubt that money was reclaimed with interest most of the time. But Herman's career never ran entirely smoothly, and Tim was to lose several thousand dollars backing him. Few Tammany politicians would have tolerated failure on that scale. But the friendship that had grown up between Sullivan and Rosenthal never appeared strained.

Herman's first job as one of Big Tim's gambling lieutenants was as the proprietor of a small-time crap game on the East Side. He did well enough at this to set up as an off-track bookmaker in Far Rockaway, at the farthest extreme of New York's public-transportation network, and for several years commuted daily from his home in Manhattan to Long

Island. By now touching thirty, Rosenthal had grown into a garrulous and rather bumptious character, clean-shaven, with the remnants of good looks, but running increasingly to fat and more and more convinced of his own importance. Herman, his friends would recall, was always full of grand ideas for getting rich, a man whose vaulting ambitions were invariably beyond his reach.

Nonetheless, oddsmaking was one of the few occupations for which Rosenthal had ever shown real talent, and after a year or two under Tim's protection he did begin to make a better living. By 1907 his little empire had expanded to include a string of poolrooms on Second Avenue, where the stretch of road between Houston Street and Fourteenth was known as "the Great White Way of the Jewish East Side." He also moved onto the racetracks themselves, setting up betting stalls at Belmont and at Jerome Park. At about the same time, he took over the concession to run gambling at the Hesper Club.

Within a year or two, Herman became extremely rich. The gambler himself was heard to boast that he was worth $200,000, and it could scarcely be denied that he now maintained himself in style, with a suite of rooms in a Broadway hotel costing some $25,000 a year—a sum in itself fifty times the salary of the average New Yorker—and an amply indulged taste for fine food and expensive clothes. Viña Delmar, the observant nine-year-old daughter of one of Rosenthal's oldest friends, remembered the gambler as "quite chubby . . . but dressed beautifully in a gray suit, a silk striped shirt, and a collar even stiffer and snowier than Papa's." Others, less tolerant and no doubt more jealous, spoke of Rosenthal as "a flashy, greedy, loudmouthed braggart."

Unfortunately for Herman, his flush years did not last long. The flow of profits from the racetracks came to an abrupt end in 1909 with the decision of the state assembly in Albany to ban gambling on horse racing throughout New York—a new law that coincided disastrously with a sharp increase in competition among East Side gaming houses. First New York's racing fraternity led an exodus to Canada and Kentucky, and the local racetracks all closed down; then

Herman found the revenues from his downtown stuss joints badly squeezed. A younger, tougher generation of East Siders had begun to press for a slice of the action on Second Avenue. Their appearance resulted in a series of violent disputes, and soon the peace that had long been maintained by Big Tim's gambling commission began to erode. Profits slumped, and the danger of doing business downtown rose.

Turning, as he always did, to Sullivan, Herman borrowed heavily to open up a new concession miles away, in Far Rockaway, Long Island—the place where he had begun his career years earlier. This time, however, the local gamblers had better connections with the police; Rosenthal's new club was swiftly raided and closed down. He tried again, on the Upper West Side of Manhattan, this time going into business with a fellow member of the Hesper Club named Beansey Rosenfeld. The two men opened a stuss house in the district known as "Little Russia" and ran it profitably for a while. But the partners soon fell out, and their place was raided and closed down.

Big losses on new premises and lost profits on old ones soon stretched Rosenthal's hitherto-ample resources to the limit, and, to make matters worse, Tim Sullivan himself was also having problems. Tim's difficulties were caused by the declining influence of Tammany Hall—which after 1905 found itself increasingly marginalized by the continuing influx of Jewish, Italian, and Eastern European immigrants with their own political affiliations and even social-welfare programs. As Tammany's power waned, and it concentrated its dwindling powers of patronage in the hands of a few old favorites, men such as Herman Rosenthal found themselves marginalized and harder-pressed to obtain both protection and funds. The police, ever alert to subtle shifts in power, reacted by putting pressure on businesses that had once been sacrosanct, and Rosenthal's gambling houses were among them.

Slowly but surely, then, Herman's money ran out. True, Rosenthal could (his friends related) still be touchingly generous. One boyhood companion, who had grown up to become a poverty-stricken vaudeville artist, recalled that—desperate for money—he tracked his old friend down to his stand at a racetrack and wagered his last few dollars on a sure thing. When the horse won but was disqualified, Rosenthal took up a collection among the other gamblers at the track and, despite having been wiped out financially himself in the same race, forced several hundred dollars on his friend. But things were definitely getting tougher, and the police and East Side rivals were no longer the only enemies that the gambler had to worry about. By the first months of 1909, Herman was also receiving the unwanted attention of New York's brash district attorney: a tough, driven lawman by the name of William Travers Jerome.

Jerome had been a power in the city for a decade. A cousin of Winston Churchill, described by one legal historian as "the most unusual jurist Manhattan had ever seen," he had made his name as a junior counsel working with John Goff during the Lexow inquiry. Jerome's reward for his work on that commission had been a position as a judge and a deserved reputation as one of Tammany's most implacable foes.

Jerome had been a revelation during his first years in office, displaying all the push and pugnacity of his famous relative. Prior to his election as DA in 1901, New York's district attorney had been hardly more than a cipher and his office a dumping ground for minor machine politicians who could be relied upon to do as they were told. Little work was done by any of the staff, and gamblers who enjoyed Tammany's protection had no reason to fear investigation. Jerome changed all that, turning the DA's office into a vigorous force for reform.

It was far from easy work, and the legacy of years of official neglect was palpable. When Arthur Train—one of the young lawyers brought in to replace the Tammany placemen who had run the department—first cleaned out his office, he found his desk stuffed full of ancient indictments that had never been acted on and piles of forgotten legal proceedings stored "in wastebaskets, pigeonholes, in the backs of drawers and on the floor." There was no system, and important papers continued to turn up in odd places for months. But the new district attorney began to work his way through the backlog, issuing a blizzard of indictments and keeping his own name in the papers by pursuing high-profile cases against prominent men. Jerome's reward for creating a template that thousands of other DAs would follow in the coming century was a personal popularity so great that he clung onto office for nearly a decade.

As Herman Rosenthal knew from bitter personal experience, Jerome's initial impact was considerable. So great were New York gamblers' fears of what the reformers might do that all the city's gaming clubs, stuss houses, and poolrooms shut down the moment the new DA and his boss, the reformist Mayor Seth Low, took office, and for almost three months not a wheel was spun or a card turned throughout the five boroughs. Most places did eventually reopen as it became apparent that even the district attorney still had to obtain evidence and build a case before he could actually prosecute. But even when Tammany regained control of the city—with, in effect, a mandate from voters to leave gambling alone—Jerome continued to make high-profile raids for years. He still courted the press as well, raiding clubs armed with a Bible in one hand and a revolver in the other, waving the pistol over his head and theatrically threatening to "shoot the next man who moves" while his men blew open safes in search of incriminating documents.

After the Tammany election victory of 1904, naturally, the DA's effectiveness was not what it had been while the reformers were in power; there can be no doubt that Jerome himself was gradually worn down by the Democrats' obstructiveness and the near impossibility of securing convictions from judges who were all too often part of the Hall's corrupt system. But even with Tammany in office, gamblers could never rest entirely easy. Some raids, some arrests, and some convictions were a desirable thing to have on the Democrats' record come election time, and since the city's richest vice lords remained on the whole inviolate, it was men of Herman's lesser clout who had the most to fear.

True enough, Rosenthal experienced little trouble while Big Tim reigned supreme. But by the last months of 1908, undermined by the arrival of a fresh influx of Eastern European immigrants in his East Side strongholds, Sullivan's power was wavering, and in January 1909, Jerome—by then entering his last few weeks in office—subjected Herman to some inconclusive questioning and extracted a promise that the gambler's various premises would be opened for inspection. Rosenthal foolishly ignored these warning signs and continued to run his houses wide open in defiance of the law. The raids that ensued were savage: Jerome, backed by a squad of fourteen brawny policemen, descended on both addresses simultaneously and pretty much destroyed them. "Axes," the *New York Times* reported the next day, "were plied, doors broken down, and walls torn open." Seven men were arrested on the spot, and Herman himself was detained a few days later. The damage to the clubs was such that they could not reopen, and, to make matters worse, Rosenthal himself was indicted for attempted bribery. He had, it seems, made clumsy efforts to buy off the DA's process server.

Herman was in trouble, and matters were scarcely improved by mounting difficulties with the illegal off-track-betting service that was still his principal source of income. Rosenthal had been able to retain some of his old high-rolling clients for as long as they were losing. But he now lacked the funds to pay out to major winners. He reneged on a $5,000 loss to Charles Kohler, the piano magnate, and when his old friends at the Hesper Club—where he now ran the gambling concession—loaned him the funds to settle the debt, he defaulted on their repayments, too. Many of the Hesper's members were so disgusted by his actions that they took themselves and their business around the corner to a new gaming club just opened by the Sam Paul Association.

The declining fortunes of the club and the rowdy behavior of the younger Hespers—many of whom were little more than gangsters— drove away more respectable members, and by 1909, Tim Sullivan and his henchman cousin Little Tim had both resigned their memberships. The pretense that the place was a social club was abandoned soon thereafter, and—under Rosenthal's stewardship—the once-proud East Side institution became just another tawdry gaming joint, less wealthy, less influential, and much less remunerative than it had used to be. The Hesper limped along for a few more months, eventually closing in April 1911 when fifty policemen burst through its armored door with axes and destroyed its fixtures and equipment so utterly that the interior was beyond repair; even Big Tim's precious letter, in its golden frame, was damaged in the fracas.

By then Rosenthal's plight was desperate. Drained of resources, assailed on all sides by the police and rival gamblers, and increasingly unsure of protection, he had long ago been forced out of his hotel suite and into paper collars and cheap clothes. His income from gambling had all but dried up; his savings were gone; indeed he owed money, and not merely to Tim Sullivan. Nor did there seem to be much prospect that matters would improve.

Less than two years after boasting of a wealth exceeding most New Yorkers' dreams of avarice, Herman Rosenthal was broke, and the gambler could not be blamed for wondering why his luck had changed so drastically. But the answer, he realized, was obvious: The police and the district attorney always seemed to have plenty of information regarding his activities; each new effort he made to reestablish himself soon became known to the authorities. That had to mean that somebody, somewhere, was informing on him, and the only people with a motive to take Rosenthal down were his fellow gamblers. In his own mind, Herman had little doubt who was responsible. He suspected "Bridgey" Webber.

Once, twenty years earlier, Herman and Bridgey* had been friends.

The two men had shared a childhood on the Lower East Side, and if they were not by all accounts particularly close—Webber's

---

*His real name wasn't Bridgey, of course. It was Louis. He had earned his nickname at the turn of the century by indulging in an all-too-public affair with a two-hundred-pound prostitute called Bridget.

family was more religious and much better off; Rosenthal was older by two years—they had certainly known each other fairly well, an acquaintanceship that deepened as they drifted into the half-light world of politics and gambling. Like Rosenthal, Webber had gotten his start while still of school age, though his specialty, at age fourteen, was the ominously advanced crime of kidnapping pet dogs. By the time he was twenty, Bridgey was running what was said to be the largest opium den in Chinatown. His premises down on Pell Street seem to have catered to a predominantly Chinese clientele, which would have made Bridgey unusual at a time when many of the Westerners who dabbled in opium did so with an eye not to New York's addicts but to wide-eyed tourists: parties of slummers, their heads filled with wild stories of Tong gang wars and white slavery, who thronged the district looking for thrills and who—for a suitable fee— could be shown around a dingy apartment decked out with drug paraphernalia and peopled by louche men and women pretending to be opium fiends. Whatever the truth, however, Webber did not remain in the dangerous and insecure drugs business for long. By about 1900 he had moved into the altogether safer world of gambling, opening a number of stuss houses in the Jewish districts along Second Avenue. Having married into money—his wife's collection of jewelry alone was reputed to be worth some $10,000—Bridgey had sufficient cash to do up his premises in style. The rewards were considerable, and before long his gambling clubs were generating an enviable income. They also placed him in competition with his old friend Rosenthal.

It was, those who knew both men agreed, an unequal contest. Webber—a slight, fastidiously dressed man with a long nose, sharp chin, bow lips, and bulging eyes—had always been the sharper, more aggressive of the two, and he was willing to go just as far as Herman, and probably further, in order to protect his interests. "He does not look like a gangster nor a gambler," a crime reporter at the *Evening Post* observed in 1912. "His manner is rather that of a quiet young clerk—one even of studious and sedentary habits. Yet his record shows him to have been a factor in East Side gambling and feuds since he was old enough to be recognized as somebody."

The first shots in the war between the friends were fired not by Herman but by Webber. Around 1908 he opened up a stuss house just along the road from Rosenthal's most profitable club and proceeded to drain much of its business. At about the same time, the former dognapper accepted a commission from the local precinct captain and began collecting graft payments from his fellow gamblers on the Lower East Side. The police chief must have been a canny man; certainly Webber had every reason to ensure that Herman and other rival gamblers made their payments on time, in full, and without exception.

In any event, appeals to reason failed and tempers flared. When Rosenthal's stuss house closed in the face of Bridgey's competition, Herman was so desperate and so furious that he hired a street tough by the name of Spanish Louis to take care of his rival. Louis came cheap because he was no more than an ambitious pimp, seduced by the romance of crime, and handy with his fists.* Melodramatically attired all in black and—as one contemporary recalled—affecting a broad-brimmed sombrero, "a brace of heavy Colt's revolvers, the most massive artillery in gangland, and a pair of eight-inch dirks, which he thrust into special scabbards built into his trousers," the would-be gangster waylaid Webber late one night toward the end of 1909 and beat him almost to death. While the hired thug worked Bridgey over, Herman lurked in the shadows and watched.

Rosenthal's message to his rival had no apparent effect; Webber's stuss houses remained open while the injured gambler recovered. Few East Side gamblers were surprised when, soon afterward, a bomb

---

*He was, one New York paper wrote, "big bodied and muscular and could deliver more knockouts with his right than any man his size or double it for that matter." In civilian life Spanish Louis had gone by the name John Lewis, but he claimed to have been born in Argentina and spun tales to his acquaintances of his noble Spanish blood. In fact—at least according to the crime historian Herbert Asbury—he was born into an Orthodox Jewish family from Brooklyn.

detonated outside the busiest among them, blowing off much of its facade. Then, when Bridgey emerged at last from the hospital, Rosenthal paid for him to be attacked once again. This time the assailant was an established enforcer known as "Tough Tony" Ferraci, who caught up with Webber on voter-registration day, blackjacked him, and broke his jaw. When Tough Tony was picked up by the police and charged with carrying a concealed weapon, it was Herman Rosenthal who turned up at the station house to bail him out. Webber and his partisans drew the obvious conclusion.

Bridgey was too clever to respond to Herman's flailing attempts to resolve their rivalry in kind, but neither did he forgive them, and he went to work surreptitiously to undermine Rosenthal's businesses in whatever way he could. First Spanish Louis—who received an invitation to call on Herman one night, only to find his patron's door mysteriously barred—met his end at the hands of several assailants who hailed him as he was waiting on the doorstep and cut him down as he fled onto a side street. Next Sam Paul, one of Bridgey's oldest business associates, stepped up the pressure by luring many of Rosenthal's remaining customers into his own East Side stuss houses. Webber proceeded to plunge Herman into further trouble by calling on his connections with Tammany. It helped that Bridgey was not part of Big Tim Sullivan's faction at the Hall (he was a partisan of the Irishman's clever cousin Little Tim instead) and that he had a first-rate understanding of the mechanics of city politics; in any event, such protection as Rosenthal might have enjoyed from the police was quietly removed, and shortly thereafter the first in a long series of well-informed, pseudonymous letters, signed by a certain "Henry Williams," arrived at City Hall. The missive denounced Herman as a leading gambler and thoughtfully provided precise details as to the whereabouts of his remaining premises.

The consequences were predictable. Williams's letter was passed on to police headquarters, where no fewer than three special anti-gambling squads stood by to act on such pseudonymous tips. There it found its way onto the desk of the man commanding the most active of all these units: a cop just then making a name for himself by cracking heads and raiding clubs throughout Satan's Circus. Manhattan's papers had been awash for several months with news of this man's exploits, and by the winter of 1911, he had probably put more gamblers out of business than any other officer. He was the most admired policeman in the city. His name was Charley Becker.

CHAPTER 5

STRONG ARM SQUAD

THE EVENTS THAT BROUGHT Becker to a desk at police headquarters and command of New York's most famous "Special Squad" had their origin a decade earlier, in the summer of 1902. Mayor Seth Low's reform administration was still in power in the city. Rosenthal was as yet a minor figure in the closed world of East Side gambling. And Charley Becker, the best part of a decade into his police career, was setting out to make a stand.

The Becker of 1902 was, the evidence suggests, a more or less despondent man. Physically he was in his prime, twenty-nine years old and possessed of a physique hardened by years on the beat: broad-shouldered, barrel-chested, with fists like typewriters. ("He could kill a man with a punch," an admirer once remarked, intending the observation as a compliment.) Professionally, though, Becker was becalmed. His decision to abandon the old style of policing had not borne fruit; months, stretching into years, of conscientious work had yet to earn him a promotion that was becoming overdue, and like many of his colleagues he found himself increasingly demoralized by the long hours he was required to work and by the capricious behavior of senior officers who tacitly encouraged graft but were quick to distance themselves from the taint of corruption when vice was exposed. To make matters worse, Mayor Low and his reformers had made little headway in tackling the department, as the thousands of patrolmen who voted for them had wished. Most captains still actively discriminated against men whose loyalty was less than absolute. A favorite trick, during Low's mayoralty, was to use the old two-platoon system to inflict extra duty on such officers, calling them out of reserve and onto the streets at all hours of the day and night. This was particularly hard on married men, who were already fortunate if they slept at home one night in every four. "Captains and Sergeants," Becker himself told a reporter from the *New York Times*, "have too much discretion in some matters, and the men are made subservient to them."

Becker was not alone in feeling poorly treated, and this no doubt explains his willingness to talk directly to the press. By 1902, indeed, morale throughout the police department was at its lowest ebb in years. Thanks to a vaguely worded piece of law, no full promotions had been made since 1899, and the ranks were becoming clogged with acting captains, sergeants, and roundsmen who had no idea whether their new positions would ever be ratified. Additional demands were also being made on patrolmen's pockets, thanks to a new form of graft—introduced in the dying days of Mayor Robert Van Wyck's administration—that required men to pay up to $25 every time they transferred precinct. And Low had done little to stamp out another long-standing abuse: Politics, more than ability, still determined men's careers. This was a particular problem for Republicans such as Becker, who remained a minority on the force.*

The upshot of all this dissatisfaction was the so-called Revolt of the Cops, an inconclusive uprising in the spring and summer of 1902 that brought Becker a degree of prominence, at least within the ranks of the police. Stirrings of discontent had actually begun a year earlier, when the Patrolmen's Benevolent Association first made a determined attempt to secure the introduction of a three-platoon system intended to limit men to eight hours' duty at a stretch. Three

---

*Asked by an investigating committee whether a man's affiliations affected his chances of promotion, Police Commissioner York, of Tammany, guilelessly replied, "Oh, things being equal, it certainly does—and it ought to. I'd favor a Democrat every time if circumstances were alike. . . . Every day in the week and every hour in the day."

platoons would have prevented a number of the most injurious abuses of the system and, by ensuring that officers worked to a predetermined rotation, would have let the men's families know when their loved ones would be home. But although two separate attempts to bring in the new scheme were made, both were unsuccessful. Aside from any other considerations, the costs involved meant that the idea was abandoned almost as soon as it was tried.

What was telling about all this was not so much the failure of the campaign for three platoons as the determination shown by ordinary patrolmen, who felt angry enough at their treatment to stage what amounted to industrial action—strictly enforcing the excise laws throughout the city on one April day, thus stopping the flow of graft and annoying their bosses—and approve substantial contributions (amounting, potentially, to $60 a man) to fund their doomed campaign. Plainly, this unprecedented defiance owed much to the activities of a small number of militants, who not only talked colleagues into supporting the campaign but collected so much money that the PBA was able to set aside $150,000 to lobby for a bill in Albany and a similar sum to bribe New York's pliant bosses. These leaders were, in fact, not officers of the Benevolent Association but ordinary patrolmen. Prominent among them were William Drennan of the Seventeenth Precinct and George Ryan of High Bridge station. The third leader of the cops' revolt was Becker.

Becker's role in the affair was an important one, and in the course of the campaign he exhibited considerable organizational ability, a facile tongue, and the sheer bloody-mindedness required to persist in the face of threats. Evidently he also enjoyed a good deal of personal popularity in his own precinct and was known to other officers throughout the city, for in the spring of 1902 he was elected as spokesman for the First Platoon—that is, for half of all the policemen on the force.

What drove Becker to involve himself in the revolt is less well documented, but his grievances were obviously rooted in his own persecution at the hands of a vengeful precinct captain. "Among the experiences recounted" at one mass meeting of patrolmen, a reporter wrote,

> was that of Charles Becker of the One Hundred and Twenty-fifth Street station, who presided at the meeting of the first platoon. . . . It is just about a year ago that Becker was transferred from the Madison Street station. According to the story related, Becker at that time had the temerity to lead a revolt similar in character to the present one. With a number of other policemen of the Madison Street Precinct he told the captain that he was unwilling to stand for the manner in which things were going. The captain is alleged to have replied that unless Becker and his friends ceased causing him (the captain) trouble, they would be either broken or transferred. Becker persisted in the stand he had taken, with the result mentioned.

It is not too much to suggest that the part that Becker played in the cops' revolt influenced his whole career. For one thing, it made him fearless; by August 1902, while still a mere patrolman, he was meeting face-to-face with New York's police commissioner, John Partridge, to plead the case for three platoons.* For another, the agitation surely injured him, since it marked him out to his superiors as a potential troublemaker. Though he was never censured and no disciplinary action was taken against him, senior officers made their displeasure felt in other ways. Promotion remained hard to come by: Becker spent ten years as a patrolman—longer than the average at a time when men who had real political clout, or whose acts of heroism drew them to the attention of the police commissioners, might expect to become roundsmen in only

---

*Becker's efforts were successful, too. By the end of 1902, the ineffectual Partridge had been dismissed and Francis Greene, the new commissioner, had adopted modifications to the Two Platoon system that—while still requiring men to devote an average of twelve hours a day to the department—did allow them to work to a fixed rotation and take sixteen hours off every other day.

four or five—and when he was eventually recommended for sergeant in 1905, Commissioner McAdoo took one look at his file and refused to authorize his elevation. In the interim Becker was also subjected to the NYPD's usual method of taming recalcitrant officers: frequent transfers to new precincts. These punishments were probably no more than minor irritants; there was no long exile to Goatville, no dismal posting outside the island of Manhattan. But Becker, who had been serving at the Madison Street station when agitation for the three-platoon system got under way, nonetheless found himself despatched first to the Upper West Side, then to 115th Street, and finally to Charles Street in Greenwich Village. Each of these postings meant disruptions to his daily life. Rather more significantly, though, for the patrolman's career, the round of transfers brought Becker into the orbit of the man who would become the greatest enemy he had on the force: the department's great pariah, Captain Max F. Schmittberger.

New York's police had never forgiven Schmittberger for his testimony before the Lexow Committee seven years earlier. Lexow's revelations concerning the system of purchase that existed within the NYPD had been bad enough. But it had been Schmittberger's careful dissection of the Satan's Circus graft that laid bare the workings of the department. Without the captain's sworn testimony, Counsel Goff would probably have failed in his attempts to persuade ordinary New Yorkers that their police force was thoroughly corrupt, and there might have been no Fusion administration and no Commissioner Roosevelt. True, some police officers had benefited in consequence, and most of those who had joined the police during the reform years had no love of grafters or the graft. But even the most honest of policemen despised officers who broke the oaths that each man swore at his initiation. And every New York cop had experienced at least some ridicule as a result of Lexow's hearings. Most blamed Max directly for this.

Schmittberger himself was not immune from the taunts that rang in the ears of Manhattan's policemen in the wake of his testimony. His worst moment, he once told the reporter Lincoln Steffens, came when his own children, who had been tormented in school, came home one night demanding, "Say, Pop, is it true this stuff they are saying? It's all lies, ain't it?" But the disgraced captain was, in addition, ostracized by almost all his colleagues, prevented from marching in the annual police parade by a vengeful Bill Devery, and forced to adopt the strictest economies in order to keep up the mortgage on the expensive house he had bought when flush with the proceeds of corruption.

Grateful for the testimony that had helped to bring down Byrnes and Clubber Williams, reformers such as Steffens and Charles Parkhurst were by now Schmittberger's only allies, and the captain had no real choice but to become an honest man. In the course of the next few years, Schmittberger was sent to clean up several corrupt precincts, with good results. He also became the police department's acknowledged expert on crime in New York's black and Italian districts—where it was said "that mothers used to quiet their children by threatening that 'Cap'n Max'll come and ketch you.'" Even Boss Croker found a use for him, as a living symbol of Tammany's supposed willingness to mend its ways.

Whether Schmittberger really regretted the old days any more than Croker did remained a matter of opinion. Steffens and several of the police commissioners who controlled the department after 1900 were sure he had reformed. But another faction, made up of opposition politicians and cynical reporters, argued that Max had not gotten better, merely smarter. He was honest, these men said, when the times called for it. But when reform was voted down and Manhattan thrown wide open, the captain plunged back into the department's corrupt ways with as much enthusiasm as the next man.

Whatever the truth, there is no doubt that many senior policemen ached for the chance to catch Schmittberger in some wrongdoing. The captain was carefully watched for signs of misconduct, and the junior officers in his precincts were similarly disposed against Lexow's most celebrated witness. Certainly Becker, whose friend Clubber Williams had been cruelly exposed by Max's testimony, had every reason to take against him when—thanks to the transfer roundabout—he wound up in Schmittberger's Upper West Side precinct in April 1901.

Unlike most of the captain's enemies, however, the patrolman was not content merely to mutter against Max. Within a matter of weeks, Becker had hauled in several saloonkeepers for violations of the excise law without clearing things with Schmittberger first. Since it was clear that the premises in question could only have remained open with the approval of the precinct captain—and since it was hard for all but the most gullible to believe that the owners were not paying for the privilege—the arrests exposed Schmittberger to further criticism. Max lost no time in dealing with the situation, and within days Becker was on his way again, transferred out of the Upper West Side to another district far uptown. He resented Schmittberger's high-handed treatment sufficiently to file charges of malfeasance against his superior. The captain countered with affidavits of his own, and though the matter was eventually smoothed over and all the charges dropped, there was bad blood between the pair thenceforth.

Under ordinary circumstances, a falling-out between a precinct captain and a mere patrolman would have been a matter of no moment. On this occasion, however—thanks perhaps to Becker's sudden prominence in the department—the beat man's antipathy for Schmittberger was noted, with dramatic consequences for both men's careers. In the course of the next five years, the pair would be pitted against each other twice more, and Becker's determination to pursue a vendetta against his old enemy would make him the favorite of a future police commissioner.

The second confrontation between the two men began two years later, in the first days of 1903, when the district attorney's office launched a formal investigation into Schmittberger's activities. Becker was one of several patrolmen assigned to a new Headquarters Squad formed to uncover graft in the captain's new station house on East Fifty-first Street. Whether or not Schmittberger was making real efforts to stamp out vice in this heavily corrupt district, gambling and prostitution certainly continued to flourish along the borders of Satan's Circus. No firm evidence of Max's complicity emerged, but it did not take long for Becker and his colleagues to discover that several of Schmittberger's men were implicated in the white slave trade. An eighteen-year-old orphan testified that a beat policeman who had promised help had instead escorted her to a brothel, where she was kept "practically a prisoner" for sixteen weeks. Schmittberger denied all knowledge of the affair, and no charges were brought against him. But the headquarters men had raised further doubts about his character.

Becker's work on the East Side was recognized soon afterward with elevation to the rank of roundsman—a promotion that came through in November 1903, ten years almost to the day since he first became a policeman. For a short while, his career prospered, and in the summer of 1904 he added luster to his reputation by saving a man from drowning in the Hudson River. James Butler had toppled into the water at West Tenth Street after suffering an epileptic fit. Becker jumped fully clothed into the Hudson after him, earning the police department's highest award for bravery, the Medal of Honor, and a special commendation from Police Commissioner Greene.

Even so, the Headquarters Squad was soon dissolved, and Rounds-man Becker might still have languished for years in the outer reaches of Manhattan had it not been for the good fortune that set him in pursuit of Schmittberger again. By the early spring of 1906, three years after the men's paths had last crossed, Max had finally secured himself a long-delayed promotion to inspector and been placed in overall command of policing New York's entertainment district. He was a powerful figure now, and with Tammany back in power there were suspicions that he was once again collecting graft throughout Satan's Circus. The task of investigating Schmittberger went to a new deputy police commissioner, Rhinelander Waldo, who, to make sure that the inquiry was zealously pursued, searched out a sergeant and two roundsmen with strong motives for hating their target. Each member of this new "street-cleaning" detail—a New York reporter later explained—was "known to feel that Schmittberger had done them wrong at some point in their police careers." One of the two roundsmen detailed to the squad was Becker.

In 1903, Schmittberger had known that he was being investigated. In 1906, headquarters was a good deal more discreet. On the afternoon of June 29, 1906, Becker, with Sergeant Robert McNaught and Roundsman Philip Faubell, mustered fifteen patrolmen, handpicked from downtown precincts, on an East Side pier—a ruse, the *Times* reported the next day,

> intended to give the impression that the police were going on a steamboat excursion. Then a large covered van appeared. With the sign "Storage" on the side of it, it looked innocent enough to fool anybody. . . . The policemen were told they were to have a ride, and after they got into the van the big doors were shut tightly.

Led by the three street cleaners, who traveled in a cab, the converted furniture van drove to an address on West Fifteenth Street and parked. The men inside poured out, armed with sledgehammers and axes that had been placed inside the vehicle. Urged on by McNaught, they battered down the front door of the largest gambling club on the street, while Becker and Faubell crept up onto the roof and took hatchets to a locked fire exit. Brandishing revolvers, the two roundsmen rushed down into the body of the building and detained the gamblers who ran the house, while their colleagues burst in through the front and rounded up 50 of their customers.

The street-cleaning squad carried out three more raids that day, the most dramatic being the last, on premises at 147 West Forty-first Street, where newly fitted armor-plated doors defeated all their efforts to gain entry and Becker was forced to smash his way into the premises through barred basement windows with the aid of sledgehammers. A further 75 gamblers were discovered huddled inside, taking the total arrested in a single day to 145. The profusion of gaming clubs operating openly in Satan's Circus, and the ease with which the police had raided them, was yet another indictment of Schmittberger's policing, and the next morning the city's newspapers trumpeted that the "Furniture Van Raids" had done in the inspector. Three days later

Schmittberger was transferred out to Staten Island and warned that he faced charges and a likely police trial.*

From Becker's perspective the results of this third brush with Max Schmittberger must have seemed satisfactory. He continued to serve with the street-cleaning squad for a while, carrying out raids on gamblers for two more months, and in January 1907 was advanced to the rank of sergeant—a promotion made, over the heads of a number of more experienced roundsmen, as a reward for good work in Satan's Circus. There, however, his career stalled again. Becker spent most of the rest of the decade performing mundane duties in precincts up and down Manhattan. His service included desk work downtown and an unglamorous spell of duty with the Traffic Squad.

For once, however, Becker did not care; he may even have welcomed the less onerous duties he was now assigned. There were, at least for a while, simply too many distractions in his own tumultuous private life, most of which stemmed from the deterioration of his relationship with his second wife. The marriage was all but over by the first weeks of 1905. And in March, Letitia sued him for divorce.

The Becker marriage had been unhappy for some time. There had been no more children to follow Howard, who was five by the time his mother went to court, and according to the second Mrs. Becker her husband had been compulsively unfaithful to her almost since their wedding day. There had been numerous casual conquests, among them several girls whom the policeman had met along his beat, and a few more serious affairs. The attentions that Becker paid to an Irish girl named Alice Lynch, his wife sourly observed, "were of the devoted sort."

---

*In the end Schmittberger wriggled free again. His lawyer protested that the raids were part of a conspiracy, hinted darkly at the motives of Becker and the other members of the street-cleaning squad, and argued that the inspector's only "crime" was the technical one of endorsing the reports of the local precinct captain, who had certified the district clear of vice. It was a Pyrrhic victory, however, for Schmittberger was never let loose in Satan's Circus again.

"Charley Becker was not a good husband," Letitia concluded a few years later.

> [He was] a quick-tempered man, headstrong and with a will of iron. At times he would take me into his confidence, and at other times he would endeavor to deceive me. He was away from home most of the time. Long after I knew that he was not keeping his marriage vows, when he had cast me aside to devote himself to other women, I stuck to him. I did this for our son. I was a mother and that always came first . . . [but] his actions became such that any self-respecting woman could no longer call him husband. I finally was simply compelled to sue for divorce.

Legal separations were still unusual in 1905, and neither party could hope to avoid the taint of scandal. Nonetheless, Becker did not contest his wife's suit and may even have cooperated with it, since the court papers suggest that he allowed himself to be discovered alone with another woman in a hotel room. (Adultery was then the only grounds for divorce in New York State.) So anxious was he to be rid of her that he voluntarily entered into an agreement that required him to pay her a large sum in alimony and child support. This ensured that the case was concluded swiftly, and the couple's divorce became final in June 1906. According to family lore, Becker's older sibling, Paul—a forty-eight-year-old bachelor—agreed to minimize the fuss by wedding his brother's wife and getting her and her son away from the city. It is certainly true that Letitia was next heard of in Reno, Nevada, where she and Paul Becker married in August 1909. Paul supported his new family by working in the mining business.

There can be no doubt that Charley Becker's eagerness to be divorced owed much to his involvement with another woman. The affair with Alice Lynch had cooled by 1905, but Becker soon transferred his affections to her sister, Helen, a petite and pretty schoolteacher a year younger than he was. Unlike the strong-willed Letitia Stenson, Helen was tender and supportive. She soon became the most important person in Becker's life.

Helen Lynch was the daughter of a saloonkeeper and had lived in New York for three decades. By 1905 she was working at Public School 41 on Greenwich Avenue, where—according to an autobiographical sketch set down in 1914—she met Becker on his rounds and he courted her at the school gate. "In the afternoon he would come for me, and we would take a drive, or we would go to luncheon," she recalled. Within a few months of first meeting, the couple was engaged; a year later, when the divorce came through, they married.

Charles and Helen Becker were similar in many ways. Both had grown up in modest circumstances; both were clever and articulate—the position of teacher was one of the few open to educated women at the time. And, though each had nine brothers and sisters, both felt oddly solitary. "When I was little," Helen reminisced, "my father thought that no other children were quite good enough for me, and I got the habit of keeping to myself. Until I met [Charles] I had been very much alone—I never had a woman friend that I confided in very much. My only friend was my husband." Perhaps because of all they had in common, the couple seem to have been genuinely happy. There are no hints that Becker embarked upon further affairs after 1906, and the tone of the letters he and his wife exchanged when separated remained warmly affectionate. "He," one journalist discovered, "called her My Queen and she called him Charley-boy or Charley-lover."

For the first time, Becker was an attentive husband. Unlike many New York policemen, whose idea of off-duty recreation was a visit to a saloon, a brothel, or a ball game, he made a point of returning to the couple's small apartment at the end of each patrol, and when Helen transferred to P.S. 90 on West 148th Street to take charge of the "overage graduating class"—a group of "backward pupils" with more or less severe learning difficulties—her spouse took an active interest in the children's progress. "He would often correct papers for me, or write out report cards, and he knew the name of each girl in my class. Each day I would tell him everything that happened."

There were, nonetheless, strains on the new marriage. Becker spent a lot of money on his wife—"We used to drive a good deal in the parks and out in the country," she recalled, "[and] he would often take me out to dinner at restaurants and then to the theater"—and there never seemed to be much to spare. Matters were complicated by the divorce, which certainly drained Becker's finances; well over a quarter of his $2,000 annual salary went to Letitia in alimony, and even after her remarriage there were still child-support payments to make. According to the second Mrs. Becker, her former husband could ill afford to formalize their voluntary arrangement and threatened that if she ever attempted to make the payments the subject of a legal order, he would "force her into the jurisdiction of the New York courts." Even when Helen's income was factored in, she and her husband did not believe themselves comfortably off, and for three years she taught night school to earn extra money, traveling all the way from their apartment on West 165th Street down to the southern tip of Manhattan to complete what amounted to a fifteen-hour working day. "During our seven years of married life," she later recalled,

> I did all the housework, the cooking, the cleaning, everything except the washing, and I taught school besides. . . . I always got up at six o'clock in the morning. . . . We never had a servant, and our rent never exceeded forty dollars a month. . . . That does not look as if we were very rich.

Shortage of cash led Becker to search anxiously for new ways of making money, and—for a policeman rising in the force—the only likely source was graft. Three successive Tammany election triumphs—in 1903, 1905, and 1909—undid so much of the work of the reformers that many New York cops were once more dabbling in corruption, if not so openly, so profitably, or in so organized a fashion as they had during the 1890s. By the last years of the decade, money flowed into the choicest precincts from nearby gaming clubs and brothels much as it always had; if anything, Charles Murphy's decision to dissociate the Democrats from prostitution meant that larger sums were available to the police than ever before. All indications are that Becker's desire to stay clean wavered accordingly. Whatever the policeman's real views on the matter, though, he had little opportunity to make much from corruption before 1910. Neither desk jobs in downtown precincts nor assignments to the Traffic Squad offered real potential for profit. Becker was forced to look on in frustration as others raked in the graft instead.

All this changed, however, in 1911, a year that saw Becker achieve a degree of prominence in Manhattan for the first time in half a decade. Oddly enough, he owed this opportunity—indirectly at least—to a man who was not merely one of the most remarkable figures in the history of the city but perhaps the fiercest critic of its police. Becker's unlikely benefactor was none other than the new mayor of New York: Judge William J. Gaynor.

Mayor Gaynor was in his early sixties when he took office on the first day of 1910, old for a public servant. A scrawny, bearded Irishman, twice married, once divorced, and renowned in his Supreme Court days for standing foursquare behind the Bill of Rights, the judge had long dreamed of making his mark upon the city. But he had not actually embarked upon a political career until a few months earlier, when Boss Murphy had concluded that Tammany's best chance of victory in the forthcoming elections lay in producing a candidate of unimpeachable integrity. Gaynor fit the bill—perhaps rather too well. Incorruptible, unbiddable, and fair (not to mention so austere that he covered the three and a half miles between his Brooklyn home and City Hall on foot each day in every weather), the newly elected mayor infuriated his sponsors by flatly declining to dispense the expected patronage to Tammany. To Boss Murphy's vexation, moreover, he was soon so popular that he was virtually immune from attack.

New Yorkers loved Gaynor for the punishing hours he worked, for his unqualified support of the working man, and for the blunt advice he famously dispensed to all who asked for it. It was not uncommon for the mayor to occupy a quiet hour by summoning a stenographer and reeling off tart replies to his many correspondents. To a man who wrote to pass on lurid gossip: "Dear Sir, I care nothing for common rumor, and I guess you made up the rumor in this case yourself. Very truly yours, W. J. Gaynor, Mayor." To a woman who requested help in finding a husband: "I regret to say that I do not know anyone I can recommend to you. You can doubtless make a better selection than I can, as you know the kind of man you want. Of course, it may be very hard to find him, but no harder for you than for me." And to a man from Arkansas City who wrote in search of a wife: "How could I recommend any good girl here to you? You may not be so attractive as you think you are."

The mayor's other marked attribute was a ferocious temper. Thin-skinned and famously cantankerous, Gaynor became even more irritable after a botched assassination attempt in August 1910 left him with a bullet immovably lodged in his larynx, his voice reduced to a rasping whisper and his body racked by hour-long spasms of coughing.* From that date on, he vented his anger ever more volcanically on anyone in range. The mayor might, on a good day, be sweet-natured and reasonable. For the most part, though—as the *Sun* observed—he "fought without gloves, he liked to swat; he was more than a 'good hater,' he was a pitiless scorner of many; and he turned not the other cheek but the other fist to those who assailed him."

There was plenty for Gaynor to do. In the six years since Seth Low's fall, Tammany had packed New York's government with greedy partisans, many of them hopelessly unqualified for the jobs they held. The mayor swept these men aside, "booting the leeches and drones off the municipal payroll with the efficiency of a patented eviction machine," and replaced them with competent professionals selected for their ability. He reduced costs by firing hundreds of freeloading supernumeraries and pledged to "crush into the earth" officials caught pillaging the public purse.

---

*The moment of the shooting was captured for posterity by a photographer for the *Evening World*, who happened to be composing a portrait of the mayor when his would-be murderer (a former dockworker laid off as a result of Gaynor's cost cutting) pressed a revolver to his neck and fired. When the resultant print—destined to become one of the most celebrated news photographs of all time—was placed on the desk of the *World*'s editor, Charles Chapin ("a man who, according to his staff of reporters, had a legendary imperviousness to human suffering, especially theirs"), his response was exultant: "Blood all over him! And exclusive, too!"

Gaynor's greatest efforts, though, were directed to reforming the police. The mayor ordered an end to arbitrary arrests, pointing out that nearly one in four of those detained in New York (60,000 out of 262,000 in 1909) were released without charge within a day. Observing that the NYPD routinely broke up strikes and dispersed meetings organized by socialists and anarchists, he instructed officers to protect pickets and marchers, so long as the protesters obeyed the law. And when he discovered that a squad of patrolmen had smashed its way into a poolroom on Park Row, destroyed all its equipment and arrested sixteen people without the appropriate warrant, he not only set the prisoners free and denounced the cops' actions as "mob violence" but advised the gamblers concerned that they would have been justified in resisting arrest "to the last extremity." Throughout his term in office, Gaynor also made a habit of descending unexpectedly on New York's magistrates' courts, where he searched through piles of writs and affidavits in search of breaches of due process. These measures worked. By the end of 1910, the number of arrests had fallen by a third, police behavior had noticeably improved, a number of the force's most unrepentant clubbers and grafters had been summarily dismissed, and morale among the rank and file was soaring.

That left the problem of graft, which—for all Boss Murphy's stance on prostitution—remained a vital source of revenue for the political machines. Putting an end to decades of corruption was an intractable problem, the mayor candidly admitted, not least because so many dubious practices had become so thoroughly ingrained. Gaynor's solution was to weed out grafting politicians along with corrupt officials. "As soon as I became mayor," he recalled midway through his term,

> I began with one department after another to rid it of politics and graft, for they go hand in hand. . . . Graft had been deep-seated here for over 40 years in most of the departments [but] I think it will be admitted that I have driven [it] out of nearly all of them.

Gaynor's first target was the most visible manifestation of the graft: violation of the Sunday closing law. By 1910 several thousand taverns and bars were trading on the Sabbath. Many did so openly, lights blazing; the rest preferred to adopt at least a veneer of discretion, shuttering their front windows and admitting patrons through a welcoming rear door. The problem was so widespread that it "touched the whole police force, and had defied the efforts of other mayors to abolish or even control it." It was widely rumored that several million dollars of Liquor Dealers' Association (LDA) dues found their way directly into the pockets of New York's district bosses. Millions more were collected by ordinary patrolmen on the beat.

"The way it worked," one writer explained,

> was simple. A policeman, observing a saloon open and crowded on Sunday, would walk in and announce that his duty required him to arrest the bartender or owner, or both, for breaking the law. If the bartender slid a few dollars across the mahogany, the policeman would forget about his duty, accept a drink, and move along. But if the bartender balked, he was collared and marched to the station house to ruminate in a cell overnight. Then he would be put to the expense of engaging a lawyer and a bail bondsman (usually those recommended by the arresting officer) and suffer the ignominy and annoyance of a trial on trumped-up charges, and pay a fine. Meanwhile, his bar remained closed while his competitors were serving the customers he had lost.

It was not surprising, in such circumstances, that most bars chose to pay up.

Gaynor's solution to the saloon graft problem had the virtue of simplicity. First he called in the LDA and ordered its members to cease paying protection money. Then he issued instructions to the police, forbidding patrolmen, on pain of dismissal, from entering licensed premises or speaking to their owners. Uniformed officers, Gaynor instructed, were to observe while walking the beat what bars were opening illegally and were to report violations not to their captains but directly to the district attorney's office, where intelligence would be collated and indictments prepared. Plainclothes detectives were permitted to venture into premises that kept a rear door open but were forbidden to make on-the-spot arrests. There was, in short, to be no contact whatsoever between policemen and tavern keepers, nor any opportunity for precinct captains to blackmail the owners of the city's bars by threatening to close them down. In this way Gaynor hoped to cut off the graft at its source.

Remarkably, the plan worked. Fierce pressure was placed on inspectors and captains to enforce the mayor's new orders, and, to the surprise of most New Yorkers, violations fell to a mere handful within a fortnight or so. Stubborn owners were dealt with by the plainclothesmen, and by the beginning of 1911 saloon graft had been practically wiped out for the first time in living memory. One barman, who had spent thirty-five years working in New York's liquor trade, testified that he had never known a time "when the laws were so nearly enforced in their intent as they are today. Mayor Gaynor has done away with the collector who used to come around from 'the man higher up.'" The city's newspapers were effusive in their praise. "We do not remember who it was that cut the Gordian knot," wrote *Outlook* admiringly, "but his name might have been Gaynor."

Of course, the drying up of saloon graft did not mean an end to police corruption. The majority of crooked officers simply looked elsewhere for funds, chiefly to the age-old staple of raking in payments from gambling and prostitution. These trades, being already illegal, were more difficult for the mayor to legislate. But Gaynor was convinced that what had worked for the saloon business could be made to work elsewhere, too, and that spring he set about reordering the way in which the NYPD policed vice. The mayor's solution, once again, was to strictly limit the number of men tackling the problem, but this time he went further than he had before. "It was," he explained to one newspaper editor toward the end of his term, "an awfully difficult task. . . . We tried to cope with this by narrowing the contacts of the department with the sources of the graft. I could see no other way. [In the end] we narrowed such final contact down to a single point, namely, the Commissioner himself."

Gaynor's new strategy was truly radical. Responsibility for the suppression of vice had hitherto lain with New York's fifty or so precinct captains, each of whom had gathered information and ordered raids in his own district. In theory at least, the advantage of this system was that each captain possessed the local knowledge required to maintain strict control over gambling and prostitution in his precinct. In practice, as we have seen, the majority had always exploited information for their own ends, permitting favored houses to operate so long as they maintained appropriate discretion, raking in graft in the form of protection payments and deflecting or ignoring the complaints of angry citizens. Transferring responsibility for policing brothels and gaming clubs to police headquarters and forbidding precinct cops from mounting raids meant that captains could no longer offer ironclad protection and opened up the possibility of collating intelligence from all five of the city's boroughs. Gaynor hoped that this would make it easier to curb graft and deal with the most influential madams and gamblers, some of whom controlled premises all over the city.

The mayor's policy had its disadvantages, however. For one thing, only a tough and vigorous police commissioner could make it work. For another, it demanded the creation of special squads of ordinary patrolmen, based at headquarters and reporting directly to the commissioner himself. These men would conduct the raids that had hitherto been carried out at precinct level and—properly led and supplied with detailed information—might well succeed in closing down establishments that had hitherto enjoyed police protection. Placed under the command of any but the most incorruptible of men, however, the proposed headquarters squads could become a serious embarrassment. Whatever the deficiencies of the old system, crooked police captains had at least been forced to restrict their grafting to a single precinct. Gaynor intended the new squads to operate throughout New York. An ambitious man devoid of scruples could use that sort of opportunity to levy graft in quantities that even Clubber Williams had never dreamed of.

Plainly, then, the choice of commissioner was crucial, and Gaynor spent some time pondering the move. What was required, he concluded, was a man of undoubted integrity, a proven leader with some experience of organizing special squads. Only one likely candidate existed, and in the last week of May the mayor announced his decision. His choice was the man who five years earlier had drafted Charley Becker into the assembly of grudge-bearers that had brought down Max Schmittberger. The city's new police commissioner would be Rhinelander Waldo.

Waldo was an attractive candidate in many ways. He was independently wealthy, possessed impeccable manners, and belonged to the East Coast elite—his name was in the *Manhattan Register* and his mother, a habitué of the Waldorf-Astoria hotel was (as a reporter noted) "one of *the* Rhinelanders." All of this made it seem inconceivable that the new man would yield to the temptations of graft. Better yet, although he scarcely looked the part (in his mid-thirties, the new commissioner still possessed a featureless baby face and favored brilliantined hair), Waldo had a military background. He had graduated from West Point, served with the U.S. Army in the Philippines, and, in addition to his short spell as deputy police commissioner, had run the New York Fire Department for several years.* He also had a passion for police reform, having spent some months in London and become convinced that the reputedly incorruptible British police should become the model for the New York force. Finally (a point not lost upon the mayor), Waldo was less forceful and more biddable than his predecessor, a tough Brooklyn judge named James Cropsey, who

---

*A job that had, just two months earlier, put Waldo in charge of tackling the notorious Triangle Shirtwaist fire, a hideous conflagration that claimed the lives of 146 mostly young, mostly female garment workers trapped on the upper floors of a building off Washington Square in which the doors leading to the fire escapes had been locked in an attempt to prevent pilfering.

had angered Gaynor by standing up to him. If nothing else, the new commissioner's staid upbringing and impeccable manners would stop him from challenging the mayor in the press.

Waldo arrived at police headquarters on Centre Street late in May 1911. The new commissioner was apparently too busy putting Gaynor's plans into action and too naïve and too busy plotting reform to notice that his own office was filled with dubious officials loyal not to the forces of modernity, nor even to Mayor Gaynor, but to the sachems of Tammany Hall. His deputy commissioner, George Dougherty—who had charge of the Detective Bureau—was a former Pinkerton detective gone bad who had become an active grafter; his secretary, Winfield Sheehan, a onetime cub reporter with the *New York World*, was even more slyly influential. Sheehan had used the contacts he'd made during his years as a journalist to position himself as point man for several influential politicians who needed to wield influence over the police. Among his closest acquaintances was Big Tim Sullivan, who was (it would emerge years later) using Sheehan to administer the flow of graft collected from gambling houses in the city. Throughout Waldo's time at police headquarters, Sheehan covertly represented the police on the infamous "commission" Sullivan had established to regulate gaming in Manhattan, sitting alongside state senators from Brooklyn and Manhattan. He kept an agreed percentage of the graft himself, and even the generally cautious newspapers of the day were prone to note that he seemed mysteriously affluent for an official living on a salary of $75 a month. But if Waldo ever heard the rumors that swirled around his assistant, he made no attempt to investigate them. A man of independent means who lived in the finest style himself, he apparently saw nothing unusual in a secretary who maintained a fancy bachelor apartment and employed a Filipino manservant.

Deficient though his powers of observation may have been, Waldo was an energetic administrator. In his first few months in office, no fewer than four new units were created. First came a new Vice Squad, then the so-called Secret Squad, established in June 1911 to carry out undercover work among Manhattan's criminals. There were also two Strong Arm Squads, set up to suppress New York's gambling houses. Waldo took no chances in selecting their leaders. The first of the Strong Arm Squads was led by "Honest Dan" Costigan, the second by the equally incorruptible Lieutenant Riley.

Establishing special squads based at headquarters had been tried before, of course. New York's first-ever Strong Arm Squad had been set up as early as 1853 by Richard Walling, the outstanding figure in police history in the years that separated High Constable Hays from Clubber Williams. Its purpose had been the suppression of the street crime perpetrated by the boldest of Manhattan's gangs. In Commissioner McAdoo's time, the department had put together an Italian Squad to tackle an explosion in violence and extortion among Sicilian and Neapolitan immigrants and a Vice Squad, under Costigan, to break up poolrooms. But neither raiding nor the use of strong-arm men had ever worked for long. Raids invariably raised hackles—not only at Tammany Hall, which stood to lose financially from the suppression of vice, but also among all those concerned by the infringement of civil liberties. And the members of the various squads had, as McAdoo admitted, to be watched constantly and transferred frequently to keep down corruption.

Nonetheless, all went well for a short time, and Waldo, emboldened by his success, decided to create yet another unit, this time to crack down on the street-corner toughs who still ruled over some parts of the city. His decision was prompted by complaints from a Wall Street lawyer who had been appointed to administer several houses held in trust on East Ninety-seventh Street. Deciding to visit his new properties, the man was alarmed to discover that the surrounding district was controlled by the Car Barn Gang, a group of rowdies recruited from the East River docks. The Car Barners—who were led by a former Sunday-school student by the name of Freddie Muehfeldt—were heavily armed and so confident in their power that they brazenly posted placards around the borders of their domain ordering the police to keep out. Seeing these, the Wall Street man prudently declined to exercise his rights, turned back, and placed a call to Waldo, who sent half a dozen officers up to East Ninety-seventh Street to find out what was going on. The patrolmen were promptly set upon, beaten up, and stabbed—not fatally—an affront that no commissioner, least of all an ex–army broom like Waldo, could afford to ignore. Within days he had pulled together what became known as the Special Squad, a group of twenty "huskies" whose sole duty, the newspapers were informed, was "to travel about the city and hand out generous doses of strong-arm medicine to any and all who show unmistakable signs of being in need of it." To take charge of the new unit, Waldo needed a man with physical presence, a commanding personality, and the willingness to bend, if not to break, the rules. Casting his mind back half a decade to his days as a deputy commissioner, his choice fell on Charles Becker, who by now held the rank of lieutenant.* Early in the second week of July 1911, Becker was plucked from the Madison Street precinct and given command of the Special Squad.

Becker's first task was to break up the Car Barn Gang—an assignment he completed successfully, though not without running considerable risks. Smashing his way into the gang's headquarters at midnight with six men, Becker narrowly escaped serious injury when one of Muehfeldt's gangsters, up on the first floor, hurled a large iron pot full of boiling water at his head. Several Car Barners were arrested in the ensuing fracas and the remaining members rounded up a few nights later when the lieutenant cannily timed a second raid to coincide with one of the gang's marathon drinking sessions. After that the Special Squad moved on to tackle the Gophers, a murderous band headquartered in Hell's Kitchen, and then what one reporter referred to as "the Negro toughs of San Juan Hill," a black gang from north Harlem. Both groups were dispersed in a series of running fights in which Becker—disguised on one occasion as a longshoreman—played a leading part.

---

*Not as the result of promotion. The rank of sergeant had recently been abolished and all sergeants redesignated as lieutenants. In 1911 Becker was one of no fewer than six hundred men holding the new rank in the NYPD.

Even in 1911 the establishment of a squad of toughs whose job it was to beat up New York's hoodlums and hangers-around on street corners raised some eyebrows in the city, but Becker's conspicuous success stilled many of his critics. Whether or not the billy clubs and blackjacks wielded by the Special Squad were really likely to end the menace of the gangs (rounding up suspects as mere loiterers meant they received short sentences in the House of Correction rather than the long terms in a state prison that might have resulted from more orthodox detective work), New Yorkers did feel safer as a result of the lieutenant's efforts. Within a few weeks, Becker and his men were famous.

Celebration of the exploits of the Special Squad reached its zenith when, to reassure the public that the gangster scourge was being tackled, someone at police headquarters arranged for a journalist to interview Charley Becker and his strong-arm men. The resultant article, published in an August issue of the *New York Times*, introduced readers not only to Becker himself—"standing over six feet in his socks, tipping the scale over 200 pounds, broad-shouldered, with the eyes, jaw and fists of a fighter"—but also to a group of patrolmen so larger than life that they could scarcely have been further from the anonymous thugs imagined by their critics. Among the ranks of the Special Squad was one of the police department's few Jewish officers, Ajax Whitman—the "Strong Man of the Police Department," who was pictured in a skintight leotard and cross garters, posing with circus dumbbells. Whitman's brother Nathan was also one of Becker's men. He gloried in the title of the "Yiddish Irishman" and specialized, for no readily apparent reason, in disguising himself as an Irish laborer. Patrolman John D. O'Connor, who could no doubt have carried off that pose more convincingly than Nathan Whitman, had been bafflingly assigned instead to patrolling Manhattan's swimming spots in search of "undraped bathers"; he was photographed looking rather awkward, his brawny arms folded protectively over a Victorian-era swimming costume that hung down to his knees and his upper lip sporting a magnificently waxed mustache that could not have survived contact with sea water for long. The remaining members of the squad included the "Strong Arm Dude," M. B. Conlon; "Old Sleuth"

Faubel, who was not especially elderly and took his name from a dime-novel hero of the day; John J. Bones—who made a seedy-looking "corner tough"—and Joseph "Eat 'Em Up Alive" McLaughlin, whose attempts to disguise himself as a workingman had left him looking disconcertingly like Nathan Whitman's twin. The last member of the squad to be photographed by the *Times* was Patrolman George "Boots" Trojan, Becker's expert on gangs. Trojan was a noted bruiser described by his lieutenant as "being as good as four ordinary men to go into a muss with." The *Times*' reporter delicately forbore to mention exactly how this renowned fighter had earned his nickname.

It was not long before the exploits of the Special Squad earned Becker promotion of a sort. In October 1911, just as the cold weather came in and sent the street gangs scurrying for cover, Commissioner Waldo announced that the strong-armers would be redirected to crack down on gambling and graft. Becker's men would join those employed by Costigan and Riley in raiding roulette houses and poolrooms; henceforth, their main duty would be to shut down Manhattan's illegal gaming establishments. Becker was thus elevated from chief persecutor of the corner yahoo to a position of real power in the city. The assignment to police Manhattan gambling was his golden opportunity, and he took it.

Waldo had chosen his man carefully. Becker, he knew, was an officer who achieved results. But, more than that, he was a man of intelligence and ambition whose police career had thus far proved a disappointment. Charley Becker had never been the sort of cop happy simply pounding a beat, but despite his efforts over the years there had been no more famous cases, no swift promotion, and the lieutenant seems never to have been considered for the more prestigious and rewarding career of a detective. The flash-pan flare of fame that he had so briefly experienced during the Stephen Crane affair may have kindled an appetite within him—but, if so, the hunger raging inside nearly two decades later must have been awfully strong.

By 1911, then, Charley Becker was a man desperate for an opportunity, and the offer of that chance—Waldo no doubt calculated—should have been enough to earn his loyalty. Bringing men in from the precincts to run squads out of Centre Street had always been a tricky business, for not every officer could be relied on to act with the necessary diligence. Becker, on the other hand (as one disgruntled fellow officer spit), was a man who "would raid his own crippled grandmother if he thought it would make him look good at headquarters." His fierce ambition promised that he would be an asset to the commissioner and a threat to ordinary cops.

Waldo certainly had had no complaints about the way in which Lieutenant Becker set about his new assignment. For nine more months, his men were rarely out of the news. Between them the three "strong-arm squads" led by Becker, Costigan, and Riley launched more than two hundred raids and made 898 arrests. Most of the targets were selected by either Waldo or Mayor Gaynor, acting in response to tip-offs received from "members of the public" who were—it seems more than likely—in many cases rivals of the gamblers being informed on. All three Special Squads thus found themselves plunged into a dangerous maelstrom of opposing business interests, but Becker seems to have carried out his orders fearlessly no matter what his targets' political connections, at least twice in the face of ill-aimed fusillades of bullets. When Freeman's celebrated roulette palace on West Thirty-eighth Street was raided in February, it was the first time the club and its gentlemanly customers had been so inconvenienced in eighteen years. A few weeks later, the strong-armers burst into the Lincoln Hotel on Columbus Circle, rounded up a large number of the establishment's high-class call girls, and then proceeded to batter their way through the building, smashing down doors, until they found the place where the hotel's managers were hiding. This embarrassing disruption to the Lincoln's discreet and highly lucrative prostitution racket was a severe annoyance to the hotel's owner, Sam Paul, whose temper hardly improved when his stuss joints began to be raided, too. By the summer of 1912, the influential Paul was furious with Becker and the Strong Arm Squad and even angrier with Herman Rosenthal, whom he strongly suspected to be the mysterious informant who had been passing information concerning his establishments to the mayor.

Not all of the Special Squad's targets were politicians. Becker and his men also raided a number of dives run by crooks, including poolrooms controlled by Chick Tricker and Jack Sirocco, two of the best-known gangsters of the day. In most cases the strong-armers' methods were direct and uncompromising; having broken into a gambling house, they would produce hatchets and systematically wreck all the equipment in the place. Since the rooms were invariably classed as private clubs, the police had no right to detain their occupants indiscriminately. But they could and did carry warrants naming the people they expected to find gaming in the establishments they raided. Those who were actually discovered on the premises could be arrested.

It did not take long for New York's newspapers to pick up on the campaign, and over the winter many of the major dailies gave over hundreds of column inches to the Strong Arm Squads and their raids. Most of this coverage was devoted to Lieutenant Becker, who apparently enjoyed seeing his name in print. Early in 1912, Becker went so far as to hire his own "press agent," a fly-by-night newspaper tipster by the name of Charles Plitt, to keep reporters informed of his activities. Plitt wasted no time in filling the dailies with dramatic accounts of his client's raids, and before long even the august *New York Times* had taken to reporting the strong-armer's successes. A story published in the second week of February 1912 drew a lively portrait of one late-night action:

> Lieut. Charles Becker, head of the Special Duty Squad, met twelve of his men shortly before midnight Thursday night at Ninth Avenue and Thirty-fourth Street. They piled into waiting automobiles already partly filled with axes, sledge hammers, and other wrecking outfit. The three automobiles swung into West Thirty-seventh Street, and drew up in front of a house on the north side of the street, near Eighth Avenue.
>
> As Becker knocked at the door a little shutter opened and a Negro looked out and instantly closed the opening. As he scurried away, the axes began to fall on the door. Half the

squad started around to watch the rear exits. The police had to batter down a sheet-iron door to get into the hallway. There, another "ice-box" door confronted them. They battered this down and smashed their way into the dancing and assembly room of the "club."

There were nearly a hundred persons in the place.... Three men who had arrived early in the evening on an automobile slumming tour were very popular, for they had proved not only good spenders but excellent singers. They were members of Becker's force, and the only policemen in the place when the raiders broke in.

There was pandemonium when Becker pushed through the opening the axes had made. As the men filed in behind him, the crowd suddenly separated, and at the other end of the room a colored woman stepped from behind a partition and raising a revolver began to fire. The third shot had gone crashing into the woodwork of the door and everyone was cowering when the lights went out. Three times more the woman fired, and then Becker sprang forward with his revolver in his hand.

"Look out!" he shouted, and then other revolver shots came and the crowd in the darkness came to life and charged the narrow entrance. Becker fired above the heads of the attacking force and at the same time the policemen at the door began to fire. They drove the crowd back. The lieutenant quietly groped his way down the room until he came to Walter Herbert, Republican District Captain, who is charged with being the proprietor of the place.

"You turn on the lights," he said, and to emphasize his command he shoved his revolver against the man's stomach. Herbert did not argue. He backed against the wall and switched the lights on. More than twenty shots had been fired, but after that there was no trouble.

By now Becker's new celebrity had had a marked effect upon his social life. He came to the attention of Colonel Henry Sternberger, a

National Guard commander who made a habit of loaning out his car to police officers whom he particularly admired; soon the lieutenant was being chauffeured around town in a handsome tourer. He established friendships with several of Manhattan's best-known crime reporters, including Deacon Terry of Hearst's *American* and Fred Hawley of the pro-Tammany *Sun*. Perhaps Becker's most cherished new acquaintance, however, was Bat Masterson, sports editor of the raffish *Morning Telegraph*—a newspaper whose front-page cheesecake photographs of chorus girls and detailed coverage of racing made it the title of choice in New York's poolrooms and barbershops. Masterson was renowned throughout the country as a former Wild West lawman and gunfighter who had—so rumor had it—killed at least twenty-six men during his years on the frontier and whose encounters in western cow towns with the likes of Wyatt Earp and "Mysterious Dave" Mather had become the stuff of legend. Safely retired now to an apartment off Times Square, Masterson turned out a thrice-weekly column covering boxing, crime, and politics. He had the reputation of having scarcely missed an important fight in nearly thirty years, and his job and famous name gave him access to ringside seats. For Becker, an avid boxing fan, he made an invaluable friend.

Of course, even the relatively modest fame that the lieutenant thus attained was double-edged. Regular newspaper coverage of the strong-arm men and their exploits meant that the squad's routine brutality was also exposed. When one of Becker's men maimed an eighteen-year-old boy by smashing his arm with a pool cue, reporters noticed. More seriously, the lieutenant's assiduous courting of publicity made other policemen look bad. Costigan and Riley and their men received far less coverage than did Becker and his, and—perhaps egged on by the press—Becker's squad soon began to make more raids than their colleagues. By July 1912, nine months after Waldo's campaign got under way, they had been responsible for closing down no fewer than a hundred gambling houses: half, rather than the third that might have been expected, of the total raided across the city. Such successes reflected poorly on the other squads, whose lieutenants were vying with Becker for the rank of captain.

It was not long before Becker's displays of thrust and ambition began to make him enemies; by the summer of 1912, Sam Paul was far from the only influential gaming-house proprietor with cause to hate him. Each raid the lieutenant carried out cost gamblers money. Each item of equipment smashed had to be replaced. Each arrest meant that lawyers had to be hired and fines paid—and there was always the possibility of prison. Nor could Becker's men expect to be applauded by colleagues who saw their own efforts passed over in the rush to praise the Strong Arm Squads. "I can say that Becker knows that he is very unpopular in the Police Department," one lawyer commented. "He has been an ambitious man."

Had mere ambition been the worst of Becker's sins, of course, he would have had comparatively little to worry about. In truth, however, the lieutenant's appointment to police vice in Satan's Circus brought with it temptation of a sort that few policemen of his generation would have been able to resist. Twenty years earlier Becker's mentor, Clubber Williams, had made his fortune in the district. Bill Devery, ten years later, had done much the same. Charley Becker—a man who was no stranger to grafting, who needed money, and who was more than halfway through a career that otherwise promised relatively little—was far too steeped in the discreditable traditions of the department to spurn such a golden opportunity. Within weeks, perhaps even within days, of his appointment, he had begun to exploit his new position for every dollar it was worth. And by the summer of 1912, with an audacity that amounted to recklessness, he had built up an extortion racket of a size and reach unseen in Manhattan for a decade.

Lieutenant Becker was in a strong position to demand protection money from New York's gamblers. With a whole squad of strong-arm men at his back and a certain leeway to conduct raids as he saw fit, he could make life impossible for those who dared to cross him. Becker had no choice but to act on the orders he received from Gaynor and Waldo, of course, and that meant that the protection that he offered was never ironclad. But there were ways around that problem: reasons a planned raid might have to be postponed, perhaps even for months, and—when the time did come—tip-offs phoned anonymously to those who had paid their assessments, advising them to hide their best equipment and warn off valued customers.* In time-honored fashion, Becker would then arrange for some elderly roulette wheels and fading faro banks to be smashed to pieces to ensure that things looked good, and his strong-arm men would make at least a handful of arrests. Only the most acute observers—and there were not many of them, either at police headquarters or among the city's journalists— would notice that few of the clubs raided by Becker actually closed down for more than a few days. Nor was it generally realized that only a tiny percentage of the gamblers arrested by the strong-armers ever saw the inside of a prison cell. It was a simple matter for the lieutenant to arrange for crucial evidence to be lost or for his men to be afflicted with conveniently hazy memories when cases came to court. Thus while nine hundred or so men were certainly arrested between October 1911 and July 1912, the charges against more than eight hundred were dropped. Of the hundred who did appear in court, the great majority were issued with suspended sentences and fined between $2 and $50—sums so small as to be no deterrent to a seasoned gambler.

Becker's corruption was not generally known, though it soon became the subject of gossip among the police themselves. Newspapers may have heard talk of the doings of the Special Squad, but they could not publish without cast-iron evidence. Gaynor and Waldo remained ignorant even of the rumors for several months at least. But it is inconceivable that Becker could have operated on the scale he did without the tacit approval of at least some of his superiors. That meant, of course, that the money extorted from the city's gamblers was shared. Each of the men who approved of the actions of the Special Squad—they apparently included Sheehan, Waldo's corrupt secretary—would have received a portion of the cash, and every precedent suggests that a large part of the

---

*Some idea of the scale of such deceptions can be found in a report issued by Anthony Comstock's Society for the Suppression of Vice, whose agents on one occasion stood by while the police raided a supposed gambling den, finding only "a crap layout worth $10." One hour later Comstock's men burst unannounced into the same establishment and seized more than $2,500 worth of high-class gambling equipment.

proceeds eventually found its way to New York's politicians. In addition, Becker must have had to pay off most if not all of the members of his squad, and a further share, amounting to perhaps 10 percent of the total collected, would have been retained, as commission, by the agents he employed to make "collections" from the gaming houses on his behalf.

It is all but impossible, in these circumstances, to calculate the full extent of the lieutenant's grafting, but his corruption was evidently staggering. Contributions were levied from at least one hundred Satan's Circus clubs, and the total collected across the city as a whole was said at the time to have amounted to $1.8 million in just nine months: the equivalent of $2.4 million a year, a figure not far short of the $3 million that the *New York Times* calculated had been raised across all five boroughs twelve years earlier. Each monthly "assessment" totaled anywhere from $50 to $500, depending on the size and profitability of a house. On one occasion Honest John Kelly,* one of the best-known gamblers in the city, parted with $2,500 to purchase protection for his string of clubs. Nor did Becker rely on extortion alone for his considerable income. Gamblers who did not meet his demands were raided and forced to watch as the cash discovered in their establishments was gathered, counted, and "confiscated," never to be seen again. According to one well-connected club owner, he was robbed of $8,000 in this manner.

Whether the payments extorted by the policeman and his associates really totaled $2 million—and it seems unlikely that they did—the amounts that Becker personally banked between October 1911 and July 1912 certainly averaged at least $10,000 a month, the equivalent of more than $155,000 a month today. No fewer than fifteen private bank

---

*Kelly's nickname—not entirely deserved—dated to his early days in New England, where in 1888 he had umpired a crucial baseball game between Boston and Providence and famously refused a $10,000 bribe. In the 1890s, he became a boxing referee and was the first to exercise the prerogative of calling off all bets if he suspected that a bout had been fixed. Kelly ran foul of Big Tim Sullivan in 1898 when he did suspend betting on a fight between "Gentleman Jim" Corbett and Tom Sharkey in which Corbett's second entered the ring, resulting in the heavyweight's disqualification. Sullivan—who had wagered $13,000 on a Sharkey victory—angrily ordered Kelly's gambling house to be raided by the police the next day.

accounts controlled by the lieutenant were eventually traced—some in his own name, others opened jointly with his wife, and a few that had been concealed under a false name. The cash paid into just nine of them totaled nearly $60,000. Some $29,615 had been squirreled away in the Corn Exchange Bank of Washington Heights between November 1911 and August 1912, and another $21,000 was deposited in other branches of the same bank between April and July. A further $3,500 was paid into the Empire Savings Bank in April and $3,000 placed in the vaults of West Side Savings in May. Other accounts and safe-deposit boxes hid amounts ranging from a few hundred dollars to $2,000. Nor did all the money Becker made find its way to a bank. In the spring of 1912, he and Helen paid $9,000, in cash, for a handsome mock-Tudor house in Williamsburg, a comfortably middle-class district of Brooklyn. They continued to live in their old apartment, but Becker began visiting his new property regularly to fix it up.

Superficially, the lieutenant's position seemed secure. There was, after all, little that Becker's victims could hope to do to halt the constant drain upon their profits; their businesses were illegal, and to make any formal complaint would be tantamount to confessing to a crime. Nor would the mayor, Commissioner Waldo, or even the newspapers be likely to believe the word of a professed criminal over that of a policeman. The least hint of dissent simply invited retribution at the hands of the Special Squad. By the end of 1911, Becker felt confident enough to abandon the inconvenient practice of collecting payments in bulky packages of cash. A handful of trusted gamblers, astonishingly, began to pay their dues with personal checks.

It was not long, nonetheless, before the first threats to Becker's security emerged. As early as Thanksgiving 1911, a journalist friend working for the Hearst newspapers warned that several of his victims were plotting to expose him. The suggestion worried Becker sufficiently for him to call on Waldo and request a transfer back to ordinary duties, but the commissioner was so pleased with the Special Squad's work that he dismissed the idea out of hand. A few months later, in March 1912, Waldo himself began to receive pseudonymous letters revealing the location of several gaming houses. After a while one of the writers—the same "Henry Williams" who had offered tips concerning Herman Rosenthal—began denouncing the strong-armers, too. In a letter dated March 27, "Williams" told the commissioner, "I would like to have you investigate quietly Lieutenant Becker. He is now collecting more money than Devery, and it is well known to everyone at police headquarters. Please do this and you will be surprised at the result."

Further denunciations followed, until Waldo felt compelled to act on them. Fortunately for Becker, he chose to do so by passing the complaints to Winfield Sheehan for investigation. Sheehan, unsurprisingly, merely forwarded them on to Becker, and he in turn boldly sent them back to the commissioner, accompanied by a polite note suggesting that he was probably not the best person to investigate himself. Whatever Waldo did with the complaints thereafter, no proper inquiry was ever established, and when further anonymous denunciations arrived at the commissioner's office, they were sent on to the officers concerned as well. Nothing was done.

Even so, Becker sensed disaster looming. He had been greedy, extorting a very large amount of money in only a short time, and probably he felt that the system he had created had started to run out of control. Once he and his associates began to levy contributions from a club, they could hardly stop, and too much was being demanded from too many influential people for the process to continue indefinitely. Worse, nothing was being done to mollify those whose businesses were being drained of cash. Becker was simply too junior to run so large a racket properly, for while he had the power to make good on his threats, he could not always keep his promises. The old masters of police protection—men such as Bill Devery—had been at least as avaricious and corrupt. But Devery had also been chief of police, and when he swore that a club would not be raided, he meant what he said. Charley Becker, on the other hand, was "just a little lieutenant" (as Gaynor once described him) and had to raid where he was told. That made the protection that he offered much less valuable. By the summer of 1912, it was only a matter of time before he upset one too many people and found himself in trouble.

Becker knew it, too. Shortly after the first letters from "Henry Williams" began arriving at headquarters, he called in to see Waldo. Once again he urgently requested a transfer, and for a second time Waldo turned him down. The commander of the Special Squad protested, but he had no choice. So Lieutenant Becker went back to work, grafting and raiding, raiding and grafting, dancing a tarantella of his own devising that by now could have only one end.

The appearance of three vigorous police strong-arm squads on the streets of New York was the worst possible news for Herman Rosenthal.

The gambler's fortunes had not improved in the long months since Gaynor came to power. His falling-out with Beansey Rosenfeld had been a violent one, and when the pair's stuss house in "Little Russia" was closed down, Herman had arranged for Rosenfeld to be beaten up by Tough Tony, the same thug he had earlier employed to "take care" of Bridgey Webber. Then, when Rosenthal attempted to reopen their old premises, Beansey's friends retaliated by sending a hoodlum of their own to bomb the club. The explosion blew off most of the front of the house, bringing Herman's attempts to operate on the Upper West Side to a sudden end. Shortly thereafter Rosenthal retreated to Second Avenue, where, with the closure of the Hesper Club, he found himself reduced to running a pair of low-grade stuss houses and his old—and still-illegal—off-track-bookmaking service. None of these three businesses made much money, and even when the income from all three was combined, it scarcely guaranteed a living.

It was not long before Rosenthal's financial worries sent him scurrying back to Big Tim Sullivan. Sullivan was struggling with problems of his own: His political power continued to decline, and there were rumors that Charles Murphy and his allies at Tammany Hall were attempting to squeeze the overmighty district boss out of the lucrative midtown graft. But Tim was still a rich man and remained unfailingly generous to his friends. Rosenthal emerged from their meeting with another loan, this one, he boasted to his friends, for the sum of $5,000. Better yet, the gambler received Sullivan's permission to try his luck in Satan's Circus.

Herman appeared in midtown Manhattan in the autumn of 1911. He was almost the first of the Lower East Siders to be permitted to do business within the borders of Satan's Circus, which had hitherto been the preserve of much-better-connected gamblers. The only other East Side figure with a presence in the district was none other than Bridgey Webber, whose connections with Sullivan's rivals at Tammany Hall had won him a concession to set up a poker parlor on West Forty-second Street and a faro house three blocks to the north. There was, in short, plenty of room in Satan's Circus for a downmarket gambler from a working-class part of town. Rosenthal, however—provocatively and more than a little rashly—chose to rent premises practically opposite Webber's faro club, purchasing the lease on a four-floor brownstone at 104 West Forty-fifth Street.

Big Tim's blessing, and his generous loan, had offered Herman one more chance to make something of himself. The signs are that he recognized that this might be his final opportunity; certainly he was determined not to fail. The new premises were done up in considerable style, three floors (and nearly all of Sullivan's $5,000) being given over to sumptuously furnished rooms offering faro and roulette. In order to save on his customary hotel bills, Rosenthal reserved the fourth floor for himself. He turned it into an apartment and installed his second wife, Lillian—a massively built woman who resembled an operatic soprano without the voice and indulged a gaudy taste in embroidered gowns, big hats, and fancy hairstyles. ("She was fat," young Viña Delmar mercilessly observed, "and she wore a purple satin dress and a pearl necklace at three o'clock in the afternoon.") Between them the couple got the establishment ready by midautumn. Herman put the word out among the gambling community, and on November 17, 1911, he opened for business.

Unfortunately for Rosenthal, his expenditure and effort were in vain. The new club was not a success; indeed, it was a catastrophic failure. The reason for this was simple: The gambler's extensive preparations had not included payoffs to the police—he hoped, presumably, for Sullivan's protection—and only two days after the roulette wheels had begun to spin, he was summoned to an urgent meeting by Inspector Cornelius

Hayes, the officer in overall command of the district. The fact that Hayes was able to make such an approach with impunity suggests that Mayor Gaynor's policy of reducing contact between the police and the vice trade was not working all that smoothly; in any event, he and the gambler sat down in the back room of a local restaurant, where, according to Herman, Hayes demanded payments totaling $1,000 a week and threatened to close him down forthwith if the cash were not received. Rosenthal, who had no money left, refused, with inevitable consequences. On November 19, a squad of Hayes's men descended on West Forty-fifth Street, broke down Herman's door, and smashed all his equipment. The damage was so extensive that the gambler had no choice but to remain closed. He had been in business just four days.

Rosenthal must have sensed that this was practically the end. He was nearly penniless. He had run afoul of the Satan's Circus police. He had exhausted the patience of half the influential gamblers in the city—among them Beansey Rosenfeld, Sam Paul, and Bridgey Webber—angering his enemies enough that one or another was sure to take a certain pleasure in keeping the police informed of his activities. Worse, he owed a fortune to Tim Sullivan and now had no means of repaying it. Herman's one chance of clearing his debts, paying off the police, and restoring his own battered finances was to reopen his club and run it free of hindrance for quite a while. To do that required police protection, and if Hayes and the men of the vice precincts would not provide it, there was only one man who could. Rosenthal had no choice but to turn to Charley Becker.

It is impossible to state with any certainty how Becker and Herman met. Rosenthal must have heard of the activities of the Strong Arm Squads, and very likely he was perfectly aware—either from fellow gamblers or as a result of arrangements made to keep his Second Avenue stuss houses in business—that the lieutenant sold protection. But in a pair of affidavits made in July 1912, Herman gave conflicting accounts of their first encounter, stating on one occasion that he and Becker met in the course of a police raid on Second Avenue in the autumn of 1911 and on another that their initial meeting took place at an Elks' Club ball held some weeks later. The truth, insofar as it can now be ascertained, is probably that Rosenthal did note Becker at work during the raid but did not talk to him—"I had had my experience with the cops," he once remarked of this encounter, "and had no desire to widen my circle of acquaintance among them." The first time that the two men actually spoke seems to have been at the Elks' Club formal held on West Forty-third Street late in November. By then, of course, Inspector Hayes had altered Herman's views concerning the desirability of making friends with the police. The gambler was now keen to make Becker's acquaintance.

"We had," Rosenthal would say of this initial meeting, "a very good evening, drank very freely, and became very good friends." A good deal of conversation passed between the two, and some of it no doubt concerned the protection Becker and his men could offer in Satan's Circus. The two men (again in the gambler's account) arranged a second rendezvous to take the matter further. They met, "by appointment," at the Elks' Club New Year's ball.

"We had a fine evening together," Herman's version of events continued,

and had a lot of champagne to drink. Becker and I had been talking together through the night and he seemed very anxious to win my friendship. . . . Later in the morning we were all pretty well under the weather. He put his arms around me and kissed me. He said, "Anything in the world for you, Herman. I'll get up at three o'clock in the morning to do you a favor. You can have anything I've got." Then he called over three of his men . . . and he introduced me to the three of them, saying, "This is my best pal and do anything he wants you to do." We went along and we met pretty often, and many nights we would take an automobile ride, and he told me then that he wished he could put in six months of this [grafting and] he would be a rich man. He was getting hold of a lot of money. I told him then, "Don't you think you are taking a chance by me being seen with you so often?" And he told me I don't have to fear. "But when that 'guy' down at headquarters (meaning Waldo) puts it up to

me about meeting you, I'll simply tell him that I am meeting
you for a purpose—to get information from you."

Whatever the veracity of Rosenthal's affidavit, there is no reason
to doubt that he and Becker did talk business. The problem, from
Herman's point of view, was that he had little to offer. His premises on
West Forty-fifth Street were still closed, and likely to remain so until
he found a further source of cash. That made it pointless to agree to a
simple payment of protection money. Becker, in any case, was by now
getting more ambitious, and after several further meetings—Rosenthal
would claim that the pair met up occasionally throughout January and
February 1912—the two men reached a more interesting arrangement. Becker, it was agreed, would inject sufficient capital into the
club to allow it to reopen and provide it with protection when it did.
In exchange, Herman would hand over no less than one-fifth of his
earnings to the grafting lieutenant.

This agreement may well have been unprecedented; at least no
similar example is known of a serving police officer becoming a sleeping partner in a gaming house. The only reasonable explanation for
Becker's willingness to take such an enormous risk is that he knew his
days with the Special Squad were numbered and he hoped, by insisting on such rigorous terms, to make large additions to his bank balance quite quickly. The details of the agreement reached between the
two are also interesting. Becker, who appears—with reason—to have
doubted that Rosenthal would keep his side of the agreement, insisted
on installing a trusted man to manage the club and ensure that the
stipulated 20 percent was paid. Herman, meanwhile, was forced to
secure the agreed-upon $1,500 loan by taking out a chattel mortgage
on his household goods, made payable to Becker. Evidence that the
lieutenant had gone into business with the gambler would eventually
emerge with the discovery of this document, made out in the dummy
name of "John J. Donohue."

Rosenthal received his money in the spring and—with, apparently, a further sum wrested from Big Tim—reopened the West
Forty-fifth Street club on March 20. For a while Becker was true to

his word; the premises went unmolested, and Herman heard nothing more from Inspector Hayes and the Satan's Circus police. But Bridgey Webber found out soon enough that his enemy was back in business, and he wasted little time in causing further trouble. Within a few days of the reopening, anonymous letters reporting the existence of the club began appearing in Mayor Gaynor's office. They were signed by the same "Henry Williams" who had been so busy causing trouble for both Becker and Rosenthal the previous year.

The eagerness of Herman's fellow gamblers to inform on him exposed Becker's weak position once and for all. A few days after the first letter was received, Rosenthal would recall, "Lieutenant Becker met me by appointment and told me what a hard job he had got in stalling Waldo. That Waldo wanted to 'get' me." The policeman did what he could to hold off the commissioner, pleading for time to "gather evidence." But by the middle of April, the pressure to act was becoming too great to resist. Becker's solution—common enough in the not-too-distant past, and probably one he had used more than once since taking command of the Special Squad—was to stage a high-profile raid designed to satisfy his superior.

Most gamblers, being realists, accepted this sort of action as inevitable and were happy to take the long-term view that it was better to accept some damage and some lost business than it was to anger their protectors. Rosenthal did not. Short of money yet again—the tremendous drain on profits imposed by Becker himself can hardly have helped—he simply could not contemplate even the temporary closure of his club, much less the cost of replacing yet more smashed equipment. Becker did his best to make his partner see sense. "He told me," Rosenthal recalled, "that I must give him a raid. He said, 'You can fix it up any way you like. Get an old roulette wheel and I'll make a bluff and smash the windows. That will satisfy Waldo, I suppose.' I told him then that I would not stand for it. That if he wanted to raid me he would have to get the evidence. That I would not stand for a 'frame up.'"

Rosenthal's intransigence was a severe embarrassment for Becker, whose commitment to the pair's business relationship certainly did not extend to putting his police career at risk. But a direct order from Waldo could scarcely be ignored. Pausing only to promise Rosenthal that he would stall the commissioner a little longer, Becker wasted no time in setting up a raid. Possibly he felt that he could smooth things over with his partner later; possibly he did not care. There seemed, after all, to be little Herman could do to hurt him. Who would take the word of a confessed criminal over that of the most admired police lieutenant in New York?

The Special Squad raid on 104 West Forty-fifth Street took place shortly after 10:30 P.M. on April 17, 1912. Rosenthal was not on the premises at the time, for reasons that evidently still outraged him when he came to set down his version of events some three months later:

> [Becker] called me on the wire at my home and he told me to go and see a certain party at half past ten in the evening at 59th Street and Broadway at a place called Pabst's. When I reached Pabst's there was nobody there to meet me. Then I suspected something was wrong, so when I came back to my home, I found the windows broken, the door smashed in, and the patrol wagon waiting outside. I wanted to go in, [but] policeman James White told me to go away, not to come. "It's all right," [White said.] "Everything is all right. It's Charley making the raid, and it's all right."

The anguished Rosenthal retreated to a spot across the street and waited for the police to leave. Then he ascended the steps into the club, past the wrecked gaming rooms and up to his own apartment, where his wife repeated White's message, adding, "Charley said he had to make the raid to save himself." According to Lillian Rosenthal, Becker had done what he could to calm her, promising that he would reimburse the couple for the cost of all the damage done: "Tell Herman to get down to the St. Paul building tomorrow and get the papers [for the chattel mortgage] from the lawyer. You tell him I am standing the expenses of this raid. You tell Herman he and I are even, and I'll see him tomorrow."

Under the circumstances Becker's offer must have been more than Rosenthal had hoped for; few other New York gamblers, after all, had ever received reimbursement for what was generally seen as one of the risks, and one of the costs, of running an illegal business. But the lieutenant's deception, and his willingness to break what Herman saw as a promise to keep stalling on the raid, left scars. To make matters worse, one of the two men arrested in the course of the raid had been Rosenthal's teenage nephew, a boy with no police record whose prospects might be severely blighted by a conviction for gambling.

Becker and Herman met again in court the next morning. The encounter was a frosty one. "Charley," Rosenthal said, "wanted me to waive examination [and said] that he wanted to make the raid look natural and that he would turn it out in the Grand Jury room"—a trick perfected by the likes of Clubber Williams that was standard practice for the grafters of the period. "I said, 'Can I trust you?' He said, 'Why, it's all right. You can.' So I had the case adjourned until the next day to think the matter over [and then] waived examination."

Herman's decision no doubt came as a relief to Becker, who must have feared the consequences of his partner's answering questions under oath. But it did Rosenthal himself no good, and Becker's willingness to forget about repayment of his loan made no difference in the short term to his serious predicament. The gambler's anger grew considerably over the succeeding week as his club stayed closed, his chief source of income remained frozen, and, worst of all, Becker reneged on his promise to take care of the grand jury. When an indictment was handed down against Rosenthal's nephew, Herman insisted on another meeting. Becker instructed him to hire a cab, drive to a prearranged location, and pull over to let him in. "We rode downtown very slowly," the gambler recalled, "talking over different things, and we finally had an argument. When we left, we were on very bad terms."

CHAPTER 6

LEFTY, WHITEY, DAGO, GYP

THAT NIGHT, AND EVERY night thereafter, the gambling house on West Forty-fifth stood empty. Shorn of funds, short of friends, and stripped of police protection, Rosenthal could not simply refit and reopen, as he had hitherto contrived to do. His club was still shuttered and locked in June 1912, when Viña Delmar and her father rode over from Brooklyn on the first really hot weekend of the New York summer.

It was a Sunday, the girl recalled, and West Forty-fifth seemed preternaturally deserted. The Saturday-night gamblers and roisterers who had woken the street as they stumbled out of their saloons and clubs at three or four or five in the morning now lay slumped on lumpy mattresses in dirty rooms, asleep; the churchgoers were still at church; and the remaining inhabitants of the West Forties were seeking refuge from the sun indoors. Even so, the girl observed, the neighborhood retained a whiff of menace, not least in the vicinity of Rosenthal's ruined premises, which still awaited repair:

> The street was very seedy. Most of the other brownstones had signs offering furnished rooms. No one sat on the steps or even used them. Not a single person came in or out of the houses. The window shades were drawn to the sills on that hot and silent Sunday. There were business establishments between some of the houses and in the basements of a few.

A chop suey restaurant, a dressmaker, a milliner, a hand laundry. [But although] Herman's house looked nicer than most of the buildings on the block . . . something had happened to his front door. There were deep, jagged marks cut into it, as though at some time he had forgotten his key and in a fury had attacked the door with a sharp and heavy instrument.

Rosenthal himself came down from his apartment to meet his visitors. The gambler was as finely dressed as ever, but apparently depressed. He "became serious almost immediately," Delmar recorded, and "his face took on a dark sadness." Her father had little doubt why this was so. His old friend was becoming desperate and had almost nowhere left to turn.

Herman's position had actually worsened since his falling-out with Becker two months earlier. Big Tim Sullivan, it transpired, had made one last attempt to succor his old protégé, offering, through intermediaries, to pay Rhinelander Waldo a substantial bribe to leave Rosenthal alone. But the commissioner had spurned the offer and, outraged, ordered the police to clamp down still more tightly on the gambler's activities. On Waldo's orders, Inspector Hayes had stationed a policeman permanently in the club itself, and relays of officers now loitered in the building around the clock, making it impossible for Rosenthal to do more business there. In the course of the next few weeks, Herman would make several increasingly desperate attempts to dislodge these unwelcome squatters—on one occasion locking the day-shift man in and relenting only when reinforcements armed with axes and hydraulic jacks appeared and on another, when the temperature was hovering in the nineties, announcing that he would light the coal furnace in the cellar and roast the waiting cop onto the street.* When Viña Delmar

---

*As the law stood in 1912, Rosenthal could have barred the waiting patrolman from reentering his premises if he vacated the building for even a minute. Once the guard on the club was lifted, the police could have reentered only by securing another warrant, which would have required fresh evidence of impropriety.

and her father called, however, the gambler and the police guard maintained a semblance of civility. "It was," the girl would write,

> a terribly hot day, and the policeman frequently patted his forehead with a large handkerchief and fanned himself with a copy of *Variety*, which, in those days, had a green cover.
>
> "Jerry, why don't you tell Lillian to get you a cold beer?" Herman asked.
>
> The policeman laughed. "I don't like strychnine in my drinks," he said.

It is hard to know what went on in Rosenthal's mind during these difficult few weeks. Much of his attention must have been given over to conjuring various schemes to get his club reopened. But it does not seem too much to suggest that as each avenue closed and his despair mounted, Herman became increasingly determined to seek retribution. His own world might lie in ruins. But he could at least take satisfaction from seeing his tormentors damned as well.

Rosenthal had long been notorious in the closed world of New York gambling for his readiness to seek revenge. His methods, too, were often criticized. On occasion, as we have seen, he felt no compunction in physically harming rivals, but the sort of beatings meted out to Beansey Rosenfeld and Bridgey Webber were not uncommon in the underworld. It was a far worse sin, in the eyes of most Manhattan crooks, to "squeal"—to make a private grievance public and involve the press or the police in what should have remained criminal affairs. Yet Herman, perhaps buoyed by his friendship with Tim Sullivan, believed himself above such concerns. For nearly three years, ever since his gambling empire first began to crumble, he had lodged repeated protests regarding his treatment at the hands of the DA and the police. As early as February 1909, Rosenthal complained that patrolmen from the local precinct were attempting to gain entry to his premises. Later that same year, he lodged an affidavit with Police Commissioner Baker, alleging that two policemen from the local precinct were pursuing a vendetta against him. In 1910 he had been a member of a deputation of gamblers who sought a meeting with Mayor Gaynor to "protest against their spoliation by policemen," and in 1911 he had railed long and loud against the closure of the Hesper Club. Now, in the summer of 1912, he began striking back against his assembled enemies by putting a reporter from the *New York Sun* on the track of the Sans Souci, Sam Paul's high-class stuss house—a deliberate piece of malice that resulted in an outraged article and prompted Waldo to have the place shut down.

The surprising thing—at least to Herman's rivals—was that he got away with this sort of behavior. For years the gambler's clout with the Sullivan clan had been such that those who crossed him frequently regretted it; the two patrolmen who the gambler had alleged were harassing him soon found themselves patrolling Staten Island. But Rosenthal did not have quite so much influence as he liked to pretend. He certainly overstated the extent of his involvement when, in 1911, he boasted of having Deputy Commissioner Driscoll dismissed from his post for ordering the closure of the Hesper Club. And—as Big Tim's power declined—even the modest level of influence that Herman had enjoyed evaporated. By the summer of 1912, his pull was nonexistent.

The gambler did his best to cause some trouble nonetheless. Sullivan had left town on an extended European vacation, a holiday arranged by relatives to keep him away from supplicants such as Rosenthal. But Herman went to Waldo and Gaynor anyway, hoping to finagle an audience in which to state his case. When both the commissioner and the mayor refused to see him, he went on to call at the district attorney's office and on the president of New York's Board of Magistrates, with similar results. No city official seemed anxious to listen to the allegations of a self-confessed criminal, a man whose record of making impossible-to-prove charges against police and politicians had earned him a deserved reputation for difficulty.

The refusal of New York's politicians to listen to Rosenthal and his tales of woe left the gambler in a difficult position. He had pinned his hopes of justice, as he saw it, on having Inspector Hayes and the local precinct captain, Day, disciplined—reprimands that would surely have lead to the withdrawal of the police from his house. Only Waldo had the power to order this, and since the commissioner would not see him, there was only one way left to pile up pressure on the man. Herman would have to place his story in the city's newspapers and put trust in the power of the press.

Rosenthal had never had a lot to do with journalists. Like most denizens of New York's underworld, he understood instinctively that newsmen were his natural enemies. Every reporter knew that wrongdoing and graft sold papers, and—barring perhaps those who worked for papers supportive of Tammany—they could be relied on to combine detailed, salacious crime reporting with the sort of prim, moral editorials that frightened politicians and led to wearisome assaults on vice. The Lexow Committee, to take only one example, might never have sat had the press not been in an uproar at Dr. Parkhurst's exploits, and the scandals of the Ice Trust and the *New York Times*' turn-of-the-century gambling exposés remained fresh in the memories of those who had lived through them. Squealing to the press was thus a worse sin even than complaining to the cops, since it was still more likely to lead to trouble for all concerned.

No fewer than fourteen dailies covered the city of New York, many of them appearing in both morning and evening editions, and between them they boasted an enormous circulation. The two biggest papers—Pulitzer's *World* and Hearst's *American*—had single-cent cover prices and sales totaling over a million. In the absence of newsreels, radio, and television, moreover, the vast majority of New Yorkers relied exclusively upon the press for news and opinion, which meant the larger titles had considerable clout that ran well beyond the confines of New York itself. Covering, as they did, the greatest metropolis in the country, the news reports and features printed by Manhattan's dailies were frequently picked up and published in other newspapers as far away as Europe.

Each paper had its idiosyncrasies, of course. The *Sun* was resolutely pro-Tammany, the *Tribune* just as solidly Republican. The *Times*, which sold many fewer copies and possessed less influence than it does today, was one of the few to give much space to foreign news.

Most titles, however, and certainly those with mass circulations, relied heavily on sensation to sell copies. Gifted owners and editors had spent the better part of a century honing a formula that worked: New York had been the birthplace of modern crime reporting and, half a century later, it was the crucible of Sunday journalism, too, with its comic strips and women's pages and its relentless parade of pseudoscientific feature articles: "The Suicide of a Horse," "Cutting a Hole in a Man's Chest to Look at His Intestines and Leaving a Flap That Works as if on a Hinge," "Experimenting with an Electric Needle and an Ape's Brain." The bustling dailies, meanwhile, survived by supplying their readers with a steady diet of sports reporting, crime, and bad behavior: the baseball scores, exotic murders, and "scandals involving men of wealth in tuxedos and chorus girls in their underwear."

In principle, then, any number of New York papers might have been interested in Herman Rosenthal's tale of vice, and the gambler was optimistic he could find a taker for his story. Having—unlike Charley Becker—no contacts with the press himself, he began by asking a friend by the name of Jack Sullivan, who worked in newspaper distribution, to make a few approaches for him.* Sullivan did his best, canvassing first the titles that he represented and then the city's other papers, throughout the latter half of June. But even he could raise no interest in Herman's allegations. Newspapermen, it transpired, were wary of printing stories based solely on the statements of a gambler. Such tales were difficult to verify and all too easily denied; under the

---

*Sullivan, a former bodyguard of Hearst's, had grown up on the East Side and been best man at Herman's second wedding. Like several of Rosenthal's friends, he was Jewish but had changed his name in order to escape the anti-Semitic prejudice of the day and stay in with the Irish-run Tammany Hall—his real name was Jacob Reich. He now ran a depot where parcels of the *World*, the *American*, and the *Globe and Mail* were broken down and bundled up for sale by thousands of adolescent vendors and liked to be known as "The King of the Newsboys." This work would not normally have given him access to any journalists, but Sullivan, like Rosenthal, was a loudmouth and a busybody. He made it his business to be in and out of newsrooms all the time and boasted incessantly to anyone who would listen about his contacts in the press.

criminal code in force at the time, moreover, they were more or less useless as evidence, since the testimony of criminals could not be admitted without full corroboration.

It wasn't until Rosenthal took up the baton from his friend and began to call in person on the news desks that anyone took him and his story seriously. Probably, though this is not certain, the gambler brought with him some sort of dossier of evidence, or perhaps a statement sworn before a notary, in order to pique interest. Whatever Herman's tactics, though, the effort proved worthwhile, for early in July he at last made contact with a man willing to listen to his tale.

Rosenthal no doubt thought that he was in luck. The journalist who sat down to go through the evidence was a young, tall, red-haired man named Herbert Bayard Swope, an extroverted and utterly self-confident reporter just making his name as one of the ablest newsmen of the day. And the paper that Swope wrote for was the biggest and boldest in all Manhattan, a title better able than any other to trumpet stories of corruption and brutality. If Herman could just persuade Swope to run his allegations, he could wreak considerable revenge on Becker, the police, and New York's gamblers. Swope, after all, had plenty to offer. All the help—ran the reporter's little joke—in the *World*.

Joseph Pulitzer's *New York World* was the leading paper of its day. Brash, bright, and physically smaller than many rival titles, it was a firm favorite among big-city commuters, who found it easy to read in crowded carriages. The *World* was also the first daily to run headlines across more than a single column and the first to illustrate its stories with photographs as a matter of routine. It was in these respects the progenitor of all modern newspapers.

Pulitzer's real genius, though, was to produce a paper everyone could read. When he acquired the title in 1883, he threw out the piousness and windy prose that had characterized news reporting until then and adopted instead a much breezier style, "putting the who-what-when-where-and-why into an easily graspable lead paragraph," and insisting on "simple nouns, vivid verbs, and short sentences." "I want to talk to a nation, not to a select committee," the *World*'s new owner told the owner of the *Evening Post* when that worthy criticized the changes; to his own staff, called to a meeting to discuss plans for the paper, he explained, "Gentlemen, you realize that a change has taken place in the *World*. Heretofore you have all been living in the parlor and taking baths every day. Now I wish you to understand that, in future, you are all walking down the Bowery."

These tactics were born of necessity. The *World* was deeply in debt and sold a mere 15,000 copies a day. Having paid $346,000 for the title—well over the odds—Pulitzer knew that circulation would have to soar if he was ever to recover his investment. Thankfully, it did. Boosted by a mass of lurid crime reporting and by popular campaigns (it was the *World* that raised the funds required to erect the Statue of Liberty), sales reached 150,000 within two years and continued to grow. By the turn of the century, the paper was being published out of a new fifteen-story office, topped off with a gilded dome, which stood only a block from City Hall and afforded the editors fine views down into the newsroom of their lackluster competitors.

The great publisher himself spent less and less time running the paper after 1887, when—burdened by pressure of work—he suffered a nervous collapse that left him partially blind. In his later years, Pulitzer developed such an acute sensitivity to noise that his infrequent visits to New York had to be spent cocooned in a darkened, soundproof room, equipped with triple-glazed windows, deep within the mansion that he kept on Seventy-third Street. But he continued to control affairs at the paper from afar, thanks in large part to his genius for selecting staff. It was Pulitzer who hired Nellie Bly, the famous "girl reporter" of the 1890s whose most celebrated feat was to best Jules Verne's hero Phineas Fogg by traveling around the world in a mere seventy-two days. On another occasion—recalled Donald Henderson Clarke, who joined the *World* as a cub reporter in 1906—the editors received a cable from Pulitzer's yacht, criticizing their newspaper for dullness. The publisher went on to propose a typically forthright remedy: "Hire the best hard-drinking reporter in New York immediately," his telegram concluded, and the *World* men found one, reeling, in a nearby park.* It was also Pulitzer who recruited Frank Cobb, a Midwest farmer's son, as managing editor of the paper. Cobb, in turn, hired Herbert Bayard Swope.

Swope would probably have appealed to Pulitzer, whom he never met. The two men came from the same town, St. Louis, and Swope got his start there on the *Post-Dispatch*, which was Pulitzer's first paper. The old publisher would certainly have approved of the younger man's eye for a story. Swope's first big break came in 1911, when he covered the infamous Triangle fire; in the spring of 1912, he made an even bigger splash reporting on the loss of the *Titanic*, on this occasion scooping all his rivals by being the first American newsman to reach Halifax, where one of the ships carrying the bodies of those lost on the liner docked.

In person Swope was a study in extremes. He was six feet one inch tall, and wiry, with a pince-nez, sharp features, and a head crowned by a blazing mop of hair. He was always neatly dressed, favoring tailored suits accessorized with canes and yellow chamois gloves, and yet a new acquaintance would invariably be struck more forcibly by a fizzing

---

*The newsman hired as a result of Pulitzer's order, the mercurial wordsmith Esdaile "Doc" Cohen, undoubtedly did shake up the newsroom. Clarke recalled that he was sitting at his desk one afternoon when "suddenly, a loud crash as of splintering wood, accompanied by a roar—which, although remindful of a lion, was identifiable as human—sounded above the click of typewriters, the rattle of the city news-tape, and the tattoo of telegraph instruments. My eyes swung to the cause of the disturbance: a large man with a large head, bald on top, blue eyes behind gold-bowed spectacles, graying mustache above wide-opened mouth, over noticeable chin. He was erect beside his desk . . . waistcoat open and flapping, he raised clenched fists over his head and said loudly and distinctly: 'God damn it. God damn the *World*. God damn all the editors. God damn Mr. Pulitzer. God damn everybody.'

"I was more than astonished; I was paralyzed for a moment. I expected that this wild man instantly would be seized and restrained until the police or operatives from the handiest psychopathic establishment arrived. But no one seemed to pay any other than amused attention. . . . He stooped, picked up a chair, dashed it to the floor with most satisfying sound effect. Then he said suddenly and quietly, with a sweet smile: 'God damn it. I'm going to buy a drink. Who will accompany me?' "

" 'Just letting off steam,' head office boy Alex Schlosser explained to Clarke. 'That's nothing.' "

energy that made him anything but elegant. The newsman was incapable of sitting still, or staying quiet for more than five minutes at a time. He regularly worked until five or six in the morning, sleeping till noon, and possessed a voice "like a dinner gong."

Swope's character was just as forceful. He was excessively ambitious: as pleasant as could be to men who might be useful to him, but to everyone else, as New York caricaturist Peggy Bacon once remarked, as "self-centered as the last dodo." He relished an audience—according to Alexander Woollcott, he "could not write a letter unless there were four people in the room"—and did his utmost to leave a distinct impression on them. He was desperate for people to remember who he was. In a revealing memoir of his old colleague, fellow reporter Donald Henderson Clarke recalled once catching Swope unguarded in the men's room. Believing himself to be unobserved, the newsman was working on his phone manner. "This is Herbert Bayard Swope," he was intoning to a mirror. "This is Herbert Bayard *Swope*. This is Herbert *Bayard* Swope."

The real secret of Swope's success was his ability to make friends of almost anyone. Even in his early days at the *World*, his acquaintances included many of the most powerful politicians in New York. But he was equally at home in the twilight world of the city's gaming houses, and probably this is what drew him, alone of Manhattan's newsmen, to Herman Rosenthal. Swope himself was a ferocious gambler, betting on anything and everything, playing poker for high stakes (so high indeed that he could not afford them), and wagering compulsively at racetracks. In consequence he knew about the stuss houses and roulette joints of Satan's Circus and understood how vice was organized and protected. In all likelihood, Swope guessed, well before Rosenthal approached him, that the NYPD knew of most, if not all, the gaming operations in the city and permitted those that paid their dues to operate discreetly. And as a seasoned reporter, he certainly sensed that—properly substantiated—an exposé of vice and corruption in Satan's Circus would play well in his paper, which had always been fervently antiauthoritarian and critical of the police.

In truth, however, Swope had another, secret, even better reason for wanting to discover what Herman had to say. In the course of half a decade as a fixture in Manhattan's gambling clubs, the *World* man had come to know Arnold Rothstein, and know him well enough to be one of the gambling lord's few confidants. The two men were the same age, had similar backgrounds, and were well enough acquainted to travel together to racetracks and gambling houses out of town; Swope had even been best man when Rothstein wed. The precise nature of their friendship was never revealed—Swope in later years became far too respectable to dwell on the matter—though perhaps he and the gambler simply shared the pleasure of "being just a little smarter than the next person," as Rothstein's most recent biographer suggests. But it seems likely that these two manipulative men swapped information. Rothstein, after all, could only benefit by supplying his reporter friend with tips when there was something he needed to make public or someone he wanted to close down. And Swope lost nothing by passing tidbits concerning politics and the police to a man who never talked to other journalists.

Whatever the truth of the matter, Rothstein learned soon enough what Rosenthal was up to. Swope's friend seems to have known the gist of his complaints before the end of June, and he became determined to stop Herman from causing trouble in Satan's Circus. Rothstein was not alone in this—"Rosenthal's ruining everything," another veteran gambler, Dave Busteed, was heard to growl angrily at about this time—but he had bigger interests than most men to protect and was perhaps more of a stickler for underworld etiquette. After all, as a third club owner told the *Evening Post*, "The trouble with Herman is that he doesn't know the rules. The rules are, you pay your license money, lay low, and play like gentlemen. When you get a hint, take it and close down. It's when fighting among the brotherhood is too noisy that the powers step in."

Arnold Rothstein shared this view. The question was how Herman could be silenced, and to this problem there could be only two answers: Rosenthal could be paid off, given money to compensate him for his losses, with sufficient extra to get him out of town for good. Or he could be shut up more permanently. Some of the gambler's growing ranks of enemies already favored the latter course, among them Sam Paul, the former gangster, and Beansey Rosenfeld and Bridgey

Webber—neither of whom, it can confidently be said, would care if he got hurt. Others, Becker and Inspector Hayes among them, had motives of their own for wanting Herman to be silenced, too.

For the time being, however, Rosenthal's story remained unpublished and his allegations against the NYPD unvoiced. There was still time for matters to be settled quietly, and Rothstein was resolved to try.

According to one journalist who knew the Rothstein crowd, it was Tammany's Tom Foley, the ruler of a downtown ward adjacent to Tim Sullivan's, who first involved the gambler in the Rosenthal affair.

Word that Herman wanted to talk to the press got out, Leo Katcher of the *Evening Post* recalled years later:

> One of the first to hear it was Tom Foley. Foley called Arnold Rothstein and told him to get hold of Rosenthal and shut him up. "Get that stupid son of a bitch out of town," Foley told Rothstein.
>
> Rothstein sent John Shaughnessy* to find Rosenthal and bring him to the Rothstein home. An hour later Rosenthal was there.
>
> Rothstein let Rosenthal know what he thought of him. The mildest name he called Rosenthal was "fool."
>
> Rosenthal defended himself. "If the Big Feller [Tim Sullivan] was here, Becker would be pounding a pavement."
>
> "The Big Feller isn't here. And if he was, he'd tell you to keep your trap shut. All you can do is make trouble for a lot of people."
>
> "I don't want to make trouble for anyone, only Becker. They ask me about anybody else, I won't tell them. Only about Becker. . . . They can't make me say what I don't want to say."
>
> Rothstein took out his bankroll and counted off $500. "[Herman]," he said, "you've got to get out of town. Here's enough money to get you out. If you need more, let me know."

---

*Shaughnessy was a pitman at one of Rothstein's gambling clubs.

"I'm not leaving town," Rosenthal said. "That's what Becker wants me to do. I'm staying right here."

No arguments could sway him. . . . Finally Rothstein gave up. He informed Foley he had been unable to muffle Rosenthal.

Arnold Rothstein's failure to talk sense into Herman gave the vice lords of Satan's Circus pause for thought. It was one thing for a disgruntled gambler to threaten to expose senior policemen; that, after all, might be only a front, an attempt to extort hush money in lieu of other compensation. It was quite another for the man in question to spurn money when it was offered and to reject a pointed warning. Rothstein and his more rough-and-ready colleagues could only assume that Rosenthal actually meant what he said and was determined to press ahead with his complaints—with all the potentially disastrous consequences that public exposure of corruption might entail.

Many New York gamblers viewed this prospect with dismay. The election of Mayor Gaynor had made life uncertain enough for most men's tastes, and the appearance of aggressive East Side lowlifes within the hallowed borders of Satan's Circus was beginning to upset the checks and balances that had kept the peace in earlier years. Plenty of faro mechanics, poolroom oddsmakers, and stuss-house owners thought Herman was dangerous and wanted him to stop. But none was more anxious to keep the squealer quiet, or more ready to take steps to silence him, than the former gaming-room manager of Rosenthal's own faro house on West Forty-fifth, a bleak and shifty card sharp by the name of "Bald Jack" Rose.

Rose, who had known Rosenthal since childhood, was an extraordinary man. Born Jacob Rosenzweig, in Poland, he was brought to New York in infancy and grew up on the Lower East Side. Leaving the city in his teens, he spent the best part of a decade in Connecticut, where he scraped together a living as a card player, a fight promoter, and even as manager of a minor-league baseball team based in Norwich and known, perhaps inevitably, as the Rosebuds. Rose had given all that up to come back to Manhattan and resume his career as a professional gambler; midway through the first decade of the new century, he was acknowledged as perhaps the finest poker player in the city. By 1910 he had accumulated sufficient capital to set up on his own and was listed as president of what was grandly described as "Second Avenue's premier gambling club," a place where Herman Rosenthal was treasurer.

All this meant that Bald Jack had a broader experience of life than did most downtown gamblers, including Rosenthal himself. But he might have remained simply another East Side ne'er-do-well had it not been for the fantastical appearance that made him unforgettable. Without the hat that he habitually wore to disguise his bizarre features, Rose looked disconcertingly vampiric, with a long and narrow skull, tightly wrapped in the chalk white skin of a New York nightbird, a sharp nose, and vivid, bloodred lips. His slitted eyes were a mesmerizing amber color and—set deep in a snakelike face—conveyed the impression of intense cunning. As for that uncompromising nickname,

> it involved no hyperbole. As a result of a childhood illness,* he had no eyebrows, no eyelashes and not a hair on his head. One of his subsidiary nicknames was Billiard Ball Jack. To cut down the shine, he wore his poll thickly dusted with jasmine-scented talcum powder.

Rose had one obvious reason for hating Rosenthal: He had lost his job when Herman's faro club was closed. But there was more to his antipathy than that. For one thing, Lillian Rosenthal was in the habit of insulting Bald Jack's wife, who had once worked as a prostitute; whenever the gambler complained of being short of money, she was wont to snap, "Why doesn't Hattie go back to her old business?" For another, Rose was a man of amorphous loyalties, who had run a stuss house on Second Avenue in partnership with Beansey Rosenfeld and was friends with Bridgey Webber. Perhaps most significantly of all, however, Herman's onetime employee was also a known stool pigeon—a police informant—who had long passed tips to the cops.

---

*Rose's alopecia was the result of a severe bout of typhus.

He was recognized in the downtown precincts as a man ready to protect his own business interests by "ratting" on other fellow gamblers. And it was in this capacity that Rose had met Lieutenant Becker.

According to Bald Jack's own account, he had first encountered the head of the Special Squad in August 1911, when a club of which he was part-owner was raided. The next day, Rose drew Becker aside at the Exeter Market Court and offered to become an informant if the policeman would agree to throw out two unexecuted warrants against the club, which could otherwise have been used to raid the place again at any time. Becker agreed, and he also arranged to have the case that he was bringing against the gambler thrown out in exchange for a bribe of $200.

After that, Rose said, "We grew quite chummy," and it was not long before Bald Jack was coopted as one of three collectors Becker kept hard at work, doing the rounds of gambling houses and gathering protection payments that he could not be seen to solicit himself. Bridgey Webber helped out, too, Rose claimed, and their "customers" included Sam Paul—who paid $300 a month—and another downtown gambler known as "Dollar John" ("a sneaky little rat—sharp eyed—and a framer"), who parted with the same. If Becker paid his collectors at the going rate, Rose would have retained as much as 25 percent of the cash he gathered, a sum that might have amounted to nearly $20,000. Whatever the truth, the gambler could certainly afford to move, at about this time, from his old apartment on East Seventh Street up to 110th Street in Harlem, which in those days was one of the most genteel addresses in Manhattan.

"All was going along smoothly," Bald Jack's account continued, until Becker met Herman Rosenthal and decided to go into business with him. When Becker needed a trusted man to watch over his investment in Herman's faro house, he arranged for Rose to be installed as manager, and the gambler kept watch to ensure that his boss received a fair cut of the revenues. But this arrangement ended with the closure of the club. By then, Rose concluded, "Herman was growing desperate; he began threatening to tell what he knew."

It is easy to see how, from the Bald Jack's point of view, Rosenthal's story might prove lethally embarrassing. For one thing, Rose might go to jail for the part that he had played in organizing Becker's vast extortion ring. For another, Herman knew enough about Bald Jack's sideline as an informant to plunge his sometime enemy into trouble with some wronged and unforgiving men.

Rose was for the most part a cool, clear-thinking opportunist. He had stayed in business by steering clear of trouble and seizing his chances as they arose. Had it not been for his own heavy involvement in the Rosenthal affair, he might have perceived that Herman's threats were mostly bluster and recognized that his old boss had no evidence to prove his allegations.

But Rose was involved, and for once he failed to think things through. The prospect of exposure, jail, and ruin panicked him. Sometime toward the end of June, he went to see Jack Zelig.

Zelig was one of the great men of the New York underworld. Though only twenty-four years old, he was an influential figure on the East Side, thanks in part to his prowess as a fighter and in part to his considerable ruthlessness. The Zelig gang controlled a swath of territory along Second Avenue and was heavily involved in numerous rackets, including the collection of protection money from stuss houses and pool rooms. Like most of the hoodlums of the day, they felt more at home flitting between the tenements downtown than they did amid the tawdry glamour of Satan's Circus. But they could be hired, by those with the appropriate connections, to act as enforcers anywhere in the city. To an East Side man like Bald Jack Rose, they seemed the obvious solution to the problem posed by Herman Rosenthal.

Gangsters of Zelig's type had appeared in New York only recently. True, street gangs had been a feature of the city since at least the 1820s, when bands of thugs with names such as the Chichesters and the Roche Guard coalesced in the Five Points. These gangs and their great rivals, the Bowery Boys, became notorious south of Fourteenth Street, though they attracted little notice elsewhere in the city until a daylong battle fought between the warring factions in 1857 left twelve men dead and was ended only—after several fruitless police charges—by the intervention of two full regiments of infantry. But, violent as they were, these early hooligans were rarely professional criminals. Most of the Bowery Boys, and many of the Five Pointers, worked for a living, perhaps as carters, printers, or saloonkeepers, and the crimes they did commit were seldom serious. The slum gangs were also avowedly political, gathering at saloons controlled by district bosses, owing allegiance to one or another of the factions of the day, and intimidating opposition voters at election time. Most came into existence to help defend a neighborhood against external threats, whether posed by rival thugs or the police. They were organized along national or religious lines and spent a good deal more time fighting one another than they did preying on ordinary citizens.

It was not until sometime in the 1870s that gangsters, in the modern sense, appeared in Manhattan. The first group to consist principally of full-time criminals may well have been the Whyos, who congregated at Big Tim Sullivan's saloon on Chrystie Street and were Democratic partisans at election time. Unlike their notorious predecessors, however, few Whyos had conventional jobs. Those who worked did so as "dive owners, and brothel and panel-house keepers." The remainder made a living as pickpockets and thieves.

The Whyos faded from view around 1895 and were succeeded by a pair of gangs headquartered off the Bowery. To the west of the old street lurked the Five Pointers, who were predominantly Italian (Paul Kelly, their brainy, Irish-sounding leader, had been born Paolo Vaccarelli). To the east lived Jewish gangsters led by Edward Osterman, a muscular street tough better known by the anglicized version of his name, Monk Eastman. Kelly, the abler of the two, was good-looking and personable, spoke three languages, looked like a prosperous bank clerk, and was clever enough to take no active part in his gang's more thuggish activities. Eastman, on the other hand, was slow and "so crude in appearance that he could model for the stereotypical crook who has continued to show up in cartoons down to the present day."

The gangster had "a bullet-shaped head, a broken nose, cauliflower ears, prominently throbbing veins, . . . pendulous jowls, and a bull neck," and his body bore the scars of so many knife and gunshot wounds that a doctor who once examined him inquired whether he had seen action in the Spanish-American War. ("No," grinned Monk. "Just half a dozen little wars down on the East Side.") Viewed from this perspective, Eastman—all brawn and little brain—can be seen as the last of New York's old-style gang leaders and Kelly as the first of a new breed of smaller, brighter, faster-thinking hoodlums who combined at least a degree of restraint with better long-term planning. It came as no surprise to those familiar with both men that Monk ended up in jail, serving ten years for a botched street robbery, while his rival retired gracefully to Harlem, dying, in 1936, as a respected citizen.

It was in Monk Eastman's day that gangsters first began to make big money in Manhattan. They ran dance halls and beer dives, worked as pimps and procurers, organized downmarket stuss games, and extorted protection payments from more respectable gamblers. A few sold drugs. And as workers throughout the city unionized and began to fight for improved conditions and wages, Paul Kelly and a Jewish counterpart known as "Dopey Benny" Fein perfected the art of labor racketeering, organizing new unions, infiltrating others, and threatening costly strikes and sabotage against employers who refused to pay them off.

The advent of so much easy money changed the New York underworld forever. The Eastmans and the Five Pointers were the last of the large gangs. Their successors were smaller, less stable, more aggressive groups, led by ambitious minor thugs who fought endless wars among themselves. Kelly's successors included a pair of violent saloonkeepers named Jack Sirocco and Chick Tricker; Eastman's was one Max Zweibach, better known on the East Side by the sobriquet "Kid Twist." Twist did not last long; he was shot down outside a Coney Island music hall in May 1908. Sirocco and Tricker survived him, but neither man commanded the loyalty of more than a handful of followers. The rest of Kelly's men joined other gangs or set up on their own. Some up-and-coming toughs had no firm loyalties, hiring themselves out to one group or another while also working for themselves. And, at about the same time, the racial loyalties that had bound together so many nineteenth-century gangs also began to dissolve. It was no longer utterly unheard of for an Irishman to work for an Italian gang or an Italian for a Jew. By 1912 gangland was more fragmented than it had been for half a century, which made it easier than ever for a ruthless, charismatic man like Zelig to scrabble his way to a position of some power in the city.

Zelig himself was an interesting study. His real name was Selig Harry Lefkowitz, and he was born, most accounts agree, into a fairly well-off family on Broome Street, in the heart of the tenements. As a youth (an East Side police detective testified) the future gangster was "not a bad boy at all—not a tough guy, I mean," and Jack could no doubt have pursued a respectable career had he wished to. By the time that he was twelve, however, Zelig had already succumbed to the lure of crime and was working Second Avenue as a "stall," a boy whose task it was to jostle the chosen victim of a "tool"—that is, a pickpocket. He was good at the job and soon picked up the tool's skills as well. Even at his apogee, in 1912, Jack was still capable of seizing a good chance to rob a victim. He was, wrote the private detective Abe Shoenfeld, an expert on East Side crime, "known as a very good tool and a very good stone-getter*—perhaps one of the best in the world."

Zelig attributed his own fall from grace to a childhood love of marbles: "One of the worst things a small boy can do is play marbles for keeps," he told one reporter. "That is the thing that started me wrong. It gives a boy his first taste of gambling and gives him an idea of getting something without working for it, which is a mighty bad thing to get a taste for." But to many of his contemporaries, he seemed made to be a gangster. He was tall for the period, at five feet eleven inches, clean-shaven and slimly built, with a handsome oval face spoiled by a squashed and broken nose. He was also markedly intelligent, always elegantly dressed in suits, high collars, and straw boaters, and reputedly a decent conversationalist. These characteristics were, however,

---

*A term for a pickpocket specializing in the theft of jewelry.

secondary to his prowess as a fighter. According to one police detective, Zelig was "bandy legged" and "raw boned," had "healthful dark fearless eyes [and a] splendid disposition." According to another, he was the toughest man on the East Side, as handy with his fists as he was with a gun. One contemporary who knew him well explained in cheerfully mixed metaphors that the Zelig of 1912 was

> a fighting terrier—the man is a demon when his blood is boiling. He can fight fifty men at once if he has them in front of him and is not taken unawares. In other words he is a wild cat. When in action he plants his feet firmly, throws out his chest (he has no stomach at all but is all bone and muscle) and when he hits with his fist it descends like a lion's paw.

It was this reputation as a brawler that first enabled Zelig to establish himself at the head of a gang. He had been little more than an anonymous sneak thief when, in 1910, he found himself surrounded by members of a rival gang while sitting down to dinner in a Chinatown restaurant. Most gangsters of the day would have beaten a hasty retreat or summoned aid. Not Zelig. Sitting alone and unprotected, the East Sider "single-handedly took on, beat up, and knocked out three of the neighborhood's most feared Italian gangsters in front of an astonished crowd of hoodlums"—the first decisive victory ever recorded by a Jewish man over the Mafia. In the annals of East Side crime, Zelig's achievement was notable in itself. But it was what the former pickpocket did next that set him apart from his contemporaries. Rather than simply boasting of his victory, or even attempting to exploit his rivals' momentary weakness, Zelig formally declared a vendetta against the presence of "foreign" gangs in the Jewish areas of Manhattan. News of his announcement caused a sensation in the closed world of Second Avenue, where storekeepers and ordinary pedestrians had grown increasingly used to being harassed by Irish or Italian thieves and muggers. Word that Zelig was actually making good on his promise sent the gangster's stock soaring even higher. Within a few months, the former pickpocket and his fast-growing gang of followers had driven so many Italian and Irish gangs out of the East Side that even honest citizens acclaimed them. Jonah Goldstein, then a lawyer, later a New York judge, wrote that the gangster had "rendered a public service," and the balls that Zelig and his men held at the popular Arlington Hall were patronized not merely by criminals, as was usual at the time, but by respectable Jewish businessmen anxious to show support and gratitude for the man who, in Abe Shoenfeld's encomium, "was the great emancipator of the East Side." Zelig, the private detective added,

> cleared the East Side dance halls and academies of Italian pimps, . . . cleared the East Side of Italians who were wont to hold up stuss houses and legitimate business places, . . . and prevented more hold-ups and other things of a similar nature in his career than one thousand policemen.

By 1912, when he was first approached by Rose, Zelig was at the height of his powers, and his popularity on the East Side was unrivaled. He had a well-developed sense of his responsibilities and was married, with a son (his wife, many East Siders were surprised to learn, was Christian, a former good-time girl named Henrietta Young). Even the police seemed powerless to stop him. Charles Becker, for one, had tried; during his days with the anti-gang Special Squad, the lieutenant had arranged for two of his men to concoct evidence against the gangster in an attempt to get him jailed for carrying a concealed weapon. Fortunately for Zelig, the attempt was a clumsy one. The gangster had swiftly been discharged and was pictured leaving the police court with a broad grin on his face.

Exactly what passed between Rose and Zelig is unknown. Bald Jack was well known on the East Side, and Zelig must certainly have been aware that he worked as a collector of graft for Becker. Possibly he was at least reluctant to involve himself with one of the policemen's men. But Rose was offering a substantial sum—$1,000 or $2,000 it seems—to have Rosenthal disposed of. Even $1,000 was a lot of money to most East Side gangsters; low New York thugs would kill a man for change, and even Zelig had murdered for $100 or less.* It does not seem to have taken Zelig long to accept the commission.

Rose's money was enough to buy the services of experienced assassins, and the four men Zelig supplied were certainly among his best. The best shot was probably Louis Rosenberg, a young, left-handed gangster known throughout the East Side as "Lefty Louie"; he had killed at least two other men. Jacob Seidenschmer—better known as "Whitey Lewis"—sometimes worked as Zelig's bodyguard; he "had been a third-rate pugilist, but under Jack's tutelage he became a blackjack artist of rare merit." The third man, "Dago Frank" Cirofici was—at least according to Val O'Farrell, a noted Central Office detective—"the toughest man in the world" and had, the writer Herbert Asbury recalled, "a girl called Dutch Sadie, who was also a noted fighter; she carried a huge butcher knife in her muff, and frequently employed it to good effect when her lover was hard-pressed."

The leader of the little group was another East Side thug—a small, deceptively slight gunman known familiarly as "Gyp the Blood." Gyp—whose real name was Harry Horowitz—was then a part-time dance-hall "enforcer" and leader of a group of burglars and pickpockets working around 125th Street. He owed his memorable nickname not so much to any act of savagery as to the combination of a swarthy, Romany complexion and a taste for fashionable clothes. But Gyp was certainly no less brutal than his three companions. "What

---

*In 1911 one informant had confessed to the police that Zelig quoted fixed scales for the commission of various crimes, the exact fee depending on the prominence of the intended victim:

Slash on the cheek with a knife . . .	$1 to $10
Shot in leg . . .	$1 to $25
Shot in arm . . .	$5 to $25
Throwing a bomb . . .	$5 to $50
Murder . . .	$10 to $100 and up

time he was not working on commissions for Jack Zelig," notes Asbury,

> or robbing drunken men in the Bowery dives, Gyp the Blood was a sheriff and gorilla at the cheap dances of the East Side; he soon became known as the best bouncer since Monk Eastman and "Eat 'Em Up Alive" McManus, which was no light praise. He possessed extraordinary strength, and frequently boasted that he could break a man's back by bending him over his knee. Moreover, he performed the feat several times before witnesses; once, to win a bet of $2, he seized an inoffensive stranger and cracked his spine in three places. He also became an expert revolver shot, and was extremely accurate at throwing a bomb, a task in which he delighted. "I likes to hear de noise," he explained.

For ten days nothing happened. Twice Rose returned to Zelig's table—"I said, 'Rosenthal is still at it, but I don't see those fellows at it'"—and twice Zelig reassured him—"They are on the job. I will see them again today." Then, at the end of the first week of July, the four gunmen tracked Rosenthal to the Garden Café on Seventh Avenue. Seeing that he was with his wife, however, and suspecting that a dark-clad figure loitering conspicuously outside might be a detective, the gangsters withdrew—though not before Herman had noticed them skulking around within his line of vision.

Rosenthal seems to have misinterpreted this incident, imagining that it was simply another effort to intimidate him, rather than a botched attempt at murder. But he was, by now, certainly frightened enough to put his own threats into action. Next morning he hurried downtown to call on Herbert Bayard Swope at the offices of the *New York World*, and with Swope's help he swore two lengthy affidavits, which the newspaper published on July 13 and 14. Both statements were, as Rosenthal intended, "dynamite." The first charged that a police lieutenant—unnamed—assigned to enforce New York's gambling laws had in reality been Rosenthal's business partner. It caused a sensation. Having assured himself of the city's attention, Herman followed up that revelation by naming Becker and two Satan's Circus officers—Inspector Hughes and Captain Day—as grafters in his second, far more detailed statement.

Lieutenant Becker was alarmed and infuriated by the second affidavit. He responded to Rosenthal's allegations that same afternoon, announcing that he would sue for criminal libel. But his anger was nothing to that of the Tenderloin's gamblers, who were all too easily convinced that Herman would bring the authorities down upon their heads. "Rosenthal's going to ruin it for everyone," one gambling-house habitué complained. And from all around him, in the gaming room, there were murmurs of assent.

The most attentive reader of the *New York World* for July 14 sat in an office on the second floor of the Criminal Courts Building. His name was Charles Whitman, and he was the city's district attorney.

A slight man of below-average height, with a thin and drooping mouth, craggy nose, wide-set hazel eyes, and wavy brown hair that he parted in the middle, Whitman had succeeded the long-serving William Travers Jerome in 1910. He was the son of a noted Connecticut pastor, fiercely moral and "obedient to fundamental ethics," and had never felt entirely at home in the city. And though he was already forty-four years old, he was relatively new to public service, having eked out a living for many years as a teacher and a lawyer of middling ability.

Like his energetic predecessor, Whitman was no friend of Tammany. He was a Republican and a onetime supporter of Seth Low, who had secured himself a last-gasp nomination as a magistrate on the day that Low left office. With no prospects of advancement under Tammany, it was not until four years later that the future DA contrived to save his fast-fading career. Capitalizing on a dispute between two Democratic factions, Whitman secured a modicum of power by getting himself elected chairman of the New York Board of Magistrates.

This close brush with political extinction seems to have galvanized Whitman, who suddenly became a whirlwind of ambition and activity.

Aping the exploits of Roosevelt and Jerome—on whom he plainly modeled his public persona—he launched a high-profile campaign against the "clean graft" payments traditionally made to the police by bail bondsmen who wished to make sure that it was their name that the cops passed to suspects in the station house. Whitman also made a point of targeting the plethora of late-opening saloons, personally touring the streets after hours and—whenever he found a dive operating in violation of the law—calling for help from any nearby beat policeman. Together the magistrate and the patrolman would raid open saloons, much to the cop's disgust, Whitman taking care the next day to keep the city's papers abreast of his activities. The press caught on soon enough, and it was not long before Whitman was being hailed throughout New York as "the raiding judge." It was this publicity that eventually helped him win election as district attorney with a majority—astonishing for a Republican in New York—of nearly 30,000 votes.

Now, in 1912, with reelection looming, Whitman was looking for a new cause: something that would reinforce his reputation as a reformer and keep him in the public eye. Rosenthal's affidavits, with their lurid revelations of police corruption, clearly had the potential to spark just the sort of furor that he was looking for. And plainly it was the district attorney's duty to investigate such serious allegations. The day that the second of the depositions was published, placing Becker's name in the public domain, Whitman summoned Herman to his office.

Of course, a politician with Whitman's well-developed instincts knew that a mere gambler's tale would never be enough to provoke a real sensation. Rosenthal would need to produce firm evidence of Becker's under-the-table involvement in his gambling house to really interest the DA, and though Whitman listened carefully to Herman's statement, he seemed to be far from impressed. Probably he could see that it would be almost impossible for the gambler to prove his charges and foresaw that the police could simply deny that what Herman claimed was true. The initial meeting between the two men lasted only thirty minutes, and it seems likely that Whitman would never have seen Rosenthal again had Swope, anxious to keep the story alive, not pressured him.

The *World* man had to push hard for a decision, even following Whitman up to Newport over the long weekend in an attempt to badger him into calling Rosenthal again and asking the gambler for better evidence. It required considerable persuasion, but eventually Swope did extract a brief statement from the DA, which was published in the *World* the next day. It didn't sound much like the Whitman whom other reporters knew, and there were plenty of men down on Newspaper Row who thought the DA's words, as published, had "a distinctly Swopean flavor."

"I have had Rosenthal's charges under investigation for some time," the statement began, inaccurately.

> I have no sympathy for Rosenthal the gambler, but I have a real use for Rosenthal who, abused by the police, proposes to aid decency and lawfulness by revealing conditions that are startling. . . . The trail leads to high places [and] the situation is best described as "rotten." This man will have the chance to tell his story to the Grand Jury.

Swope's bosses were relieved to receive a telegram containing Whitman's statement. WHAT YOU SENT SAVED THE STORY, the *World*'s city editor replied. But Swope was still not satisfied. He pressured Whitman to abandon his comfortable country-house weekend and return to New York to pursue the investigation, first hand. Eventually, worn down, the district attorney conceded the point. He boarded a train bound for Manhattan. Swope trailed him, seated in the next carriage.

According to New York gambling legend, it was after his first meeting with Whitman that Herman Rosenthal became aware that he was being followed. Badly frightened already by his encounter with Zelig's gunmen in the restaurant, Herman at last understood that his life was in real danger. "He managed to elude his trailer," recorded Leo Katcher,

> and, seeking some haven, rushed to the Rothstein home on West Forty-Sixth Street. He found Rothstein there. "I've changed my mind," he said. "Give me the money and I'll get out of town."
>
> "You've waited too long," Rothstein said.
>
> "Let me have the five hundred," Rosenthal pleaded. "I'll go 'way someplace and hide."
>
> "You're not worth five hundred to anyone any more," Rothstein said.
>
> "Then you can go to hell." Rosenthal stormed from the house.

Charles Whitman arrived back in New York late in the afternoon of July 15, hot, tired, and more than half convinced that his journey had been a waste of time.

Forewarned by Swope's excellent intelligence, Whitman was unsurprised to discover an anxious Herman Rosenthal loitering at his office in the Criminal Courts Building. The gambler had been waiting in an airless room for several hours, and his pink silk shirt and collar were stained with grime and sweat, which he dabbed away with a large handkerchief. Frightened though he was, however, he remained as stubbornly self-righteous as ever. He begged the DA to press charges against Becker.

Publicly Whitman seemed sympathetic; it was, after all, rare for any gambler to openly volunteer sensational disclosures. Privately, though, the DA was not sure there was much that he could do. There was certainly no prospect of putting Rosenthal in front of a grand jury—the only body capable of handing down indictments he could act on— without at least one witness who would back him up. But all Herman's efforts to persuade other gamblers to testify had failed. No fewer than six men, whose names he had supplied to Whitman—they included Sam Paul, Bald Jack Rose, and even Bridgey Webber—had, scarcely surprisingly, declined to be drawn into the affair. "The gamblers in this town are a bunch of quitters," the disappointed Rosenthal had told one newspaper reporter after yet another fruitless attempt to scour the dives on Second Avenue. Meanwhile the district attorney typed a statement for the press:

> This office is ready to present to the Grand Jury any evidence, properly corroborated, which involves the corruption of the police department . . . but I have no right to waste the Grand Jury's time by presenting to it witnesses whose statements consist of little more than rumor or hearsay and upon which no action would be justified.

From Becker's point of view, the press release was a relief. The DA seemed more or less ready to drop the matter. From Rosenthal's perspective, though, the press statement could scarcely have been worse news. Whitman seemed determined to shrug off complaints that he had risked his life to make.

The gambler was now fully aware of what he had done. His encounter with Jack Zelig's men at the Garden restaurant had shaken him. The discovery that he was being shadowed around the streets of Manhattan had left him very apprehensive. Now rumors were flying that harsher sanctions were being planned. "It was," Jack Rose remarked, "in the air that Rosenthal was running a big risk acting the way he did," and by that afternoon Herman himself shared that opinion.

"You'll find me dead one of these days," the gambler told the DA glumly when his statement had been made. "And you'll find they've planted a gun on me."

Whitman snorted. This was New York, he said, not the Wild West. "Oh, you may laugh," Herman shot back, "but the gangs are already around my house." Perhaps, the DA replied, but the case had such a high profile that no one would dare to take action.

Rosenthal did not seem reassured. "Better men than I am have been killed when the police wanted them out of the way," he muttered darkly. "They will get me and you'll never know who did it."

It was early evening by now, and time for Herman to go. But he still hoped to get corroboration for his statements and begged for the chance to talk to Whitman one more time. The problem, the gambler added nervously, was that he could not risk being seen calling yet again at the Criminal Courts Building. "They will get me if they see me coming here," he said.

Perhaps Whitman felt sorry for Rosenthal. Perhaps he simply wanted to get the whole affair over and done with as quickly as possible. Either way, he relented. There would be no need for the gambler to travel all the way downtown; he could come to the DA's home and complete his business there.

The two men parted shortly before eight that night with a clear understanding. Herman would call at Whitman's apartment on Madison Avenue at seven the next morning.

CHAPTER 7

"GOOD-BYE, HERMAN"

THREE DAZZLING ARC LIGHTS, white and garish, blazed in the darkness that had fallen over Manhattan, mercilessly illuminating the peeling facade of a narrow, six-story building on the north side of West Forty-third Street. Although most respectable New Yorkers were in bed by now, the temperature in the city still hovered in the eighties, and the building's two doors both gaped open. Inside, passersby could glimpse a shabby lobby, hung with cheap lace curtains, and the entrance to a dimly lit café. The sounds of chatter and laughter and of a pianist pounding out the latest ragtime tunes mingled together and drifted from the interior.

This was the Hotel Metropole, owned by Big Tim Sullivan in partnership with the gamblers Jim and George Considine,* and once one of the jewels of the Sullivan empire. By the summer of 1912, admittedly, the hotel was so far past its prime that it was close to bankruptcy. But even in its present depressed state, the Metropole had two saving graces in the eyes of its loyal customers. The first was its location, a mere fifty yards from Times Square in the heart of Satan's Circus. The second was a coveted twenty-four-hour liquor license—obtained through Sullivan's influence—which allowed the Café Metropole to remain open around the clock and attracted a lively

---

*The Considines had first partnered Sullivan years earlier, at Miner's Theatre on the Bowery. Within months they would also be in business with Arnold Rothstein, backing a sumptuous new gambling house known as the Holley Arms Hotel out on Long Island.

late-night crowd. The hotel was particularly popular with boxers, gamblers, and actresses.

A few minutes before midnight on July 15, the most notorious gambler in New York City waddled up West Forty-third and turned in to the lobby. Herman Rosenthal was clad in the same rumpled pink shirt he'd been wearing a few hours earlier at his meeting with Whitman and dabbed at his damp forehead with a bright silk handkerchief. Barely pausing to glance around, he rolled into the café and slumped down at a table for four, sweating profusely.

Summoning a waiter, Herman ordered himself a Horse's Neck—bourbon, ginger ale, and a twist of lemon—and three large Havana cigars. He seemed nearly prostrated by the heat, swatting listlessly at the clammy air with the cardboard fan he clutched in one fat hand. But the gambler's eyes were still bright and alert. The waiter who delivered his drink noted that they darted constantly from side to side, between an exit opening onto the street and the connecting door to the hotel.

Precisely what Rosenthal was doing at the Metropole that night was never fully ascertained. Certainly Herman knew the hotel well; it stood only two blocks south of his home, and he was often to be found in its private gaming room (run by Arnold Rothstein) or taking refreshment in the café. But to walk knowingly into a place filled with gamblers, men whose very livelihoods were threatened by his conniving with Whitman, was to invite—at the very least—harsh words; and to dawdle in a restaurant only hours before a dawn appointment with the DA struck some men as eccentric, even for a night owl such as Herman.

There were many, Whitman prominent among them, who were certain that the gambler was thoroughly embittered and had every intention of giving evidence as planned the next morning. But others, including some of Rosenthal's oldest friends, were equally convinced that Herman had no intention of doing anything so dangerous. These men felt sure that the gambler had come to the Metropole to keep some other appointment and that he expected to be met—perhaps by Rothstein, perhaps by some emissary from the Sullivan clan—and paid as much as $15,000 for his silence. At seven the next morning, they contended, Herman Rosenthal fully expected to be standing not at the door of Charles Whitman's apartment but on a platform at Grand Central Station, waiting for the train that would take him out of New York.

Whatever the gambler's intentions, he was plainly in no hurry to leave the Café Metropole. At around ten to one, he invited three passing acquaintances to join him, and the four men spent more than half an hour in animated conversation. When these companions rose and left, Rosenthal looked up and peered around him, scanning the faces of the other diners for people that he knew.

"What do you boys think of the papers lately?" he smirked to a knot of gamblers at a nearby table. "You aren't sore at me, are you?"

"You're a damned fool, Herman," one of them replied—or so the papers reported the exchange the next day.

A few minutes later, while Rosenthal was sipping at another drink, the door leading to the Metropole swung open and another gambler entered. It was Herman's sworn enemy, Bridgey Webber. Glancing from side to side, Webber circled swiftly around the room, brushing past his adversary as he did so.

"Hello, Herman," said Webber in a pleasant tone.

If Rosenthal was surprised to be addressed so politely by a man whom he had once tried to have killed, he gave no sign of it. "Hello, Bridgey," he returned with equal affability. But Webber wasted no more time on pleasantries. He continued his circuit of the room, leaving the café at a brisk walk by the same door through which he had entered.

Herman finished off his drink and glanced at his watch. It was now twenty minutes to two. He pushed back his chair and heaved himself to his feet. "I guess the morning papers must be up," he declared, knowing perfectly well that most of the Metropole's customers could guess the likely headlines in the press. Stepping out into the street, Rosenthal found a newsboy near the hotel entrance. He bought seven copies of the *New York World*—which led with his allegations against Becker—and took them back to the café. As he reached his seat, Herman waved the paper over his head in triumph. "What about that for a headline?" he crowed to the men at the next table, pressing copies into their hands.

Rosenthal settled back into his chair, spreading open his own *World* and smiling to himself. He read the news attentively for a few more minutes. Then, just after five to two, he was interrupted by a short, well-dressed stranger who had entered the café through the street door and come up to his table.

"Herman," the newcomer said, "there's somebody wants to see you outside."

Rosenthal seemed unsurprised to be accosted in this way. He set down his drink, gathered up the remainder of his papers, and, clutching at the last of his cigars, rose from his chair and followed the unknown man into the night.

Even at two in the morning, the streets around Broadway were generally busy, filled with revelers, gamblers, prostitutes, their clients, and the dregs of the theater crowd. During the summer months, Satan's Circus was even busier than usual, as New Yorkers sought refuge from the clammy heat by lolling outside on fire escapes or pacing the streets in search of the slightest breeze. Yet on this particular July evening, West Forty-third seemed oddly quiet.

The street outside the Metropole had begun to clear soon after Bridgey Webber left the building. By about 1:40 A.M., the taxi line near the hotel—which was always crowded in the early morning hours—had emptied as a dozen cabs were dispatched one by one on a variety of errands, most of them to the outer boroughs of New York. Several men and women who had been loitering in the vicinity of the Metropole were asked to move on by tough-looking men one passerby recalled as "East Side types." Most took the hint and walked quickly away. By ten minutes to two, there were only a handful of pedestrians outside the hotel. According to one witness, Herman Rosenthal's old partner Beansey Rosenfeld was among them. Another was an employee of Webber's who stood loitering by the hotel door.

A few minutes later, the silence that had fallen over West Forty-third was broken by the growl of a powerful automobile engine. A large gray touring car, its roof down and its headlights on, had turned left off Sixth Avenue. The car drove slowly toward the Metropole, pulling over to the south side of the street as it approached. It was a Packard taxi, registration 41313 New York—the same car, owned by Louis Libby, which had been used to shoot up Jack Sirocco's café in the spring. The driver coasted to a standstill thirty yards from the hotel, leaving the motor idling. A moment or two later, both passenger doors opened and three or four dark-suited figures got out and walked toward the Metropole, coming to a halt in the shadows opposite its entrance. The Packard's chauffeur and another man stayed in the car.

They did not have long to wait. At three minutes to two, a round figure appeared silhouetted in the doorway of the Hotel Metropole. Herman Rosenthal had come to claim his due.

Rosenthal stood blinking in the dazzle of the hotel's lights, his sweaty handkerchief protruding from a pocket, his Havana still dangling from one plump hand. Just ahead of him, a figure wearing a felt hat lifted a hand to the brim as if in signal and then darted away. Instantly the men waiting opposite hurried across the street toward him, pulling revolvers from their jackets as they came.

Herman squinted uncertainly from side to side, evidently trying to locate the man who had called him from his table. He did not seem to realize that anything was wrong. The Metropole's arc lights had blinded him—"the illuminations were as powerful as a spotlight on the stage," one man who knew the scene explained—and he might not even have sensed the arms now thrusting out toward him. His eyes were given no time to adjust; a moment later the unnatural quiet enveloping West Forty-third was shattered by the crisp staccato of several shots. The gambler was hit immediately, blood erupting from his face, his knees buckling as he crumpled facedown on the pavement. His unlit cigar tumbled from slackened fingers, somersaulting on the concrete. A thick sheaf of morning papers slipped out from beneath his arm and fell softly to the ground, shrouding his body with headlines shouting his name while, beneath the flimsy pages, a sticky, spreading pool of blood matted his hair and began to run toward his nose and mouth. In another moment the assassins were crouching over him. "I gotcha!" one of them exclaimed.

Investigation would eventually establish that at least three rounds were fired. The first bullet had missed its target and embedded itself at head height deep in the wooden frame of the Metropole's front door. But the second had struck Rosenthal in the face, passing through his cheek and jaw and shattering some teeth. At least one fragment lodged itself in the gambler's neck as he pitched forward and began to fall; and at that instant the third round had entered Herman's head an inch above the hairline, piercing his skull and destroying his brain. The fatal bullets had been fired from a range so close that burns caused by muzzle flash had etched themselves onto the dead man's skin.

At the first sound of gunfire, the driver of the Packard gunned its engine, and the slate gray car emerged from the shadows, turning a lazy half circle in the street. Rosenthal's killers leaped onto its running boards, and the vehicle moved away at a sedate pace, gathering speed as it headed east down Forty-third Street and turned left onto Madison Avenue. New Yorkers ambling along Madison watched as the vehicle accelerated noisily into the distance, the men on the running boards scrambling in as it went.

The sudden crack of gunfire had been clearly heard within the Hotel Metropole; at least one customer looked up in time to see the muzzle flashes from the murderers' revolvers. The men and women in the café who rushed to the doors to discover what had happened found the street outside already filling as pedestrians came running from as far off as Broadway. They were too late to get a good look at the gunmen but just in time to see one of the gambling types from the café walking unhurriedly onto the street. This man stepped casually over the body lying in his path, turned and bent at the waist, his hands thrust deep in his pockets as he studied Rosenthal's bloodied face. "Hello, Herman," he said, smiling. Then he straightened up. "Goodbye, Herman," the man added, and walked swiftly away.

News of the shooting spread through Satan's Circus like wild fire. By five past two, ten minutes after the murder had occurred, a crowd fifteen or twenty people deep had formed around the body. Many members of this mob were gamblers with little reason to like Rosenthal; one reached over and tugged at the corpse's shoulders, turning Herman onto his back and exposing his wounds for everyone to see. Word of the dead man's identity passed swiftly through the crowd.

It took only a few minutes for reporters to arrive. One of the first men on the scene was the owlish Alexander Woollcott—then covering police affairs for the *New York Times* but soon to become the same paper's theater critic*—who came puffing up from Broadway. Woollcott had reported plenty of murders in his time, but the scene awaiting him outside the Metropole stuck firmly in his mind. "I shall always remember the picture of that soft, fat body wilting on the sidewalk," he recalled in later years.

> I shall always remember the fish-belly faces of the sibilant crowd which, sprung in a twinkling from nowhere, formed like a clot around those clamorous wounds. Just behind me an old-timer whispered a comment which I have had more than one occasion to repeat. "From where I stand," he said, "I can see eight murderers."

The police who hurried to the scene did what they could to control the milling crowd, but chaos prevailed for nearly a quarter of an hour, and by then the heaving mass of rubberneckers had grown to be several hundred strong. Eventually Jim Considine summoned a waiter from the Metropole, and a hotel tablecloth was pressed into service as a makeshift shroud. A platoon of forty police reserves, called from nearby precincts, appeared and cleared a space around the body. Soon after that, a doctor arrived to examine the corpse; death, he concluded, had probably come instantly. At about two-thirty, the bloody cadaver was rolled onto a stretcher and loaded into in a police

---

*A few years later, Woollcott was, of course, a founding member of the Algonquin Round Table, a famed gathering of wits that numbered among its members Robert Benchley and Dorothy Parker.

ambulance, which made its way, bell tolling, to the Sixteenth Precinct station house a quarter of a mile away. After that, the vast crowd of spectators gradually dispersed. Among those glimpsed leaving the scene was Bridgey Webber, who set off at a smart pace toward Times Square.

The clean getaway effected by Herman Rosenthal's murderers was a considerable embarrassment for the police. No fewer than six officers had been within a hundred yards of the Metropole when the killing took place: One was standing on duty on Seventh Avenue, another on Broadway, and two more had paused for a moment on the corners of West Forty-third itself. A fifth man, Lieutenant Edward Frye, was walking east along the same street only thirty yards or so from the hotel, while the sixth policeman, Detective Billy File, had actually been sitting in the Café Metropole, only a few feet from Rosenthal, when the gambler rose to go onto the street. File, a burly former boxer who had once sparred with the heavyweight Jim Corbett, was off duty, and his attention was focused on the girl singer he was entertaining, but he reacted quickly to the sound of gunfire, leaping to his feet, drawing his revolver as he rose, and thrusting a passing waiter to one side as he made for the door. Finding it already blocked by a press of fellow customers desperate to discover what the commotion was about, File lost valuable seconds forcing his way through the crowd. By the time he reached the pavement, the taillights of the fleeing Packard were already receding into the distance.

Looking quickly up and down the street, File spotted a single taxi sitting parked in some shadows; its driver had been asleep for nearly half an hour and had escaped being moved on by the unofficial dispatcher at the taxi stand. Rousing the drowsy cabbie, File—joined by Lieutenant Frye—hand-cranked the cab and set off in pursuit. By the time the men reached Madison Avenue, however, the Packard was long gone. They cruised as far north as Fifty-ninth Street in search of it before abandoning the chase and returning disconsolately to the Metropole.

While Frye and File were gone, other patrolmen began interrogating members of the crowd. Several bystanders came forward to tell confused accounts of the murder; there was very little agreement between them. Some said that one killer had done all the shooting, others that two or three different men had fired. Several had seen the passengers from the Packard crossing the street, but a waiter from the Metropole said he thought a single assassin had been crouching behind one of the giant plant pots that stood outside the hotel entrance, while a pedestrian insisted that five shots had been fired from a moving car. The one thing all the witnesses agreed on was that none had gotten a clear look at the gunmen. The only descriptions the police came up with were of anonymous-sounding men with average builds and unremarkable clothes, their faces concealed beneath the brims of hats.

The best hope of tracing the killers seemed to be locating their vehicle. Automobiles were not so common in New York City in 1912 that the sudden appearance of one, driving at speed at well past two in the morning, would not attract attention, and it transpired that several men and women on both West Forty-third Street and Madison Avenue had turned to watch the murder car as it roared by. Several had noted the plate—one witness had even jumped in front of Frye and File's taxi to shout out the details as they sped past. The trouble was that bystanders recalled the number differently. By the end of the night, the police had collected no fewer than seven different versions. According to the desk sergeant who recorded the first details of the killing in the police blotter at the Sixteenth Precinct, the dead gambler

> was shot and killed by four unknown men about 24 years, white, 5 feet 5 or 6, smooth faced, dark complexion and hair, who after shooting Rosenthal jumped into a waiting automobile No. 13131 NY or 14131 NY.

Several other witnesses insisted that the number had been 43131 NY. On that basis, so far as the baffled detectives leafing through their statements could see, almost any combination of the numbers 1, 3, and 4 might be the correct one.

One witness, though, did not *think* he had the right number for the gray Packard; he *knew*. Charles Gallagher, an unemployed cabaret singer, had been walking toward Broadway when he heard the shots. Moments later the Packard had swept past him, men still clinging to its sides. He got a good look at the plates and—elbowing his way through the mass of people flocking to the hotel entrance—found Patrolman Thomas Brady beginning to take statements. Several members of the crowd were shouting out versions of the license plate—all wrong. Eventually the singer caught Brady's eye.

"No," he insisted. "41313 NY is the right number."

The policeman seized Gallagher by the shoulders, hustled him backward through the crowd, and pressed him up against the hotel wall. He did not seem grateful for the information. "You're wanted as a material witness," Brady snapped, summoning a colleague.

The second policeman hurried Gallagher away to the Sixteenth Precinct building, where he was told to give his story to a harassed sergeant. The desk man wrote it down. "Name?" he asked, and Gallagher told him. "Address?"

"I've already given it to the detective," the singer protested. "I don't want any notoriety."

At this the sergeant lost his temper. "He's a witness. Lock him up," he snarled to a patrolman, and the astonished Gallagher was hauled off to the cells.

"They didn't give me a chance to explain that I only wanted to help them," he told a *World* man the next day. "By the way they treated me I began to think they thought I was the man who shot Rosenthal."

The singer's escort fumbled with some keys, opened the door of an empty cell, and propelled him roughly into it. Gallagher slumped down on a wooden cot as the heavy door swung shut, and the authorities' best hope of solving the Metropole shooting was left fuming behind bars.

It did not take long for word of the murder to reach the better parts of town.

Rhinelander Waldo was the first senior official to learn of Rosenthal's demise; the telephone in his suite at the Ritz-Carlton rang at about 2:30 A.M. The commissioner responded to the news by barking out, "Ye Gods!" Then, assured by his assistants that the local precinct had things well under control, and deciding he would rather not disturb the irascible Mayor Gaynor in the middle of the night, Waldo went back to bed.

At roughly the same time, Herbert Bayard Swope was bulldozing his way into the Sixteenth Precinct building on West Forty-seventh Street. Like most newspapermen, Swope was a confirmed cynic, particularly when it came to the police. He knew that Rosenthal was far from popular with the NYPD, especially now, and especially among senior officers, who resented the allegations he had leveled against three of their number in the press. The *World* man looked on in growing anger at the chaos enveloping the station house; he was astonished to hear so many different versions of the license plate bandied about, and he found the desk policeman's treatment of Charles Gallagher still more of a concern. In Swope's opinion the cops were doing their best to lose the Packard's number; if they were left to their own devices for much longer, the whole investigation might easily be compromised. There was only one thing he could do. The reporter pushed his way to a telephone and placed a call to DA Whitman.

Whitman was fast asleep in his apartment on East Twenty-sixth Street when the insistent ringing of the phone jerked him awake. He stumbled out of bed and picked up the receiver. At the other end of the line, shouting to make himself heard above the hubbub of the station, Swope rattled off a hurried summary of events at the Metropole, then told the district attorney that he really ought to get over to the Sixteenth Precinct right away. Whitman demurred. Surely, he grumbled, this could wait until morning.

"No. You've got to come right now," Swope said.

"But I'm in *bed*. I've got my *pajamas* on," the DA wailed. In the end Swope was forced to hail a taxi, drive to Whitman's home, and virtually drag him into his clothes. The two men then went down to the street, got back into the cab, and headed for West Forty-seventh Street.

Thanks to Swope's intervention, the district attorney arrived at the Sixteenth Precinct not long after 3:00 A.M. He went straight to a vacant office and sat down at the desk. As he did so, the phone rang. This time the caller was the precinct captain, William Day, one of the men accused by Rosenthal of graft. Someone had finally told Day that the most sensational murder in years had been committed on his doorstep, and the captain was telephoning to find out whether it was really necessary for him to come all the way back into town from his home in Brooklyn to take charge. Having had his own sleep rudely disturbed, Whitman was in no mood to be merciful. Yes, he told the captain, ice in his voice, it certainly was. For good measure the district attorney had Day's boss, Inspector Edward Hughes, routed out of bed as well. Then he settled down to try to find out what was going on.

Whitman's first discovery was Gallagher. Hearing from Swope and several other newsmen that a vital witness had been detained, he had the angry singer brought up from the cells. It took the DA several minutes and more than one apology to calm Gallagher down and get his story, but when he did, he realized the number matched the details given by another witness by the name of Thomas Coupe, a desk clerk at the Elks' Club across the street from the Metropole. It had been Coupe who had leaped into the path of Billy File's taxi shouting out the details of the murder car; like Gallagher, he had the number right. The vital lead was passed on to a bleary-eyed Inspector Hughes as he entered the station house. Hughes hastened off to check the details in a register.

In the midst of this confusion, no one had thought to tell Lillian Rosenthal of her husband's death. The news was eventually broken by a reporter from the *American* who arrived outside Herman's apartment on West Forty-fifth Street shortly before three in the morning. The house was dark, and he had trouble gaining admittance; the patrolman still stationed inside was suspicious, thinking this was another of Rosenthal's ruses to lure the police out of his home. But at length the door opened and a disheveled Mrs. Rosenthal appeared. When the reporter told her what had occurred, she collapsed in hysterics.

"I had a premonition that something terrible was going to happen," she sobbed to her visitor. "When Herman left home I felt certain all was not right, and I told him so. He just laughed—he always laughed. He had been warned so many times, and it's true I've told him so frequently that I feared for something, that he—well, he just went." When she had recovered herself somewhat, Mrs. Rosenthal asked the newspaperman to take her to the Metropole. She threw what the reporter thought looked like an "automobile duster" over her bulky frame and slipped into some shoes. But the second she stepped out onto the pavement, she collapsed again. By the time the *American*'s man had calmed her and gotten her down to the hotel, Herman's body was long gone and there was little left to see.

Charles Becker, meanwhile, was still wide awake. He had attended the fights at Madison Square Garden earlier that evening, had a drink at a hotel, and then given several friends lifts home in Colonel Sternberger's touring car—passing only a block from the Metropole as he did so—before returning to his own apartment off 165th Street at 2:00 A.M. Helen was lying in bed waiting for him. She got up to make her husband a roast beef sandwich; Becker ate it slowly. He had just finished when a telephone in the apartment rang. He and his wife exchanged glances; the number was private and unlisted.

Mrs. Becker picked up the phone and handed the receiver to her husband. The caller was Fred Hawley, Becker's reporter friend from the evening *Sun*.

"Charley, have you heard the news?" asked Hawley.

"What news?" Becker replied.

Hawley told him. Becker seemed incredulous, asking the reporter if he was drunk. "No, Charley, listen to me," Hawley begged. "Herman Rosenthal has been killed. I am working on the story and want a statement from you. What do you know about it?"

There was a brief pause before Becker's voice came back down the line. "I don't know anything about the murder," he said, speaking with care. "But I do know a lot of things about Rosenthal. I am mighty sorry he has been killed because I had the goods on him and was about to show him up for keeps."

Hawley scribbled in his notebook. "I think you ought to come down," he finished. "I think you ought to get on the job."

Becker talked over Hawley's suggestion with his wife. "I didn't know what to do," he admitted later. "I told Hawley if I come downtown people may think that I have come down to gloat over the death of a man who has attacked me. If I don't come down, the newspapers will say that when told about Rosenthal's death I evinced no interest or emotion." In the end curiosity got the better of the lieutenant and he decided to go. It took him until three-thirty to get to the subway station at Times Square; by then the street outside the Metropole was quiet again, and he headed for West Forty-seventh Street instead. He arrived at the precinct house shortly before 4:00 A.M., just as a large, slate-colored touring car drew up outside. It was the missing Packard taxi. Several policemen jumped down, flung open a passenger door, and dragged a stocky man with dark, wavy hair into the station. The prisoner was Louis Libby; he looked very apprehensive.

A cordon of patrolmen held back the knot of reporters gathering outside the Sixteenth Precinct. Becker, still wearing his civilian clothes, brushed past them and hastened up the steps in Libby's wake. The first room that he came to was Captain Day's office, which was crowded with policemen and officials. The lieutenant was about to enter when he noticed Inspector Hughes raising a hand to wave him off. Becker backed out, startled, and as he did so, he glanced down at the figure sitting in the captain's chair. The eyes that met his were not Day's. They belonged to District Attorney Whitman.

The police had traced the Packard easily enough. The registration details supplied by Gallagher and Coupe led them downtown to a garage on the north side of Washington Square, where Acting Captain Arthur Gloster found a gaggle of mechanics cleaning cars. Accosting one of them, Gloster demanded to be shown around. The second or third vehicle he came across was Libby's Packard, which had been reversed into its parking space. Its plate, 41313 NY, was clearly visible.

"When did this come in?" Gloster asked the garage hands.

"Twelve o'clock. It has been down to Coney Island," one of them replied. The policeman reached out a hand and ran it across the Packard's hood. It was still hot to the touch.

"Keeps warm a long time, doesn't it?" Gloster observed with a grim smile.

The garage doors were all secured, and several patrolmen set off to find the taxi's owner. They traced Libby and his partner Shapiro to a boardinghouse on Stuyvesant Place and hauled both men out of bed. By the time they got back to Washington Square, Gloster had gotten the mechanics talking. One of them admitted that Libby had returned the taxi to the garage shortly after two-fifteen. When he did so, the man added, he had told them to spin the Coney Island story to anyone who asked. Gloster had heard enough. He bundled the chauffeur and his partner into the murder car and headed for the Sixteenth Precinct.

Lieutenant Becker hung around inside the station house for nearly half an hour after Libby was brought in. At one point, when he caught Whitman's eye, he told the DA he wanted to go into the station's makeshift morgue to view Rosenthal's corpse. Whitman—so he said later—at once suspected that the lieutenant was planning to plant evidence of some sort in a pocket. "Never you mind going near it," he snapped back. "I've been all over that body." Defeated, Becker retreated to the pavement outside the precinct building, where he slouched against an iron railing trading theories with waiting newsmen. Most of the reporters thought that rival gamblers had arranged the murder, but the lieutenant disagreed. "I'll lay you five to one it was some of Spanish Louis's gang," he said.

At about 4:30 A.M., Becker felt a tap on his shoulder. He turned; it was Inspector Hughes.

"Have you seen the body yet?" Hughes asked.

"No," Becker replied.

"We'll get a look at it," Hughes said, and he led Becker into the station house's yard. The two men peered through a window into the back room where the corpse was lying. It was still covered in blood. "Whoever done him, done him good," Hughes muttered. He and Becker then walked together back inside the precinct building, where they found a highly unorthodox lineup under way. Libby, dressed in greasy overalls and his chauffeur's cap, was standing in the middle of a row of plainclothes officers, all of whom were wearing suits. Unsurprisingly, Thomas Coupe, the Elks' Club clerk, had no trouble picking him out.

"That's him," Coupe declared. The clerk then gave a statement, positively identifying the chauffeur as the man who had killed Rosenthal. Libby, he added, had not been alone in the touring car but had fired all the shots.

Coupe's deposition crowned a satisfactory night's work for the police. At dawn the DA went out onto the front steps of the precinct house and gave the waiting reporters a full statement. Coupe, Whitman said, had made a firm identification and could describe the murder and the scene in detail. "He will make a splendid witness," the district attorney added. Then he ducked back into the station to continue his investigation.

In the course of the next day, things returned slowly to normal in the Sixteenth Precinct. Whitman relinquished control of the station house shortly after breakfast, returning to his usual office in the Criminal Courts Building and leaving Day and his men to get on with the tedious job of typing up statements and collating evidence. One of their first tasks was to inventory Rosenthal's possessions and move the body to the morgue at Bellevue Hospital. The contents of the dead man's pockets proved to consist of some keys, his handkerchief, and a little over $85 in cash. Herman had not been armed and had told friends he would never carry a gun, insisting, "If they are going to get me, they will get me."

Shortly after Whitman's departure, Rhinelander Waldo appeared to give his own brief statement to the press. The murder of underworld figures was not uncommon in New York, and incidents of this sort did not usually attract attention; at least six similar crimes were committed in July 1912—two on the same day that Rosenthal was shot—and none received more than a few weary lines of coverage in the press.* But the

---

*The police response was similarly muted. None of the dozen or so murderers responsible for these other killings was ever caught.

death of such a prominent informant, just hours before he was scheduled to give evidence of spectacular police corruption, was no ordinary affair, and Rosenthal's murder was the lead story in every daily paper in the city. Waldo knew that he and his men would be expected to solve the crime and that failure to bring the investigation to a successful conclusion would badly damage his career. Few were surprised when the commissioner announced that the full resources of his department would be thrown into tracing Herman's killers.

Waldo's determination to bring somebody to justice for the Metropole shooting was only increased by the knowledge that many New Yorkers suspected the police themselves of arranging the affair. The late edition of Swope's *World* reported that the NYPD had been reduced to "a state of terror" for fear that Rosenthal's death would be traced to its doors. The same paper openly speculated that the gambler's enemies on the force had organized the shooting and expressed surprise that Becker himself had yet to be suspended from duty and was apparently not even a suspect.

So far as Inspector Hughes and the men responsible for investigating the murder were concerned, however, the matter was not quite so clear-cut. Their only real leads were still Libby and Shapiro, and the two chauffeurs were refusing to say much about the events of the previous night. Most of the morning was devoted to questioning the pair, but progress remained slow.

To the newspapermen still clustered outside the station house, this was hardly surprising. Experienced correspondents who had been inside the building reported that Hughes's handling of his prisoners had been extremely peculiar. The two suspects had been let out of their cells, and reporters from several papers were shocked to find them standing in a corridor unsupervised, deep in conversation. Even when Libby and Shapiro were brought up to the interview room, they were interrogated with unusual restraint. When Aaron Levy—a lawyer with long experience of defending East Side "characters" who had agreed to represent both prisoners—arrived at the Sixteenth Precinct late in the afternoon, he was startled to discover that neither of his clients had been beaten up. "I was certainly surprised to find both men sound as a dollar when I first saw them," Levy confessed to the waiting members of the press. "Usually men who are picked up for a cowardly murder are given such a third degree that they are not very presentable in court twenty-four hours afterwards. But these two boys were looking fine."

In fact—though the reporters did not know it—Hughes had every reason to be cautious. By the middle of the afternoon, he had discovered that Libby had a solid alibi; the chauffeur had spent the previous evening in his room, and no fewer than five of his fellow lodgers came forward to confirm that they had seen him there. And, to complicate matters further, lawyer Levy decided that both his clients would give their statements not to Hughes but straight to the DA. This was clever thinking; no policeman was going to take too many liberties with Libby and Shapiro under such circumstances, at least not while the memory of Gallagher was so fresh in their minds.

By the end of a long day of questioning, then, Hughes had coaxed no more than a few scraps of information from his suspects. Libby readily admitted that he had known Rosenthal slightly; both men had once been members of the Hesper Club. He agreed that Jack Zelig was one of his best customers. But he denied all knowledge of the murder and said that he had no idea who the Packard's passengers had been. Shapiro, meanwhile, had confessed to driving to the Metropole. Hughes guessed, given the history of the car, that he must have known that his customers were gangsters. But there was no way of proving it, and the chauffeur refuted that charge indignantly. He had been as shocked as anyone, he said, when Rosenthal was shot. Shapiro even claimed not to have recognized his passengers, adding that when he had been slow pulling away in the aftermath of the murder, one of them had pistol-whipped him into driving faster—an odd thing to do to a trusted associate. An ugly bruise along the hairline on the driver's scalp seemed to support this claim.

It was only at the end of a frustrating afternoon that the police finally obtained the information they really needed: the name of the man who had phoned to book the taxi to the Metropole. The caller, they were told, was Bald Jack Rose. "The car," lawyer Levy confided to reporters after talking with his clients, "was hired from the Café Boulevard stand by telephone. The man making the call said his name was 'Jack,' and the [operator], who had rented the car many times to Rose, claimed he recognized the voice."

It was a vital breakthrough. If the police could now track down Jack Rose, he could lead them to the gunmen in the Packard; in all likelihood he also knew who had hired the men and why. But Rose was a known stool pigeon of Becker's, and the new information was important for another reason: It promised to link the gambler's employer, Becker, to the crime.

In 1912 leads of this sort rarely remained unpublished for long, and by evening most of New York's dailies had been tipped off about Rose. Only a handful chose to publicize the story, which was still uncorroborated at this point. The *World*, predictably, was one of those that did.

Swope's paper had no doubt what Rose's involvement meant. "Herman Rosenthal," it proclaimed in ringing tones next morning,

> was murdered in cold blood by the System.
>
> The System is the partnership between the police of New York City and the criminals of New York City.
>
> The System murdered Herman Rosenthal because he threatened to expose it and had begun to expose it. . . . It murdered him because he came to the *World* office Saturday night and made affidavit as to the System's activities. It murdered him because he had declared that he *would* submit his evidence to the press of New York and make public the criminal profits that the police derive from the protection of lawbreakers. It murdered him in a desperate effort to save itself from destruction.

It was left to District Attorney Whitman to add the coda that the *World* merely implied. The DA had spent the day inspecting the murder scene and trying to discover why the men on patrol near the Metropole had not done more to catch the fleeing gunmen; he did not return to his apartment until three on the morning of July 17, twenty-four hours after he had been hustled out of bed by Swope. But when he did so, the newsmen were still waiting for him.

Several reporters cornered Whitman in the lobby of the building and pressed him for a statement. They wanted to know more about Libby and Shapiro, naturally. But they also wanted to hear the DA's theories about the motive for the murder.

Whitman had by now reached some firm conclusions on the subject. He professed himself astonished that the police on duty in Satan's Circus had managed to obtain half a dozen different numbers for the murder car—"all of them wrong"—and said that he believed "there was much police interest and activity behind the slaying of Rosenthal."

"I accuse the Police Department of New York," the DA added in conclusion,

> through certain members of it, with having murdered Herman Rosenthal. Either directly or indirectly, it was because of them that he was slain in cold blood with never a chance for his life.
>
> I have the necessary proof that there were five policemen there, two were within 100 feet of it, one was within 40 feet at the time the crime was committed,* and not one of them attempted to do anything that would naturally be done by the police under the circumstances. . . . Five men were able to shoot to pieces the head of a Grand Jury witness and escape without being even seriously inconvenienced. . . . The police permitted this murder and deliberately allowed the murderers to escape.

Whitman did not add that Charles Becker was one of the members of the force to whom he was referring, but he might as well have. By the early hours of July 17, the lieutenant was already the DA's leading suspect.

---

*Whitman evidently meant Detective File and Lieutenant Frye.

CHAPTER 8

RED QUEEN

IT MAY HAVE SEEMED blindingly obvious to Charles Whitman that Becker and the New York cops had ordered Herman's murder, but others were not so sure. Rosenthal had had so many enemies that even his fellow gamblers were not entirely sure how many men had wished him dead. When Horace Green of the *Evening Post* gained access to Rosenthal's home on the night before the funeral, posing as an acquaintance, he was struck by the morbid suspicion displayed by even Herman's closest friends. "The murderers had not yet been caught," Green wrote, "[and] it was common knowledge that the criminals lurked in the neighborhood, and that, in order to avoid suspicion, they would appear among the chief mourners. Therefore, each eye was turned against its neighbor, and each man, as he passed you, asked the silent question: 'Did you shoot Herman Rosenthal?' "

The dead man's body lay in an open casket, a tribute to the undertaker's craft. Lillian Rosenthal, looking fatter than ever in a billowing crepe gown, had begged Sam Paul and Bridgey Webber to meet the funeral expenses, and her husband's old rivals had obliged. But neither man attended Rosenthal's interment, on a stuffy afternoon two days after he was killed, and only a few of Herman's friends cared to be seen in the cortege. The funeral director's men were pressed into service as pallbearers, and no more than a handful of relatives followed the coffin to the cemetery. There were some flowers but, conspicuously, no cards. "Herman Rosenthal a live gambler with a bank roll and a generous hand was a hero," Swope explained in the *World*. "Herman Rosenthal a murdered 'squealer' was a thing to be shunned."

None of these considerations, naturally, prevented thousands of curious New Yorkers from flocking to West Forty-fifth Street at the time appointed for the funeral. So dense were the crowds outside the Rosenthal apartment that Viña Delmar and her father, over from Brooklyn to pay their respects, found it impossible to get within sight of its front door. "Traffic was blocked from Fifth Avenue to Broadway," the girl recalled.

> People stood on roofs, climbed poles, and leaned from every available window to see Herman's coffin carried from No. 104. Thousands filled the streets, perspiring and struggling to draw a step nearer to the waiting hearse. Mounted policemen vainly attempted to disperse the crowds. They backed horses into groups where brawls had suddenly exploded. They scooped fainting women out of the mob. They rescued lost children and picked up a man who had died from a heart attack. They snarled and barked and, finally, by threatening mass arrests, they cleared a passage through which Herman could be taken away forever from Forty-fifth Street.

The funeral itself was subdued. There was little ceremony, and Rabbi Samuel Greenfield delivered only a short address. He made no attempt "to dignify or glorify Rosenthal beyond his walk in life," waiting reporters noted, but talked a little of the dead man's generosity to friends. Greenfield also mentioned one relative who had been too ill to attend. Herman's mother, who had depended on him for support, was dying in Brooklyn. She lay on her deathbed, raving and calling for her son, never knowing—Swope exhaled—that "her boy had preceded her on her long journey."

Viña Delmar and her father were not the only people taken aback by the public's consuming interest in Herman Rosenthal. New York's underworld, more used to gangland murders going unreported and unsolved, could scarcely remember a case like it, and the active involvement of the district attorney badly shook the murderers in the gray Packard. Zelig's men had plainly believed there would never be a full investigation of the crime, neither bothering to conceal their vehicle's license plates nor donning disguises or masks. The gangsters went hurriedly underground, and many of the gamblers who had known Rosenthal well wasted little time in leaving town. Some fled to the Catskills, others to Hot Springs, Arkansas, a popular resort renowned for harboring criminals. Among those who left New York more or less immediately were Beansey Rosenfeld, Dan the Dude, and all three of the minor gamblers who had shared Herman's fatal table at the Metropole.

The furor that erupted over Herman's shooting was, in short, unprecedented, and it owed a good deal to the city's newspapers. Every daily in the city cleared its front page to report not merely the murder but the ensuing investigation—even the *Morning Telegraph*, which as a rule preferred to discuss horseflesh and chorus girls. Still more remarkably, the story remained news for months. Hearst's *American* featured the case on its front page on 150 of the 190 days following the shooting—this at a time when it also had to make room for a World Series between New York teams, an attempt on the life of Theodore Roosevelt, and national elections. The *World* and the rest of Manhattan's dailies were not far behind. "Never in their history," one reporter calculated, had "the New York press found room for as relentless coverage of a story as it did for the Rosenthal murder."

What made the affair sensational, of course, was the rumored involvement of the city's cops. Tales of police corruption sold newspapers, and it was the tantalizing possibility that someone in authority had commanded Herman's murder that set the Rosenthal affair apart from other gangland killings. New Yorkers vividly recalled Herman's angry allegations against Becker on July 15. The gambler's death, coming as it had a mere eight hours before he was due to give a further statement to the authorities, seemed to confirm every accusation he had made.

District Attorney Whitman helped fan the flames. Having openly accused the NYPD of instigating and then covering up a conspiracy to murder, the DA was soon in the news again, melodramatically declaring Herman's shooting "a challenge to our very civilization." His well-publicized determination to crack the case resulted in a steady stream of developments, each leaked to an eager press. Editors responded by assigning their best reporters to the story, and a swarm of inquisitive newsmen were soon actively assisting Whitman in pursuing leads that had eluded him. The papers' editorial columns and cartoonists, meanwhile, seized the chance to condemn police corruption and brutality. "Never before in this city was murder done with such openness," the *American* scolded. "The tragedy seemed the limit of malignity; nothing could be worse than this." The *World* published a grim cartoon showing a hulking cop, his revolver smoking and his face hidden by a strip of cloth labeled "The System," stepping over a body sprawled on the pavement. "Strip off the mask!" the caption begged.

Swope and Whitman, who had set the whole story in motion, were the principal beneficiaries of this deluge of reporting. For Swope the affair was a godsend: the biggest story of the year, perhaps of his entire career. The opportunity to cover such a case amply justified the risks that he had taken, first in arranging to publish Herman's unproven affidavits, next in pursuing Whitman to Rhode Island and cajoling the DA into coming home, and then in routing him from his bed on the night of the shooting to take charge of the investigation. The Rosenthal shooting made Swope's name and secured for him the post of chief reporter for his paper.

For Whitman the case was even more important. Had it not been for Herman's murder, the district attorney might well have served out his term in comparative obscurity, denied the chance to resuscitate his fading career. Rosenthal's death offered the opportunity to garner headlines and present himself as a no-nonsense lawman. Throughout the ensuing weeks and months, Whitman would take considerable pains to contrast the vigor of his own investigation with the lethargy and dubious motives of the police. Whether or not the DA was really as sure as he appeared to be that the murder was no mere dispute between gamblers, he certainly did see the whole affair as an opportunity to embark on a high-profile crusade against Manhattan's cops. By taking on those perennial New York bugbears, police corruption and brutality, Whitman hoped to build himself a platform from which to launch a new career in politics, as other district attorneys and peppery judges (Gaynor included) had already done.

Looked at in this way, Lieutenant Becker made an attractive target. There was nothing to be gained, in political terms, from prosecuting Zelig's gunmen; even Rosenthal's gambling enemies, Webber and Rose, were such obvious lowlifes that their convictions would scarcely raise a stir of interest. Arresting Becker, on the other hand, would create a scandal, and convicting him was an achievable goal. It simply meant proving that the lieutenant had had a hand in Herman's murder—and pursuing Rosenthal's charges against Becker's grafting, too.*

While the district attorney was busy making statements to the press, Rhinelander Waldo was pushing hard for answers. The commissioner wanted the murder solved just as badly as did Whitman, though he no doubt hoped to prove that the police had had no role in it. Waldo's determination was due in part to a natural desire to prove to his many critics that his men could solve the case. But it evidently owed something, too, to the awkward conference he had been forced to endure with his mentor, Mayor Gaynor, soon after the shooting. "Conferring," one newsman explained, "was perhaps not the word."

---

*The benefits of taking a public stance on the police corruption were brought home to Whitman just a few days later, when he received a visit from the industrialist William Schieffelin, representative of a group of wealthy "Simon Pure" reformers. (A Simon Pure was a hypocrite who made a great public show of virtue, named after a Quaker character in an early-eighteenth-century play.) He and his friends, Schieffelin said, wanted to offer the DA financial assistance in his quest to crack down on the NYPD. The next day, Whitman let it be known he would be a lot more comfortable running the Rosenthal investigation from somewhere other than his dingy office in the Criminal Courts Building. Schieffelin obliged, and the DA spent the next five months working from a luxury suite in the Waldorf-Astoria hotel. "Whenever we had any problems," one of his staff recalled, "Whitman would pick up the phone and make a call, and a couple of hours later Schieffelin would come in with a bundle of money. Those Simon Pure fellows were really generous. They were so grateful to have someone working hard to clean up the city."

By standing at a particular spot in City Hall Park, reporters had been able to follow the progress of the interview through a half-open window in Gaynor's office:

> When the meeting began, the Mayor wore his straw hat. He took it off early in the talk, however, and was seen belaboring his police commissioner with it. Now on the head, then on the shoulders or chest, as the mood seized him. Toward the end of the talk he contented himself with poking it at the commissioner.

For all Waldo's urgings, though, it took some time to get the police inquiry on track. Of course, Inspector Hughes and his colleagues had (at least if Whitman were correct) strong motives to leave the murder unresolved, and they often did seem baffled by an array of false statements and red herrings that, taken together, gave the impression that the whole case was a muddle. The police had to sift through statements from more than one witness who claimed that uniformed policemen had been among the killers at the Metropole. Another insisted that Sam Paul had been seen sitting in the Packard taxi, and a third swore that the man who had telephoned to rent the murder car was none other than Lieutenant Becker. None of these stories checked out, and neither did the tale told by another witness who claimed that the taxi had no connection to the murder in any case— the gunmen had walked to the Metropole, he said. As for the number of assassins who had lain in wait for Herman to emerge, conflicting testimony put the number variously at one man, three, or four.

Amid all this misinformation, though, there were three or four good leads. The best hope of breaking the case seemed to lie with William Shapiro, who remained in custody at the Sixteenth Precinct station house. Hughes, unhappy with the chauffeur's continued insistence that he had not recognized his customers, had his prisoner arraigned for murder on his second day in custody, and—confronted by the chance that he would stand trial for the killing—Shapiro was soon revealing more of what he knew. He still refused to name any of Zelig's gangsters. But he did recall that Harry Vallon had been one of his passengers that night. So had a second gambler named Schepps, he said.

To Hughes and the Satan's Circus police, Shapiro's allegations made sense. The hatchet-faced Vallon was a known minor criminal who was not only a friend of Bridgey Webber's, but an acquaintance of Jack Rose's. Sam Schepps, a former pimp and opium fiend, belonged to the same circle of associates. A short, plump, bespectacled sneak, and "egotistical beyond imagination," Schepps now bought and sold fake jewelry and picked up spare change every now and then by carrying messages for Rose.

Looked at dispassionately, the chauffeur's statement clearly pointed to the notion that Rosenthal had been killed by his fellow gamblers. Bald Jack Rose had hired the taxi seen outside the Metropole. Two close associates, Vallon and Schepps, had traveled with him in the car. Vallon, in turn, was known to work for Bridgey Webber. As for Sam Paul—who was, other than Arnold Rothstein, the most influential gambler of them all—rumors had reached the police as early as July 17 that Herman's death was actually the consequence of a recent police raid on the Sam Paul Association, occasioned by a tip-off Paul believed had originated with Herman Rosenthal. It came as little surprise to anyone when a *New York American* investigation showed that at least a score of gamblers—including Paul, Webber, Vallon, Schepps, and Rose—had spent the hours after the murder together at the Lafayette Steam Baths, an all-night hangout on the East Side greatly favored in the underworld.

Whether any of this linked Becker to the murder remained a matter of dispute. Commissioner Waldo did not think so, loyally if naïvely hurrying out a statement backing the lieutenant and defending his department. But Whitman continued to insist such was the case. The DA was still not willing to let the police investigation run its course, and over the next few days he not only convened a grand jury to consider Herman's graft allegations but also created quite a stir by asking the Burns private detective agency to conduct its own inquiries into the Rosenthal affair. The police could not be trusted to find the murderer themselves, Whitman said.

Ironically enough, in these strained circumstances, it was the much-maligned Inspector Hughes who made the next important breakthrough, tracking down Bridgey Webber and hauling him in for questioning. Webber proved unforthcoming; he gave a short statement of his movements on the night of the murder that omitted anything incriminating and implausibly insisted he and Rosenthal were close friends. "I have known Herman all my life," he stated. "When I was blackjacked by 'Tough Tony' on registration day three years ago, Rosenthal took me to the doctor and took me home. People wanted to make me believe that Herman had me beaten up. I didn't believe it. I don't know anything about the murder." But Hughes was certain that Bridgey knew more than he was saying. The gambler was released, but the police kept close track of his movements.

The next suspect to turn up was Jack Rose, who walked unchallenged right into police headquarters on July 18. Bald Jack, it transpired, had spent the interval since Rosenthal's murder hiding in a friend's apartment well uptown. According to statements he made at different times, the gambler either had been lying in bed, ill and unaware that he was wanted for questioning, or—rather more plausibly—had waited for the chance to see what Shapiro was saying before making the decision to turn himself in. Whatever the truth, his appearance on Centre Street had been meticulously planned. Rose had spent much of the previous day consulting a lawyer friend with strong connections with Tammany Hall. That morning he had carefully dressed in his best clothes and had even stopped off for a manicure on his way downtown. He strolled into the lobby of the building wearing a natty gray suit and a gray silk shirt, discreetly striped with green, and swung a cane jauntily to and fro as he made his way upstairs.

Bizarrely, the *World* observed, given that half the policemen in the city were supposed to be searching for him, Rose went quite unrecognized by anyone in the lobby "despite his remarkable appearance" and was able to saunter up and down the corridors unchallenged in search of Waldo's office. The gambler was eventually directed in to see a surprised Deputy Commissioner Dougherty, who took down his age—thirty-seven—and occupation—"sporting man"—and extracted a statement as determinedly bland as Webber's had been. "There was nothing to be gained by staying back," Rose said when asked why he'd surrendered, "since I felt that I was perfectly innocent. I haven't the remotest idea of why or by whom Rosenthal was killed."

If Bald Jack's unrevealing evidence irked Dougherty at all, the deputy commissioner did not show it. But—given Shapiro's incriminating statements—Dougherty was not about to let Rose go free. He knew that the gambler had plenty more to say and was better placed than any man to solve the mystery of Charley Becker's involvement in the whole affair. When Bald Jack had finished talking, Dougherty informed his prisoner he was under arrest "on a charge of acting in concert with others to cause the death of Rosenthal." Then he stepped out of his office for a moment to arrange for a message to go straight to Whitman's office informing him of this development.

Dougherty was still discussing the matter with a colleague along the hall when his office door flew open. The visitor was none other than Lieutenant Becker, who evidently had no idea his former collector had turned himself in. Becker had (so he would later claim) called in at police headquarters to tell his boss where Bald Jack might be hiding, and he was badly shocked to discover that he was too late, stopping "as if shot" when he saw Rose already sitting there. As for the gambler:

> All of a sudden I felt, rather than saw, somebody at the door, and I may have heard a kind of hiss—I'm not sure now—but I don't think I heard anything at all—I just felt it. I looked up and there standing in the door was Becker. I shall never forget that face if I live to be a thousand years old. He never moved a muscle. He just stood there and looked. I never had been so scared in all my life. I wanted to go to the electric chair right then—anything to get away from him and his eyes.
>
> I hadn't made a single crack about Becker except to boost him. But he was afraid I was beginning to tell, and anyway I had

come to headquarters in spite of his orders. I always knew Charles Becker was a tough man, but I never knew the real sort of man he was until I got that flash of him looking at me. It didn't last more than a minute, I suppose, but I felt like I had been in a furnace, I was just burning up. He disappeared without a word, and I came to with a choke as Dougherty entered.

"What's the matter with you?" he asked in a funny way.

"Oh, nothing," I said. "I'm seeing things."

Becker had every reason to be disconcerted by Rose's sudden appearance at Police Headquarters. Bald Jack hiding out among the tenements well away from awkward questions was one thing. Bald Jack sitting confident and apparently talkative in the heart of police headquarters was quite another. The development certainly implied that Rose knew he could easily stand trial for the Rosenthal shooting and had come to Commissioner Dougherty to do some sort of deal. And indeed more or less as soon as the gambler was led away to the cells—still swinging his cane and protesting to waiting newsmen that he was merely doing his duty as a citizen by assisting the police with their inquiries—the tenor of the investigation changed.

To begin with, Dougherty stopped protecting Becker. The deputy commissioner had loyally followed Waldo's line thus far, insisting there was no evidence, other than the word of criminals, that any member of the NYPD had had a thing to do with Herman's death. "The police are too busy going after Rosenthal's killer to pay attention to the newspaper stories that take up so much of Mr. Whitman's time," he brusquely informed one newsman after the shooting at the Metropole. On July 20, though, Dougherty changed his mind, calling on the DA in the latter's offices to ask what should be done. Several of the leading dailies reported the conversation that ensued:

DOUGHERTY: Do you want me to arrest Lieutenant Becker?
WHITMAN: Not yet.
DOUGHERTY: All right. I see we agree as to who is in back of this killing.

Chauffeur Shapiro's successive confessions, meanwhile, had at last grown detailed enough for the deputy commissioner to authorize the arrest of several leading suspects. First Bridgey Webber and then Sam Paul were summoned to headquarters for questioning, Webber because, according to the chauffeur, his rooms had been the murderers' rendezvous, and Paul thanks to the various threats muttered against Rosenthal at a Sam Paul Association picnic held just before the murder. Paul's arrest coincided—to the surprise of many of the journalists covering the case—with the seizure of Rosenthal's old friend Jack Sullivan, the newspaper distributor, who had been seen lounging around Webber's poker club at around the time the four gunmen assembled. There was still no sign of Harry Vallon or Sam Schepps, and the latter was generally believed to have fled the city. But the whereabouts of Vallon became obvious when, shortly after midnight on July 23, the faro dealer followed Rose in strolling right up Centre Street and surrendering to the police, reputedly on Webber's orders. Vallon had been hiding out in the Catskills, and he proceeded to give a vague and unincriminating statement. Dougherty was not impressed, and he had Webber, Paul, Sullivan, and Vallon charged with conspiracy to murder.

By that Tuesday morning, then—one week after the shooting—the police had three gamblers and a hanger-on in custody along with Libby and Shapiro. So far as the general public was concerned, six arrests meant progress, and there was increasing speculation that the mystery of Herman's murder was about to be solved. The press coverage was tumultuous; most dailies printed extra editions to report developments, and a crowd estimated at more than six thousand strong filled the streets outside the Criminal Courts Building when Webber and his friends were brought in for questioning. "A kind of lunacy descended on the city," Viña Delmar would remember, "as one dramatic charge followed another. The days were filled with extras, which in turn were filled with rumors as well as with detailed testimony."

From Dougherty's perspective, though, things were not yet quite clear-cut. The prisoners all denied their guilt; Webber, the first to be detained, had been so certain he was not a suspect that he had asked the cab that brought him to headquarters to wait, since he would "be back in five minutes." And, taken into court the next day, the gamblers maintained their silence. Bald Jack Rose's main contribution to these initial hearings, the newsmen covering the case observed, was to turn up dressed in a "nifty" new suit: The procurer was "a symphony in brown," Swope told his readers, "from his tie to his shoes, save that he wore a pink-striped shirt," and Vallon informed the magistrate he had been "awfully drunk" on the night of the murder and could not remember much about it. Bridgey Webber devoted most of his efforts to intimidating Whitman's witnesses. At least one man, a barber who had heard the shots outside the Metropole and reached the spot in time to identify the gambler, wilted under Webber's baleful gaze and decided that he was no longer sure that it really had been Bridgey he had seen "running like hell" from the Metropole. "Didn't you just tell me in that other room that you saw Webber?" demanded an astonished Whitman. "I—I think I did," the man replied. "I am not sure about it. . . . Judge, I'm under oath, and I'm not sure now." The DA had the witness charged with perjury.

Ultimately it was Shapiro who ended this impasse. Under increasing pressure from the district attorney's men, who by July 25 were threatening to make him a scapegoat for the whole affair, the chauffeur at last made a detailed confession describing the events of the sixteenth. Shapiro's new testimony was far from complete—he still had more sense than to implicate Zelig's gunmen and claimed to have taken no active part in events whatsoever—but it was still enough to condemn the imprisoned gamblers.

"I picked up Rose and Sam Schepps," his statement began,

and drove them back to Webber's. I waited there about twenty-five minutes and was looking out of the corner of my eye when I saw Jack Rose come out of Webber's place. With him were three men. . . . Then Rose came over to where I was and as they got in I noticed that Sam Schepps was one of them and Harry Vallon was the other. The third man I couldn't make out at first because Rose kept him behind the others and held him back to whisper something in his ear. Then, when this fellow put his foot on the step, Rose patted him on the back and said, "Now make good," or something like that.

I then started with my passengers toward the Metropole and as I turned into Forty-third Street I saw Jack Rose in the shadow on the north side of the street. Someone in the car said, "There's Jack now," and one of the others said, "Close your trap, you damn fool."

I stopped along the south side of the street about one hundred feet east of the Metropole entrance. Vallon, Schepps and the third man got out of the car and Vallon told me not to move away. I felt that there was something going to happen, but I didn't know what it was. . . .

I was dozing when I heard the first shot. I had thought this was to be a "beating-up" party, but I realized it had turned to murder. There was nothing for me to do but start the car at once, which I did. The gunmen piled into the car and one of them ordered me to "beat it."

Word of Shapiro's revelations reached the imprisoned gamblers and their lawyers on July 25. The next day, a Friday, was spent in conference. Webber had become suddenly talkative, it emerged, and—hearing of this—the attorneys representing Bald Jack and Harry Vallon "advised their men to throw themselves on Mr. Whitman's mercy."

It seemed only a matter of time before all three confessed. There was still some doubt as to exactly what the prisoners would say, but even a casual reader of the daily papers realized that the DA was really interested in just one thing. Rose's lawyer, for one, saw no harm in giving the waiting throng of newsmen a taste of his client's evidence.

"Everyone knows," the attorney smiled, "that the shadow of the police hangs over this crime."

Becker's position worsened further during the last days of July with the publication of a series of devastating disclosures concerning his income from grafting.

Both the DA's office and the press had been searching for evidence that the lieutenant had been banking illicit payments for several weeks. It was—as most policemen and most lawyers knew—difficult to show that any officer had accepted bribes. Virtually all grafters were paid in cash, often via intermediaries, and took good care to keep no records that could possibly incriminate them. But over the years reformers had found ways of implying what could not be proved. Clubber Williams's career had not survived the revelation that he was the proud owner of a steam yacht and an estate in Connecticut. Lieutenant Becker's Achilles' heel proved to be his new home in the Bronx.

Reporters had little difficulty in pinpointing the property. The house, noted the *World*, sprawled over no fewer than four substantial lots and was considerably larger and more elaborate than its neighbors. It rose three stories and—most incriminating of all, to the *American*'s reporter—included an empty garage. In 1912, as the newspaper observed, no ordinary lieutenant on a salary of $2,250 a year could reasonably have hoped to buy a car.

A few among the charitable and the naïve accepted the lieutenant's hasty explanation that he and his wife had both saved hard for nineteen years to pay for the property—a response that owed much to the example set by Clubber Williams and his mysterious landholdings in Japan. But Becker and his wife had altogether less luck in answering their critics when Whitman began to uncover the details of their bank accounts, beginning with the news that Helen had paid in $3,000 in a single morning at one institution where that sum was the maximum customers were allowed to deposit in a month. A "flood of cash," totaling nearly $50,000, was subsequently tracked to nearly a score of bank accounts and safe-deposit boxes. It was far more money than the Beckers could account for, although some (the lieutenant offered) had been borrowed from his brother, some represented savings set aside from Helen's years of teaching night school, and a good proportion of the rest was cash moved, for no apparent reason, to and fro between accounts that the DA had inadvertently "miscounted."

Over the coming months, Becker's attempts to explain all this suspicious wealth would get considerably more elaborate. Windfalls from dead relatives would figure heavily. But few people, then or later, ever believed that his money had come from anywhere but the brothels and gambling houses of Satan's Circus, and in consequence the policeman lost most of what little sympathy New Yorkers might have felt for him.

The exposure of Becker's clandestine bank accounts was a severe setback for the couple—more serious, in some respects, than the allegation that he had ordered the death of Herman Rosenthal. A criminal's story of a plan to murder another crook was one thing—the policeman, for one, shrugged off those charges as just the sort of behavior one might expect from self-confessed villains. But the exposure of Becker as a grafting cop was another matter altogether. The public found it easy to believe tales of police corruption, and before long, hostile reports of Becker's dubious service with the Strong Arm Squads began to fill the newspapers. That was bad news for the lieutenant, but—more than that—it was also a serious concern to the real powers in the city. Tammany was terrified. With Whitman, a Republican, in the DA's office, the cop-hating Gaynor at City Hall, and recollections of the Lexow hearings still fresh in many people's minds, the last thing Boss Murphy could afford to sanction was another corruption scandal. When Whitman's prisoners started talking, the sachems of Tammany suddenly found themselves as one with the gamblers of Satan's Circus and the senior officers of the NYPD. Their most pressing concern became to deflect Whitman from pursuing his inquiries into their particular domains.

Under normal circumstances, Tammany looked after the police. Preserving corrupt cops from prosecution made sense: It kept embarrassing news out of the press, it guaranteed the loyalty of the men who gathered money for the Hall, and it minimized disruptions to the flow of graft.

There can be little doubt that Becker expected protection. It is scarcely plausible that the lieutenant had been able to extort tens of thousands of dollars from gambling houses with strong political connections without the approval of Tammany—or at least of Big Tim Sullivan. It follows that very large sums—at least half a million dollars, judging from the cash in Becker's bank accounts, had been channeled upward from the lieutenant's collections—sufficient, surely, for him to expect help at such a crucial juncture. And for several days after Rosenthal's murder, it did seem that Becker might walk away from the affair unscathed. He received a visit from State Assemblyman Fitzgerald, a well-known ally of Big Tim's, who told the press that Becker was obviously innocent. Waldo put out a statement declaring that he would not so much as suspend his onetime favorite without "real evidence"—which, the commissioner implied, was not likely to appear. Even William Gaynor, no friend to the police, observed that Herman's statements were scarcely to be trusted. When, on July 18, Becker was summoned to spend half an hour at City Hall, the chief topic of his conversation with the mayor was the policeman's regrettable willingness to meet Rosenthal at the Elks' Club ball; the gambler's murder was barely touched on. "Do not bend a single bit to clamor," Gaynor now instructed Waldo, "and especially to clamor chiefly created by hired press agents and the gamblers with whom you are at war, and those corrupt newspapers which have been all along and are now at the service of gamblers." It is scarcely surprising that when Becker met a gaggle of reporters the next day, he was "swaggering in his manner." The lieutenant, one newsman added, "wore a smile constantly and appeared to take his predicament very lightly."

In truth, however, Becker's position was not so strong as he believed. To begin with, Tammany Hall was no longer the monolith that it had been when the policeman had begun his career. Then Tammany had still controlled not merely the city government and the police but the judiciary as well. Two decades later time and scandal had loosened the Hall's grip on power, and Charles Murphy, its new boss, depended far less on the police for help than had his nineteenth-century predecessors. All this made it less likely that the Hall would come to the rescue of a corrupt policeman, no matter how valuable his services had been.

To make matters worse, Becker badly underestimated Whitman's determination to drag him into the Rosenthal affair. The lieutenant seemed to have expected that the statements of "mere criminals"—no matter how damaging—would not be taken seriously by the DA or the press, and it seemed not to have occurred to him that the sworn depositions of several gamblers, not one, might be enough for Whitman to take action. And while Becker recognized that his adversary would seek to generate political capital from the case, he was taken aback by the speed with which the district attorney rounded up Herman's enemies and contrived to get them talking.

Perhaps the biggest mistake that the policeman made, however, was to depend on Big Tim Sullivan. Becker's faith in Tim's ability to damp things down in Satan's Circus was not unfounded; Sullivan had kept the peace for years, to the benefit of police, politicians, and gamblers alike. Despite his long friendship with Rosenthal, moreover, the Tammany man had nothing to gain by permitting the gambler's murder to become a scandal. But—no doubt quite unknown to Becker, who lacked political connections and had met Big Tim in person only once—by the summer of 1912 the boss's power was nearly gone, his health suddenly in terminal decline. Visitors to Sullivan's headquarters at the Occidental Hotel were left to cool their heels in the bar, casting bored eyes over the famed erotic fresco on the ceiling; Tim was far too ill to see them.*

Late that July—at the very time a fit and healthy Sullivan might have used his influence to see that Herman's murder was swiftly tidied up— Tim passed the point of no return. He spent the last days of the month incapacitated by symptoms that included "bouts of manic depression, delusions of food poisoning, violent hallucinations and threats of suicide." In August he was no better. And in September, soon after attending the funeral of his estranged wife, Sullivan suffered a complete nervous breakdown and was hurried out of town to be confined in a private sanatorium in Yonkers. He was only forty-nine years old, and even his enemies had expected him to rule over the vice district indefinitely. Now he was gone, and with his family in disarray, Mayor Gaynor indifferent, Rhinelander Waldo weak and ineffectual, and Tammany

---

*Sullivan succumbed rapidly to his illness. The symptoms first emerged in April 1912. Shortly after Rosenthal was shot, he had to be confined to his home; six months later he was certified insane. The disease that crippled him was never publicly identified, but members of Tim's own family believed that he was suffering through the last stages of syphilis.

distracted by the looming squabble over the Sullivan legacy, no power in
the city could stop District Attorney Whitman. Any attempt on the part
of Becker's superiors or the Tammany sachems who shared his graft to
offer him protection risked giving the dangerously powerful DA an
excuse to broaden his inquiry. Long before the end of July, rumors began
to sweep along Fourteenth Street. If it would only shut up the DA, the
whisper ran, the politicians planned "to let Becker take the brunt of
things," "to have him 'take the splash,' to 'let him drop.' "

The signs were already there for those who wished to see them. A few
days after the murder, Becker had been stripped of the command of
his Strong Arm Squad and reassigned to a desk at headquarters. The
squad itself was broken up; two-thirds of the policeman's men were
transferred to Dan Costigan's command and the rest did mundane
clerical tasks alongside their former chief. The *Sun*, which maintained
a cozier relationship with Tammany Hall than did most of its rivals,
took to reminding its readers of the identity of the major suspect in
the case, running a panel headlined WHAT BECKER DID YESTERDAY. And
a reporter who called to find the lieutenant closeted with his attorney
noted that the easy smile was gone. Becker, the newsman told his
readers, now had "stern lines in his face, and his manner was nervous."
"I am not going to make any statement whatever," he scowled when
the journalist knocked. "I am not going to say a single thing." His
lawyer hustled the man out of the room.

By now the New York press was scenting blood. Posses of
reporters ambushed Becker on his daily journey to and from the
office. Others combed through yellowing files of clippings to rake up
scandals from his past. Swope—well informed as usual—was the first
to pose awkward questions about the lieutenant's dismal marital history, and when a rumor reached Newspaper Row that Becker had
killed himself, a large pack of journalists hurried to Deputy Commissioner Dougherty's office to get a comment and were disappointed to
see the man himself come down the steps, decidedly alive. "Well,
boys, I have committed suicide, as you can see," the policeman shot
sarcastically as he clattered past them, face set grim.

Becker clearly felt the pressure mounting. Soon after Rosenthal's death he publicly proclaimed his willingness to testify before Whitman's grand jury on police corruption—a decision that would have meant waiving his immunity from prosecution. Refusal to cooperate, Waldo had advised him, would be no different from confessing guilt. The dailies also got wind of Becker's summons to another meeting with his superiors, and when the lieutenant emerged onto the street, he was instantly mobbed by reporters firing questions. Once again Becker brushed his interrogators angrily aside and stalked away, flashbulbs popping all around him. But (noted the *Tribune*'s man) on this occasion he at last lost his temper with the swarm of newsmen trailing him:

> As he left City Hall, photographers followed, taking pictures of his back to the considerable amusement of passers-by. Every few steps, Becker would whirl on them in fury, snarling, "Arrest that man!" to no one in particular. We were reminded of nothing so much as the Red Queen, in *Alice in Wonderland*.

There was some temporary respite on July 22, when Becker received another permanent assignment, this one to an obscure precinct in a corner of the Bronx. His new station house was on Bathgate Avenue, near 177th Street, far enough from most reporters' beats to keep them at arm's length for a while. The locals were not too happy to have such a notorious character billeted on them—a few vocal community leaders protested that the posting was an insult to the borough—but Becker himself was probably happy enough to be away from his tormentors. He was assigned clerical duties once again (it was simply too much trouble to send him anywhere in public) and spent the next week engaged in "roundsman's work," sorting papers at a desk placed conveniently in full view of the precinct captain.

Being absent from headquarters brought problems of its own, of course. Becker was no longer in any position to hear of developments in the Rosenthal affair as they occurred, much less to know what might be going on in Whitman's office. No doubt friends and colleagues on the force kept him informed as best they could. Yet the lieutenant had little option but to follow most events through the pages of the daily press, which continued its blanket coverage unabated into the last week of July.

On the whole, the news was bad. Deputy Police Commissioner Dougherty was now openly discussing the likelihood that Becker would be charged with murder, "smashing his fist down on the desk in front of him," one paper said, to emphasize his point and voicing the opinion that "any farmer sitting under his own apple tree with a straw in his mouth" could see that the lieutenant had a lot to hide. Honest Dan Costigan was popping up before Whitman's grand jury, complaining that Becker had deliberately ruined several of his carefully planned raids.* And William Shapiro's memory of the events of July 16 was still improving day by day. The chauffeur now gave a vivid account of how Harry Vallon had leaped back into his cab after the shooting, brandishing a smoking revolver. Vallon, Shapiro added, had struck him over the head with the gun while ordering him to "step on it."

Whitman still had no firm evidence of Becker's guilt, nonetheless, and the DA wasted no time in using these admissions to pile further pressure onto the imprisoned gamblers. Someone, they were told, would have to stand trial for the Rosenthal shooting, and charges could not be long delayed. The case for their guilt was already strong. But (Whitman added with nicely calculated emphasis), "If they can help the people get the men behind this thing—if one of them can help me assure Becker's punishment and aid justice further—I'd have no hesitation in trying to get them clemency. Why punish the small fry? It's the big fish who should be punished."

The district attorney's message was clear enough. The three gamblers could face the courts themselves. Or they could denounce Lieutenant Becker as the man who had demanded Herman's murder.

---

*On at least one occasion, Costigan testified, he and his men were interrupted in the midst of searching a suspected gambling house when Becker came crashing through a side door minus a warrant—thus neatly invalidating all the evidence that they had gathered. The implication was that the panicking owners of the club had placed an urgent phone call as soon as Costigan appeared, reminding the lieutenant of the protection money they had paid, and Becker had responded by hurrying straight over.

Rose and Vallon were the first to be convinced that their one hope of avoiding trial was to turn in Charley Becker. Their old friend Webber took only a little longer to reach the same conclusion. According to Shapiro's latest statements, the gunmen who had murdered Rosenthal had been marshaled inside Bridgey's poker rooms, a block away from West Forty-third Street, and had stepped out of his front door straight into the waiting Packard taxi—details that, taken together with Webber's mysterious appearance at the Metropole only a few minutes before Rosenthal was killed, were amply sufficient for Whitman to threaten the onetime dognapper with an indictment for murder.

By Sunday, July 28, the three men—grouped, thoughtfully, in cells adjoining one another—had talked the matter through and conferred with their lawyers. Several witnesses would eventually come forward to claim they had heard snatches of the conversation that passed between the gamblers; according to these men, the members of the trio swiftly concluded they had no choice but to go along with the DA. "My God," Webber was reported to have cried, "I can't stand this any longer! Why, they're trying to send me to the chair. Look here, just how bad do they want Becker? What'll they do for me if I give him to them?" To which Bald Jack Rose replied, "I would frame Waldo, the mayor, anybody to get out of here."

That evening Rose, Vallon, and Webber were summoned to the hotel suite Whitman was using as an office. A group of reporters waiting outside were told that the DA planned to subject the men to another round of questioning, but it did not take the newsmen long to divine the way that things were going. At eleven, one of Whitman's aides stuck his head around the door and announced that none of the men would be returning to their cells that night. All three had been granted permission to sleep, under guard, on Whitman's sofas.

The next morning, after breakfast, the deal was done.

Charles and Helen Becker had risen a little earlier than usual that Monday. It was hot again and greasy, the air limp with the threat of an approaching storm, but the policeman did not care. He and his wife were finally ready to move into their new home, and Becker had spent nearly the whole weekend completing all the necessary chores. He had finished work on the interior, hung the shutters, and even put in some work on the garden, where—at least so Helen averred—the lord of Satan's Circus planned to spend his leisure hours cultivating vegetables. Only a single job remained, and that morning Becker ceremonially completed it. At about 7:30 A.M., just before the start of his shift, he called at his property, took out a screwdriver, and carefully affixed the street number, 3239, to the door. An hour later he was back at his desk at the Bronx precinct house, telephoning his wife to say that all was ready for their move.

On Bathgate Avenue, the day eased by. Downtown, though, out of Becker's hearing, things were moving at a sharper pace. By noon the twenty-three men of District Attorney Whitman's grand jury had almost finished their work for the day. The morning had been spent listening to yet more evidence of police corruption—on this occasion details of Becker's raid on Herman Rosenthal—but the testimony had been quickly disposed of and the whisper was that the jurors would be discharged till Tuesday morning. The members of the jury took an early lunch, after which the hoped-for permission to go home came through. The same did not apply to Whitman's men, however, and by 3:00 P.M. the district attorney's offices were frantic with activity. Lawyers darted in and out, bringing in statements and bearing out court papers. The DA sat closeted with Webber's attorney. Soon afterward the lawyer left to report to his client and the imprisoned gamblers were brought back from the cells.

The interrogation that ensued lasted for several hours; later the district attorney would tell a group of reporters that he had battered at the trio relentlessly, "pounding one against the other until they all broke down and said Rosenthal was shot in front of the Metropole by a hired gang because Lieutenant Becker wanted it done." The truth was more calculating and less dramatic. The meeting was long, but it remained thoroughly businesslike and was devoted largely to going through each part of the gamblers' statements until Whitman was sure he knew exactly what each man would say. Soon after supper the DA emerged and the cluster of newsmen who had been waiting for him learned that Sam Paul had just been released from prison and all charges against him had been dropped. Webber, Vallon, and Rose, meanwhile, were to go before the grand jury.

It took some time to summon back the jurymen for this extraordinary session. "Sixteen members are needed to return an indictment," the *World* reminded its readers, and it was not until nearly 7:00 P.M. that the necessary quorum was assembled and the gamblers brought in. Despite the relative lateness of the hour, it was distressingly close inside the courtroom; the storm that had threatened to break all day was gathering, black clouds rolling in from the horizon to seal in the humidity and heat. A group of nearly two dozen reporters, who had been made to wait outside, sprawled about in upright chairs, tugging at loosened collars and easing damp shirts away from sticky skin. Inside the room, though, no one gave much thought to the discomfort. The grand jury sat transfixed by Bald Jack Rose, who had taken the stand ahead of his companions—which was only right, because Rose had the most to tell.

"What he said," one newsman wrote,

shot straight home. His every word was about Becker, and his story was based upon intimate knowledge of the policeman . . . He detailed how Becker, six weeks ago, told him that Herman Rosenthal had lived too long, that Rosenthal had to be put out of the way, and that the man who did the job had nothing to fear because he, Becker, was a power in the Police Department. So Rose went out and spread the word that the strong arm commander said that Rosenthal must be killed. . . .

The four men who pistoled Rosenthal by this arrangement were Whitey Lewis, Lefty Louis, Dago Frank and Gyp the Blood. Rose admits that he rounded them up that night and saw that they were poised for the crime. . . . [He] called Becker up by phone a few minutes after Rosenthal was dead on the sidewalk in front of the Metropole. He told Becker it was a horrible thing. He said that it was more than he expected.

He was frightened clear to his heart and he was afraid to stir without a word of confidence from his master. And Becker said over the telephone while he was making preparations for a hurried trip down to the Tenderloin: "Oh, don't worry. I'll protect you. There won't be much fuss over this. . . . What do you think I am in this department? I can do as I damn well please."

Webber and Vallon, who followed Rose before the grand jury, offered corroboration for parts of Bald Jack's story. Webber admitted that he had supplied $1,000 with which to hire the gunmen—Rose was temporarily short—and confirmed that the four gangsters Rose had named had received as much again when Rosenthal was dead. Vallon added that he had acted as a go-between, carrying messages to and from Bald Jack. He was silent about his presence at the Metropole, and in any case both judge and jury had heard enough. At 8:00 P.M., an indictment was handed down authorizing Becker's immediate arrest.

Perhaps the strangest part of the proceedings was the dread displayed by the three gamblers when they heard that the policeman would soon be joining them in the cells. Webber had "cold fear" imprinted on his face, one reporter wrote, and Vallon also appeared scared. The men, added the reporter from the *Sun*, looked

as if a vast weight had been lifted from their minds, [but they] were nevertheless in desperate fear. It was a terror that was obviously not assumed. There was nothing theatrical about it. They were glad a load was off their souls, but they dreaded what might happen to their bodies.

"For God's sake," said Rose, the hand he held up trembling as if from ague. "Don't send me to [prison] tonight. Maybe you think I'm a fool. But I swear I believe that I'd be killed some way if I went there."

DA Whitman stepped in swiftly. There was no need for the men to be returned to prison, he offered. They could spend one more night sleeping in his office. Four of the New York County detectives assigned to his department were detailed to watch them. Another three set off for the Bronx by train just as the storm broke in full earnest. They reached Bathgate Avenue shortly before 8:30 P.M. and went straight into the station house for Becker. Incongruously enough, the tough street cop was busy cleaning a typewriter when they came for him.

The evening climaxed in appropriately Gothic fashion when Becker arrived at the Criminal Courts Building down on Centre Street. It was after 10:00 P.M., and rain was falling in sheets as the lieutenant was bundled out of the nearest El station and into the sagging monstrosity constructed at such cost to the city by Boss Tweed. By now, long after working hours, the stone interior of the building was deserted, and the ominous rumble of approaching thunder echoed along its shadowed corridors as three detectives propelled their prisoner toward the one court that remained in session. "Every now and then," noted the man from the *New York Times*,

> flashes of lightning threw into painful relief the tense faces and figures of the Grand Jury, assembled in extraordinary session at night for the first time within the memory of the oldest court attendant. . . . As this youthful appearing man in a tan suit approached the bar there was a nervous twitch in the muscles of his face, and the vivid flashes of lightning which now and then electrified the courtroom showed Becker standing strained, nerved to meet whatever might befall him.

The hearing itself took only a minute. Attorneys representing Rose, Webber, and Vallon sat to one side of the room; they "looked seriously pleased with themselves," another reporter noted. Becker said nothing as the indictment for murder was read to him; "a set grin was on his lips," thought Swope of the *World*, "but in his eyes there was the signal of collapse." He left it to his attorney, John Hart, to enter "the normal pleas of not guilty," and the lawyer added a request for time to confer with his client before he was led off to the Tombs prison, which stood next door. "I do not think I have the power to grant that request," replied the judge, but Hart was assured that he would get the chance to talk things through with Becker in his cell that night.

With that, the lieutenant was given into the custody of bailiff Joseph Flaherty, who—as chance would have it—was a former policeman who had served under Becker's command. Flaherty led the way, shuffling out of the courtroom, back along the gloomy corridors and across a low and narrow walkway that led directly from the Criminal Courts to the Tombs. The bridge arched over the main courtyard of the prison, passing over the spot where condemned men had once been executed on the gallows, and it was known, perhaps inevitably, as the Bridge of Sighs. At the far end stood a heavy gate. Flaherty knocked loudly, and with a rattle of bolts and a chink of keys, the door swung open.

Charles Becker stepped inside and was swallowed up in utter darkness.

CHAPTER 9

TOMBS

THE TOMBS PRISON, TO which Becker had been consigned, was one of New York's grimmest landmarks. It was a bleak and crumbling monolith, fashioned entirely of granite, and stood on the site of the old Collect Pond—which, more than a century earlier, had supplied the city with its drinking water. The pond and its surrounding marshes had never been properly drained, and the first prison buildings on the site had been erected on wooden piles crowned by a platform of hemlock logs that promptly subsided under their weight, cracking the foundations, warping the cells, and leaving the lower levels permanently dank and occasionally ankle-deep in muddy water. Decades after its completion, the building still sprang leaks continually and was popularly said to rise and fall with the tide.

The Tombs might have been designed to break its inmates' spirits. It had earned its portentous name because the architect of the first prison to stand there had patterned its forbidding exteriors after an old Egyptian mausoleum. This original Tombs had been pulled down and replaced a few years before Becker arrived there, but many New Yorkers still agreed with James Gordon Bennett's description of the place as "a loathsome and dreary charnel house," and the interiors were as cramped and gloomy as ever. By 1912 the Tombs was used chiefly to detain prisoners on remand; it was supposed to have a capacity of no more than 350 men, but overcrowding was severe and the actual number of inmates was generally at least 2,000. To make matters worse, the cells themselves had no windows and were so narrow that there was barely sufficient room for a man to stand between his iron cot and the wall. There was no running water, no sanitation except for tin pails, very little natural light, and the sole ventilation of small chimney flues that led up to the roof above. In summer, the temperature inside the building soared into the high nineties, and inmates were kept locked up for twenty-three hours a day. Even the Tombs' own doctor conceded that "a man confined in one of these cells invariably suffers an impression of crushing weight closing in from all sides."

There were four floors of cells. As a rule, the handful of convicted prisoners occupied the bottom tier while those awaiting trial on various charges were billeted on the remaining three, with suspected murderers on the second floor, burglars and arsonists above them, and lesser offenders on the fourth and highest level in the smallest cells. Becker, for whatever reason, was assigned Cell 112, on the lowest, dankest tier, and it was there that his wife found him on the morning after his arrest.

Helen Becker had been out shopping when her husband was detained, and first heard of his arraignment from the superintendent of her apartment block on 165th Street. "A little later," she recalled,

> some lawyers came, and a friend of my husband's, a newspaper man, who brought Charley's revolver and his keys that had been taken from him. I tried to find out what my husband had been arrested for, but they said they did not know. They said that the wife of this newspaper man was coming to spend the night with me. I said it was not necessary—I did not know this woman and I preferred to be alone; but they insisted, and finally she came and spent the night. . . . I was not as disturbed as one would think—although I did not sleep well—because I could not believe that Charley was in any serious difficulty. My one idea was to see my husband and find out what had happened.

The next morning, Becker's reporter friend arrived—it was probably Fred Hawley of the *Sun*—and escorted Helen downtown to the

Tombs, where the pair braved the large crowd that had assembled by the prison gates. ("They were there on account of my husband," the policeman's wife confessed, "but the reporter told me they were always there. He wanted to reassure me. I knew nothing about prisons at this time.") After a short wait, Mrs. Becker was escorted down to the lower levels to visit her husband in his cell. She traveled to the prison—a ninety-minute journey from her home—seven times a week from then until the day her husband came to court.

From Monday to Saturday, Helen was permitted to see Becker for nearly two hours a day; the couple spent most of their time talking over the details of the case and preparing for the trial. On Sundays, when visiting was not allowed, Helen would turn up anyway, bringing in Becker's favorite food—usually a roast chicken, homemade bread, and fruit ("Charley is very fond of fruit")—and ask one of the warders to take the meal to him. She spent the rest of her free time tackling a deluge of unwanted mail. "From now on," she would say, "I shared my husband's notoriety. Letters came from all over the country—begging letters, religious letters, crazy letters." Word of Becker's grafting, and of the fortune the policeman was supposed to have banked, only made matters worse. "All sorts of people were ready to help me in my trouble if I would send them a few hundred dollars. One person in Portland, Oregon, wanted $10,000. Another wanted an artificial leg. . . . One day I received a letter from a man who told me to be at Grand Central Station at a certain hour, carrying a roll of paper under my left arm for identification. I must have two hundred dollars ready and hand it over when a young man claimed it. Unless I did this, the letter said threateningly that four men would call upon me. As a matter of fact, a man did call, and, being alarmed and unprotected, I had him arrested; but I dropped the case when he turned out to be a weak-minded youth whose head had been turned by newspaper reports on my great wealth."

As for Lieutenant Becker, his principal complaint was the lack of opportunity for exercise. He was taken out of his cell twice a day and allowed to run up and down the stairs for half an hour. The remainder of his time was spent either working on the case or studying the daily papers with increasing irritation. He was particularly irked by the suggestion that he was not eating well. "I haven't missed a meal," he exploded. "A guilty man would look haggard about now—that's what they're trying to say."

Becker received only two visitors other than his wife. One was a reporter from the *New York Times*, the other Hawley of the *Sun*. They wrote that the policeman looked "more massive than ever" in the confines of his cell and retained "the grip of a bear" when he shook hands. He was publicly confident of an acquittal, the newsmen added. "I have no fear of its not turning out right. . . . The whole thing will be tried, and it won't be tried in the papers, either. There is a lot that the public don't understand. It is largely a political squabble."

Becker's arrest, one newspaper observed, was "the greatest shock the police ever had." The news, added the *New York Times*,

> flashed from police station to police station by a system of underground telegraphy, and Becker's predicament was known throughout the force almost before he had reached the Criminal Court building. Everywhere throughout the department it occasioned consternation. Never before, perhaps, had "the system" faced a situation so fraught with possibilities of trouble to itself.

Almost immediately, journalists noticed changes in the city's cops. "Where on Monday," a reporter wrote, "there had been assertive garrulity was now worried reticence. Smug complacence yielded to restless inactivity. Frown succeeded smile. Full tones made way for whispers."

It scarcely helped that the NYPD had been more or less the last to hear of Becker's arrest and arraignment. District Attorney Whitman had carefully kept the details of his plans from Dougherty and Waldo, more in the hope of mining a rich seam of publicity than because he seriously suspected that Police Headquarters might preempt him or, worse, somehow tip off the lieutenant. Dougherty received the news from Swope sometime after Becker had arrived in court. Waldo was sitting quietly in his club, enjoying a late-night snack, when informed of the same developments. He "immediately had looked ten years older," the reporter who conveyed the news observed.

Badly stung by Whitman's triumph, the police responded by redoubling their efforts to find Jack Zelig's missing gunmen. The four murderers had gone to ground in different parts of the city more or less as soon as word had reached them of the whirlwind of outrage sweeping through Satan's Circus, and though the authorities had plastered large areas of Manhattan with "Wanted" posters describing the men, they remained elusive for some time. Zelig, too, was no longer to be found in his usual haunts and was generally thought to have skipped town. But the Police Department had been far from idle since Rosenthal's murder. One positive effect of the close relationships that had sprung up between gamblers, gangsters, and individual policemen was that the NYPD could call on plenty of contacts in the underworld. The police were short neither of informants nor of leads to the whereabouts of the missing men.

The first member of the quartet of gunmen to be captured was Dago Frank Cirofici, who—being Italian rather than Jewish and not normally a part of Zelig's gang—quite possibly received less protection than was accorded to Gyp, Whitey, and Lefty Louie. Cirofici was picked up at a boarding house on West 134th Street; the arrest came as the result of a tip-off telephoned to Dougherty, and the gangster gave the police no trouble. When the detectives detailed to arrest him entered the room, they found Frank slumped on his bed in a stupor, lying alongside a similarly catatonic girlfriend named Rose Harris. Two bags, packed with traveling clothes, sat in one corner of the room, and an opium pipe, still warm, lay beside the couple; Cirofici had smoked so much of the drug that he was still more or less unconscious when he was bundled into a cell at police headquarters and did not fully revive until the next day. Dougherty came down to question his prisoner anyway, but after putting Frank "on the grill" for two hours, the Deputy Commissioner had to admit that the gunman's responses had been "rambling and incoherent." Harris, who was sufficiently alert to answer questions by this time, insisted that she could give her lover an alibi for the night of the murder.

The capture of Cirofici left the police no closer to locating the remaining gunmen, and someone—probably a friend of Dago Frank's—took swift action to warn potential informants of the dangers of their actions. Four days after the gangster was captured, two Italian thugs walked into the Café Dante, a saloon and gambling den much frequented by Cirofici. The men burst into the card room on the third floor and shot dead the Café's owner, one Giacomo Verella, a former dealer in ostrich feathers. The police soon concluded that the murder had been an act of revenge. Verella, they discovered, employed a retired police detective to manage his bar and was known "to be a friend of many members of the Police Department." He had asked his patrons one too many questions about Frank's likely whereabouts and paid the inevitable price.

Whether or not the police had cultivated Verella as a stool pigeon, they certainly seemed to be extremely well informed about the gunmen's movements. Cirofici had been arrested only a few hours before he had planned to leave the city. Whitey Lewis, the second of the four gangsters to be captured, was actually standing on a rural railway platform, waiting to board a train that would take him west, when he was stopped. The arresting officer was a detective who had been shadowing him for days disguised as a farm laborer.

According to George Dougherty, Lewis's capture was the "logical outcome of a general plan we mapped out within a couple of days of the murder." The police, Dougherty explained, had been watching a boarding house owned by Bridgey Webber's brother in the Catskills and had been able to identify their target as he passed through from a group photograph that the gunmen and their wives and girlfriends had unwisely posed for days before the shooting at the Metropole. As for "Whitey Jack," he had recovered his composure by the time he was hustled into the police station in the nearby town of Kingston. The former pickpocket was shifting a large wad of chewing gum from cheek to cheek and—asked by the desk sergeant if he had ever been arrested before—responded: "I guess yes; a thousand times."

The capture of two of Zelig's gunmen fueled yet further loud headlines in the New York press and gave fresh impetus to a story that might otherwise have vanished from the front pages after Becker's arrest. In the minds of many people in Manhattan, the apprehension of Dago Frank and Whitey Lewis seemed to confirm much of what Whitman had been saying. Some skeptical New Yorkers had publicly doubted that such apparently outlandish characters as Gyp the Blood had any existence outside the fevered minds of the DA and his informants. News of the arrest of Cirofici changed all that, as Viña Delmar well remembered:

> When that extra flooded the streets, the city reacted in stunned surprise. Then there actually was a Dago Frank! The driver hadn't been creating characters to promote himself with Mr. Whitman. Excited discussion was still under way when the newsboys were shouting again. A saloonkeeper . . . was now dead. In his own barroom he had fallen, with eight bullets in his heart.
>
> Few people cared about the saloonkeeper, but the possible significance of the murder disturbed everybody. Had he and the betrayer of Dago Frank been one and the same? If so, who had killed him? Friends of Dago Frank? Or, more chillingly, was this an unemotional, businesslike murder calculated to insure, through terror, the silence of other voices?

It was probably no coincidence that Jack Zelig's closest associates, Gyp the Blood and Lefty Louie, proved to be harder to locate than the other gunmen. The Police Department's intelligence on the final pair of wanted killers was noticeably less complete than the information they had uncovered concerning Lewis and Cirofici, and for well over a month, both the NYPD and Whitman's office wasted a good deal of time checking out worthless leads and false reports of sightings. Louie and Gyp were said to be in the Catskills, in Syracuse, in Worcester, in Boston, and sometimes yet farther afield; at one point Whitman dispatched several expensive Burns detectives to Central America in response to a tip that the pair were touring Panama. Police watched for the men at a fruit store in Methuen, Massachusetts, and at a "trotting meet" in Salem. It was not until September 14, fully two months after Rosenthal's death, that the two were finally located, and when they were, it was in an ordinary-looking Brooklyn apartment where—it transpired—they had been hiding more or less ever since the shooting.

Like their companions in crime, Gyp and Lefty Louie put up little resistance to the police. They "had just seated themselves at table for supper," Herbert Swope was able to inform his readers, "when the door panels cracked and the detectives forced their way into the apartment with drawn revolvers. The little company . . . were taken utterly by surprise. They simply sat staring mutely at their captors. 'Gyp the Blood' found his tongue first. 'Drop the guns!' he cried to the detectives. 'We're not going to start anything.' " The two gunmen, who had been lounging in casual clothes, insisted on changing into suits before they were led away. Gyp, who had mislaid his hat, created such a fuss about it that one of the policemen lent him his for the ride to the station.

As Dougherty explained it, the gangsters had been captured because they could not bear to live without their wives. On several occasions, the police had followed the two women onto the elevated railway, only to lose them when they unexpectedly alighted and jumped into vehicles that had been waiting for them. It had taken a substantial operation, involving numerous cars and motorcycles and the stationing of men at every road and railway exit along the eastern border of the city, to locate the gangsters' hideout.

By now, relations between the police and the DA had reached something of a low. Whitman, perhaps irritated by the failure of his own detectives to find the missing gangsters, publicly accused Waldo's officers of playing games. The police had always known exactly where to find the suspects, he charged. Probably the DA was angry that the four men had not been picked up sooner; he would have had more time to build a case against them if they had. In the end, Whitman had felt unable to wait any longer and, with only Lewis and Cirofici actually in custody, he persuaded a grand jury to indict all four men for murder on August 21.

Whitman's scrupulously laid plans were now coming to fruition. The existing indictments against Becker and Shapiro were renewed at the same time, and—to the surprise of many New Yorkers—Jack Sullivan, the bumptious "King of the Newsboys," found himself charged with conspiracy to murder on the same day; he had previously been held merely as a material witness. There did not seem to be any real evidence that Sullivan had been plotting against Rosenthal, and the case against him would eventually be quietly dropped. For a few days, though, the new indictment loomed large over the case. The one credible reason for charging the newspaper distributor—Becker's supporters howled—was to intimidate a potential witness. Sullivan was, after all, the only one of Whitman's suspects to insist that he knew nothing to suggest that Becker had any involvement in the case. He had declined all offers of a deal, which made him potentially dangerous. The threat of prosecution (so the policeman's lawyers speculated) was intended to keep him out of the Becker camp until after the trial.

Whitman's last public act that August was to put Jack Zelig in front of a grand jury. Zelig had not been seen in New York for more than a month, and there were many who speculated that he would never be found. But on August 15, a man answering to the gangster's description was picked up in Providence, Rhode Island, on the charge of pickpocketing one of the passengers on an electric streetcar. It was Zelig, shorn of his followers and almost all his power, forced to return to his old profession of sneak thief. Several years of inactivity had done little for the old pickpocket's dexterity, however, and Thomas Griffiths—the passenger in question—soon noticed the disappearance of his wallet and $65 in notes. Zelig almost escaped; giving a false name, he was granted bail before the local authorities realized who he was and disappeared after "a man named Goldberg"—whom one might guess was a local lawyer who had received funds by wire from New York—put up his $2,000 bail. But the gangster was recaptured before he could leave town, held over the weekend, and sent back to Manhattan six days after his arrest. He arrived home in New York just in time for the grand jury session that Thursday.

Zelig, who was well known for his nerve, made the best of a bad situation. He turned up at the Criminal Courts Building on August 22 immaculately turned out in a tailored suit, stiff collar, and straw hat, and informed anyone who would listen that he had long planned to honor his obligation to testify and was assuredly not under arrest. He claimed to know nothing whatsoever about the Rosenthal affair and calmly denied any involvement in the gambler's bloody murder.

"Herman Rosenthal was my friend," the gang lord assured a large crowd of reporters. "If I was not in the predicament I am at the present time, I would make it a point to find out who did the killing and break his leg for him." Zelig added that he held Jack Rose, not Becker, to blame for his current predicament; it had been Bald Jack, he thought, whose evidence had resulted in his arrest in June. True, Rose "well knew my friends would kill him" if Zelig was actually convicted,* but wasn't it well known that the bald gambler would "hang his own brother to clear his own skirts"? As for the four gunmen accused of actually shooting Herman: "I know them by sight, and I think they are decent chaps compared with this man Rose." Turning to leave, the gangster added, as a parting shot, "I know [Rose] framed me, and I don't believe that Becker knew anything about the frame up of me. I am under no obligations to any of them." Then he was gone.

District Attorney Whitman spent the next few weeks preparing feverishly for the trial.

He wanted the proceedings to start quickly, while Manhattan was still in a frenzy of excitement over the murder, for that could only help his case. And he wanted his potential jurors to be able to come to court knowing as much as possible about the allegations spilling forth from Rose and his companions. Not many New Yorkers, Whitman knew, felt much sympathy for the police. But many citizens were equally unwilling to believe the evidence of criminals. By publicizing the

---

* "Would avenge you, you mean," Zelig's lawyer hurriedly interjected at this point. "That's what I said, avenge me," replied his client, grinning.

details of Becker's character, his grafting and his brutal ways, the DA hoped to make his witnesses' behavior credible. So, for the best part of a month, Bald Jack was hauled before the grand jury almost daily to recall his version of the Rosenthal affair, while the city's papers filled their pages with news of the lieutenant's secret bank accounts and the dubious record of his Strong Arm Squad. Grand jury testimony was privileged, of course, which meant that Rose's appearances were a useful way of giving evidence that would never be admissible in court—the details of Becker's grafting, for one thing, and Bald Jack's highly colored recollections of his boss, for another. To no one's surprise, a good deal of this material found its way into the press.

The steady drip of damaging testimony was such that some newspapermen eventually challenged the DA about it. Whitman denied that he had actually leaked any of Rose's supposedly confidential testimony. But he also reminded one reporter that there was nothing illegal about a district attorney releasing reports of grand jury testimony. Even more conveniently for Whitman, it *was* illegal for those who had testified to correct any of the statements the DA chose to ascribe to them. Repetition of anything that had been said on the witness stand, it transpired, was a violation of the oath of secrecy administered when evidence was taken—as Dan Costigan discovered when he attempted to correct no fewer than a dozen errors in the statements Whitman had attributed to him in a press release.

Of all the evidence assembled for the prosecution case, Bald Jack Rose's charge against Becker was far and away the most damaging. Having taken the decision to speak out in exchange for Whitman's promise of immunity, the garrulous stool pigeon now seemed to be determined to paint his former boss in the blackest tones imaginable. Bald Jack's thirty-eight-page, handwritten confession (promptly passed to Herbert Swope) consisted principally of a striking portrayal of the sinister conspiracy he insisted had been hatched to do away with Rosenthal. Nothing that Webber or Vallon had to say could match the horror of Rose's allegations—"the mission of the other two," it was said, "being to nod their well-barbered heads vigorously." In addition, Vallon's admitted involvement in the murder and Shapiro's implication that the faro dealer had been one of the shooters, made Whitman anxious not to place undue weight upon his testimony.

According to Rose himself, his decision to disclose every detail of the plot against Rosenthal was in some sense a principled one. Bald Jack seemed anxious to establish that he was not simply a "squealer"; he had decided to talk, he said, only after Becker had repeatedly threatened his life. "While I was in the Tombs," the collector told Swope in one of a series of exclusive interviews that Whitman set up for the *World* man, "Becker sent word to me that my life wouldn't be worth a dime if I started to squeal. Five or six other cops sent me the same message. . . . I waited until absolutely sure that Becker had put me in the bag and was tying it up. Then I hit in self-defense, and I'm going through with the thing."

Rose's claim that he and his fellow prisoners had been threatened in their cells struck many New Yorkers as credible, whether or not the men concerned had any real intention of making good on their threats. Webber, it was said, had been woken one night by an electric torch being flashed in his face, to hear a darkened figure in the shadows hiss, "Now remember, you'll get just what Rosenthal got if you make so much as a crack against men who have been your friends, and you can tell the others that it goes for them, too." Rose, meanwhile, had apparently been accosted in a conference room by an anonymous "messenger" who bent down and whispered in his ear, "The best thing for you to do is kill yourself."

Whatever the truth of the matter, the confession that Rose handed to Whitman on August 6 was as detailed and as compromising as the DA could have hoped. Beginning with a lengthy account of the manner in which he and Becker had first met, Bald Jack went on to describe his work as the lieutenant's graft collector before bringing up the ugly rumors that had begun to float around the East Side after Zelig went to prison for carrying a gun. Terrified that the gang lord would come to the conclusion that it was he who had betrayed him to the police, Rose had rushed to seek advice from Becker. "Well he said if you do Zelig a favor he will do one in return," ran Bald Jack's barely punctuated, poorly spelled confession. "Find out his friends and tell them if they want to save Zelig and themselves that Rosenthal is the man who is stirring up all the trouble in N.Y. and I want him murdered."

According to Rose's account, the gambler could not believe at first that Becker meant it:

I said do you mean you want Zelig's friends to go . . . and threaten him that they will beat him up? why no he said. I want him murdered shot, his throat cut, any way that will take him off the earth. he went further he said if anybody will Murder Rosenthal nothing can happen to them. he would take care of that. and if these men down town don't accept the job tell them that not one of them will be left on my roundups. . . . I will frame every one of them up and send them up the river for carrying concealed weapons.

Of course, the gambler added, "all this [occurred] while I was only thinking of my position the fear of the vengeance of the crowd who . . . were accusing me of Jobbing Zelig." Rose, in short, felt he had no choice but to obey the lieutenant, but he had never met Zelig and had no experience of procuring murder. Instead he had gone to see his friends Vallon and Webber and begged them to help; through them, he had been put in touch with Whitey Lewis and Lefty Louie. Bald Jack had supplied some money in order to get Zelig bailed, and the gangster's followers, in return, had agreed to murder Rosenthal.

There was plenty more to Rose's deposition—Becker, the stool pigeon wrote, had cunningly arranged matters so that the murder would be written off as a dispute among gangsters—but the lasting impression left by Bald Jack's account was of a policeman so consumed by his own importance that he had believed himself invulnerable. "He said if [Rosenthal] only could get croaked that night how lovely everything would be . . . don't worry no harm will come to anyone . . . he said if I saw the squealing _____ I would of liked to take my knife out and cut a piece of his tongue out and hang it on the Times Building as a warning to possible future squealers."

Even after the shooting, Rose explained, the lieutenant had continued to assure him all was well: "I kept getting messages from Becker . . . advising me to sit tight and not worry as he was looking after everything including my family." But "I was sorely troubled and the talks I had with my [attorney] convinced me that I ought to tell all . . . and Vallon and Webber were only anxious to join in and tell all as we realized we were tools and were going to be made the scapegoats."

Bald Jack's lengthy confession was, thus, hugely incriminating—perhaps sufficient in itself, if the gambler was actually believed, to secure Becker's conviction on a charge of conspiracy to murder. But District Attorney Whitman faced one all-but-insuperable problem in permitting Rose, Webber, and Vallon to tell their story on the stand. New York law clearly stated that the evidence of criminals was not admissible as evidence where it concerned events in which the witnesses themselves had been involved. There was clearly every reason why such a provision should exist; without it, any group of crooks might conspire to place the blame for a crime upon some hapless colleague. But Whitman knew he had no chance of prosecuting Becker, let alone of pressuring the lieutenant into betraying "the men higher up," unless he could produce an independent witness—a man with no apparent involvement in the Rosenthal affair—willing and able to corroborate what the three prisoners were saying.

As things turned out, the solution to the DA's problem was Sam Schepps. The rotund and bespectacled "fake jewelry man," a friend of Webber's and sometime "lobbygow"* to Rose, whom chauffeur Shapiro had identified as one of the passengers in the fatal Packard taxi, had fled town soon after the murder—on the advice, it would emerge, of Bald Jack's lawyer. That meant he had not been a party to any of the negotiations entered into by Whitman's trio of gamblers. Just as conveniently, Schepps was picked up, on August 10, in Hot Springs, Arkansas, as Whitman was beginning the tricky process of

---

*A contemporary term, derogatory in tone, used to describe some insignificant factotum of a more important man.

piecing together his case. The fugitive had called in at the local post office to mail a letter, unaware that the postmaster, Fred Johnson, was also a United States deputy marshal with a keen eye for famous faces. Schepps's photograph had been emblazoned across half the papers in the country when it was announced he was wanted for questioning, and Johnson had harbored doubts about the stranger in his town for days. When the arrest was made, the marshal had his prisoner searched and quickly discovered proof that he had indeed found Schepps. Even more intriguingly, the arrested man was carrying a letter from Jack Rose, and the envelope he had brought with him to post contained the lobbygow's response.

Bald Jack's missive was a short note begging Schepps for help. "Dear Sam," the letter began, "I don't know what you have heard or read, but it has got down to the stage where the electric chair stares us in the face." The gambler went on to explain the negotiations he had conducted with the district attorney and swore that he had extracted Whitman's promise that the same guarantees of immunity would be extended to Schepps. "My advice to you is to let me send a representative of the district attorney to bring you here," Rose finished. "This would prevent the police getting you and putting you through a third degree." Schepps, for his part, appeared suspicious that Bald Jack's letter was a trap: "Your letter followed to me and contents noted. All I can say is I am mighty sorry it has turned out this way for you, dear old pal. . . . What you asked of me I considered very carefully and looked at it from all sides, and find I am in very bad regardless of the leniency you say Mr. Whitman holds out for me. That you had a guilty knowledge of the facts before its perpetration is a fact from your confession. So why do you want me to corroborate a few lies[?]" Schepps had, in other words, been dubious as to the wisdom of surrendering, not least because he and his friend had had no chance to agree on a story: "I am willing [to come only if] you will expect me to tell the truth and nothing but the truth, or else to write word for word what you expect of me."

Now that Schepps was in custody, however, circumstances changed. Within hours of the arrest, the plump con man's lawyer was closeted with Whitman in New York, agreeing to what were evidently favorable terms for his client's full cooperation. "DON'T TALK TO ANY PERSON UNTIL YOU REACH NEW YORK AND SEE WHITMAN, WITH WHOM SATISFACTORY ARRANGEMENTS HAVE BEEN MADE IN YOUR BEHALF," the attorney wired to Hot Springs. While Schepps waited for one of the district attorney's staff to come and fetch him, he was detained not in jail but in the town's plush Marquette Hotel, and when the first New York newsmen to reach the resort arrived, they found the man they had come to see relaxing in a nearby steam bath.

To use Schepps as a corroborator, Whitman first needed to dispose of several inconvenient pieces of testimony linking his new witness to Rosenthal. Shapiro's statement that Schepps had traveled with him in the "murder car" was one. Another was Rose's unfortunate confession that he had handed his lobbygow the $1,000 required to secure the four gunmen's services, and that Schepps, in turn, had passed the cash to Gyp the Blood (the fake jewelry man had been popularly referred to as "the murder paymaster" by the Manhattan papers after that). Once Schepps was back in New York City and had signed the papers agreeing to testify in exchange for the usual immunity, both witnesses changed their stories. Bald Jack said his earlier statement had been the result of "too hasty recollection." In fact, he now remembered clearly, he himself had paid off Lefty Louie.

Realizing how vital Schepps was to his case, Whitman left nothing at all to chance. The lobbygow was sent to join Webber, Vallon, and Rose in the cells, where—so Becker's attorneys would allege—all four men were given ample time to talk through the case and align their evidence. The DA himself went down to Hot Springs to take depositions from any potential witnesses to whom Schepps had talked, a maneuver that had the effect of making it difficult for the defense to obtain useful testimony in the resort. And by the time the case was ready to go before a jury, Schepps had been maneuvered into a bizarre but legally imperative position. He was now a "nonaccomplice corroborator": a man who just happened to have been present more or less throughout the planning of Herman's murder but who had not overheard a word of the discussions taking place between Webber,

Rose, and Vallon—not to mention Lieutenant Becker, of course. Yet (or so the district attorney would contend), this accomplished con man had been too naïve to realize at the time what all the whispered conversations meant. Nor had he actually participated in the planning or aided in the commission of the crime.

By the time that Schepps appeared in jail, his privileged status was attracting the envy of his friends and fellow prisoners. Whitman's key witness had not been charged with the capital crime that the three gamblers in the cells had been indicted for—the worst offense logged against him was vagrancy—and had experienced none of the terror that Vallon, Rose, and Webber had felt when they suspected they were facing execution. Schepps, moreover, received a weekly "salary" from Whitman, and—according to one journalist, who saw the correspondence—was permitted to send out to a store on Fifth Avenue for luxuries including "an eiderdown, two feather pillows, a large rug, two folding chairs, and six pairs of white silk socks at $2.50 a pair." When this extravagance became known, the "murder paymaster" acquired a new nickname. Schepps was now "the Beau Brummel of vagrants," a man whose "faultlessly cut clothes of a modish pattern" put even the well-dressed Jack Rose in the shade.

"It's not fair," Webber moaned, according to the *American*. "How come you get the special privileges?"

"That's because you aren't the corroborator. I got pulled in last and got to be the corroborator," said Schepps.

"I wish I'd of been pulled in last. Then I could of been the corroborator," Bridgey sighed.

In truth, none of Whitman's witnesses had much cause for complaint. While Charles Becker languished in his narrow cell and Zelig and his gunmen hid out in their various apartments, farmhouses, and hired rooms, Webber, Vallon, Rose, and Schepps were living rather more comfortably. The gamblers, having successfully persuaded the DA that their fear of retribution was genuine, had been sent not to the dank and depressing Tombs but to the smaller, much more modern West Side Prison, a building up on Fifty-third Street that soon became known to the press as "Whitman's Ritz." They spent most of their time out of their cells and were allowed to play cards, organize athletic contests among themselves, and receive a succession of laundrymen and tailors who combined to ensure that the gamblers remained expansively well dressed. Spurning the ordinary prison fare, the men ordered in their meals from Delmonico's and other fancy restaurants.

Like Becker, the gamblers and their friend Schepps were also permitted visits from their wives. The amenities in the West Side Prison were evidently superior to those in the Tombs, however, for early in August, Bridgey's wife, Pearl Webber, was able to throw a party in the jail. When Becker's lawyer, Hart, got to hear of this, he was nearly apoplectic, sarcastically suggesting to one newspaper reporter that the four witnesses were living the lives of emperors: "All the delicacies of the season make up their repast. Chiropodists are furnished to treat their feet and manicurists to cut and highly polish their fingernails. Tutors are provided to instruct them in the modern classics. American Beauty roses adorn their cells each day."

The advantages enjoyed by Whitman's witnesses were certainly not limited to their superior accommodation. The three gamblers and their associate also enjoyed first-rate representation. James L. Sullivan acted as attorney for Rose and Vallon, and the man who had cannily bundled Sam Schepps out of town was known to have excellent contacts at Tammany Hall. Schepps himself was represented by the equally well-connected Bernard Sandler. Bridgey Webber, however, trumped his companions by securing the services of Max Steuer, a renowned advocate, famous for his modest demeanor and undemonstrative style, who was (the *New York Times* observed) "called by some the greatest criminal lawyer of his times." Steuer (who, oddly, had been quoted in several newspapers to the effect that he would never get involved in the Rosenthal affair) was best known for being Big Tim Sullivan's attorney. He accepted $10,000, in cash, as a retainer from Bridgey's wife.

Charles Becker's advocates were not in Steuer's league. John Hart, who had been the lieutenant's lawyer for several years, was a former assistant in the district attorney's office of no special distinction. He and Becker realized that they needed to bring in someone with a higher profile—not to mention more experience with murder trials—but the two men struggled to find a man prepared to take the case. Hart's first suggestion was that Becker hire his old boss, William Travers Jerome, and there can be little doubt that the former DA would have made a formidable adversary for Whitman. Unfortunately for Becker, however, Jerome refused to take the case unless his client made a clean breast of his grafting. This the policeman would not do—in part, it seems, because he feared a jury would believe almost anything of a man who had confessed to enriching himself from vice and in part because he still held out the hope that he could simply go back to his old job in the event of an acquittal.

The next lawyer to be suggested was Martin Littleton, a stocky genius with "a kind of magic in his language," but Littleton had been Max Schmittberger's attorney and had faced off against Becker in the police trials of 1906. He declined to get involved. In the end, Becker was forced to settle for his third choice: an old-style Tammany lawyer named John McIntyre, whose extensive experience of capital cases (he had been practicing for nearly forty years) was offset by a florid, windy style. It was widely supposed that McIntyre had been the choice of Helen Becker, an Irishwoman herself, and that Helen had been impressed by the attorney's successful defense of two Fenian terrorists, tried in London years earlier for plotting to blow up the Houses of Parliament and with them Queen Victoria. If McIntyre could obtain an acquittal in London on a charge like that—the argument went—he might do equally as well for Becker.

The Tammany man took the case early in August and with it a retainer of some $13,000. Exactly who had paid his fee remained a matter of speculation. There was a strong rumor that Tammany Hall itself had footed the bill, on the strict understanding that no mention would be made in court of Big Tim Sullivan or any other sachem who might or might not be living off the proceeds of Satan's Circus vice, but not a shred of evidence of such a deal ever materialized. Given the rapidity with which the Beckers' secret bank accounts were stripped of their assets at this time, it seems much more likely that Helen Becker paid McIntyre with the proceeds of her husband's grafting.

The remaining members of the defense team scarcely matched McIntyre in experience. Apart from Hart, who stayed on as an assistant counsel, Becker employed two lawyers in their twenties, Lloyd Stryker and Paul Whiteside. Stryker, in particular, would go on to a distinguished career. But in 1912, neither man had any real experience with murder trials, and both had been in private practice for less than three years. With little money available to pay the fees of other assistants, Becker found himself forced to depend heavily on his wife for unpaid legal aid.

Had Helen Becker not existed, one eminent New York reporter noted, "it would have been impossible to invent her." She was too perfect, with her simple clothes, modest demeanor, and unshakeable faith in her husband—"a character" (recalled Viña Delmar, whose mother was one of Helen's most fervent admirers) "so unbelievably pure, courageous, and devoted that her equal had never been met outside the pages of a sentimental novel." Newspapers, particularly the women's pages, lauded Mrs. Becker even as they lined up to condemn her husband, and her popularity rose still further when it became known that—after seven years of marriage and at the age of thirty-eight—this delicate wisp of a woman was expecting her first child. "The fascinating thing about Mrs. Becker was that she had not been created by a lawyer, who hoped to soften public attitudes toward her husband," Delmar thought. "Mrs. Becker was just naturally so saintly that one could only marvel. . . . She had chosen to teach children crippled in mind or body. She had systemized her life so that marketing, cooking and house cleaning were all capably managed without stealing time from her husband, her classroom, or her never-ending search for ways to improve the future of unfortunate children."

Fortunately for Helen, her pregnancy and her prior service qualified her for a full year's leave of absence from those pupils, which she immediately dedicated to helping with the case. She began by carrying messages from her husband to McIntyre, progressed to spending long nights alone working through piles of legal documents, and before long was making her own attempts to locate new witnesses. Small wonder that what impressed Viña Delmar most

> was Mrs. Becker's present course of action, her gallant search for what she believed to be a hidden truth sufficiently powerful to free her husband. . . . This quiet, respectable girl had taken to walking the streets of the Times Square district after midnight, seeking out people who might be in possession of useful information. It was reported that she would smile shyly at a cab driver, a doorman, or a newspaper vender and say, "I'm Helen Becker. Can you help me? Is there something you know which you have not told? Or have you heard of someone whose silence is working against my husband?"

Of course, not everyone believed in Mrs. Becker's utter goodness even then, not when it emerged that—on the day after her husband's arrest—she had set out for the commercial district armed with a bag full of bank books and had meticulously consolidated more than $18,000 of the couple's tainted savings into a single, readily accessible, account. But no one who knew Helen doubted that she was the sort of woman any man would want as his wife, were he facing the possibility of execution. "New York in 1912," Delmar pondered, looking back, "was no gentler than it is today, nor was it more perceptive. Few knew that they were facing a woman indomitable enough to try anything, intelligent enough to know there is self-forgiveness for everything except inaction."

Thanks at least in part to Helen's efforts, Charles Becker continued to hope for an acquittal as August shaded to September. It was still rare, after all, for any New York policeman to be convicted in a court of law, and lawyer McIntyre assured him that Whitman's case was far from watertight in some respects. Even the DA had to admit that Becker did not know Jack Zelig and had never once set eyes on the four gunmen. McIntyre also expected to demolish Whitman's central argument in court. The notion that a police officer might have wanted

Herman Rosenthal dead was one thing, the Tammany attorney said, but the idea that the shooting was a case of murder by proxy, twice removed, was surely considerably less plausible. Becker seemed reassured. "They have no one to testify against us but criminals," a fellow prisoner heard him tell one visitor in the Tombs. "No jury on earth is going to believe them."

Becker would have been a good deal less optimistic had he known the lengths to which District Attorney Whitman was going to obtain a conviction. Aware, as any good lawyer should be, of the flaws in his own case, the DA had spent the last week of August and early September working hard behind the scenes to tip the scales of justice in his favor. First, he appointed Assistant District Attorney Frank Moss to help prosecute Becker; the bearded, pious Moss had huge experience of trying cases of police corruption dating back to his days as a junior counsel on the Lexow Committee of 1894. Next, Whitman nudged Justice John Goff, another veteran of the Lexow investigation, into launching a judicial inquiry into the apocryphal story that the police had found letters from Charles Becker on each of the arrested gunmen. He also approved, although he did not instigate, the creation of yet another municipal investigation into police corruption. The Committee to Investigate Police Graft—brainchild of a Republican alderman by the name of Henry Curran—began hearing evidence from a long parade of witnesses that August.

Little came of either Goff's hearings or the Curran committee, and Goff eventually concluded that the rumored Becker letters did not actually exist. But the twin investigations added greatly to the clamor in New York that summer, and, by September, no fewer than five separate inquiries into police corruption were running in the city. Goff's, Curran's, and Whitman's own grand jury hearings attracted most of the attention, but Mayor Gaynor had formed a special committee of his own, while a group of "concerned citizens," meeting on August 12, had voted to fund their own private inquiry into the misdeeds of the police. This flurry of activity suited the district attorney perfectly. It would have been a brave New Yorker who insisted, in the weeks leading up to Becker's trial, that there was nothing wrong with the city's police.

Had Whitman confined himself solely to stoking up public opinion against the police, he would have done Charles Becker's prospects a good deal of harm. As it was, the DA still had one more ace to play. In normal circumstances, the lieutenant would have been tried late that coming autumn in New York's Court of General Sessions. But in the third week of August, Whitman went to see John Dix, the Governor of New York State, and persuaded him to transfer all the cases arising out of Rosenthal's murder—including the Becker prosecution and the separate trial planned for the four gunmen—to the State Supreme Court of New York County. This had the effect of removing the lieutenant from the purview of the General Sessions judges, whom Whitman felt were lenient and unreliable. It also placed Becker under the jurisdiction of none other than Justice Goff.

There could scarcely have been a more ominous choice. Goff—cold-hearted, humorless, and so short as to appear stunted—had made his name two decades earlier exposing Clubber Williams and Inspector Byrnes, and nothing that had happened since had revised his low opinion of the police. By now living on a farm upstate, where he kept rare breeds of heron, he was a confirmed cop-hater, who had always taken considerable delight in persecuting corrupt officers. As a Supreme Court judge, he built a fearsome reputation for indulging what one of Becker's lawyers termed "the most odious vice which is incident to human nature, a delight in misery merely as misery." Goff was (in the opinion of Newman Levy, an attorney who played no part in the Rosenthal affair) "the cruelest, most sadistic judge we have had in New York this century."

The judge's dislike of the police was bad enough. Even more alarming, from Becker's point of view, were the close ties he had built to Whitman's office. Goff was an old colleague of Frank Moss—the two men had worked together for Dr. Parkhurst's Society for the Suppression of Crime and then for the Lexow Committee—and knew the DA himself well enough to invite Whitman to the farm upstate; the pair spent the time talking over the issue of police corruption and, by Whitman's own admission, "ironing out a few kinks in the Becker case" as well. There were many in New York's legal community who felt that the judge should disbar himself from Becker's trial. Goff, naturally, disagreed. The case, he ruled, would go ahead as planned.

Well, almost as planned. Whitman's final maneuver, soon after Goff's appointment, was to prevail upon the judge to bring Becker's trial date sharply forward, to September 12—less than two months after Rosenthal's death and only a week after the lieutenant was formally arraigned for murder. This, one reporter observed, gave the defense team "probably the shortest allotment of time in history for the preparation of a major criminal case," and McIntyre was predictably outraged. He hurried before Goff, pleading that his preparations for the trial were not complete and pointing out that several hundred prisoners arraigned months earlier than his client were still awaiting trial. Becker, the Tammany man added, could not hope to get a fair hearing "in the midst of clamor and hysteria," and while public opinion was being prejudiced with "diabolical and infamous lies." Goff threw out the petition, and it was only by scrambling to obtain a hearing before a second Supreme Court justice that McIntyre eventually succeeded in obtaining a postponement. It was no more than a partial victory, though. Thanks to the DA's maneuverings, Becker's trial would still get underway disconcertingly quickly. Proceedings were now scheduled to commence on October 7, 1912.

Whitman and McIntyre both completed their preparations for the hearings early in October.

The district attorney's case was relatively straightforward. Whitman would rely on his collection of minor gamblers and lowlifes to implicate Becker in the planning of Rosenthal's murder. Jack Rose would be the prosecution's most important witness; his testimony, Whitman hoped, would persuade the jurors that there had been a conspiracy to end Herman's life and that the police lieutenant had led it. To do this, Rose would have to explain not only how the scheme was conceived, but also how and where the plans were laid. He would describe meetings between Becker and the gamblers at which the murder was discussed, and detail the manner in which the assassins themselves had been recruited and paid. Webber and Vallon—the DA planned—would back up Rose, and Schepps would corroborate the story.

John McIntyre, meanwhile, was in a far weaker position than the DA. The old Tammany advocate knew it would be hard to convince a jury that his client had played no part in the conspiracy to murder Rosenthal, if only on the general principle that it is notoriously difficult to prove a negative. Securing Becker an acquittal, moreover, meant surmounting two nearly insuperable obstacles. First the defense would have to refute the prepared statements of Jack Rose— no easy matter, when the gambler's recollection of the dates and times required to plan a point-by-point defense remained conveniently vague. Then McIntyre and his team would have to persuade the court that Becker was a man of integrity and honor, incapable of ordering Herman's death.

In this respect, the attorney's task was rendered all but impossible by his client's history of grafting. Jerome had been right about one thing: failure to make a clean breast of the corruption issue fatally hamstrung Becker's case, not least because it made it virtually impossible for the lieutenant to testify in his own defense. The second Becker was under oath, McIntyre realized, Whitman would expose him as a criminal. Evidence of his corruption and his secret bank accounts would all become admissible. And no jury was likely to believe that a man banking $40,000 a year or more from vice—twenty times his annual salary—was incapable of murder. Innocent or guilty, Charles Becker risked conviction on a capital charge because he was a grafter.

Soon there was only a week to go before the opening of the trial. Then six days, five days, four. The papers filled with talk of the tactics likely to be adopted by the prosecution and defense. Most newspapermen and the majority of ordinary New Yorkers, it seems safe to say, believed Becker to be guilty, although a good proportion of their number also guessed that he would somehow be acquitted—as policemen, in their city, mostly were. In Brooklyn, Viña Delmar's family was split on the issue; the girl's father was convinced Becker was guilty, her mother just as certain he was innocent.

There was the usual idle speculation regarding surprise witnesses. Whitman was known to have sent a man all the way to London to fetch back Thomas Coupe, the Elks' Club clerk who had watched the Packard taxi flee the Metropole; perhaps he knew something vital and incriminating.* As for the defense, Becker had prevailed upon his old friend Bat Masterson to catch a train to Arkansas and take depositions there to undermine Sam Schepps.

The greatest mystery of all was Zelig. Details of the gangster's testimony to the grand jury six weeks earlier had still not been released, heightening uncertainty as to exactly what the man might say if and when he came before the court. Lawyers for both sides announced that Zelig would appear for them. According to Whitman, he was planned to be "the principal witness for the state"; the gangster, Swope heard,

> would have testified that Rose and Vallon came to him several times, saying that Becker wanted Herman Rosenthal removed and asking him to provide the necessary gunmen. Zelig would not have admitted he did furnish the men, but his testimony concerning what Rose and Vallon told him would have been a strong and substantial corroboration of Rose's confession.

According to McIntyre, however, this was nonsense. Why had Zelig not been subpoenaed by the DA, and perhaps jailed to prevent another flight, if his testimony was so vital? "The fact is that Zelig had

---

*Or perhaps not. According to the City Hall reporter Andy Logan, the DA's man and the desk clerk "were discovered some time later at London's luxurious Savoy Hotel where they had been living for several weeks while they labored, more or less arduously, over the terms on which Coupe would agree to return. Eventually the desk clerk accepted a check for five hundred dollars and a round-trip first-class ticket good on any Cunard liner. The two men would arrive back in New York too late for Becker's trial but in time for that of the four gunmen. . . . In the end [Coupe] was never called to testify in either, and he eventually used the other half of his ticket to go back to Liverpool, where he reportedly invested his five hundred dollar payoff in a thriving pub."

been subpoenaed as a witness for the defense . . . to refute statements by Rose that Becker had requested Zelig to furnish the gunmen," the old attorney said.

As things turned out, the thorny issue of the gangster's loyalties would not be put to the test. Shortly after eight on the evening of October 5, not much more than a day before the lieutenant's trial was scheduled to begin, Zelig was sitting at his usual table at Segal's International Café on Second Avenue when the telephone rang. The caller was a woman the gangster knew, a manicurist who ran a salon a few blocks to the north. Probably Zelig had a relationship of some sort with her; in any event, she asked him to call at her apartment. Joking about the girl's request with several of his friends, Zelig left the café and hopped on board a streetcar heading up Second Avenue. He found a seat toward the front of the carriage, alongside a right-hand window.

As the trolley rattled north, the gangster was too preoccupied to realize that he was being followed. The moment he had emerged from the International Café, a small-time crook by the name of "Red Phil" Davidson had darted from a nearby doorway and run after his streetcar, catching it as it slowed and leaping onto the running board. Clinging tightly to the outside of the carriage as it hurried along, Davidson edged forward until he was only a foot or two from Zelig's seat. He then drew a .38 Smith & Wesson from his pocket, placed the barrel of the gun behind the gangster's right ear, and fired. Zelig slumped forward, bloody and dying, while Red Phil jumped down and fled in the confusion. As he hurried along Fourteenth Street, however, the assassin was spotted by a patrolling policeman and arrested.

Zelig's body was taken to a nearby morgue. The contents of his pockets proved intriguing. They included four letters, heavily blood-stained, from the imprisoned gunmen, assuring their leader that they were doing well in prison, and a highly incriminating collection of papers relating to the Becker case. One was an "advertizing contract" signed by Libby and Shapiro, stipulating that Zelig would be paid $100 a month from the proceeds of their taxi business. Another scrap of paper listed the home address of a lieutenant of police, and two others the full details of a pair of witnesses to the shooting at the Metropole—just the sort of information that a man who wished to influence the outcome of a trial might need. One thing that wasn't found during the search was the $500 in cash that the gangster had been handed as he left the International Café; Zelig's money, as was usual in cases of this sort, was almost certainly stolen by the police.

News of the gangster's shooting broke within a few minutes of the murder and, the *New York Times* reported, "staggered the District Attorney as a physical blow might have done. He threw up his hands and exclaimed: 'My God, what next? I don't know what to do.' " Whitman, the paper added, had been warned only the previous day by Bald Jack Rose that "Zelig will never live to see the trial start. Watch. He'll be the next one they get." The *World* and other Manhattan dailies, meanwhile, rushed out extras to hullabaloo the murder. Second Avenue "was in uproar" when word of the attack came through.

Most of the talk, of course, concerned the motive for the shooting. Red Phil's wife said that he had drunk heavily the previous night and seemed "highly excited" in the morning; there were many who felt this meant that he had planned the killing. Some theorized that Davidson had been acting under orders from the Jack Sirocco crowd, who saw the run-up to the Becker trial as the perfect moment to revenge themselves on Zelig without attracting much suspicion. Most, though—given the portentous timing of the shooting—took the view that Zelig had actually been killed to stop him from telling what he knew about the Rosenthal affair. Zelig, in this interpretation of events, had joined Herman Rosenthal as a victim of Lieutenant Becker's ruthlessness, and suspicions that Davidson had been "put up to the job" hardened considerably when it was discovered that the gun he had used to kill his victim was a police-issue revolver.*

---

*How this weapon found its way from the NYPD to Davidson was never properly established. Its former owner, Patrolman Christopher Maher, claimed to have left it accidentally in a saloon a year and a half earlier. The bartender, traced and questioned, swore he had returned the missing pistol to its owner; and a pawnbroker from Jersey City came forward to admit that he had sold the gun to the assassin. The pawnbroker did not disclose, however, how the gun came to be in his possession.

Manhandled to the nearest station house, the killer himself was adamant that the murder had had nothing to do with the Becker case; Zelig had cheated him out of $400, he explained. But it did not take detectives long to discover that none of Red Phil's acquaintances believed a word of this story; the idea that a lowlife such as Davidson—a pimp with a sideline in poisoning horses—had ever had so much money to his name was laughable, they said. In later statements, the killer changed his story and claimed that Zelig had blackjacked him the day before and stolen a mere $18, but even this tale was disputed. According to several East Siders who spoke to the press, Red Phil and his victim had fought when Davidson suggested Zelig was "a stool pigeon for Becker." The police—publicly at least—insisted that the shooting was no more than "a private and personal matter," the result of a dispute between criminals, and this was the line taken by the Manhattan press.

The mystery of Jack Zelig's death was never properly resolved. Red Phil, tried for the killing, pleaded guilty and so avoided giving any evidence that might have offered clues as to his motive. He was rewarded with conviction on a charge of second-degree murder and released after serving just twelve years. As for Zelig himself, the gangster got a full-blown East Side funeral, "with 40 carriages of mourners" and a crowd supposedly 10,000 strong milling outside his apartment. He left a wife and son and little money, a reputation as the great protector of the Jewish quarter, and a considerable question mark over his true role in the Becker-Rosenthal affair.

"Jack Zelig," detective Abe Shoenfeld wrote, in what amounted to a eulogy,

> is as dead as a doornail. Men before him . . . who had been the leaders of so-called gangs were as pygmies compared to a giant. If they were to stand alongside of Zelig they would consider it an honor.
>
> This man cleared the East side dance halls and academies of Italian pimps. . . . He cleared the East side of Italians who were wont to hold up stuss houses, and legitimate business

places. He cleared the East side of Italians who could be seen walking through the streets with Jewish girls—whom they were working into the business of prostitution. He has prevented more holdups and things of a similar nature, in his career than one thousand policemen. . . . He died as he lived [and] while his friends are sorry he was killed by one of his own race, they rejoice that he was not killed by an Italian.

As the thousands of mourners wound their way back from Zelig's interment in Brooklyn, the newsmen assigned to cover events for their papers hurried off to file their stories. It was midafternoon on October 7, which meant there was ample time for those working for the morning titles to file reams of copy. And on any other Monday, a funeral such as Zelig's would have received extensive coverage in the press.

On this day, though, a far bigger story was brewing in New York—one so big that the gangster's funeral was thought worth no more than a paragraph or two. On the far side of the East River, in the Criminal Courts Building, the trial of Police Lieutenant Becker was getting under way.

CHAPTER 10

FIVE MINUTES TO MIDNIGHT

THE JURY GATHERED IN the courtroom leaned forward slightly as District Attorney Whitman rose to deliver his opening statement. "The murder of Herman Rosenthal," the DA began, "was the most cunning and atrocious of any time and any country. . . . We are going to claim that the real murderer, the most desperate criminal of them all, was a cool, calculating, grafting police officer." With this, Whitman gestured to the bulky figure sitting in the dock. Lieutenant Becker, who was wearing an ill-fitting dark gray suit that clung damply to him in the Indian-summer heat, did not return his gaze.

Judge Goff's sweltering courtroom occupied part of the first floor of the same Criminal Courts Building, just in front of City Hall, where Becker had been arraigned. By the early autumn of 1912, the shoddy workmanship that had gone into the structure was plain for all to see; the external walls had sagged and buckled, and there was talk of condemning the courthouse once and for all. "It is," wrote the lawyer Arthur Train,

> one of the gloomiest structures in the world. . . . Tier on tier it rises above a huge central rotunda, rimmed with dim mezzanines and corridors, and crowned by a glass roof encrusted with soot, through which filters a soiled and viscous light. The air is rancid with garlic, stale cigar smoke, sweat and the odor of the prisoners' lunch. The corridors swarm with Negroes, Italians, blue-bloused Chinese, black-bearded

rabbis, policemen, shyster lawyers and their runners, and politicians, big and little.

Goff's courtroom had seen many famous trials. Those with long memories recalled that it was the same one in which a captivating showgirl named Nan Patterson had been acquitted for the murder of her wealthy lover, a much older man who had (the girl successfully averred) committed suicide by shooting himself in the back while the couple was sequestered in a hansom cab. But the Becker case was something else entirely. The oldest New Yorker could scarcely remember a prosecution like it. It was "the trial of the century," several newspapers suggested, and public interest was such that accounts of the evidence occupied the first, second, and third—and sometimes fourth and fifth—pages of every Manhattan daily for the duration of the proceedings. Nor was interest in the case confined to New York. The Becker case featured as prominently in virtually every American newspaper, large and small, and in most of those published in London and Paris, too.

The proceedings got under way promptly at 1:00 P.M. on October 7. Becker had spent the morning discussing the case with a guard from the Tombs and taking an active part in a final pretrial conference with his lawyers. The principal topic of conversation was undoubtedly the best way to handle the selection of the jury. The lieutenant had definite views on the sorts of jurors who would offer him the best chance of acquittal: He wanted married men, preferably blue-eyed and tall. Married, because he wanted the jury to reflect on the enormous consequences a guilty verdict would have for Helen and her unborn child; blue-eyed because "blue-eyed men are the most intelligent"; and tall because, as McIntyre explained, "Becker, as a big man, didn't want to run the risk of entrusting his fate to a little man who might have a grudge against all six-footers."

These stipulations slowed the process of jury selection considerably, and so did the long list of questions Becker's attorneys insisted on putting to each potential juror. Some were sensible and obvious—McIntyre asked every candidate if he was related to any member of the prosecution team or had a grudge against the police. Others were more revealing. Each man, when he stepped forward, was interrogated as to whether he had met Inspector Schmittberger. McIntyre also wanted to know if he was prepared to convict on the testimony of accomplices. Whitman's oddest challenge, meanwhile, was to an apparently ordinary businessman who informed the court that he had been out of the country from mid-July until the beginning of September. When the potential juror admitted that he had not read a single word of newspaper coverage about the case, the DA stepped briskly forward and had the man ejected from the panel.

With so many questions to ask, and so much at stake, the selection of the Becker jury took far longer than usual. At the DA's request, a special "blue ribbon" panel, 250 strong and made up of well-educated jurors, had been assembled for the case. Two-thirds were automatically disqualified when they confessed that they had already made up their minds about the case; this number doubtless included many who simply did not relish deciding a case involving gangsters and powerful policemen. The remaining candidates were weeded out more slowly. After two full days of questioning, only eight jurors had been seated, and McIntyre had used all but a handful of the thirty peremptory challenges he was permitted. A further hundred prospective jurors had to be assembled, and the twelfth and final member of the panel was not seated until early on the fourth day of the trial.

It is, to say the least, debatable whether the pains McIntyre took over the selection of the jury were justified. They certainly enraged Judge Goff, who had long possessed a reputation for being "willing to sacrifice almost any legal nicety to get proceedings over and done with." Goff had canceled a planned holiday to take the case and made it clear early in the proceedings that he wanted the entire hearing over and done with in a maximum of two weeks—an astonishingly short time for a case of such importance. It would (as the judge himself observed) set a new speed record for a major murder trial. With almost a quarter of the available time already gone, Goff ordered the court into day and night sessions, a decision that meant proceedings dragging on well into the evening, sometimes as late as 11:00 P.M.

The long sessions exhausted jurors and attorneys alike and made it harder for the men in the jury box to focus on the facts. To make matters worse, whenever McIntyre or one of Becker's other attorneys dwelled on a piece of evidence or strove to hammer home an advantage, their attempts to create an effect would be interrupted by Goff's urgings from the bench that they should "go along," "get along," that "time is too precious."

Late nights and long hours were not the only problems confronting Becker and his lawyers. Conditions inside the courtroom were thoroughly uncomfortable. The case had attracted so much attention that every one of the two hundred seats that could be crammed inside was filled, and overcrowding was exacerbated by the inclemently hot autumn weather. As temperatures inside the room rose into the high seventies, a handful of electric fans were brought in to help swirl the muggy air, but several of the jurors complained that they were having difficulty hearing testimony over the whirring of the blades. Goff had the fans turned off and, when the sounds of passing horses and roller-skating children drifting in from the busy street outside proved equally distracting, ordered all the windows sealed as well. Before long, everyone in his court was sweating and swiping at the lifeless air with court documents or newspapers. And as the case proceeded under its stifling blanket of humidity, Goff added one further refinement. "Have the shades drawn low," the judge hissed in his characteristic thin whisper. "There is not enough gloom in this courtroom."

The character of Justice Goff loomed large over the proceedings from the start. The judge glared down from the dais at one end of the room, a martinet who reveled in his power over a one-room kingdom. The sheer force of his personality lent him considerable presence. "Upon the bench," recalled Lloyd Stryker, one of Becker's junior attorneys, "sat an old man with white hair and piercing, cold, blue eyes. A superficial glance might have given the impression of quiet kindliness and serene benignity. Some said that he resembled a figure in a stained-glass window, yet how mistaken and how tragic an allusion this was. . . . He had a cold heart and a sadistic joy in suffering.

From his face the mask of benignity was soon laid aside, and as I gazed up at the bench, I felt like some four-footed denizen of the jungle that suddenly stares into the cold visage of a python."

From the perspective of those who encountered him in court, Goff's principal attributes were a hair-trigger temper and an invincible sense of his own rightness. With the possible exception of Whitman, all the attorneys in the room were terrified of the judge's snappish flares of irritation and unwillingness to tolerate the least hint of dissent. "That saintlike son of a bitch," State Assemblyman Abraham Levy once called him, while a City Hall reporter recalled that "distinguished members of the bar, at the height of their careers, confessed to waking up in their beds in a cold sweat, having heard in nightmares the sound of that low, sibilant voice saying, 'Buzz, buzz, buzz, buzz, *guilty*!'—a verdict he pronounced, it seemed to them, with joy."

Strangely for a man with such an awesome reputation, Goff was poorly qualified to be a judge and possessed at best a shaky grasp of legal technicalities. An Irish immigrant who had first arrived in the country as a child in the wake of the terrible famine that had struck his homeland during the 1840s, he had been forced to leave school at an early age in order to help provide for his family. Though Goff did later take night classes at Cooper Union, the celebrated public college in downtown New York, he remained more or less self-taught and never obtained any formal degree. Even the judge's politely worded entry in the *Dictionary of American Biography* confesses that "he could never be described as a scholar" and "was not profoundly learned in the law." Goff's real talent, his partisans observed, was as an "uncanny prestidigitator": a cunning manipulator of procedure who had a thorough understanding of human nature and rarely bothered with the legal niceties that hamstrung less bullheaded men.

From the first day of the trial, Goff orchestrated the proceedings to suit himself. A publicity fiend who adored to see his name in print, the judge barred the general public from his court in order to increase the space allocated to reporters. Testimony dragged on for hours at a stretch, sometimes without breaks for lunch or dinner. The recesses that were granted were short in any case. "A sufferer from ulcers, Goff made do with a bowl of milk and crackers and a swig of Irish whiskey at mealtimes," one reporter wrote, "and saw no reason to make allowances for others whose appetites were stronger than his own." Fifteen minutes for lunch and a slightly longer break at suppertime were typical throughout the trial.

In person Goff was tall, quiet, darting, and mercurial, and it quickly became clear to most observers that Becker's choice of attorney had been a mistake. John McIntyre—florid, corpulent, and prolix—irked the judge intensely. Oddly enough, the two men shared nearly identical backgrounds; both were Irish, and both had supported revolutionary Fenian independence movements in their youth. But there the similarities ended, and McIntyre's overwrought interjections soon began to fray Goff's famously short temper. On only the second day of the trial, when the defense attorney protested one too many of the judge's rulings,* Goff turned on McIntyre in fury and warned him that "the interruptions which have occurred may have exceeded the bounds of propriety." If McIntyre persisted with his objections, the judge snarled, he would have him arrested and ejected from his court. After that exchange, Becker's relatives and friends were not the only ones to feel that Goff displayed a heavy bias against the defense.

With jury selection at an end, Charles Becker prepared carefully for his day in court. Wisely deciding to present his most serious and sober side to the twelve jurors, he entered the room at McIntyre's left hand, looking almost scholarly with a small pair of pince-nez glasses perched on the bridge of his nose. The policeman had dressed entirely in black—even, the *Sun* noted,

> to the four-in-hand scarf worn in the low collar that exposed his full, muscular neck . . . He approached the railing in with long strides, throwing glances this way and that over the

---

* "Mr McIntyre," the *New York Sun* observed of the passage of the trial that preceded this exchange, "was many times over-ruled. He kept the stenographer extra busy entering exceptions to the Justice's decisions."

crowd. His glances found the person that he sought, his wife, who sat well forward. He smiled slightly, nodded just percepti- bly, and passed on as she waved smilingly.

The next time Becker rose to his feet it was to enter a formal plea of not guilty to the charge of murder, and the rest of the press corps at last had the opportunity to take a good look at the man they'd been writing about in so much detail for so long. New York newspapermen generally disliked and distrusted the police, and many of the reporters assigned to cover the trial were distinctly unimpressed by the big lieu- tenant's presence. "The personality of Becker is not a pleasing one," the man from the *American* observed.

> The defendant is powerful of physique, his heavy body topped by a bullet-like head. There is no hint of the finer things in life in his make-up. His hands are hairy, sinewy; his black hair has not a touch of gray in it. His large nose . . . reveals to the stu- dent of physiognomy the fact that arrogance and relentless pursuit of any object are the strongest features of his being. Charles Becker is steeped in the memory of the power that was his. His gaze is brilliant, sardonic, menacing. I am very glad that someone dear to me will not sit on that jury and hold the life of Charles Becker in his hands.

With Becker's plea recorded, Whitman rose to deliver his opening statement. Goff, meanwhile, seemed more preoccupied by the activi- ties of Becker's wife, who took a chair inside the rail leading to the judge's chambers that placed her directly opposite the jury. Helen was by now visibly pregnant and looked—one smitten newspaperman reported—"small, charmingly feminine, and cheery" in her beaver hat and a blue silk suit that several observers pointedly remarked looked rather too expensive for a mere policeman's wife. She sat there almost motionless throughout the DA's hourlong address, gazing beseech- ingly at each juryman in turn. Goff evidently considered this an attempt to influence proceedings, for when Whitman sat down, he ordered Mrs. Becker over to the far side of the room, a few seats along from the jury benches, where the members of the panel could not see her. "That," she remembered a few months later, was "the one day I thought I should lose my strength and sink to the floor . . . I had to walk across the room with every one staring at me. I almost fainted."

The opening stages of the prosecution case were not dramatic. Whitman spent a little time outlining events outside the Metropole, calling a series of witnesses whom McIntyre did not bother to cross-examine. Patrolman Brady and Detective File described hearing shots and finding Rosenthal lying on the pavement, dead; a police surgeon and a doctor detailed the gambler's wounds. The next two witnesses—Jacob Hecht, a waiter at the Metropole, and Louis Krause, another waiter who had been outside the hotel when Rosenthal emerged—described the murderers. Hecht had seen one man raising a pistol with three others lurking behind him. Krause described the way in which another man leaving the Metropole appeared to signal to the gunmen, and said he had seen three gunmen and noticed Bridgey Webber running from the hotel.

Krause's evidence was the first to damage Becker's case. The waiter insisted that he had watched Jack Sullivan approach Rosenthal's body, roll it over, and then "turn to one of the shooters and laugh." Since Sullivan was expected to appear as a witness for the defense, this was a potentially serious problem for McIntyre, and the lawyer spent some time trying to shake Krause's story. The defense attorney raised eyebrows with the revelation that the waiter's lawyer was James Sullivan, the same man who represented Bald Jack Rose. But it was Krause who landed the first really telling blow of the proceedings. He had testified before the coroner that he could not be certain who had gunned down Rosenthal. Now he unhesitatingly identified three of Zelig's men. How, asked McIntyre, with studied insolence, could he be so certain of their faces?

"I am a waiter," Krause shot back. "It is my business to remember faces."

McIntyre did what he could to discredit the stream of prosecution witnesses, but without a great deal of success. He asked one loiterer outside the Metropole—who had confidently identified one gunman despite his confessed difficulty in seeing without glasses—whether it was true that Whitman had paid him $2,500 for his testimony; Goff disallowed the question and had it stricken from the record. Whitman thus triumphed in the opening exchanges, and in general the DA handled the judge far better than did his opponent. He hustled through his witnesses as rapidly as possible—this had the added advantage of allowing him to gloss over any inadequacies in their testimony—and the case that he outlined was strikingly straightforward. Acute observers in the press box noted that very little of it concerned Becker, whose name had not yet been mentioned at all in more than a day and a half of testimony.

Whitman's main preoccupation at this stage of the trial seemed to be to produce the four imprisoned gunmen as frequently as possible—ostensibly in order to allow his witnesses to identify the men. In fact, this was scarcely difficult; far from having the quartet displayed as part of some conventional police lineup, Lefty, Whitey, Gyp, and Dago Frank were hauled into court in chains, over the Bridge of Sighs, and arrayed together in the dock. Lewis, who had white-blond hair, was impossible to miss, which made it a comparatively simple matter for a succession of the DA's witnesses to work out who was who. Even then Thomas Ryan—the taxi driver whom File had found asleep outside the Metropole—had second thoughts when brought face-to-face with the killers. Shooting a glance at Lefty Louie (who stood "with lips drawn back until the white strong teeth glistened savagely" and looked "like some wild animal at bay"), Ryan stammeringly declared that he was no longer quite sure of his identification.

"The parading of the gunmen in and out of the courtroom," it was later pointed out,

> was most likely done to establish the evil nature of the characters involved in the murder and, by showing them off within a few feet of Becker, to encourage the jury to think of him as part of the gang. The gunmen were an ugly looking crew and had not been favored with the special attentions of the tailors,

barbers, and manicurists said to be in regular attendance on Bald Jack Rose and his fellow gamblers. The question before the court, however, was not whether the gunmen had killed Rosenthal but whether Becker had had a hand in it.

Judge Goff's renowned vindictiveness was sharply on display throughout this phase of the trial, and most of it was directed toward McIntyre. "This is a court of justice," he snapped at the defense attorney after one particularly windy intervention. "It is not a place for a display of eloquence or emotion." But Goff reserved his greatest scorn for McIntyre's repeated attempts to have evidence prejudicial to his client ruled inadmissible. The attorney's repeated protests at the parading of the four gunmen drew an especially sharp response: "You may consider," the judge hissed, "in each instance [that] you have made an exception and that I have overruled it. That will expedite matters." Reporting this exchange the next day, one New York paper remarked that Goff "kind of dripped each word on McIntyre so that it foamed up a little before the next one fell."

Whitman's next two witnesses also came into court wearing handcuffs. Jake and Morris Luban were petty thieves and forgers, then awaiting trial in New Jersey on fresh criminal charges. Morris Luban claimed to have been in the lobby of the Metropole on the night of the murder and said he could identify three of the gunmen. Considerably more damagingly for the defense, Morris also related that he had been lounging in the Lafayette Baths some three weeks before the shooting when he noticed one of his old acquaintances, Jack Rose, entering the steam room with Lieutenant Becker. Both men, he testified, were naked, and had greeted him politely before returning to their own conversation.

"Did you hear them say any words one to each other?" Frank Moss asked.

"I did. Becker spoke."

"Give the words he said."

" 'If that bastard Rosenthal ain't croaked,' " replied Luban (whose words were censored in the daily press), " 'I'll croak him myself.' "

This was the first evidence that the court had heard of Becker's involvement in a conspiracy to murder Herman, and over the next few days the meeting in the Lafayette Baths would become one of the three main planks in Whitman's argument. McIntyre, rising to cross-examine, chose not to dwell on the unlikelihood that a policeman with so much to lose would have spoken quite so unguardedly in front of strangers in a public bath. He focused instead on Luban's dubious motive for appearing for the State.

Was it not true, McIntyre asked, that Luban had previously offered to testify as a witness for Becker? That he had sent not one but four letters to the defense proposing to exchange evidence for help in getting out of jail? And that he had offered to prove not that the lieutenant had conspired to murder Rosenthal but that Becker was the victim of a "frame-up"?

"When I came over here," the forger grudgingly accepted, "I expected some favors from the State of New York." When McIntyre asked him what he had been doing at the Metropole that night, Luban replied that he had gone to the hotel with a girl named Annie after taking in a show at Hammerstein's Theater. McIntyre was able to show that Hammerstein's had not been open on the night of the murder.*

The demolition of Morris Luban's highly dubious evidence was a blow to Whitman's prospects, and the district attorney was probably happy to hear Judge Goff call an end to the proceedings for the day. He and his assistants regrouped overnight and decided that the best way to repair the damage done by McIntyre's cross-examination was to put a more reliable witness on the stand. The obvious choice was Bald Jack Rose, who was probably the quickest witted of the prosecution witnesses and by a distance the most memorable. Unlike Luban, who had arrived in the Criminal Courts Building from his prison cell in Jersey only minutes before he was scheduled to testify, Rose had

---

*In the letters referred to, Jake Luban attributed to Jack Rose the words ascribed in court to Becker. Two weeks after Morris Luban testified, another sibling, Alexander, visited the Brooklyn district attorney to demand the return of the $3,000 bond he had posted on his brother's behalf. "The family is through with him," Alexander Luban said. "Morris is no good. . . . I'm sure he was nowhere near the bath at the time he described."

been in the DA's custody for weeks, and there had been plenty of opportunity for Whitman to go over the details of his evidence.

Bald Jack cut a compelling figure in Goff's court the next day. A further hundred spectators had somehow crammed themselves into the already-crowded room to watch the gambler's entrance. When Rose appeared, he was "a symphony in medium dark blue, perfectly groomed, his head lightly powdered," and "shaven to the blood." The gambler delivered his evidence in a colorless monotone that—many of those present found—somehow rendered the evidence he gave more rather than less bloodcurdling. Goff had ordered the windows in the court closed again, and the atmosphere in the room was "super-heated" as the cadaverous Rose, cutting a thoroughly bizarre figure in the grime-filtered light, took his oath to tell the truth and embarked upon a well-rehearsed account of Becker's treachery.

Despite the infernal heat, Bald Jack was a cool witness. He described in measured terms his own first meeting with Charles Becker, his recruitment to assist the lieutenant with his graft collections, and his own long association with Herman Rosenthal, for whom he had worked off and on for twenty years. He explained Becker's falling-out with Rosenthal. And, under Frank Moss's careful questioning, he recalled numerous instances in which the police lieutenant had first hinted, and then stated openly, that he wanted Herman murdered.

It had been "weeks" before the shooting, Bald Jack said, that he had first met Whitey Lewis and Lefty Louie in the Bronx to discuss the business. "Do you mean," he recalled Lewis asking, "that you want someone croaked?" "I told them that *he* did," Rose carefully explained to Moss, "and they didn't even ask the name of the intended victim, but said that they were ready to do the job if Zelig approved of it."

There were several interesting features to Bald Jack's evidence. Rose said that it was he who had scared the gunmen out of killing Rosenthal in the Garden restaurant, telling them that a Burns detective was watching them as they gathered outside; the gambler insisted that he had never wanted the shooting to take place. He explained that Dago Frank had been a late addition to the murder party, recruited at the rooms where he loafed about with Whitey, Lefty, and Gyp because the other three had been briefly absent when Bald Jack called. He also claimed that Becker had sent him into the Tombs to ask for Zelig's help. According to Rose's testimony, the lieutenant had seemed utterly unperturbed when his collector proposed to bring the more experienced Vallon in on their plot. Becker was, Rose added, equally happy for Bridgey Webber to be included in the burgeoning conspiracy and raised no objections when Sam Schepps unexpectedly turned up at one of the plotters' meetings. By that time (at least if the prosecution witnesses were to be believed), the fact that Becker was arranging Herman's murder was known to Rose, Vallon, Webber, and Schepps, not to mention Zelig, his four gunmen, and any number of curious eavesdroppers at the Lafayette Baths.

Lieutenant Becker, Bald Jack went on, had grown increasingly impatient as he had tried tactic after tactic to delay the planned assassination. By Rose's own account, he had done as much as any man reasonably could to persuade his boss to abandon the plot: "Why, Charley, don't excite yourself. This man Rosenthal is not worth taking any such chance with." Becker, though, had been insistent: "[He] called at my house and said, 'Rosenthal is still at it, but I don't see those fellows at it.' I said, 'They are on the job. I will go and see them again today.' "

The crux of Bald Jack's evidence came when Moss began to question him as to the detailed planning of the murder. In order to obtain the conviction of Becker, the prosecution had to show that the lieutenant had met with Rose and his fellow gamblers and formally discussed how best to dispose of Rosenthal. Rose, moreover, would have to place Sam Schepps in his usual uncomfortable role of playing no part in the murder scheme yet being somehow present when the matter was discussed. And according to Bald Jack, this was precisely what had occurred one night that June or July—he could not begin to remember the exact date—on a street corner in Harlem.

Justice Goff by now was "half on his feet, craning his neck down from the podium" to better hear the evidence. Becker—the gambler went on—had been ordered to raid a crap game on West 124th Street.

He had asked Rose and Bridgey Webber to rendezvous with him at a spot on the corner of West 124th and Seventh Avenue to go over the arrangements for Rosenthal's murder. This meeting, henceforth generally referred to as the Harlem Conference, had also been attended by Vallon. It was on this occasion that Schepps unexpectedly turned up with Webber and—the story went—loitered half a block along the street in a spot where he could see, but not hear, what was going on.

Frank Moss spared no effort to alert the jury to the fact that this was a critical passage of evidence. The Harlem Conference, Rose explained, had taken place shortly before 10:00 P.M. The conspirators "sat on a board across [a] vacant lot talking about Rosenthal." The lieutenant had just heard of Herman's attempts to arrange a meeting with DA Whitman, which added to his urgency to have matters resolved. "Take charge of this thing, Bridgey," Rose recalled him saying, "and see that it is done for me." When Webber professed himself less than keen to get involved, the lieutenant had reassured him: "There is nothing going to happen to anybody that has any hand in the croaking of Rosenthal," he said. The Harlem meeting concluded, Bald Jack added, with Webber grudgingly agreeing to visit Zelig's men. "With Bridgey on the job I think we will get quick results," Rose recalled assuring Becker as the conspirators dispersed.

The picture that Rose drew of the Harlem Conference was grotesque—"like that in which Macbeth had plotted with his hired murderers," observed the literate Lloyd Stryker—and clearly highly damaging to Becker. So was the gambler's recollection of a second meeting between the policeman and the associates, which Bald Jack said had taken place at the Murray Hill Baths, just up the street from Webber's clubhouse, soon after the murder. Becker had been "all smiles" by this time, his collector recalled, and congratulated his fellow plotters on a job well done. He described visiting the West Forty-seventh Street station house and gazing down at Rosenthal's bloody corpse. "Don't worry, Jack," Rose recalled him saying. "He is dead and that is the end of it. The only thing to do now is to see that those fellows get away and lay low for a few days until this thing blows over."

Bald Jack took nearly four hours to give his evidence to a hushed and attentive court, and by the time that he had finished, many of those present were persuaded that Becker was indeed guilty. The doubts raised by Morris Luban's devious evidence the previous day had been thoroughly assuaged; Rose's statements were so detailed and dispassionate it was hard to believe he was not telling the truth. Above all, the *New York Times* declared, the gambler's description of Becker "gloating over the body of the dead Rosenthal in the back of the West Forty-seventh Street station delivered a smashing blow to the battlements of the defense." The *Sun* could only agree:

> Nearly every man and woman in the court room shuddered. Rose had spoken in a quiet, absolutely expressionless tone, which intensified the dreadful visualization he was making. . . . Lieutenant Becker did not blanch or quail. But he was visibly exerting strong self-control. His jaw set like a rock. One could see the muscles stiffen. Sweat streamed from his face. One hand gripped his chair, the other the table in front of him. . . . No human being could have been subjected to a worse ordeal, but the accused man faced three hundred pairs of eyes without flinching.

Almost everything about Rose's evidence had been memorable. On the stand the gambler had spoken in a voice so quiet that everyone in the room had to strain to catch it, creating the impression that his was by some distance the most important testimony of the trial, and his accounts of the lieutenant's plotting had grown more, rather than less, outlandish since he first confessed his involvement in the killing: "I don't want him beat up, I could do that myself," Bald Jack now remembered Becker snarling. "Cut his throat, dynamite him or anything. . . . Don't be particular when you do it, break into his house and get him there if you want. . . . What do you care who is around? Walk up and shoot him right in front of a policeman if you like." McIntyre had done what he could to stem the flow of vitriol. "Every few moments," one reporter noted, "there would be a rhythmic interruption in the courtroom. McIntyre: 'Objection.' Goff: 'Objection overruled.' McIntyre: 'Exception for the record.' "

Judge Goff's steadfast rejection of these protests meant that McIntyre did not have the chance to get at Rose until his cross-examination of the gambler began early in the afternoon. Bald Jack had to withstand this battering for nearly six and a half hours, without any recess for dinner. More than four decades later, Lloyd Stryker still vividly recalled the scene that played out in Goff's court on that long-ago October Saturday:

> At half-past two, Mr. McIntyre began his cross-examination. He continued without a break or a request for an indulgence until six in the evening. I shall never forget that afternoon. It was a steaming day and in a stifling courtroom, hour after hour, our chief counsel relentlessly pressed on. . . . He was a master of every field of cross-examination, but he excelled perhaps in that in which he now engaged: the discrediting of a witness by showing from his own mouth that he is unworthy of belief. Every question searched some dark chamber of this rascal's life, reached into the putrid cesspool of his past, turned the light upon his meanness, his depravity, and his crimes. . . . It was a slashing and a brilliant effort. [McIntyre] laid his questions on as with a lash. . . . His collar wilted and sweat streamed down his face as he confronted one of the worst men who ever lived.

Many of the others present in the court that day were less impressed than Stryker by McIntyre's style of questioning. Becker's attorney was certainly thorough, adding layer upon layer to his portrayal of Rose in his effort to show the gambler in an unflattering light, but his efforts to develop themes and build up the momentum of his interrogation were persistently thwarted by Whitman's objections and by the inter-cessions of Justice Goff. This time virtually all of the objections raised were sustained. McIntyre asked no fewer than five times whether Rose admitted to procuring Herman's murder without obtaining an answer.

Bald Jack was equally obstructive when it came to giving a response to more innocuous questions. It took the defense counsel fifteen minutes to get Rose to agree that he was born in Poland, and twenty to define the term "lobbygow" as it applied to his associate Schepps—all of it time that might have been better spent tackling more crucial issues. Nor was Bald Jack any more forthcoming when Becker's lawyer tried to explore his enmity for Rosenthal. The most that McIntyre elicited was a terse denial that Herman had ever called him a "bald-headed pimp" and a rejection of the suggestion that Rose himself had had Rosenthal gunned down "because he said that I was living with a woman not my wife or that my children were illegitimate."

Judge Goff, Stryker thought, went out of his way to protect Bald Jack on the stand. Rose had given his evidence to Moss "under the friendly nods and encouraging smiles of the prosecutor's judge. . . . He was fawned upon by the court. By every look and intonation, the judge revealed how much he wanted to obscure the fact that this man was not only a cunning, shrewd, calculating, dangerous criminal, but a self-confessed murderer who, in return for his testimony, had secured from the District Attorney an agreement whereby he would go scot-free." Now, with Rose under cross-examination, Goff stepped in just as Rose was getting rattled. McIntyre's persistent efforts to portray the witness as an unreliable crook were halted when "the judge leaned down and suggested that the witness might well plead the Fifth Amendment to this kind of thing. . . . Rose shook off all such questions from then on."

Goff's most decisive interventions, though, came later in the proceedings. Counsel McIntyre—an overweight, unhealthy fifty-seven—began to show signs of flagging around 6:00 P.M. He had been on his feet for nearly four hours, and as he reached the crucial point of questioning Rose on the gamblers' time together in the Tombs, he began to lose his train of thought. "I am tottering on my feet," the lawyer told Goff "in a strangled voice." "I feel thoroughly exhausted, and if I continue now I may not be able to come back here Monday. I may collapse at any moment." The judge insisted that he press on with his examination.

McIntyre, although now visibly distressed, did his best to comply with Goff's command:

> "Didn't you go down on your knees . . . in the Tombs and swear by the grave of your dead mother that Becker had nothing to do with the 'affair'?"
>
> "No."
>
> "Did you not say to Jack Sullivan in the counsel room that to implicate Becker was your only chance?"
>
> "No."
>
> "Didn't Jack Sullivan say, 'What can you squeal about?' and didn't you say, 'The newspapers are hollering for Becker'?"
>
> "I did not say anything like that."
>
> "Sullivan did not say, 'You bald-headed——, are you going to frame up someone?'"
>
> "There were ten in that counsel room."

Several times between 6:00 and 8:00 P.M., Becker's lawyer repeated his request for an adjournment, but Goff would not relent. The judge was apparently enjoying McIntyre's growing discomfort—a product, it now appeared, not merely of exhaustion but of lunch. "One of Justice Goff's curious attributes," a reporter noted, "was that he had the continence of a camel. McIntyre did not. He had been forced to stay on his feet in the courtroom since two-thirty in the afternoon without a chance to go to the men's room and was beginning noticeably to fidget." The judge's behavior was, Lloyd Stryker thought, "cold, calculated, deliberate oppression."

At last, at 8:45 P.M.—six and a quarter hours after the cross-examination had begun—the defense counsel reeled and clutched at the corner of his table.

"Your Honor," McIntyre gasped, "I am utterly exhausted. I am unable to do my full duty to my client. Won't your Honor please accede to my request?"

"Why, Mr. McIntyre," Goff smirked, "you are stronger than you were this morning." He denied the defense request for a continuance. McIntyre repeated that he could not go on. "Order was disregarded," one watching newsman noted. "Over and over again Mr. McIntyre shouted that he was worn out, that the proceeding was not fair."

John Hart jumped to his feet and offered to take over the examination. Goff regarded him balefully.

"I do not wish to listen to you, sir," he snapped. Then, to McIntyre: "No good reason whatever appears for an adjournment. There yet remain three hours. Counsel may have them."

"I cannot go on," the defense attorney groaned.

"Have you no more questions? If not I will declare the cross-examination closed and excuse the witness."

When McIntyre began to protest once again, Goff turned to Rose and discharged him,* thus denying Becker's lawyers the chance to recall Bald Jack to the stand. McIntyre staggered off toward the men's room. Amid all the heat and the discomfort, the old attorney had lost track of his line of questioning. He had not so much as touched upon the Harlem Conference.

Justice Goff's conduct and his frequent intercessions had marked the Becker trial almost since its outset.

Other judges noticed it. Goff, one said after going through the trial transcripts, had vigorously "intervened to protect the People's witnesses on cross-examination," had "objected to and excluded questions asked by the defendant's counsel," and on one occasion—when McIntyre asked the district attorney "to concede a fact on which there was apparently no dispute"—had nonetheless stepped in and ruled for Whitman ("No, I will not let him concede it"). At the same time, Goff had been

---

*This was not the first time that Goff had intervened to halt a cross-examination during the Becker trial. Toward the end of McIntyre's questioning of Morris Luban, the judge had peremptorily ended the examination. On this occasion, too, John Hart had risen and asked to be permitted to continue in McIntyre's stead. "No," Goff said, and ordered an adjournment.

generally lax in permitting Whitman and his team to make repeated references to Becker as a "grafter" who was collecting protection money from gambling houses in Satan's Circus. These allegations, while true, were based on evidence that was not admissible in court, and the judge had been quick to put a stop to the defense's efforts to affix similarly negative labels to the district attorney's assemblage of gamblers and forgers.

The members of the jury probably barely noticed such legal niceties. But all twelve jurors were certainly aware that in the Becker trial the prosecutor and the defense attorney enjoyed very different relations with the judge. It was common, at least during the first days of the hearing, for Goff and Whitman to huddle together in conference during any breaks in testimony, discussing the judge's stewardship of the grand-jury hearings into police corruption; the *Evening Post* even published a short article applauding the "rapport" that had grown up between the pair and the "pleasant picture they made conferring on the bench, with Whitman's brown head bent close to Goff's silvery one." McIntyre, in contrast, became the frequent subject of the judge's wrath: "Mr. McIntyre, you know better than to object," Goff barked at one juncture, and, at another, "There is no necessity in being so explosive about it!"

Throughout the case Goff undermined most defense attempts to show Rose and his fellow gamblers in a less-than-flattering light. One of his most decisive interventions was to prevent McIntyre from introducing Rose's conflicting statements in the case as evidence; without access to Bald Jack's earliest statements to the police, the defense was not able to point out the dozens of discrepancies in his changing versions of events. Goff was also vigilant for anything that hinted that the prosecution witnesses had colluded, at one point disallowing eighteen successive questions put by McIntyre and at another preventing the defense from exploring the free-and-easy conditions under which Rose, Webber, and the others had been locked up in the West Side Jail.

Later, in what ranked among the strangest aspects of the trial, Goff apparently grew concerned that his repeated overruling of the defense's questions might form the basis for a possible appeal. He summoned McIntyre to the bench and told him that he could recall two of his witnesses and ask them more than twenty of the disputed queries after all.

When the defense attorney refused, remarking that a "last-minute addendum" to his case, taken entirely out of the context, would scarcely benefit his client, Goff turned to the prosecution table. Since the defense refused to pose the questions, the judge ruled, a district attorney would do so in its stead.

Frank Moss had spent the best part of two months striving to place Charles Becker in the electric chair. Now, under Justice Goff's cockatrice glare, the assistant district attorney rose slowly to his feet and began asking questions of a witness on his enemy's behalf.

Proceedings in the Becker case resumed on the morning of Monday, October 14, when Bridgey Webber took the stand. He was just as self-controlled as Rose ("Webber's story," a watching journalist reported, "was as cold and emotionless as it if came from a frozen heart"), but his evidence came, inevitably, as something of an anticlimax, and it contained some statements that were frankly unbelievable—not least Bridgey's contention that none of the imprisoned gamblers had read a single newspaper article about their case in more than a month in jail.

Webber did corroborate several of Bald Jack's most important statements. Like Rose, he testified that Lieutenant Becker had demanded that Rosenthal be "croaked," and, like Rose, Bridgey claimed to have warned the policeman not to proceed ("Charley, that is a pretty serious thing—having a man murdered"). Yet the gambler added almost nothing, other than a better idea of the time, to Bald Jack's account of the Harlem Conference. On cross-examination McIntyre asked some questions about Sam Schepps and his role in the Harlem meeting, but the defense attorney did not take issue with the idea that the conference had taken place.

Harry Vallon, who followed Webber onto the stand, was little more illuminating. He, too, could not be certain when the Harlem assignation had occurred, though he did relate some extra details. He and Rose had stood around chatting with the lieutenant while they waited for Webber to appear, the faro dealer said; as he recalled it,

"Becker was telling us he was going to raid a crap game. There was a little colored boy on the other side of the street and he called him over and spoke to him." Sam Schepps, Vallon went on, had been nowhere to be seen, but Bridgey had assured him that Schepps was there, and he believed him. McIntyre had no more success shaking Vallon's story than he had Rose's and Webber's.

The final prosecution witness of any moment was Schepps himself. The self-satisfied fake-jewelry man took the stand first thing next morning, resplendent in a new suit and a neatly done bow tie that "made him look," a reporter thought, "more like a prosperous department store auditor than a man recurrently dependent on Bald Jack Rose for sandwich money." Spectators in the courtroom noted that Schepps presented his testimony with a marked intelligence that boded ill for Becker. "His sharp eyes," the *Sun* man wrote, "glinted behind his nose glasses and his glances darted sideways. He folded his fingers together and tried to cross his legs, a proceeding frowned upon by the court officer who stands at the witness chair. He wore a blue suit . . . and black low shoes and he carefully drew up his sharply pressed trousers so that his white silk socks would be exposed."

Schepps's testimony had been keenly anticipated; months of "dodging detectives in the Catskills and his stay among admiring citizens in Hot Springs had given him a kind of reputation second only to that of Rose." Moss took him briskly through his evidence, and Schepps responded readily—albeit "in a grinning and insolent manner" at first. Later in the proceedings, when John McIntyre rose to cross-examine, "he became more and more pugnacious and more and more determined that counsel for the defense should not get the better of him."

McIntyre's chief tactic was to lure Schepps into the admission that he had played some active part in the conspiracy—a confession that would have destroyed Whitman's entire case at a stroke. The district attorney seemed unconcerned, however, scarcely bothering to interject, and indeed "his favorite chick of a witness seemed to be able to get along without coddling." Schepps nimbly dodged the defense attorney's traps, "carefully excluding himself from private conversations between Rose and Webber" and maintaining that he had never heard either man say anything especially incriminating; they had "whispered in each other's ears" whenever they had wanted to talk over the details of their plan, he said. McIntyre's efforts were hindered, once again, by Goff, who ruled that several of the smiling con man's early depositions were inadmissible as evidence. This denied the defense the chance to show up some serious discrepancies. In court, for example, Schepps claimed barely to know the defendant, remarking that he had "probably said three words to Becker in his life." To Whitman, some weeks earlier, he had boasted of a far more intimate acquaintance, saying that he had known the policeman for years and even called upon him several times at home.

"Were you a deaf and dumb partner?" McIntyre "almost shouted," goaded to the point of madness by a long stretch of this questioning.

"They never made a confidant of me. When I realized that I wasn't wanted, I walked away," the lobbygow replied. Later in his testimony Schepps implausibly added that on one occasion he had left the room and simply stood out on the pavement "from lunch time until evening" while Rose and Vallon stayed inside, plotting the details of the murder.

What, McIntyre asked him, had the gamblers discussed with Zelig's gunmen as they drove about the city? "Oh, the sun came up and the clouds were in the sky and things like that," the con man smilingly responded. Well, McIntyre pressed, surely he'd been at least a little suspicious when Webber had burst into his poker rooms on the night of the murder, calling, "Herman's at the Metropole," and the four gangsters went tearing out? "No, why should I be suspicious?" Schepps returned indifferently. "He put on," a watching journalist observed, "a little corner of the mouth smile at this point which was trying to McIntyre's self-control. 'Don't laugh at me,' counsel demanded. 'You're treating this matter as a joke.' "*

The principal danger, from DA Whitman's point of view, was that his corroborator would take this studied insolence too far and actually undermine the prosecution case. This point was brought home to

---

*McIntyre's annoyance was understandable. "Try and think again, Mr. Schepps," he had urged a few minutes earlier as the witness blandly dodged another pitfall. "I don't have to think very hard to answer your questions," Schepps had scornfully retorted. "I'm answering them all right."

Schepps during the lunch break, and—one newspaper reported—
"the only reason [he] did not do serious damage to the State was
because he got some heavy kicks during recess. . . . Schepps radiated
all morning; in the afternoon he gave forth less froth and more
facts. . . . He is free from the taint of guilt in this case, but no doubt his
character, as given by himself, leaves something to be desired from the
standpoint of respectability."

Respectable or not, the vital point was that Schepps emerged from
six hours of cross-examination with his story—and Whitman's case—
intact. He had not made a favorable impression on the spectators in
the courtroom; his testimony had been too smug and too smart-alecky
for that. But he had borne out Bald Jack Rose and Bridgey Webber, as
the district attorney had intended that he should. By the time Schepps
stepped down from the witness stand, the twelve jurors were more
than half convinced of Becker's guilt.

Charles Whitman produced a total of nearly forty prosecution witnesses and devoted well over a week to going through their evidence.
John McIntyre swore in almost exactly as many on Becker's behalf, but
their testimonies detained the court for much less time: for five days,
rather than eight. This was only one of several indications that the
defense was struggling to make a case.

McIntyre's main difficulty lay in finding a weakness in the DA's
parade of testimony. Schepps's pivotal role as corroborator for the
State had been one potential chink in the armor, but it was otherwise
surprisingly difficult to tear the prosecution's argument apart.
Whitman had staked his chances of obtaining a conviction on the
contention that Charles Becker had attended the Harlem Conference and met again with the conspirators at the Murray Hill Baths
after the murder. That meant McIntyre needed to prove that Becker
had not been—in fact, could not have been—present at these meetings. But Whitman's witnesses had been so uniformly equivocal about
the date of the Harlem Conference (according to Schepps it had taken
place in May or June; according to Rose sometime in June or July)
that it was practically impossible to show that Becker could not have

traveled up to West 124th Street to attend it. The defense was forced to focus the bulk of its efforts on discrediting the prosecution's witnesses and on the Murray Hill Baths affair.

Things might have been different had McIntyre felt able to put Becker on the stand. As it was, the lieutenant's unwillingness to testify appeared intrinsically suspicious, not least to a jury of New Yorkers more or less brought up to distrust the police. It also robbed the defense of both a structure and a heart. Far too much time was devoted to a stream of indistinguishable witnesses, each of whom had been called to discredit a tiny portion of the prosecution case. Probably the policeman's lawyer was aiming for a cumulative effect—the suggestion that the DA's case was full of holes. In fact, the impression he conveyed was of a choppy, petty argument, not a principled defense of some great truth.

Justice Goff hardly helped, again. McIntyre had planned to open his case by calling on William Travers Jerome, the former district attorney, and Police Commissioner Waldo—two witnesses of unimpeachable integrity. Goff disallowed their evidence.* Fred Hawley, the *Sun* reporter, was sworn in next and testified that he had been with Becker for all but five minutes of the time between 3:30 and 7:30 A.M. on the day of the murder. This, if true, meant that Becker could scarcely have attended the meeting at the Murray Hill Baths, and—under cross-examination—Hawley scored a considerable blow by adding that he had not informed Whitman's office of his evidence

---

*Jerome's testimony, while slight, was actually intriguing: Jack Rose, at one point in his evidence, had recalled taking a call from Lieutenant Becker and indulging in a long, incriminating conversation in which Becker had advised him to "lie low" for the few days after the murder. Quite unknown to the gambler, Jerome had happened to be present when this call was placed. He was prepared to swear that the conversation had lasted less than sixty seconds, which—had the jury believed him—might have gone some way to discrediting some of Bald Jack's other recollections. Goff disallowed his testimony on the grounds that while Jerome remembered Becker picking up a receiver and asking to speak to Rose, the former DA could not swear that the man who had come to the phone really was the gambler. Waldo attempted to testify that it had been he, and not Lieutenant Becker, who had ordered a police guard to be placed in Herman's house—a revelation at variance with the central thrust of Whitman's evidence. Goff ruled this testimony irrelevant.

"because I did not care to have the district attorney know what I was going to testify to." Too many defense witnesses in too many other trials had been scared off with threatened indictments for the reporter to take that risk. Whitman was sufficiently enraged to call Hawley's response "the most insulting statement ever made in an American court," and he demanded to be sworn in himself. Under questioning from Moss, he testified that while Becker had been at the West Forty-seventh Street precinct house at 3:30 A.M., he had not been there after 4:00. Notionally, therefore, Becker *had* had sufficient time to visit the baths. The jury was left little wiser by the whole exchange.

McIntyre's most interesting witness was Jack Sullivan, "a short, burly man with the face of a bulldog and two odd, bald spots at the front of his head" that reminded one newsman in the press box of "little red horns." The newspaper distributor, still himself under indictment for murder, was brought down from Whitman's Palace to give evidence and supplied a great deal of testimony regarding the relations among Rose, Vallon, Webber, and their friends. Clearly still much angered by his own arrest, Sullivan could scarcely be prevailed upon to stop talking. The most significant difference between his evidence and that given by the imprisoned gamblers, though, was the distributor's willingness to answer any question put to him by either the State or the defense. McIntyre made this point well, asking Goff to instruct his witness "that since he was under indictment for murder he could refuse to answer any question. Sullivan replied that he would answer any question." But the evidence he gave was scarcely breathtaking. Most of it concerned conversations overheard in the West Side Jail. These certainly implied that Rose and his cohorts had conspired to frame Becker for Herman's murder. But, the jury must have wondered, was the blustery Jack Sullivan—little red horns and all—really more reliable than Bald Jack Rose?*

---

*Probably he was. Sullivan, unlike Rose and the other gamblers, never signed one of Whitman's immunity agreements and remained in jail until May 1913, when he was released. At that time Whitman told the press that the distributor's trial for murder would begin soon. It never happened, but the indictment remained on Sullivan's record until his death a quarter of a century later.

McIntyre had expected great things of one other anticipated witness. William Shapiro, the chauffeur of the gray Packard, had been subpoenaed to testify for the defense. Becker's lawyers planned to ask him some detailed questions about the passengers he had transported to the Hotel Metropole on that July evening three months earlier—an assemblage that, according to the driver's early deposition, had included both Jack Rose and Sam Schepps. An admission of this sort would do serious damage to Whitman's carefully promoted notion that Schepps had no foreknowledge of the murder. Once again, however, the DA smartly outmaneuvered the ponderous McIntyre. A few minutes before Shapiro was scheduled to appear, Whitman requested an adjournment. When the trial began again, it emerged that during the short interval Whitman had persuaded Justice Goff to reconvene his grand-jury investigation into police corruption and call Shapiro before it. At the district attorney's recommendation, the chauffeur had then been granted immunity from prosecution. He now appeared not to testify for Becker but as a rebuttal witness for the prosecution.

In these dramatically changed circumstances, few people were surprised to hear Shapiro recant his earlier testimony. Schepps had been nowhere near the murder car, he said, and nothing that McIntyre could say would shake him from that story. The real puzzle, to those who recalled the sensation that had followed the driver's original arrest, was the timing of the DA's last-minute offer of immunity. Whatever Whitman's reasoning, though, his masterly maneuvering had denied McIntyre a final opportunity to do real damage to the prosecution case.*

Certainly the defense fared little better with its remaining witnesses. A long stream of former policemen and apartment-house neighbors spoke glowingly of Becker's character; others attacked the

---

*Writing decades later, Andy Logan, the *New Yorker*'s fabled City Hall correspondent, probably got as close to the real answer to this puzzle as anybody when she hazarded, "Since Shapiro's lawyer, Aaron Levy, had been on hand for the final negotiations that had ended with Becker's indictment, it seems probable that his conversion had been plotted months before. *Five* formal immunity agreements might have seemed rather much, and this present maneuver took care of the matter nicely."

integrity of Luban, Vallon, and Bridgey Webber. But none of this did anything to undermine the credibility of Sam Schepps or Jack Rose. McIntyre had found one witness from Hot Springs willing to swear that Schepps, in conversation, had not exactly denied involvement in the murder. But watery testimony of this sort was never going to sway the jury. Not a single witness touched in any way on the events of the Harlem Conference. As McIntyre's defense drew to a close, it became increasingly clear that Becker's fate would rest, as the lieutenant had always said it would, on the stark choice confronting the jurors. Who would the twelve men in the jury box believe? A brawny, brutal, utterly corrupt policeman? Or three self-confessed murderers and their oil slick of a corroborator?

John McIntyre rose to deliver his summation at ten o'clock on the morning of October 23. He had been granted four hours to make his final plea, but—no doubt to the relief of those who had listened to two weeks' worth of the Tammany man's rhetoric—required no more than one to state his case.

It was not one of the defense attorney's finer performances. Granted, he had little material to work with. But McIntyre's stentorian appeal to the jury's patriotism—"I am defending an American, not a murderer"—did little more than underline his failure to make much of a dent in the prosecution case, and his summation confused many of those crammed into the court by arguing that the four gunmen, who were not on trial, might not have murdered Rosenthal.

The defense made some good points, to be sure. Morris Luban, as McIntyre pointed out, had testified "he never saw Becker but once in his life and then he was in street clothes. But he comes here and tells you he was able to identify a nude man in a room filled with steam." The idea that a man of the lieutenant's obvious intelligence could have organized a murder quite so clumsily was ridiculed. But, once again, no reference was made to the really crucial points of Whitman's case—to the Harlem Conference or the meeting at the Murray Hill Baths, without which there could be no conviction. The defense attorney's final message to the jurors was a simple appeal to reason—or prejudice, perhaps: "Remember, it is the filth of the earth that accuses him." His client seemed less than impressed. As McIntyre ranted on, the *Evening Post* observed, "Becker became manifestly nervous. He moved about in his chair. He broke into a sweat. When the lawyer finished at last, he looked greatly relieved."

There was a short recess before Frank Moss stood to summarize the prosecution case. At least one newspaper pointed out that the assistant district attorney was far more balanced than McIntyre had been—"restrained, courteous and fair. . . . When he quoted testimony, he quoted all that bore on the point in question, inverting nothing, suppressing nothing"—thus contriving to imply that he had the stronger case. Moss's summation was carefully constructed to rebut that just made by the defense. Four men had fired at Rosenthal, the prosecutor said, and there was no doubt that they were Zelig's gunmen. Rose had been nothing but a puppet, carrying out Becker's orders because he was terrified of what would happen to him if he shirked. Schepps was merely "an accessory after the crime," and Becker had "prostituted himself as a policeman"—the closest that Whitman and his men dared come to mentioning his earnings from the graft.

The bearded, earnest Moss cut such an upright figure that very few of those in court noticed his occasional recourse to subterfuge. But the assistant district attorney pulled a neat trick when he dismissed Jack Sullivan's testimony that the killers had discussed the possibility of framing Becker in the distributor's presence—"I ask you to consider the improbability of that. . . . Is Rose a fool?"—without drawing attention to the fact that his own case rested heavily on similar contentions. According to the prosecution, after all, Becker had been so drunk with power that he never bothered to disguise his intention of killing Rosenthal and openly discussed his plans in front of strangers. Moss's view of Bald Jack was considerably more respectful. Rose's crucial testimony, he told the members of the jury, could be relied upon, not least because it matched precisely the evidence he had given to the grand jury. This last suggestion was such a naked lie that McIntyre leaped to his feet, "choleric with rage," to interject by shouting, "That claim is not true, and the assistant district attorney knows it!"

The twelve jurors got a night to think over the evidence before Judge Goff delivered his charge the next morning. Most of the spectators in the court, and many of the newsmen, still believed that the case was finely balanced at this point, Whitman's plainly superior presentation of the prosecution argument being offset by the plainly dubious character of so many of his witnesses and the presumption of innocence that still lay in Becker's favor. McIntyre and his team reassured their client that the outcome would be a hung jury or an acquittal. In the district attorney's office, meanwhile, no more than five men among the entire staff of several dozen expected anything but a verdict of not guilty.

Goff's charge to the jury changed all that. It badly damaged Becker's hopes. Most of the judge's three-hour discussion of the evidence consisted of a formal instruction to the jury on a variety of points of law. But his recapitulation of the evidence, more than one reporter thought, was far from neutral. Each plank in the prosecution case was presented as fact. The meeting at the Murray Hill Baths was discussed as though it had happened the way the prosecution said it had, not as though it might never have occurred. The Harlem Conference likewise. Even Morris Luban's evidence was given renewed credibility, and the forger's account of the threats issued by Becker at the Lafayette Baths was repeated without comment. Becker, the judge concluded this portion of his charge, had telephoned Jack Rose on the day before the murder to tell him, "There is still time. It will look as if the gamblers did it."

Goff's instructions regarding Rose and Schepps were no more helpful to the defense. Goff ruled that no testimony proved that Schepps had had foreknowledge of the murder; the jury should not conclude that the fake-jewelry man was in any way an accomplice in the murder. Bald Jack's reliability as a witness went unquestioned. Toward the end of his discussion of the case, the judge even read "at some length and with apparent interest and pleasure from Rose's testimony" before closing with the admonition that "Becker, in law, must be held responsible for everyone who acted in pursuance of his instructions." It was, the lieutenant admitted to the newsmen who clustered around him for a comment as the jury filed out, "virtually a direction to find me guilty."

The Becker jurors retired to consider the evidence shortly before 4:30 P.M. The policeman and his supporters waited for the verdict in the sheriff's office along the hall; the district attorney and his men settled down in a separate room a little way away. John Becker, by then a lieutenant of detectives, sat close to his brother; so, too, did Clubber Williams, old by now and rather drunk. Helen's brother, John Lynch, and a small group of friends and defense lawyers stood or sat awkwardly nearby. Sandwiches and coffee were brought in, but few people felt hungry, particularly when the strains of lustily sung martial hymns came drifting down the corridor from the DA's office. Frank Moss, it transpired, had organized the junior members of the prosecution team into an impromptu Christian chorus.

Time slunk by. Prior to the judge's charge, Becker had been optimistic of a favorable verdict; he had even asked Helen to wear her best dress to court so they could go out to celebrate that evening. Now he felt more equivocal, and so did his wife: "Lawyers and everyone," Mrs. Becker would say,

> kept reassuring me right along . . . but while we were waiting for the jury to come in, I was nervous and did not feel like talking to people. Charley and I sat in the sheriff's room hour after hour, waiting. People crowded in to see us and speak to us, and they brought rumors that the jury had disagreed or that the last vote was so and so. It was very annoying, for they really knew nothing about it.

Now it was 8:00 P.M., now 10:00, now 11:00. The panel had been out for six and a half hours. Each tick of the clock raised Becker's spirits a fraction higher. It was common knowledge that juries took more time to bring in not-guilty verdicts than they did to find a man guilty as charged.

It was five minutes to midnight when news finally reached the sheriff's office that the verdict had come in. Becker was led away down a set of stairs while Helen hurried back along the hall, but the jurors' sudden reappearance had been so unexpected that she reached the courtroom late and found it already full.

"I ran as fast as I could," the schoolteacher recalled,

> but when I reached the door it was closed and they would not let me in. An attendant gave me a chair and I sat down with people pressing around me—for they all knew who I was. I waited three or four minutes—it seemed a long time—and then the door flew open.
>
> A reporter rushed out shouting "Guilty!" He saw me just as he spoke and felt sorry for me—he told me afterward. But he could not stop the word, or alter the fact. They had found my husband guilty of murder in the first degree.

CHAPTER 11

RETRIAL

"WELL," SAID EMORY BUCKNER, the eminent Republican, "that does it. That makes Whitman the next Mayor of New York."

The outcome of the Becker trial proved highly satisfactory to most of the participants. Whitman emerged from the Criminal Courts Building as the most celebrated district attorney in living memory, his reputation burnished and his career enhanced.* "Telegrams of congratulation poured in upon him from all over the country in scores," Swope reported, "[and] letters by the hundred came from friends, admirers and even strangers." The reforming Committee of Fourteen, which had spent a decade crusading against New York vice, passed a resolution declaring him "one of the great heroes of the age." On New Year's Eve 1912, the DA was guest of honor at a dinner for more than a thousand people held at the Astor Hotel. There he was toasted by Senator William Borah: "Well done, thou good and faithful servant. You have been faithful over a few things. We will make you ruler over many."

Whitman himself relished the attention; indeed, there were hints, after the triumph of the Becker verdict, that he had his heart set on

---

*"The man of the hour," Viña Delmar wrote, "was District Attorney Whitman. He was getting more attention in New York than Mr. Woodrow Wilson. After all, Whitman's promises already had been kept, his deeds accomplished. One could read almost anywhere that he was the champion of civilization and that morality had triumphed only because Mr. Whitman had not rested."

something grander than a mere mayoralty. "I'd like to be Governor," the DA told the man from the *Evening Post*, who noticed the "snap in his broad powerful jaws and a glint in his choleric hazel eyes," and so many New York Republicans saw Whitman as a man with the potential to run successfully for high office that several committees were swiftly formed to raise the money needed to launch the crusading anti-vice campaigner on a national political career. A fund-raising dinner was organized at the Café Boulevard downtown, which was—no doubt coincidentally—the very spot where chauffeurs Libby and Shapiro had once had their taxi stand. Whitman was cheered to the echo when he rose to make a speech and promised that his first step would be to run for mayor. Only then, he explained, would he have the power to reform the police, "an evil which threatens the existence of civilized society. Beside it, all other questions seem to be of minor importance."

Whitman did run for mayor the next summer, but as it happened his political career got off to an unexpectedly shaky start. In Democratic New York, no Republican could hope to be elected without standing on a Fusion slate of the sort that had swept Mayors Strong and Low to power. In 1913 the Fusion forces had two mayoral candidates to choose from, Whitman and a young Irish-American alderman named John Purroy Mitchel. When they cast ballots, the vote went 44 to 43 in Mitchel's favor. Whitman was confirmed as the Fusion candidate for a further spell in the DA's office, but he let his supporters know that he hoped to run again, this time against William Sulzer, the Tammany governor of the state, in the gubernatorial election of 1914.

Whitman was far from the only man to emerge from the Becker prosecution with his reputation gleaming. Frank Moss, the earnest hymn singer, became a huge hit on the reformist chicken-in-a-basket circuit. And John Goff was widely praised for his handling of what one newspaper correspondent called "a great trial, . . . a model trial." The judge invited a dozen pretty young society women to watch the sentencing, and when they arrived in court, "wearing bright-colored silk gowns and large hats," he graciously entertained them in a side room, serving them cordials and—as a special dispensation—permitting the windows to be opened and the blinds drawn up.

A few minutes later, as his guests gazed up at him adoringly from an enclosure just below the judge's dais, Goff sentenced Becker to die in the electric chair.

Lieutenant Becker lost just a little of his fabled self-control when he heard his sentence pronounced. Reporters in the courtroom saw him flicker almost imperceptibly and suck in a breath. But the moment passed. "Becker, with death staring him in the face," Swope wrote, "was the same stiff-jawed, level-eyed Becker yesterday that he used to be when at the zenith of his power as master of Satan's Circus. Only for fractions of moments did he show emotion in his hard, heavy countenance. Then the emotion was either sympathy for his wife, or utter, bitter contempt for those whose testimony resulted in the verdict of guilty."

The courtroom, which had been noisy before the verdict was brought in, was suddenly so quiet that everyone in the room clearly heard the snap of handcuffs as the sheriff fixed them to the policeman's wrist. Then a clerk stood, told the defendant to raise his right hand, and asked him to swear to his name, age, nationality, and religion. "Have you ever been convicted of a crime?" added the clerk. Becker started to say "No," then paused and corrected himself. "I have never been convicted of a crime *before*," he managed.

The lieutenant retained sufficient self-control to walk briskly away with the sheriff, looking now (one prosecuting attorney complained) as though he were about to have a good conduct medal pinned on him. He was taken back to the sheriff's room, where he found Helen already waiting, too discouraged to talk. After half an hour, word came that the prisoner was to go back to the Tombs. A crowd of reporters were waiting in the corridor, and Becker—having remained silent for so long—seemed more than willing to talk to them. "They have convicted an innocent man," he told the reporter from the *Sun*.

I can prove this and I will do it when I get a chance. There is not the slightest question but that these men who testified against me were all liars, the worst of perjurers. They perjured their souls black, and I can prove it.

The next day another crowd of friends and relatives gathered to witness Becker's departure from the city. The lieutenant was to be sent to Sing Sing prison—a notoriously grim and brutal jail, worse even than the Tombs, but the only place in New York State at which executions were carried out. The well-wishers included Becker's brother John, several of his sisters, some farmers who remembered Charley as a boy and had come down from Callicoon Center to offer their support, and a clutch of colleagues from police headquarters, many of them with their wives. Few, even the toughest beat policemen, maintained much self-control as the condemned man was hustled off toward the railway station.

"Everybody was crying but us two," Helen Becker said.

You see, once when I visited Charley before the trial, I noticed the wife of another prisoner crying; and right then I made up my mind that I would never get hysterical and cry and annoy my husband. It does no good and it distresses people. I have made many visits to my husband since then, but I have never broken down or cried before him, although I have felt like it.

We said a few words and then they took him across the bridge, and later on he was driven to the Forty-second Street station in the prison wagon. I went on the subway, and I got there ahead of the crowd, and when I told the gateman who I was, he let me go aboard the train before the others. . . . When my husband reached the train a big crowd was following him. He was handcuffed now, and guarded by seven sheriffs. There were dozens of reporters and we were all packed into the smoking-car. I was the only woman there. They let me sit in the seat beside my husband. One reporter leaned over so close to us that his head was almost between Mr. Becker and me. . . . We could have no private conversation.

Alighting from his train at the village of Ossining, Becker found that he was expected to walk the three-quarters of a mile from the railway station to Sing Sing itself. The crowd that had been waiting for him at the station trailed along behind him and merged seamlessly into another throng already gathered by the prison gates as the little party arrived. Becker, who stood head and shoulders taller than most people in the crowd, was the sole focus of attention.

Warden James Clancy was waiting by the gate with several of his guards, and the jailers cleared a path for Becker and the sheriffs as they approached the jail. "When I saw my husband coming up the hill with a string of reporters after him," Helen Becker continued,

> I almost broke down, but I controlled myself. A prison guard came to me and said, "Better go away and avoid these reporters. Come back in half an hour." So I went away and when I came back they took me down to the death house where my husband had been brought. We went through a long stone passage with iron doors and little iron windows where people peek out at you, and when we passed the punishment cells I had a feeling I almost wished Charley had died before he came here. Finally we stopped before a cell, and there was my husband. I never saw such a look of agony on anybody's face— a gray look. He did not say anything—he could not talk—and they told me to come back the next day. I did come back, and this was the beginning of many visits to the death house.

Sing Sing was indeed an awful and depressing place, ninety years old and as famously unsanitary as the Tombs itself. The prison hunched on the banks of the Hudson, thirty miles north of New York (hence the expression "sent up the river"), and was completely enclosed within high walls. Massive cell blocks, hand-hewn by Sing Sing's earliest prisoners from the dirty gray marble that abounded in the district, loomed five stories high on either side of grimy concrete walkways. The largest of these blocks contained nothing but row upon row of windowless, one-man cells—eight hundred in all, each measuring no more than seven feet long by three feet wide, fronted by thick, close-hatched iron grilles, and equipped with nothing more than a cot, a chair, a jug, and a slop bucket.

Conditions in Sing Sing were, in fact, past their worst by the time Becker arrived there in the autumn of 1912. "Lockstep," a time-honored but degrading method of marching inmates together in long, shuffling crocodiles, had been abandoned at the turn of the century, and the inmates' traditional uniform of black-and-white-striped jackets and trousers—made famous by cartoons and early movies, and traditionally used to distinguish among prisoners*—went the same way five years later. Sing Sing inmates were now dressed in gray trousers and shirts, topped with small round caps, and many of the harsher punishments that had been used to maintain discipline in the nineteenth century—including near drownings and the hanging of malefactors by their thumbs—had long been discontinued.

The jail nonetheless remained horribly depressing. Men spent as much as twenty-three hours a day locked up in their cells; there were few opportunities for exercise, and virtually all games were banned. The primary recreation—especially popular among the jail's large population of illiterates—was checkers, played on the paper boards that most prisoners kept by their beds, by men who called out moves to neighbors in adjacent cells. Inmates were entitled to only one bath and one shave a week, and few survived long years of this regime without displaying at least some signs of mental anguish. According to Dr. Amos Squire, who became prison physician not long after Becker first arrived at Ossining, one of his principal duties was "to knock on the door of each dark cell daily to discover if the occupant had fallen ill, or lost his mind."

In an attempt to spare ordinary prisoners from the even more oppressive atmosphere on death row, the dozen or so murderers in the condemned cells were sequestered in a brand-new block that had been erected a little distance from the main bulk of the prison. The Sing Sing death house was regarded, in the prison service, as a model of its kind. It had its own cells, kitchen, and hospital and its own power

---

*The system was a simple one. First offenders wore one stripe, second offenders two, and incorrigibles with four offenses or more to their names sported the completed "zebra" uniform.

supply (for all the lurid rumors, it was simply not true that lights in the village dimmed whenever an execution took place)—even a room where the bodies of condemned men were autopsied after their electrocution. Becker spent half an hour a day in the house's narrow, cinder-floored exercise yard (his daily routine was to run around the yard half a dozen times and while away the remainder of his time slamming a ball against the wall) and was given more or less unfettered access to newspapers, pen, and paper. In some respects, then, death-house regulations were less stringent than those in the prison proper. But the looming inevitability of execution, and fear of what the procedure would entail, was profoundly unsettling. According to Squire, the sound the death-row prisoners dreaded most was the insistent rasping noise that reverberated from the autopsy room as he sawed off the top of an executed prisoner's skull.

The weeks and months in Sing Sing passed slowly for Charles Becker. He was permitted to receive visitors no more than once or twice a week, and there were limits to the number of letters each man could send and receive. But the inquisitive newsmen who followed his progress reported that he adapted well to the conditions. The once-corrupt and brutal cop, they wrote, had found a measure of redemption within the bleak walls of the prison, displaying, in extremis, reserves of character and decency that surprised those who had never known him well.

Not only did Becker discover, on death row, true pleasure in reading for the first time in his life (his favorite work was *Measure for Measure:* "There is so much in it that fitted my case, and some terrific passages on death in it, too"*); he also helped and comforted the men in the other condemned cells. "He found," one New York journalist concluded,

> qualities in himself that he had not drawn on before. No formal social life was permitted among the men in the death-house,

---

*Another favorite was Captain Scott's South Pole diary, which Becker apparently clung to as a symbol of the freedom he had lost. The diary certainly provided him with a bizarre form of release: "One thing I would like to do after clearing up the Rosenthal case," he told a disbelieving newsman, "is go to the North Pole. That diary of Scott's is one of the greatest things ever printed."

but every sound carried. He began to read aloud in the evenings—Western stories were especially popular among the prisoners, he said. As he built up seniority, Becker became a kind of counselor to the other men on the block. In a small, grotesque world, he had reached the top at last.

The condemned man's principal preoccupation during his first months in Sing Sing was marshaling a case for an appeal, and his first difficulty was in finding new attorneys. John McIntyre had resigned from the case shortly after the verdict on his client was announced, and John Hart had left New York to practice law in California. Becker himself was now in straitened circumstances; the whole of his money, it appears, had been expended on his defense, the cost of which had apparently topped $20,000. Funding for an appeal was obtained by remortgaging the house at Olinville Avenue, but even then the lieutenant could no longer afford a lawyer of McIntyre's repute. His choice eventually fell on Joseph Shay, a vocal and enthusiastic attorney who came cheap but had little experience of the criminal courts. Shay had hitherto specialized chiefly in personal-injury cases and on one occasion had been suspended by the New York bar as a chronic ambulance chaser.

As Becker whiled away the hours in the Sing Sing death house, his wife struggled to adapt to life without him. The big house on Olinville Avenue was in a lonely spot, she found, "and sometimes I have thought that it has a sinister air, with its gray walls painted over in broad red lines that form strange oblongs on dull concrete. Few people pass here and rarely a carriage or an automobile. At night the street is dark and quiet under the rustling trees." She could not even think of the place as home, "for my husband has never lived there."

Soon after moving in, Helen began to suffer from a bizarre series of accidents and setbacks. When the new house was broken into on her first night in residence, she obtained a guard dog she called Bum. But "Bum bit a milkman, and the milkman put the case in the hands of a lawyer named Rosenthal—think of that!—and finally a policeman shot poor Bum." Then, shortly before Christmas 1913, Mrs. Becker's maid, a girl named Lena Schneider, contrived to smash the glass top shielding her employer's dining room table and, "reading her discharge in the broken pieces and utterly forlorn," committed suicide in her room by swallowing sixty grains of corrosive sublimate.* The policeman's wife bought herself a pet canary for company after that, but the bird died, too.

Worse followed. By the winter of 1912, Helen, who was now thirty-eight, was heavily pregnant with her first child. In January there were complications. She was taken to the hospital, where she spent four weeks under observation and endured a prolonged labor before giving birth, on February 1, by caesarean section—a very dangerous procedure at the time. It did little good. The Beckers' baby ("It was a little girl, just what I wanted") was overdue and weak, and the child died later the same day. Charles Becker had liked the name Ruth for a girl, but his wife called the baby Charlotte and had her buried at Woodlawn Cemetery in the Bronx.

When word of her daughter's death got out, Helen was deluged with messages of sympathy. But it did not take the newspapers long to discover that there was another side to her story. Charlotte Becker's death, one reporter wrote, "had been the result of a decision made in the delivery room by her mother. She had been given the choice of saving her life or the child's, and had chosen her own. She did not deny this."

Inevitably, Mrs. Becker forfeited the public's sympathy, and the earlier, friendly mail gave way to letters denouncing her as a betrayer of the ideals of motherhood and even as a murderer. "One correspondent pointed out that there were now two cold-blooded murderers in the family. Another mentioned Lady Macbeth." Helen tried hopelessly to explain that she'd had little choice:

> The birth of my baby was delayed, and the long wait was terrible. At the last moment I was told I had to decide whether to take a chance on my life or the baby's. I had no more than a minute or two to balance my instincts against the situation. If I died, and my husband's appeal failed, the child would soon

---

*Bichloride of mercury, a highly toxic fungicide.

become an orphan. Then again I thought of the position my husband was in, there in prison under sentence of death, and I knew that my life would be more help to him than the baby's. So I decided that if there had to be a choice, my life was to be saved.

The attempt did her little good. New York's opinion of Helen Becker changed irrevocably after her baby's death. Once the school-teacher had been praised as an ideal wife and partner: loyal, nurturing, supportive, and womanly. Now she seemed something altogether steelier. Sitting in her parents' apartment in Brooklyn, even little Viña Delmar caught the mood:

> I know Mamma pictured Helen Becker lying in a hospital bed sobbing her heart out for the dead baby. I do not think it was that way for Helen Becker at all. I am sure she interpreted the loss of the child as a clear sign from Heaven that nothing was to hamper her hard struggle to save Becker. I think she concerned herself with the religious aspects of the baby's birth and death, rejoicing that life had not fluttered away before the sacraments could be administered. I think that then Helen Becker had lain quietly upon her pillow, wondering who could get her an interview with President-elect [Woodrow] Wilson.

In his cell in Ossining, meanwhile, her husband wept—the only tears that he had shed since his arrest.

Becker's hopes were dealt a further blow when the trial of Whitey Lewis, Lefty Louie, Dago Frank, and Gyp the Blood began three weeks after his conviction. The same judge, Goff, presided, with predictable results. This time the case was over in only a week—the gunmen had been unable to afford expensive representation—and the jury returned its guilty verdict in slightly under half an hour, "a speed unprecedented in the history of first degree convictions in the county," according to the most ancient court official the swarm of pressmen could locate.

There were abundant echoes of the Becker trial in the proceedings. Jack Rose was once again Whitman's star witness, outlining in hushed tones the steps that he had taken to recruit the killers, and Goff, too, was his usual self, hurrying things along at a great pace and delivering a jury charge that left little doubt he believed the four men guilty. The gunmen were vocal in their condemnation of Justice Goff—"The jury would have convicted a priest after that stuff," was Whitey Lewis's reaction to Goff's summation—and particularly angered by the judge's habit of referring to them solely by their nicknames. Certainly Goff's convenient verbal tic lent a distinct air of East Side menace to the proceedings, and a dock containing Lefty Louie, Whitey Lewis, and Dago Frank undoubtedly appeared a good deal more authentically criminal than one holding Louis Rosenberg, Jacob Seidenschmer, and Francis Cirofici. "Surely," Harry Horowitz's lawyer groaned, in a rare moment of effectiveness, "it is a wonderful aid to the conviction of a man, presumed innocent, to have him described by the trial judge himself as 'Gyp the Blood.' "

Each of the four defendants had denied, under oath, having anything to do with Lieutenant Becker, but most New Yorkers ignored this inconvenient fact and felt that the slew of guilty verdicts confirmed that the right decision had been reached in Becker's trial. Few, outside the gunmen's immediate families, expressed much regret when their appeals were all rejected and the members of the gang were executed in April 1914. Whitey Lewis was the only one of the four to die loudly protesting his innocence—"They're perjurers," he insisted as the straps were tightened around him. "I swear by God I didn't fire a shot at Herman Rosenthal"*—and Lefty Louie, who had received a good deal of religious instruction while in jail, went so far as to compose an open letter, warning "other East Side boys" of the dangers of falling in with the street gangs of the slum districts. Dago Frank, the odd man out, who had been a late recruit to the conspiracy and who had consistently denied playing any part in the killing, was dragged

---

*This was very likely true. Lewis was a notoriously poor shot who probably would not have been trusted to hit Herman even at close range.

kicking and struggling to his death, a crucifix clutched tightly in each hand. The other men went quietly and unaided. It took less than half an hour to kill them all.

The bleakness of the gunmen's end and the tedium of Becker's drab Sing Sing existence contrasted sharply with the lives of the four gamblers whose evidence had placed the doomed men in the death house.

Shrugging off public disquiet that several self-confessed killers were to go free, Whitman honored the immunity arrangements he had offered his key witnesses and released all four the day after the verdicts in the gunmen's trial came in. Sam Schepps was released from custody at lunchtime on November 21, 1912, and promptly announced his intention to leave New York. But the reporters in attendance displayed far more interest in the release of Rose, Vallon, and Webber, which followed a few hours later. Webber, the newsmen wrote, was released just in time to join his ermine-clad wife on board a liner sailing for Havana, and even Bald Jack Rose—who had spoken on the witness stand of his fear that friends of Zelig's would come gunning for him—seemed in the highest of high spirits.

> Bridgey Webber had a case of champagne brought in. Newspapermen wandered up and down the cell blocks interviewing keepers and other inmates about the habits of the four celebrities. . . . Fifteen hundred people clogged 53rd Street to watch the departure of the three gamblers. Beautifully pressed, smelling of lavender water, and each swinging a cane, Bridgey, Vallon and Bald Jack climbed in to a large touring car—not a Packard—that awaited them at the door. "I will be at the office of my lawyer, to meet any gangsters who might care to see me," Rose shouted out of the window as the car started up, and they rode off towards Second Avenue in fits of laughter.

If Bald Jack and his friends ever really feared violent retribution from either Becker or the remnants of Jack Zelig's gang, they certainly recovered their nerve quickly enough. Rose and Vallon were often noticed strolling through Satan's Circus during the early months of 1913, and Sam Schepps went so far as to renege on his promise to leave town and opened up a jewelry store on Broadway. It was there, on one hot afternoon, that Helen Becker came by appointment to meet Jack Rose and plead with him to tell the truth about her husband. Rose, scarcely surprisingly, proved unresponsive, and Schepps, equally predictably, seemed most concerned to boast about his own importance. "I hold the secret of the Becker case, and I will tell the Governor if he asks me," the con man told a small group of reporters, adding sotto voce that there was not really that much he could do: "Do you want that I should go so far as to bring Charley Becker back to Broadway and I take his place in the electric chair?"

Becker, for his part, placed no faith in Schepps and his coterie of criminals. For nearly eighteen months after his conviction, however, the lieutenant was buoyed by news from both New York and Albany and seemed confident that there was still a chance of an acquittal. One positive development concerned Joseph Shay, Becker's ineffectual, ambulance-chasing lawyer, who suddenly resigned from the case citing the unexpectedly demanding nature of criminal practice, to be replaced by a more eminent, able, and harder-working litigator by the name of Martin Manton. Becker's new attorney, who had earned the nickname "Preying" Manton for his ability to set cunning courtroom traps, was considerably more expensive than Shay, and Helen Becker was forced to pay his bills by signing over the deeds of the couple's house to him. But Manton had one inestimable advantage in her husband's eyes. He was the law partner of a renowned orator called Bourke Cockran, an influential Democrat who had been Grand Sachem of Tammany Hall for the fours years from 1905 to 1909. Cockran had had a falling-out with Charlie Murphy after that, and his partnership with Manton was "mainly an office-sharing arrangement," anyway. But he was a celebrated advocate, and Becker no doubt felt that even a tenuous link with Tammany was better now than no link at all. Manton got quickly to work, and soon proved his worth by digging up several important new witnesses.

Even better news came from Albany in January 1913 when a group
of the lieutenant's friends and supporters engineered a meeting with
the new governor of New York State, William Sulzer. Sulzer, a
protégé of Big Tim Sullivan's, agreed to reexamine the Becker trial
and was presented with "a mass of affidavits and other evidence
to prove his innocence." The governor apparently possessed
privileged information—perhaps it came from Sullivan himself—for
he assured the deputation that he "knew some things bearing on the
case" and asked Becker's supporters to wait for the verdict of the court
of appeals. If the policeman was refused a second trial, Sulzer promised, he would step in to save him.*

Helen, who was permitted to visit her husband in the death house
for ninety minutes every week, noticed a definite improvement in the
condemned man's demeanor after that, and so did the newspaper
reporters who occasionally trooped up to Ossining to file updates on
the case. "Becker," said the *Herald*, "behaved almost as if he was the
Czar of the Tenderloin once more. With Manton on the case he had
recovered much of his old chestiness and swore he still expected to be
released."

By the first months of 1914, then, Becker's prospects appeared
considerably improved. Manton's work on his client's appeal was well
advanced, and there were ample grounds, the new attorney promised,
on which to argue that the policeman had been denied a fair trial,
from the court's failure to admit key pieces of evidence to Justice
Goff's apparent eagerness to help the prosecution. Then there were
Manton's new witnesses. Unlike McIntyre and Shay, the new defense
team had done considerable spadework and managed to uncover a
mass of fascinating testimony. Among Manton's discoveries were the
two men who owned the car in which Webber and Schepps had sworn
they were driven to the Harlem Conference (their names, somehow in
keeping with the case, were Moe and Itch) and the superintendent of a

---

* "I intended to commute Becker's sentence," Sulzer added a decade later, "and then to
  pardon him. I was convinced of Becker's innocence without considering the affidavits
  submitted."

building that stood just across the street from the one vacant lot then present on West 124th Street. According to the chauffeurs, they'd had no doings with any of the gamblers on the June evening Whitman had belatedly established as the date the conference had taken place—which put the witnesses' account of the fatal meeting into considerable doubt. And according to the building superintendent, the lot where the fatal meeting was supposedly held had been a thirty-foot-deep hole in June 1912. How, Manton queried, was it possible that the four gamblers who had testified against his client could have failed to mention such a dramatic landmark?

Of course, Charles Becker did not have things all his own way during the long months following the verdict, and just when the lieutenant and his defense team had begun to feel genuinely confident of their chances, the prospects of an acquittal darkened once again. One severe blow landed in the late summer of 1913, when William Sulzer fell out with Boss Murphy. The dispute between the two men did not last for long; when Sulzer refused to offer Tammany several attractive pieces of patronage that Murphy thought his due, the boss, in an impressive show of political muscle, simply had the governor impeached and replaced with a more pliant deputy. That removed the safety net that Becker had depended on. Then Whitman got to work undermining Manton's new evidence for the defense.

With the gubernatorial elections coming up, there was no way that the DA could possibly afford to let the case on which his reputation had been built disintegrate, and Becker's old nemesis proved more than willing to match "Preying" Manton trick for trick. More or less as soon as the policeman's attorney had submitted his imposing dossier of evidence to the court of appeals, stories began to crop up in the press hinting that the district attorney, too, had much improved his case. Over the course of the next few weeks, prosecution witnesses popped up at strategically placed intervals, announcing one after another that they had been approached by Becker's agents and offered vast sums—$2,000, $5,000, $10,000—to testify for the defense. The fact that several of the men concerned, including the Luban brothers and Sam Schepps, had been so badly compromised by their maulings in the first trial that Whitman would scarcely dare to call on them again made no apparent difference. Soon after that, a number of lowlifes who had testified at the gunmen's trial began alleging that they, too, were being pressed by the defense. At least one witness claimed that Becker's brother John, the detective, had coerced him into perjuring himself, and each in his own way implied that the Becker brothers hoped to keep the four gangsters alive pending an appeal. After that, Swope and the *World* pitched in with a series of alarmist stories alleging that the lieutenant's old friends at police headquarters were raising a huge defense fund in Satan's Circus. The vision of Gyp the Blood and his companions dodging their appointments with the electric chair, and of hordes of brothel keepers and gamblers digging deep into their pockets to save a corrupt cop proved nicely calculated to revive New Yorkers' inbred fear of the police, and by the time the Becker appeal was heard, few citizens recalled that Whitman and his team had not produced a single piece of evidence to prove any of the claims.

One other fundamental change occurred in the political landscape of New York while the court of appeals considered Manton's dossier. Tim Sullivan died, mysteriously, at the beginning of September 1913. His lunacy had become more marked over the summer, and he had taken to running away from his asylum and making for the railway line into New York, where he would hitch rides on freight trains heading for the city and wander along the waterfront or into the lobby of his old headquarters at the Occidental Hotel. According to "Commodore Dutch," the old Bowery bum to whom Tim had once granted permission to set up a racket, he would "just sit in the lobby and stare until they come and took him away." "I seen him one day," the Commodore recalled two decades later, "and I went over to him and I said, 'Jesus Christ, Big Tim, old pal, ain't there something I could do for you?' He just sat and stared at me. It broke my heart."

Eventually, on August 31, at the end of an all-night card game that put his guards to sleep, Tim disappeared for good. For two weeks New Yorkers speculated as to his whereabouts; then the policeman required by law to take a last look at each body lying unclaimed in the Bronx morgue lifted the sheet covering an unidentified and badly mangled corpse. It was Sullivan. He had been run over by a train on the night he vanished—probably trying to hop another freight. There were rumors, though, that Big Tim's death was somehow linked to the Becker case and that someone had made sure the old Tammany boss was "taken care of" before he could tell what he knew of Rosenthal's murder. The brakeman who'd found Sullivan lying by the tracks was questioned and said the body had been cold. He believed that Tim had been dead before he was cut to pieces by the train.

The funeral, in any event, was among the most spectacular New York had seen, and 25,000 people followed Sullivan's coffin to Old St. Patrick's, where the streets had been scrubbed clean in honor of the occasion and eight priests officiated at a requiem mass.

While these minor earthquakes shook the political landscape of New York, the legal fight for Becker's life proceeded at the traditional tortuous pace. It took the court of appeals more than three months to consider the evidence assembled by Shay and Manton, and the policeman had been in the death house for over a year when the court's decision finally came down on February 24, 1914.

Word of the ruling, when it did arrive, surprised almost everyone. Becker's conviction was overturned—not by a narrow majority, or on some legal technicality, but by a six-to-one majority of the appellate judges in a verdict generally regarded as "one of the most slashing in the history of the court." The court censured the district attorney's office for whipping up a climate of public hysteria, and Goff's conduct during the trial itself was criticized across seventy-seven strongly worded pages.

Much fault was found with the evidence in the case. Whitman, the appeals court ruled, had acted improperly in arranging for the release of men such as Jacob and Morris Luban—who had been in prison prior to the trial—to enable the men to take the stand as witnesses, and had been even more at fault for promoting Sam Schepps as a corroborating witness. The slippery con man, judges of the superior court concluded, was almost certainly an accomplice to the murder of Herman Rosenthal; the notion that he could possibly have been an independent corroborating witness was "opposed to the overwhelming weight of evidence." Indeed, the very idea that any of the DA's principal witnesses had given independent and unbiased evidence appeared implausible, given the "ample opportunities that existed for collaboration on the evidence they were to give under their life-saving agreement to convict Becker."

The lieutenant's motive for committing murder came in for equally severe scrutiny. Becker, it was pointed out, had "expressed himself as quite indifferent to Rosenthal's efforts" to several different witnesses, and he appeared to have no reason to suppose that Herman's desperate attempts to interest Whitman in his allegations would have dangerous consequences. As for the Harlem Conference, the justices of the court of appeals clearly doubted that it had ever taken place.

The meat of the court's long ruling, though, was its protracted criticism, from a legal standpoint, of the actions of Whitman and Goff. The DA was found to have wrongly made "prejudicial suggestions" that could only have damaged Becker's hopes—the suggestion, to potential members of the jury, that the defendant was "a cool, calculating, grafting police officer," for instance. Goff, meanwhile, was taken to task for his indecent haste and numerous instances of bias, the most serious of which—the judgment hinted—was the failure to treat the opposing teams of attorneys equally. Goff's determination to cut short McIntyre's cross-examination of Bald Jack Rose was cited in support of this contention. The appellate judges were also clearly worried by his charge to the jury—which outlined "most effectively" the case for the prosecution while ignoring "any arguments or evidence in behalf of the defense." Indeed, the justices of the appeals court noted,

without exception every appeal made by defendant's counsel . . . for an adjournment was denied, whereas applications of a similar character on the part of the People were quite uniformly granted.

"I emphatically deny," Judge Nathan Miller concluded in his concurring opinion, "that we are obliged to sign the defendant's death warrant simply because a jury has believed an improbable tale told by four vile criminals to shift the death penalty from themselves to another."

District Attorney Whitman's position, those who digested the court of appeals' ruling could see, now appeared unenviable. Several of his most important witnesses had been thoroughly discredited—not least Schepps, whose corroborating evidence had been the sole thread on which Whitman had dangled the tale of the Harlem Conference. The disgrace of Morris Luban similarly rendered the story of Becker's noisy consultation at the Lafayette Baths inadmissible as evidence. To make matters worse, several senior Republicans began to mutter that the DA's "availability" for higher office would be badly compromised by failure to convict Becker in a retrial.

For more than a week, indeed, the very idea of trying the lieutenant again for Rosenthal's murder seemed utterly implausible. Manton, cornered by the press, proclaimed his belief that his client would now simply be set free, and even the *New York Times* observed that "Mr. Whitman did not believe a second conviction would be possible in view of the decision handed down by the court."

It was, perhaps inevitably, Herbert Swope who steadied the DA. The *World* man, like Whitman, stood to lose some of his hard-won reputation if the Rosenthal case collapsed, and he was adamant that Becker had to stand trial for a second time. Swope also discerned an ugly public mood. Many New Yorkers remained convinced of Becker's guilt—Goff's mishandling of the lieutenant's trial was a mere technicality, these people thought—and the reporter had little compunction in stoking this undercurrent of hatred. What the *Times* termed Becker's "sincere belief" that he would one day be set free became, in the *World*, the policeman's "taunt that Whitman would never dare to try him again."

It took only a few days of this coverage for the renewed public clamor for a retrial to become so deafening that the DA felt thoroughly emboldened. Becker, he announced in the first days of

January 1914, would certainly be tried again; it was in the public interest. He and his staff would press the case as best they could "in spite of the terrible handicaps under which the prosecution must now labor." Accordingly, a retrial was ordered and a new judge installed. And in May the whole process began again.

One consequence of the verdict handed down by the court of appeals was that Becker became a private citizen again. He could no longer be kept at Sing Sing, and it was decided to transfer him back to the Tombs, where he could be held for his own safety while awaiting a second trial.

The reporters who had traveled up to Ossining to see Becker reunited with his wife noted that a curious reversal had occurred. The lieutenant, who had exchanged his prison clothes for an ordinary suit for the first time in more than eighteen months, looked significantly older than before. But his wife—on whose face, unchivalrous newsmen observed, numerous "harsh lines" had begun to appear—once again looked carefree and a decade younger.

There had been a massive fall of snow the previous evening, and the party had to travel from the prison to the railway station by sleigh. The Beckers' carriage was followed by nine more sleighs filled with guards and journalists, and as the caravan slid off past the cell blocks in a hiss of snow, bells jangling in the clear air, "from the hundreds of slitted windows came a roar of cheering as, to a man, the convicts yelled their good wishes to a man who had got another chance, . . . an uncanny sound of concerted gladness coming from the dismal buildings." Helen, her cheeks "scarlet with cold and pleasure," confessed that she had never been so happy in her life.

Charles Becker's second trial for murder opened on May 5, 1914. Whitman had returned to lead the case for the prosecution; the DA could no more afford to let a man as earnest and unflashy as Frank Moss handle the trial than he could imagine squandering the political capital he had gained. Martin Manton marshaled the defense. The new judge was Samuel Seabury, an anti-Tammany Democrat who, like

Goff, had made his name crusading against police corruption. Seabury—whose "snow white hair," wrote the *World*, "neatly parted in the center, contrasted with his ruddy complexion and flowing black silk robes"—had once been the youngest judge in New York. Now, at the age of forty-one, he seemed prematurely aged, and "his air of severe judicial probity gave the room a far different atmosphere from the days when the outrageous Goff sat in the same high-backed chair."

The second trial was more sober, more measured, and—both the press and the spectators in the Criminal Courts Building agreed—a much more close-run thing than Becker's first. "So tense was the courtroom," wrote a reporter for the *New York World*, "that even a shrug of the judge's shoulders during the testimony, or a smile of incredulity or a lifting of the eyebrows would have swung the case." In this charged atmosphere, Manton was generally held to have outdone his predecessor, McIntyre, bringing home the implausibilities in the prosecution case to good effect, while Whitman's performance was generally lackluster.

The DA had nonetheless done remarkably well to rescue his failing case. He produced the same long stream of witnesses to the events outside the Metropole and then capped them with Jack Rose, who took the stand on the eighth day of the trial and "acted like a man who is bored to death with repeating a story which rose from his mouth as easily as water from a spring." Rose's evidence regarding Becker's bloodcurdling threats, attentive reporters noted, was indistinguishable from that which he had presented at the lieutenant's earlier trial, but Manton devoted a lengthy cross-examination to pointing up several dozen discrepancies between Bald Jack's earliest depositions and the statements he now made in court. Becker's attorney scored several valuable points, but, unfortunately for the policeman, he concluded his examination by making the fatal mistake of posing an open-ended question.

"When you were planning this murder, did not your conscience prick you?" Manton demanded of Rose.

"My conscience was under the entire control of Becker," Bald Jack replied to a scattering of applause from the public galleries. This barb was considered a solid blow to the defense.

Rose's place on the witness stand was taken by Bridgey Webber, who did his best to explain away the bizarre anomaly that Manton had discovered regarding the gigantic excavation at the site of the Harlem Conference. After taking a hasty recess, Webber responded that there had been a small area along the edge of the pit where the gamblers had stood. The fact that neither Bridgey, Rose, nor Vallon had ever mentioned the thirty-foot hole that they were standing next to was played down ably by Whitman, and Webber was excused to allow Vallon to take the stand. The faro dealer's evidence, too, was much the same as it had been before, but on this occasion Vallon did recall a good deal more about the "little colored stool pigeon" he remembered hanging about while Becker and the gamblers talked.

The meaning of Vallon's suddenly improved memory was not at all clear to those listening in court at the time, and the true reason for his careful description of the teenage boy did not emerge until the last day of prosecution testimony. By then, most of those in court agreed, Whitman's case seemed weaker than it had before. Thanks, no doubt, to the savaging he had received at the hands of the court of appeals, Sam Schepps was never called to give evidence at the second trial. That meant that no one but accomplices had testified to hearing Becker say or do anything that might connect him to the murder. The lieutenant's supposed appearance at the Lafayette Baths was likewise never mentioned before Justice Seabury, and his alleged meetings in Harlem and at the Murray Hill Baths still rested on the unsupported testimony of Jack Rose and his two friends. A large number of reporters wondered why Whitman had even introduced their evidence, since the judgment of the appeals court had made it clear that no jury could convict without hearing evidence from a corroborator. It was, with carefully judged timing, only on that final afternoon that Whitman came up with dramatic new testimony that something had indeed been discussed one June night on the corner of West 124th Street and Seventh Avenue. This time the DA had fixed a specific date for the rendezvous: June 27. He also had a new corroborating witness.

Whitman's surprise witness was the "little colored stool [pigeon]" Harry Vallon had mentioned in passing at Becker's earlier trial. His name was James Marshall, and he was a scrawny "buck and wing dancer"—a tap dancer—who had picked up some money occasionally by supplying tips to the Strong Arm Squads about gambling houses up in Harlem. Superficially, at least, the evidence that Marshall gave that afternoon seemed unimportant; he testified that he had been with Becker on the night in question and had seen him talking on the street with a man in a hat, whom he identified as Bald Jack Rose. Nothing in the dancer's testimony hinted at the topic of conversation, but the simple fact that Marshall had seen Rose and Becker talking deeply impressed both judge and jury. It suggested that Vallon's testimony was true. And it implied that Jack Rose's story of the Harlem Conference was correct.

Marshall's unexpected appearance on the stand put a stop to Manton's bullish talk of not bothering to mount a defense, a line the attorney had been spinning to the press ever since the trial started. But the case that the defense mounted seemed much the same as that formerly assembled by McIntyre. Jack Sullivan—more vocal than ever—spoke once again for Becker, and a number of East Siders appeared to testify that Rose and Webber had been actively gathering donations from their gambling friends to help get Herman out of town. But none of the new witnesses were of good character, a fact that Whitman carefully brought out on cross-examination.

Most observers felt after all this that the Becker case remained finely balanced. Both sides announced that they confidently expected victory. But not everyone in Whitman's office was quite so certain as their boss was. In the days before the final pleas were heard, at least one assistant district attorney—a man named Billy De Paul—was noticed "going around town saying it was a good thing for Whitman that he didn't have to submit the case to a jury of his own staff." The prospects for an acquittal, Manton reassured his client, were solid.

All this changed when Seabury made his charge to the jury. The judge, who had hitherto remained impassive—he had, the *World* said, "sat throughout the case as if his face was carved of stone"—was just as aware as Whitman of the political importance of the Becker case. Having privately agreed to run for office on the Democratic ticket—and

gauged the prevailing hostility of the New York press to the defense—
he delivered a summation that accepted almost all of the main planks of
the prosecution's argument. Becker's junior counsel was so upset that
he leaped to his feet as soon as Seabury had finished: "I object to the
whole charge on the grounds that it is an animated argument for the
prosecution!" the lawyer cried.

Becker's retrial had taken a fraction longer than Goff's hearing—
nineteen days rather than seventeen—but, thanks largely to Marshall's
new evidence and to the judge's summation, this jury required even
less time than Goff's had to find the policeman guilty: merely an hour
and a half. Many of the journalists covering the case were shocked—
the majority thought the policeman guilty, while agreeing there was
scarcely evidence enough to justify a conviction. Manton and the
defense team were stunned into silence; they were certain they had
done enough to win.

Becker, wrote Edwin Hill of the *Sun*, "had himself under magnificent control" as he awaited the verdict.

> His iron nerve was not bending. Those who watched him did
> not see a sign of agitation. He was breathing slowly—you
> could see that from the rise and fall of his powerful chest—and
> smiling slightly as he glanced towards his counsel. He took the
> blow without a quiver.

Helen Becker—mindful of the awful experience of the first trial—
had awaited the verdict in an anteroom. Once again she knew without
hearing the words. "After a time," she said, "I saw people coming out
of the courtroom slowly and dejectedly, and my heart sank, for I realized that we had lost again. I could see by the way they walked that it
was bad news. After good news, people walk briskly."

CHAPTER 12

DEATH HOUSE

ECKER'S SECOND CONVICTION for murder was practically unprecedented. Retrials, as several papers pointed out, almost invariably resulted in either a mistrial or an acquittal. There had been only one other case of a repeat conviction in the entire history of New York State.

The policeman's bitterness was exacerbated by the fact that he had again been found guilty of murder in the first degree. At the end of his earlier trial, his own defense team had insisted that it would accept only two verdicts: not guilty or guilty of first-degree murder. McIntyre had hoped this announcement would push the jury toward an acquittal. Manton—perhaps less confident, perhaps simply less hubristic—had made no such stipulation and the jury (noted Hill of the *Sun*)

> could have saved Becker's life even in finding him guilty if they had wanted to show mercy. Justice Seabury had told them they could choose among three degrees of murder, and two of those degrees would have meant imprisonment. But like twenty-four men who had gone before them, the first Becker jury and the gunmen's jury, they believed that Jack Rose told the truth. . . . Becker and his counsel never thought there was a chance in the world that twelve men after the Court of Appeals decision would send Becker to the chair.

The throng outside the courthouse was just as large and just as hostile to the policeman as they had been nearly two years earlier, but this time there was no comforting crowd of friends and relatives to offer Becker their support. The lieutenant and his wife had waited alone in the sheriff's office for the verdict, and Becker was taken back to Sing Sing by car, the members of his escort explaining that they had heard worrying reports of an angry mob assembling at Grand Central Station. This time the condemned man was led to a cell on the death house's upper tier that had not been used for several years. It was much smaller than the one he had occupied before the second trial and had no fitted toilet, only a slop bucket. "That's one of the hottest cells we got," a keeper observed unsympathetically. "And it looks like a hot summer coming up."

One thing had changed for the better at Sing Sing since Becker left it for New York City: A new warden, Thomas Mott Osborne, had arrived at the jail. Osborne was a craggily handsome and wealthy patrician from Auburn, in upstate New York, who had spent much of his youth as an active Tammany Democrat. After a spectacular falling-out with Boss Murphy, he had abandoned politics and developed an unquenchable passion for prison reform, fueled perhaps by memories of a childhood tour of the enormous prison in his hometown, which had left him with nightmares of being chased down darkened streets by an escaped prisoner. Some of the new warden's concerns, admittedly, could only have been held by a man of Osborne's elevated social class— he was outraged at the idea that prisoners were forced to sleep in their underclothes, rather than being issued pajamas—but he was the first Sing Sing warden not to owe his appointment to patronage and the first to be a genuine reformer. Almost all of Osborne's predecessors had been outsiders foisted on the prison by Tammany as a reward for services rendered—their numbers included "a steam-fitter, a coal dealer, a horseman and a drunkard (by avocation if not by profession)"—the majority of whom, despairing of the prospect of controlling their brutal charges, had ruled through a system of harsh discipline, rigorously enforced. In most cases, however, "brutality and incompetence [had] seemed to go together—so much so that suspensions and removals were incredibly frequent." A warden of Sing Sing lasted on average less than a year, a fact that did much to explain the prison's enduring reputation as a hellhole that sucked prisoners in and destroyed them.

Thomas Mott Osborne arrived at Ossining determined to change all this, and his root-and-branch reforms improved the lot of every prisoner, even those confined to the death house. Some of the changes were purely superficial—the warden saw to it that the thick drifts of litter in the yards were removed—but others were so radical that they still appear astonishing more than a century later. By far the most dramatic was the creation of a prisoners' association that Osborne named the Mutual Welfare League (MWL). Membership in the league, Osborne stressed, was a privilege and not a right, earned by continued good behavior. But so convinced was the new warden that no man was beyond redemption that he ceded much of the responsibility for discipline within the prison to an MWL committee, which sat in judgment on malefactors even in cases of attempted murder.

Remarkably, the system worked. Osborne's first day at Sing Sing, the *New York Times* observed, "was a success in every way. There were no incendiary fires, no riots, and no strikes—all marks of the coming and going of wardens in the past." Within days the new prison governor was mingling contentedly with men who had been forbidden to approach within fifteen feet of his predecessors. To the horror of his guards, Osborne even went so far as to decline the loaded revolver other wardens had invariably carried with them on their rounds.*

Osborne, with his fervent belief in men's potential for redemption, had long been an opponent of the death penalty and swore early during his incumbency that he would never be found in the death house when a man was being executed. But the new warden did distinguish between ordinary prisoners and men convicted of a capital crime. Many of his reforms, from the right to receive visitors on Sundays to

---

*Osborne was well known to many of the prisoners. One of his most famous experiments, undertaken a year earlier, had been to spend a week in the Auburn jail as a prisoner himself, an experience that resulted in a book, *Within Prison Walls*, and only enhanced the warden's natural sympathy for the men in his charge. The prisoners, in turn—so Osborne's biographer asserts—"trusted him completely. His absolute confidence was all the protection he needed."

the dispensation to purchase postage stamps, never applied to the men in the death house; nor were condemned men permitted to join the Mutual Welfare League. Almost the only privilege extended to them under Osborne's rule was the right to hear regular Sunday-evening concerts, and even then the death-house men remained segregated from the other prisoners. Gazing curiously at Becker as he passed through the tiers of condemned cells—the brawny policeman stood, literally, head and shoulders above most Sing Sing inmates and was an object of intense curiosity throughout his time in jail—Osborne found himself repelled by the prisoner's appearance: "In spite of the handsome face and splendid physique there was a hardness about the eyes and mouth that spoke of unscrupulousness, even cruelty." Such a man, the warden thought, might easily stoop to murder. But as he got to know Lieutenant Becker over the succeeding months, Osborne changed his mind. The policeman, he became convinced, could still be redeemed:

> The doomed man would sit for hours at the door of his cell reading aloud to his fellow prisoners, whiling away the dreadful monotony of the period between sentence and death. There was, too, something manly about his attitude. He liked to talk . . . about his own case, yet never tried to appeal for sympathy with hypocritical avowals of repentance. He admitted certain crimes—chiefly concerned with graft—but not the murder of Rosenthal.

Talking matters over with his prisoner, Osborne found himself unexpectedly convinced of Becker's innocence. "Certain features of the crime," he thought, were not in keeping with the lieutenant's character: "If such a man had set his mind on murder, he would have made a better job of it. Certainly he would never have put himself at the mercy of several accomplices."

Becker's existence in the condemned cells could scarcely have differed more utterly from the life he had led in Satan's Circus. It was thoroughly tedious. Opportunities to exercise remained limited, and the policeman's principal recreation was clipping his way through the pile of newspapers brought to him each day. His reading matter continued to reflect an unspoken yearning to be rid of the stone confines of his prison: tales of expeditions to the Amazon jungle, histories of Central America. And there was something new as well: At some point during his incarceration, Becker underwent a religious conversion, abandoning the nominal Lutheranism of his youth for a more active Catholicism under the tutelage of Father William Cashin, Sing Sing's much-loved chaplain, and Father James Curry, an elderly priest from an East Side parish who made regular trips up to Ossining to see him. Before long the lieutenant was helping Cashin to conduct his nightly Bible classes in the death house. Becker, Cashin confided to one reporter who had come to visit, "had been of the greatest assistance in comforting and preparing men who were going to die." "Look here," the prisoner hurriedly returned, "I don't want to be made a white angel or anything of that kind."

Becker was permitted to send letters three times a week. Those he dispatched to his family generally sought to stress his innocence and reassure them that he was doing well. "I am writing," he noted to his nephew Gus Neuberger, "to tell you that though I am convicted, I am as innocent of this horrible murder as you are, as God is my judge . . . I say this to you, Gus, so that you may not hang your head in shame for any act of mine . . . I am feeling as good physically as I could want, but you may know the mental strain is simply awful, the shame of the thing is what weighs heavily on me." On a few occasions, however, even Becker's determined optimism deserted him. "It does seem," he told a niece, "as if fate had decreed nothing but misfortune and woe for our family, death, disgrace, trouble, & destruction seem to be the watchwords. . . . If it wasn't for my Helen & poor old mother,* I tell you I wish myself [dead], for I am tired of man's inhumanity to man. Life is but a burden from the cradle to the grave."

It was probably only in his letters to Helen that the condemned man felt free to reveal still more of himself, though he certainly repressed much of his fear and concern in order to spare his wife's

---

*Becker's mother, Mary, was then ninety-two years old, blind, and had not been informed of her son's conviction—she was told "police business" was keeping him from visiting her.

feelings. Isolation and the inexorable approach of death did, however, unstop emotions that men of the period did not often express. Becker wrote sometimes of the stifling Sing Sing regime, but more often of love and of intensely imagined romantic scenes that seemed increasingly unlikely to be realized.

"Queen of my heart," he began one wistful letter home,

I've been thinking of you the best part of the night, in fact you are never out of my mind, but somehow you seemed nearer and dearer to me than ever. . . . I do want and love you so much that my heart seems loaded and my head feels like bursting with love and thoughts of you. I think of you sitting on the porch and in my mind's eye you look lovely but sad. I try to fix in my mind how you'd look if you saw me coming in at the gate. You always were such a bunch of sunshine when I came home . . . I often think back to the dismal years before I met you, and I can't recall any pleasure in life except that which I've known since I met you. I love to sit in reverie and recall all the beautiful times and days we enjoyed together—the many talks, the drives, the places we visited, our home coming, and the words you said, the question you'd never fail to ask and, when answered properly, the look of satisfaction I'd see on your face made me happy beyond words. . . . Sweetheart, let us not lose faith or heart. This must come right, and you and I live out our lives together.

Helen, for her part, wrote to her husband every night, just before going to bed. Knowing how empty days in the prison could be, she corresponded at length, often covering eight or ten sides of papers. "I try," she explained, "to put in amusing things, jokes that I have heard or read, and bits of gossip that will cheer him up." But, like her husband, she instinctively avoided distressing topics, including her departure from the house on Olinville Avenue in the autumn of 1914. In an attempt to recoup some of his unpaid legal fees, Martin Manton had put the property up for rent, and Mrs. Becker was forced to move into a much smaller apartment on University Avenue in the Bronx. She shared it with her twin brother, occasioning mild sensation among a number of neighbors who assumed she had taken up with another man before her disgraced husband had so much as been electrocuted. Fortunately for Helen, her sense of the ridiculous helped her to see the humor in such situations:

> Another bad time was riding to school in a White Plains car. I often feel discouraged on street cars; I don't know why—perhaps it is just because there is nothing to do but just sit there and think. On this day it seemed as if almost everything that could happen to me had happened. My husband was under sentence of death, I had lost my baby, our money was gone, my housekeeper had killed herself, my mother had died, my dog Bum had bitten a man and been shot, my pet canary had died. Then I thought: "Well, anyway, I am not blind. There's something to be thankful for, that I am not blind."
>
> The very next morning I woke up with a sore eye. That struck me as funny and I wrote it to Charley in my next letter. I am glad I have a sense of humor. I think it has often saved me from suffering.

By the summer of 1914, Charles Whitman's life was anything but boring. Almost as soon as the district attorney had heard the verdict in the second Becker trial, he turned his attention to furthering his own political career. The triumphant prosecution of that eternal Manhattan bugbear, a venal senior policeman, made Whitman far better known than his rival Republicans, and this time he had little difficulty in capturing his party's nomination for the governorship of New York State. The DA's timing proved admirable; the impeachment of William Sulzer had resulted in the accession of an unpopular Catholic governor named Martin Glynn, and this, combined with a sharp decline in support for Theodore Roosevelt's breakaway Progressive Party, made the Republicans far more electable in 1914 than they had been two years earlier. By autumn the safely Protestant Whitman, with his reputation as a fighter against corruption, had taken a strong lead over his rivals. On election night he carried the state by 145,000 votes, which was regarded as a landslide.

The former district attorney's ambition was still not satisfied, however. From his first day in Albany, Whitman viewed the governor-ship of New York as little more than a stepping-stone to higher office. The gubernatorial mansion had long been regarded as a way station on the road to Washington, and the new governor's stunning popular-ity in Democratic New York—which coincided, as it happened, with a dearth of attractive Republican candidates elsewhere in the country—persuaded Whitman that a nomination for the presidency was not out of reach. Before long his ambition had become so naked and so con-suming that it was something of a joke. The rising young Tammany Democrat Al Smith publicly charged that Whitman whiled away his time "sitting in the Capitol at Albany with a telescope trained on the White House."

Inevitably, Whitman's political ambitions distracted him from the workaday politics of New York State. The governor's first year in office was unremarkable, and his policies struck many voters as better calculated to secure national popularity than they were to serve local needs. For many New Yorkers, indeed, the onetime DA—whose exploits they had followed with such avidity at the height of the Rosenthal affair—began to appear a remote figure. As early as six months after his election, some of Whitman's most vocal supporters were beginning to abandon him. A few journalists and some members of his staff observed that the governor had begun drinking heavily. In several important quarters, his popularity waned.

In the first months of 1915, however, the manner in which the governor did his job remained of consuming importance to at least one of his constituents. As chief executive of New York, Charles Whitman, in person, sat in judgment on every prisoner on death row in the state—and that, of course, included the man whose trials had made his election possible. When every other recourse had been explored and the last possible appeal exhausted, the one person still able to save Becker's life would be the man who had twice gotten him convicted of murder.

The condemned man had not yet abandoned all hope nonetheless. Martin Manton was laboring away on the paperwork required to lodge a second appeal—some five hundred pages of depositions and complicated legal arguments—and there were still occasional developments in the original case as well. By far the most significant of these erupted quite unexpectedly just before Valentine's Day, when— for a scant few hours at least—a sensational development threw the entire Becker affair into turmoil and promised to demolish the prosecution case once and for all.

It was James Marshall, Whitman's crucial witness in Becker's second trial, who inadvertently raised the defense team's hopes. Nothing had been heard from the elusive tap dancer since the guilty verdict had been given, and in January, Marshall had quietly moved down the Atlantic coast to Philadelphia, renting a small apartment with his wife. In the second week of February, though, the couple had a violent falling-out. They argued, and a drunken Marshall struck the woman hard enough to send her running to the police. Having sworn out a complaint against her husband, the battered Mrs. Marshall still felt angry enough to plunge her partner into further trouble. Marshall, she told the policeman taking down her statement, had often boasted to her that he had perjured himself in a big trial in New York. What trial? The Becker case, she said.

It was Martin Manton's good fortune that two local newspaper reporters happened to be loitering around the station house when Mrs. Marshall made her confession. The newsmen recognized the Becker name at once and, sensing an exclusive of sensational proportions, hurried down into the cells where Marshall had by then been incarcerated. The buck-and-wing man, seemingly glad of the attention and still a little drunk, freely admitted perjury: He had been paid to testify by Whitman's office, he now said. The newsmen raced off to write their stories, and an hour or two later a telegram bearing the news arrived at Manton's offices. It was from the editor of the *Philadelphia Evening Ledger*, and it requested a comment.

Manton responded speedily. MARSHALL'S STATEMENT MOST ASTOUNDING, the attorney wired back. ABSOLUTELY NEWS TO US HERE. UTMOST IMPORTANCE TO DEFENDANT AND ADMINISTRATION OF JUSTICE. TAKING THE FIRST TRAIN TO PHILADELPHIA.

It was late afternoon by the time that John Johnson, one of Manton's assistants, rushed into the *Ledger*'s offices, where the dancer sat waiting with a commissioner of oaths and several of the paper's staff. Marshall still appeared cooperative, and he willingly swore a statement setting out his relationship with district attorney Whitman. The DA, Marshall said, had traced him to his new home in Washington and dispatched an assistant district attorney by the name of Frederick Groehl to offer payments totaling $355 in exchange for testimony.

It was the nature of the testimony itself that really raised eyebrows among the waiting journalists. Marshall freely admitted to knowing Lieutenant Becker, whom he had occasionally supplied with information about the gambling houses on 120th Street. But he was equally adamant that he had never seen Bridgey Webber, Harry Vallon, or Jack Rose until shortly before the policeman's second trial. "The first time I met Mr. Groehl," the stool pigeon added,

> was in his office in the Criminal Court Building at which time he told me that he wanted me to testify in Becker's case and say I saw Becker at 124th Street and Seventh Avenue in New York. . . . He told me he had plenty of evidence that the man to whom Becker was speaking was Jack Rose, but he wanted as many witnesses as he could get, and therefore he wanted me to swear that Becker was speaking to Jack Rose.

Groehl's statement was, of course, an outright lie; Whitman had no other witnesses who could testify to the Harlem Conference other than Sam Schepps, whose fragile credibility had just been utterly demolished by the court of appeals. But the lure of cash, combined with a threat of prosecution for perjury (Whitman had gotten hold of some "false affidavits" dating back to Marshall's stool-pigeon days) was enough to persuade the dancer to testify. Marshall, by his own admission, had a hazy recollection of events on the night of the supposed Harlem Conference, said he "did not know that the man speaking to Becker was Jack Rose except from what Mr. Groehl told me and what I had read in the newspaper," and had had to be coached intensively before giving testimony at the policeman's trial. But he had completed his assignment successfully and been permitted to leave town. Now that he was speaking out, he feared that some unspecified "bodily harm" could well befall him.

Of course, the New York district attorney's office had little need to resort to the crude tactics of physical violence. On the same day that news of Marshall's affidavit appeared in the New York press, assistant DA Groehl materialized at the apartment up on East Seventy-sixth Street rented by the dancer's mother. Happily for Groehl, he had no sooner walked through the apartment door than the telephone rang. The caller was none other than the district attorney's reluctant witness, phoning with the news that he was back in town. Seizing the receiver, Groehl informed Marshall that he had better get up to the apartment as rapidly as possible; almost certainly mention was made of the fact that the threatened indictment for perjury could be easily revived. "He then stated to me," Groehl swore in a later deposition, "that he wished to make an affidavit reaffirming the testimony given by him [at] the trial."

James Marshall retracted his retraction later that same Sunday. He had been "drinking heavily" and was "very much intoxicated" when he struck his wife, he now insisted, and he was still drunk when the Philadelphia newsmen had gotten their statement from him hours later. It had been John Johnson, the dancer now alleged, and not the New York district attorney's office, who had offered payment for his story—an astonishing $2,500 in total. Johnson had dictated his statement for him, Marshall added, and then fooled him into signing it.

Deprived of the buck-and-wing man's dramatic recantation, the defense team made little headway with Becker's renewed appeal for a retrial. Justice Seabury's handling of the case had been so much less inflammatory than Goff's that it was much more difficult than before to argue that the proceedings had been biased. Manton tried his best to make the case anyway, devoting the final dozen pages of his argument to a condemnation of the judge's "extreme partiality." Nearly two-thirds of his submission, though, was devoted to a dissection of the prosecution case, discussing the same matters of fact that had so exercised the court of appeals almost two years earlier. Whitman's successors in the district attorney's office had done much the same, and it came as a considerable surprise to both sides that on this occasion the court showed practically no interest in the weaknesses of the opposing cases—that, it now ruled, was exclusively a matter for the jurors.

In fact, the appeals court's principal concern—it declared in an opinion only half as long as the decision that had previously gone in Becker's favor—was the procedure of the trial: a purely technical consideration. Seen from this perspective, the second Becker hearing had been successful and well run, the judges ruled, and Seabury's concluding charge to the twelve jurors scrupulously fair. That meant that there were no legal grounds on which an appeal could possibly be granted. The court of appeals' decision affirmed the verdict of the lower court, and Becker's execution was rescheduled to take place early on July 12.

Most New Yorkers heard the decision without much surprise. Becker himself, when he was told of it that evening, seemed prepared; he had guessed, John Johnson said, that someone would have rushed in to inform him earlier if the ruling had gone his way. But the court of appeals' opinion was remarkable nonetheless. For one thing, the new verdict exactly reversed the one handed down two years earlier—the court had voted six to one for a new trial in 1913 and now stood six to one against it. For another, no fewer than five of the seven judges on the panel had heard both the Becker appeals, and four of them had actually reversed themselves, voting against a third trial just as decisively as they had voted *for* a second. James Marshall's astonishing ballet of retraction and counterretraction had scarcely been considered; the affidavit that the dancer had given Johnson, utterly repudiating his testimony at Becker's retrial, was only "somewhat inconsistent" with his earlier statements, the court now ruled.

Becker's handful of remaining partisans howled that the shifting opinions of the appeals court justices could be explained only by

Whitman's recent elevation to governor.* But it was hard to prove that this was so, and in strictly legal terms the court's verdict was probably correct. The technicalities, in any case, mattered little to the condemned policeman in his Sing Sing cell. All Becker knew was that his last realistic hope of freedom had been torn away. For several days after the appeals court verdict was announced, Father Cashin reported from the death house, the condemned man was "overcome by a frantic and futile anger," laced no doubt with despair.

Several enterprising reporters, meanwhile, sought out Bridgey Webber in the new home he was renting upriver in New Jersey. "My sympathies are with Becker," the former poker baron said without evident sincerity. "Of course there's no chance for a pardon. Governor Whitman certainly can't pardon the man he prosecuted."

By the beginning of July 1915, less than two weeks before the scheduled execution date, Becker's lawyers were close to exhausting the few options that remained to them. The one piece of good news was that Martin Manton's distinguished law partner, Bourke Cockran, had agreed to take the case. Working without pay, the veteran attorney promptly applied to the United States Supreme Court for a writ of error, which, if granted, would have meant a retrial. Whitman's offer of immunity to five confessed criminals had been unconstitutional, Cockran said.

Like most of the defense team's tactics, Cockran's motion did no more than delay matters for a while. His application was denied within a week, and soon after that, Whitman rejected a direct appeal for clemency. Still Cockran did not give up. He got Becker's execution date pushed back to late July, then helped to organize a petition that was circulated at a constitutional convention in Syracuse, asking the governor

---

*As governor, Whitman wielded almost total power over appointments to the court of appeals. It was surely noteworthy, critics said, that Frank Hiscock—a Republican judge who had been scathingly dismissive of Goff's handling of the first Becker trial—voted silently with the majority during the second appeal and that Hiscock soon afterward was promoted to be the court's senior judge, at a considerably enhanced salary.

to cede responsibility for deciding the policeman's case to the Board of Pardons. Manton, meanwhile, petitioned for the creation of a special panel of court of appeals judges to reconsider the evidence. The former district attorney rejected both of these proposals out of hand. To Whitman's enemies—there were a growing number of them, now that he was well into the second year of his governorship—this was the signal that he was prepared to harry the lieutenant to the chair. To his supporters, notably Swope of the *World*, it seemed merely common sense. No one knew more about the Becker case than Whitman.

Cockran's last resort was a motion for a new trial, brought on July 23 before the Supreme Court of New York County. It was accompanied by an order to show cause, requiring the district attorney's office to give reasons a third hearing of the case should not be granted, and by several fresh pieces of evidence. One was Charles Becker's own account of the entire Rosenthal affair, a thirty-eight-page handwritten deposition, along with an almost equally lengthy cover letter addressed to Whitman. Another was an affidavit sworn by Harry Applebaum, who had long been Big Tim Sullivan's private secretary and closest aide. Cockran saw to it that both documents were released to the press, where aficionados of the Becker case fell upon them eagerly. The lieutenant's story was the one they read most avidly: Here at last, after Becker had sat silently through two full trials, was the testimony he could, and perhaps should, have given. But it was Applebaum's affidavit that caused the real sensation. Sullivan's confidential aide acknowledged, for the first time since Herman's murder, that the late ward boss had been intimately involved in Rosenthal's gambling affairs. He also recalled some conversation between Becker and his collector, Bald Jack Rose, that—at the very least—threw floods of light on the relationship between the two. Many who read Applebaum's statement felt it pointed firmly to Rose as the principal agent behind Herman's murder.

Becker's own account of the Rosenthal affair was given added credibility by the condemned man's refusal to beg the governor for yet another stay of execution: "I do not desire a delay," he wrote, "that can merely serve to prolong an agony which is already almost unendurable." Becker's memoir contained the expected protestation of innocence and covered his experiences in Satan's Circus from the moment of his appointment to the old Special Squad. The policeman enlarged considerably on his relationship with Bald Jack Rose and on the difficulty of recruiting and managing stool pigeons to obtain the evidence required to launch raids on gambling houses. His principal revelation, however, concerned the manner in which Big Tim Sullivan had become enmeshed in the Rosenthal affair.

Tim, Becker recalled, had wanted to protect his old friend Herman and permit him to run his gambling houses in the entertainment district. He had spoken to Commissioner Waldo on the subject and somehow obtained the impression that Waldo had agreed to leave Herman unmolested. Then, sometime in January 1912, Sullivan had decided to make sure that Rosenthal would receive the necessary protection by summoning Lieutenant Becker to meet him. Becker (so his own account ran) made no rash promises, merely pointing out that Waldo himself ordered all his raids, and that if the commissioner was content to leave Herman alone, he and his Strong Arm Squad would have no reason to have dealings with Tim's favorite. All of these conversations had, of course, been overtaken by events. But there can be no doubt that Becker was deeply impressed—even awed—by his encounter with Sullivan, not least because (as he himself explained) Big Tim's "influence in the Police Department, no matter who might be its head, was believed to be unbounded. A policeman who succeeded in enlisting his favor was considered sure of promotion." For this reason, the lieutenant pointed out, when Big Tim asked him to promise not to bring his name into the Rosenthal affair, he took the vow he made particularly seriously. This was why, at least in part, Becker had felt unable to testify in either of his trials.

The revelation that Big Tim Sullivan had offered Rosenthal protection shocked a few New Yorkers, though it would scarcely have come as much of a surprise to the average habitué of Satan's Circus. But the second part of Becker's statement—an account of the last few hours before Herman's murder—certainly was news, not least because, so the policeman recalled, he had been summoned to see Big Tim once again the night before the shooting. Harry Applebaum had tracked him down, with Bald Jack Rose's help, and the three men had ridden in Sullivan's car down to Sixtieth Street, where Tim maintained a private office. "We went up two flights of stairs," Becker wrote,

> and on [my] entering his room, he asked me, "What about this Rosenthal affair?" I said, "There's nothing of it." He said, "It must not be allowed to go any further. Rosenthal has gone so far now, he can't be stopped. He must be got away."
>
> "That," I said at once, "would be the very worst thing that could happen to us. Everybody would say that either you or I had caused his disappearance, and naturally it would seem that, if we induced him to leave [town], it must be because he had something discreditable to reveal. Now, everything he could say has already been said or published. It is absolutely necessary to my position in the department that his statement be faced and disproved."

By itself this statement of Becker's, explaining precisely why he had not wanted Rosenthal dead, was not worth much. It was certainly insufficient to prompt the Supreme Court to review his case. But Harry Applebaum's supporting affidavit, which supplied confirmation for almost all of the points that Becker made, also described a revealing moment that had occurred during the automobile ride downtown. Out of loyalty to his old boss, Applebaum had been hesitant to come forward with his evidence before either of Becker's trials. Now, though, with Sullivan dead and the lieutenant only hours from the chair, he had decided to speak out "for the purpose of setting right before the public many erroneous impressions" and to explain why he believed that Jack Rose was to blame for the murder.

Applebaum, as he recalled it, had become increasingly concerned by Rosenthal's erratic and indiscreet behavior throughout the spring of 1912 and, with Sullivan's approval, had spent several days talking to Herman and persuading him to get out of town. One day before the murder, Herman had at last agreed to abide by Big Tim's wishes, and Becker had known that he would soon be on his way because Applebaum himself had told him about Rosenthal's decision. It was Becker's certainty that the whole affair was about to die down that made Tim's aide quite sure that he would never have done anything so rash as to arrange to have the gambler murdered. Indeed, Applebaum clearly recalled the conversation that had passed between Becker and Jack Rose that evening:

> On our way down I told Becker that Tim wanted to do any-thing he could to help out the situation; that I had been talking with Rosenthal and he was willing to do anything that Tim asked him to do. Rose told me how Herman had been talking about his wife. He was very bitter over it, and made the remark that "someone ought to croak Rosenthal." I immediately protested at such a thought, and Becker spoke up and said, "No, they hadn't. He wants to be left alone. No friend of mine must harm a hair on his head, for if they do it will be blamed on me, and I can beat this thing all right."

In fact, the one thing that Applebaum and Becker disagreed on was Herman's true motive for leaving New York. The secretary believed that Rosenthal felt indebted to his mentor, Sullivan, "so that it was not necessary to bribe him" to leave town. Becker, for his part, was equally certain that Arnold Rothstein and the Satan's Circus gambling frater-nity were paying Herman handsomely to do so: "It was a matter of common reporting in every newspaper office," the lieutenant wrote in his letter to Whitman, "that a sum of money had been raised, probably by Rose, from the gamblers to get Rosenthal away, that Rosenthal refused the sum offered, but consented to go away for a larger sum. It was for this larger sum that he was said to have been waiting at the Metropole when he was called out."

That, Becker clearly believed, explained why the troublesome gam-bler had risked going to West Forty-third Street on the night of his death. It also solved the puzzle of why Herman had so obediently fol-lowed the messenger sent in to fetch him when he was summoned to his death. The only mystery remaining was who precisely had ordered the assassination. Plenty of people had had a motive for wanting Rosenthal silenced, after all: Arnold Rothstein, for one, and Rosenthal's hated rival, Bridgey Webber, for another. Becker and Applebaum nonetheless both felt certain that the real culprit had been Jack Rose, the man who, rumor in Satan's Circus had it, had been assigned to take the gamblers' payoff to the hotel.

At some point, the policeman and the politician guessed, Bald Jack had taken a good look at the thick rolls of dollars in his hands and decided that it would be a crying shame to pass all that cash to Herman—not least because for a mere $1,000 Rose himself could pay off Zelig's gunmen and have Gyp the Blood and his three friends dispose of the man who had so insulted his wife. Rose, both Becker and Applebaum felt certain, had simply kept the balance of the money for himself, pocketing a sum that could easily have amounted to as much as $15,000.

A few people, well versed in the ins and outs of the Rosenthal affair, felt that Becker's statement and Applebaum's affidavit answered several of the most puzzling questions still hanging over the case. Unfortunately for Becker, the members of this small group were mostly former colleagues, friends, family, or members of his own defense team. The New York papers reveled in the chance to drag the now-dead Sullivan's name into the mire in a way they had longed to, though never dared to, while the Tammany man had been alive, but they still gave little credence to the remainder of the evidence. And none seemed to think that a new trial was justified—certainly not at this late stage.

In strictly legal terms, the newspapers were right. Justice John Ford, of the State Supreme Court, spent the best part of a week considering the documents that Cockran had submitted to him—a delay that once again raised Becker's hopes—and the policeman's attorneys were able to use the delay to get one last postponement of the execution date, which was now pushed back to July 30. On the twenty-eighth, however, after five long days of thought, Ford ruled in favor of the prosecution. Cockran's motion was denied, he said, on the purely technical grounds that Becker's statement and Applebaum's deposition were not actually "new evidence," the only sort that would allow the case to be reopened. The lieutenant, Ford explained, had been free to testify to his dealings with Tim Sullivan at either of his trials.

The news was brought to Becker in his death-house cell at ten-thirty that evening, a little less than thirty-six hours before the scheduled execution. Assistant Warden Charles Johnson found the policeman hunched, waiting, on the edge of his cot and, leaning forward to place his head next to the bars, whispered, "Charley, I have bad news for you. Your appeal has been denied." The deputy warden pushed an arm through the bars of the cell and took the prisoner's hand in his, but Becker did not take his eyes off the floor. "Denied, denied," he murmured. Johnson thought that he seemed "in a daze."

"Well," Becker said, his grip on the warden's hand tightening convulsively, "I'll die like a man, anyhow."

In the Bronx, meanwhile, word of Justice Ford's decision reached Mrs. Becker's apartment. Helen did not hesitate. There was nothing now that her husband could do to save himself, but she had not yet exhausted her own arsenal of appeals. She picked up the telephone and dialed Manton's private number.

"I would like to see the governor," she said when he replied.

Charles Whitman was the one man who could still save Becker's life. As governor he possessed the power to commute any death sentence handed down in New York to life imprisonment, or, moreover, to issue an outright pardon. There was even a recent precedent for the commutation of a disputed sentence: In Atlanta, a month earlier, Governor John Slanton had refused to sign the death warrant for a pencil-factory manager named Leo Frank, convicted on the most circumstantial of evidence of murdering a fourteen-year-old girl. Whitman no doubt knew all about the Frank case—newspaper coverage of the man's arrest, trial, and conviction had rivaled that accorded to the Becker-Rosenthal affair—and he would certainly have been aware of the uncanny parallels between Leo Frank and Becker: Both men had been convicted on the unsupported evidence of confessed criminals who would otherwise have faced the death penalty themselves, and both bitterly professed their innocence. From Whitman's perspective, however, the manner in which news of the commutation of Frank's sentence had been greeted in Georgia must have weighed more heavily than any fine consideration of innocence or guilt. A howling mob had stormed the governor's mansion in Atlanta, forcing Slanton to call out the National Guard and, a few days later, to flee the state for his own safety.

Mrs. Becker cared little for all that, of course. All she knew was that Whitman could still reprieve her husband. For months she had rejected out of hand the mere idea of a personal plea to the governor, and Becker had said he would rather go to the chair than see his wife humble herself in such a manner. Now, though, with her husband's execution a scant few hours away, fear and despair had altered Helen's mind.

Manton arranged for Mrs. Becker to see Whitman in Albany. She and John Johnson caught a train from New York early on the morning of July 29 and arrived at the governor's mansion a few minutes before noon. Whitman was not there; he had overlooked an appointment to review a contingent of the National Guard at Peekskill, miles away. An aide placed nervous phone calls, and eventually Helen was told that the governor would still see her if she could meet him at Pough-keepsie, more than seventy miles from Albany, that evening.

Mrs. Becker caught another train, and she and Johnson arrived at their destination a little before six. Helen appeared drawn and tightly wound, and her mood was not improved by the large crowd of curios-ity seekers that assembled in the main street as word of her arrival spread. She was ushered away from the gawkers and shown into the parlor of a small hotel, where she waited for nearly two hours while her lawyer rehearsed his arguments for a stay of execution. Whitman listened impassively and denied Johnson's application.

It was dusk by the time the governor finally consented to see Helen, and then he was so drunk he had to be supported by two aides throughout their fruitless interview. Helen spent nearly twenty-five minutes pleading for clemency, even dropping to her knees to beg; Whitman slurred that there was nothing he could do. She retaliated in the press: "The governor was in no condition to understand a word I said," she told one astonished journalist. Another reporter gained admission to the hotel room to get Whitman's side of the story and found the governor just as Mrs. Becker had described him, "leaning limply over the side of a chair" in an alcoholic stupor.

By then Helen was already gone. It was nearly 8:00 P.M., and the only available train would not get in until after 10:00, so Johnson hired a car to drive the forty miles to Ossining. The journey proved remarkably eventful. In his anxiety to get away, the driver stalled the engine outside the hotel, offering the bolder members of the waiting crowd the chance to clamber up onto the running boards and peer at the passengers sitting in the back. Then the party made a wrong turn and wasted more than an hour searching for the correct road. In the end it took three hours to get to Sing Sing, and throughout the frantic drive Johnson and Mrs. Becker grew increasingly apprehensive. The lawyer worried about the meeting he had scheduled with Warden Osborne. Helen feared that she would arrive to find the prison gates locked against her, and her husband would be forced to face his last few hours alone.

Sing Sing had already prepared for Becker's death.

Invitations had been dispatched in the middle of July to those chosen to witness the execution. There were three dozen in total, and they went to doctors and to a sanitary engineer, to representatives of the press, and to the operators of several wire services. One, scarcely surprisingly, was sent to Swope of the *World*, but the reporter—doubtless to his chagrin—was recuperating from a bout of rheumatic fever, and his doctor had forbidden him to attend.* Swope sent another *World* reporter in his stead; the man arrived at Ossining bearing a large sheaf of handwritten instructions setting out in considerable detail exactly how the story should be covered. Preparations were also made to cater to the needs of the large body of newsmen expected to descend on Sing Sing without the benefit of invitations. Linemen spent several days installing additional telegraph wires and Morse-code senders in a shack opposite the death house.

---

*Swope had, however, attended the execution of the four gunmen. He had sat perched like some gangly bird of prey in the front row, and—one journalist wrote later—"other reporters there insisted they were surprised he didn't at the last moment step forward and pull the switch himself."

Inside the condemned cells, white curtains were fitted across the bars of all the cells that Becker would have to pass on his way to the execution chamber so that the other inmates would not be able to see him as he walked by. In the execution chamber, guards tested each piece of equipment. The lieutenant's electrocution was scheduled to be the first at which a new system of signals would be used, as the *New York Times* reported:

Instead of the old method, by which the executioner signaled with his arm to the man in charge at the power plant, there is a little electric button behind the chair, and above it is tacked a placard bearing the following gruesomely suggestive instructions: "Five bells, get ready; one bell, turn on the current; two bells, turn on more current; three bells, turn on less current; one bell, shut off current; six bells, all through."

New York's newspapers remained predominantly hostile to the condemned man. The *Times* spoke for most of the Manhattan press when it observed that Becker's death sentence was a punishment not just for Herman's death but for the arrogance Rosenthal's killer had displayed during his strong-arm days: "He paid for the times when 'Big Tim' called him 'Charlie.' He paid for his one-time power, that almost of a dictator, over the underworld of New York. And he paid for his pride in all this." Several dailies had issued their reporters instructions to study Becker carefully for signs of weakness or incipient collapse; in the end, opinion seemed evenly divided between those who thought that the policeman continued to display an "iron nerve in the face of doom" and those who discerned the onset of a nervous breakdown.

The lawyers were more generous. Bourke Cockran paid tribute to his client's astounding self-control: "His hand is just as cool and his voice as steady as can be." John McIntyre said that he had never previously doubted the verdict of a jury in a murder trial. "But in this case I say that if Becker is executed tomorrow I will carry to my grave the conviction that at least one innocent man has suffered the death penalty." And Joseph Shay, another of the lieutenant's old attorneys, released a statement of his own: "I believe that Becker is dying a martyr, and that his innocence will be established in time, perhaps by the deathbed confession of Vallon or Webber. Rose is too low to confess even on his deathbed."

Becker himself was woken early on his last morning. At 8:00 A.M. his prison clothes were exchanged for special black cotton shirt and trousers, made without metal buttons or wire stitching; he was given black felt slippers instead of shoes. A guard shaved a spot on his temple, ready for the electrode. Another appeared carrying a pair of shears and neatly slit Becker's trouser leg almost to the knee. When the time came, this would allow the death-house guards to affix a second wire to the condemned man's calf.

The next portion of the day was passed in writing: a love letter for his wife, a final statement for the press. At two in the afternoon, the policeman saw his relatives for the last time. His brothers John, the detective, and Jackson, now a Wall Street broker, found him sitting in his cell gazing at a small photograph of Helen that he kept on the wall. The meeting was so difficult that the two men were relieved when one of the other prisoners along death row broke the awkward silence by singing "Rock of Ages." Becker joined in with the chorus.

Helen Becker reached Sing Sing, pale and breathless from her journey, soon after 11:00 P.M. Her husband had been waiting for her with increasing anxiety for most of the evening. Becker was so popular in the death house that he had received special permission to spend more than an hour and a half with his wife in the warden's room. The guards, who had been given strict instructions to keep their eyes on the prisoner constantly, turned their backs as the couple embraced for the final time. "No condemned man at the prison had ever had such sympathetic treatment," observed the *World*.

Helen left the prison at 1:30 in the morning, and Becker was returned to his cell. "I am tired of the world and its injustice to me," he told Father Curry, the New York priest. "My happy life has been ruined; I have not been given a chance a mere dog would get." Warden Osborne, coming to say good-bye at 2:30 A.M., found his prisoner awake and sitting on the edge of his cot, "his chin sunk in his hands." At 4:00, Father Cashin heard Becker's last confession, which contained no admission of guilt and ended with the firm assertion, "I am sacrificed for my friends."

The execution was set for 5:45 A.M. Outside the walls a double line of guards poked long sticks through the fence that marked the limit of the prison grounds to keep back the crowds assembling there. Inside, the executioner—a small, sharp-faced, balding electrician dressed in a gray sack suit, a striped shirt, polka-dot tie, and pointed patent leather shoes—checked his equipment for the final time.

Becker was the hundred and sixteenth prisoner to die at Sing Sing since electrocution was first used to execute a man in August 1890. The victim on that occasion had been an ax murderer named William Kemmler, who was accidentally subjected to "a far more powerful current than was necessary" and died "in convulsive agony," flames jetting from the base of his spine and purplish foam spewing from his lips. The technique for electrocuting a man had been refined somewhat since then, but it was still common for the death house to fill with the odor of burning flesh and scorched hair as the moistened electrical conductors placed against the condemned man's skin dried out. A lengthy electric shock could "turn blood into charcoal and boil a brain." When a prisoner was ready to enter the chamber, he was issued thick muslin underwear, and little wads of cotton would be forced into his ears and nostrils to prevent scalding brain fluids from spurting forth uncontrollably when the current was applied.

Thomas Mott Osborne, who had vowed never to be present when a man in his charge was being executed, walked away from the death house at 5:00 A.M., leaving Deputy Warden Johnson to bring the policeman from his cell. Becker, who was still awake when Johnson came for him, went quietly to his death. A dozen steps took him from his cot to the door leading to the execution chamber. At 5:42 the witnesses clustering inside saw a narrow red door swing open, and the condemned man entered the room. He walked with a strange, hobbled gait, his knees locking involuntarily. His face was a mask.

The chair, surprisingly insubstantial, stood on a thick rubber mat almost in the center of the room. There was no glass and no partition to separate Becker from the witnesses who had come to watch him die, the nearest of whom sat only ten feet away. The electric chair itself, the man from the *American* observed, "had had a double coat of varnish and its metal fixtures had been burnished for the occasion." Straps dangled loosely from its arms and legs, and a heavily insulated wire hung from a goosenecked fixture above it. The policeman's guards, anxious to spare the condemned man the agony of a lengthy wait, hurried so much with the buckles that they neglected to secure one of the restraints that stretched over his chest. Becker's last words, uttered as another leather strap was fastened across his mouth, were a recitation of the Catholic litany: "Into Thy hands, O Lord, I commend my spirit."

Five bells rang, then one. The executioner took his hands out of his pockets and threw a long wooden lever on the wall. The raucous drone of electricity filled the room, a green flash shot from the equipment, and Becker's muscular body lurched forward against the straps, his head twisting sideways and upward as though attempting to escape the shock.

Charley Becker was the largest man ever brought into the execution chamber at Sing Sing, and it may be for this reason that his electrocution was horribly botched. Too little current was applied at first, so that the death agonies became protracted. The temperature within the dying man's body rose to 140 degrees Fahrenheit, the loose strap across his chest burst open, flames were seen to spurt from his temple, and despite the administration of 1,850 volts for a full sixty seconds, Charles Farr, the death-house doctor, found Becker's heart "not only still beating, but pounding strongly." In the end it took nine minutes and three separate jolts to kill the prisoner, though the representative of the *World* observed that "to those who sat in the gray-walled room and listened to the rasping sound of the wooden switch lever being thrown backward and forward, and watched the greenish-blue blaze at the victim's head and feet and the grayish smoke curling away from the scorched flesh, it seemed an hour." The whole affair was described in later years as "the clumsiest execution in the history of Sing Sing."

* * *

As the reporters who had gathered to witness the execution filed out of the chamber, they were handed copies of Becker's final letters. The first was addressed to Governor Whitman:

> You have proved yourself able to destroy my life. But mark well, Sir, these words of mine. When your power passes, the truth about Rosenthal's murder will become known. Not all the judges in this State, nor in this country, can destroy permanently the character of an innocent man.

The second letter was a final testament. Becker had spent much of the night memorizing it, in the hope of being allowed to deliver it himself, but the guards had not permitted this.

"I stand before you," this statement began,

> in my full senses knowing that no power on earth can save me from the grave that is to receive me, and in the presence of my God and your God I proclaim my absolute innocence of the crime for which I must die. You are now about to witness my destruction by the State . . . And on the brink of my grave, I declare to the world that I am proud to have been the husband of the purest, noblest woman that ever lived, Helen Becker. This acknowledgment is the only legacy I can leave her. I bid you all goodbye. Father, I am ready to go.

> CHARLES BECKER

When most of the reporters had left, Becker's corpse was removed to the autopsy room for the usual examination, arms dangling, head hanging back, legs swinging. Dr. Farr stripped the black cotton shirt from the lieutenant's hulking body and was startled to discover that it concealed the little photo of Helen that Becker had kept on the wall of his cell. The dead man had pinned it to his undershirt, with the face turned inward, over his heart.

EPILOGUE

T HIRTY MILES AWAY, in New York City, Arnold Rothstein sat at his usual table in Jack's twenty-four-hour café, just down the street from the Hotel Metropole. At twenty minutes to six, the conversation at the table slowed, then stopped, and each member of the gambler's party fumbled in his waistcoat for a pocketwatch. Rothstein's was large and made of gold. He set it on the table before him and gazed at it in silence, watching as the hands swept their way inexorably toward the time set for Becker's execution.

At 5:45 A.M. precisely, the gambler picked up the timepiece, snapped shut its cover, and led his friends out into another New York morning.

"Well," he said evenly, "that's it."

Becker's corpse was brought back to New York City late that afternoon. Three men heaved the heavy coffin up the steps to Helen's new home at 2291 University Avenue in the Bronx shortly before 4:00 P.M. and laid it gently on a table in the parlor. A small crowd soon gathered outside, made up in part of girls who had been playing tennis on the nearby public courts. There was not much to see, but, one newspaperman reported, "from within the apartment house came the incongruous sounds of a woman crying and the faint tinkle of a piano."

The next day was a Sunday. A steady stream of messenger boys bearing flowers from Becker's lawyers, Helen's pupils, and the Sullivan clan called at the third-floor flat throughout the morning. A handful of Becker's friends were invited in to the apartment to view the body, among them old Clubber Williams, in his seventies by now, who called twice and whose wreath—bearing a ribbon reading IN RESPECT FOR CHARLEY—was set in a place of honor at the corpse's feet. None of those who made their way out of the house and past the assembly of waiting pressmen could bring themselves to mumble the usual comfortable platitudes about the cadaver, for there was nothing calm or peaceful about Becker's face. The marks left by the execution were all too obvious, from the roughly shaven head to the burns where the electrodes had been placed. The undertaker had done what he could to conceal the lieutenant's injuries under heavy greasepaint, but they remained visible even so. A scorched patch of skin on the left side of the forehead was particularly prominent.

There was one new story for the papers to report. Mrs. Becker's hatred of Charles Whitman had come to such a head during the disastrous interview in Poughkeepsie that she had resolved, during the lengthy journey home, to denounce his actions publicly. As soon as she returned to New York, Helen commissioned a local engraver to produce a handsome silver plate, seven inches by five, for her husband's coffin.

CHARLES BECKER

the inscription proclaimed,

MURDERED JULY 30, 1915
BY GOVERNOR WHITMAN

A single journalist was granted access to the Becker apartment and allowed to view the coffin on condition that he pooled notes with his colleagues, and the story made all the city dailies the next morning. "The plate," one report concluded, "is screwed to the upper, removable section of the casket's top. When the lid is put in place, the plate will be above the face."

Whitman's office wasted little time in taking action when this bit of news emerged. Within a matter of hours, a party of three senior policemen, led by an inspector, appeared at the apartment and gravely informed Helen that the inscription amounted to a criminal libel on the governor. The plate was unscrewed and taken to Police Headquarters on Centre Street, where it was preserved as evidence in case Whitman chose to sue. In the end the governor had the sense not to press the matter further, and Helen's family soon obtained a replacement, this one made of aluminum and inscribed with nothing more than Becker's name and date of death.

The interment was arranged for the first day of August. It was an abominably hot, close day, the worst of the year so far, but even the muggy beating of the sun was not sufficient to deter another gigantic New York funeral crowd, this one an estimated ten thousand strong, from descending upon University Avenue. The press of humanity was so great that the street became entirely blocked shortly after dawn.

No more than a hundred members of the throng that gathered to gawk outside the Becker home had any acquaintance with the dead policeman. The remainder were simply thrill seekers. "A championship series baseball game or a hippodrome spectacle would not have brought out a more noisy and disorderly crowd than that which attended the Becker funeral," the *American* observed.

Women with babies in their arms gathered outside the apartment house soon after sunrise in order to obtain advantageous positions for viewing the funeral cortege when it started for the church. The crowd held its ground until many dropped to the pavement with exhaustion. Women engaged in heated arguments as the coffin was borne through their midst, and above the din was heard the crying of suffering infants—children whose parents or caretakers had forgotten all about them in their momentary frenzy.

Two women fainted and had to be carried away when the coffin, borne on the shoulders of six stalwart men who are now or were formerly members of the Police Department came down the narrow stairway, was pushed waveringly through the throng and finally lodged safely in the hearse. The crowd blocked the way and it was at least twenty minutes before the mounted policemen could clear the street sufficiently for it to start for church, three blocks distant. Then a footrace took place. Men, women and children threw dignity to the winds in their mad desire to be among the first to reach the church.

Moving picture operators and photographers raced along in the vanguard, while many ignored the "No trespassing" signs as they made for the church across lots, through bramble bush and rag weed.

The church of St. Nicholas of Tolentine could hold seven hundred people, but at least fourteen hundred crammed into the building to hear Father George Dermody, an old friend of the Beckers', conduct the requiem mass. There was no sermon and no eulogy. Those forced to wait outside could in any case hear nothing of the service over the hubbub of the mob, and there were further ugly scenes when the mass was over and mounted police were forced to charge the crowd repeatedly to clear a passage for the hearse. Matters were little better at Woodlawn Cemetery, where onlookers trampled down the flowers laid on other graves and dozens of women hitched up their skirts and clambered unsteadily onto tombstones to obtain a better view.

There was another short delay at the entrance to the graveyard. A uniformed attendant emerged from the gatehouse to bar the way and refused to allow the cortege into the grounds until the inflammatory inscriptions attached to several gaudy floral tributes had been removed. One elaborate flower-covered cross, with the words SACRIFICED FOR POLITICS picked out in letters nearly a foot high, was pulled from a hearse and the offending words removed. A wreath, sent by Becker's doctor and emblazoned with the slogan TO THE MARTYR, was similarly defaced. Only then was Helen permitted to make her way into the cemetery, where a fresh grave had been dug for her husband next to the plot that held the body of their baby daughter.

It was noon by the time Charles Becker was lowered into the ground, and by then the thermometer stood at eighty-four degrees and it had become "the most depressingly hot day of the season." Wreaths and mourners wilted in the sticky heat, but there was no ceremony and the grave was soon filled in. Helen, heavily veiled, stood almost motionless beside it. Only the intermittent wrenching of her shoulders betrayed the fact that she was weeping.

* * *

The whole Becker scandal had been so grotesque and so protracted that it helped to pitch New York into another of its periodic spasms of reform. The mayoral election of 1913—held three months after the sudden and unexpected death, from heart failure and the lingering effects of his shooting, of Mayor Gaynor on an ocean liner off the coast of Ireland—saw the forces of Tammany Hall swept aside by John Purroy Mitchel, who won a large majority campaigning on the reformist Fusion ticket. Mitchel was only thirty-four years old when he was elected, making him the youngest mayor in the city's history, but he was already a veteran of New York politics and canny enough to know that a fresh crusade against municipal graft would play well with his voters. His administration cut waste and introduced improved accounting practices designed to make it more difficult for patronage and corruption to spread unchecked. The appointees ejected from their offices were replaced, by and large, with competent professionals.

Among those who lost their jobs in this way was the hapless Rhinelander Waldo. The new police commissioner was Arthur Woods, a protégé of Theodore Roosevelt's who boasted a Harvard degree in administration and had already been a deputy commissioner for a while. Under Woods's leadership the police department was extensively reorganized. The three-platoon system that Becker had fought for was at last introduced, and with it the eight-hour day and a guarantee of more time to spend at home with wives and families. Great efforts and large budgets were devoted to training. A new detective college was established. Beat cops were sent to lecture in schools, and neighborhood children were recruited into a Junior Police organization with the result that delinquency declined and relations between the police and the community began to improve at last. A police loan fund was established so that officers who found themselves in financial difficulties were not forced to turn to graft to bail themselves out. Slowly at first, and then more swiftly, the old perception of the law as a force for oppression, and of the NYPD as a venal body devoted largely to its own interests, began to change.

The effects of this reform were felt within the ranks of the police as well. Encouraged to think of themselves as useful public servants, thousands of men who had never been presented with the temptations that corrupted Becker, who had restricted themselves principally to clean graft, and who, like Max Schmittberger, cared about the taunts their children suffered in the playground, responded with enthusiasm. Both the morale and the efficiency of the force improved. Mitchel grew fond of quoting one letter he received from a patrolman: "You have shown us how to be better policemen and better citizens. You have elevated us to a position of honor in the community, and enabled us to again walk the streets with heads up, eyes to the front, and fit to look any man in the face."

Of course, corruption still existed. Few of New York's thousands of crooked cops were punished in the wake of Becker's trials; the Curran Committee, which finally delivered its report in 1913, struggled (as had the Lexow investigation before it) to place credible witnesses on the stand, and its fifty-two recommendations—which included a more secure tenure for the police commissioner and the creation of a central complaints bureau—were in any case voted down by the Democratic majority on the Board of Aldermen. Nearly two-thirds of Curran's proposals were, in fact, quietly waved through a few months later in order to sweeten Tammany's record on corruption. But the $40,000 expended on his hearings resulted in fewer than twenty indictments, and though four inspectors and six other officers did go to jail for grafting and another twenty either were sacked or resigned from the force, the great majority of guilty officers escaped punishment again. Over the next four years, a new department of internal affairs, known as the Confidential Squad and led by the freshly promoted Captain Costigan, uncovered hundreds of cases of corruption, most still involving the levying of protection payments from brothels. Tellingly, if unsurprisingly, the men drafted to the squad were highly unpopular among their colleagues. "Its members were called rats," one squad officer, future Police Commissioner Lewis Valentine, recalled. "I have been called that name many times." When—with the awful inevitability that afflicted all New York reform administrations—Mitchel was voted out of office at the end of 1917, the Confidential Squad was instantly shut down.*

The election of Mayor Mitchel had been no fluke nonetheless. The Fusion triumph of 1913 was actually a product of slow changes in the fabric of the city that not only reshaped the way politics in New York worked but severely reduced the graft available to precinct captains and eventually doomed the seemingly all-powerful Sullivan clan to electoral extinction.

Tammany had first felt the ground shift beneath its feet years earlier. The consolidation of the five boroughs of Manhattan, Queens, Brooklyn, the Bronx, and Staten Island into a single metropolis back in 1898 had altered the balance of power in the city once and for all. From then on, the votes of the laboring masses of Manhattan, which had kept the Hall in power for years on end, had to be weighed against those of the Republicans, anti-Tammany Democrats, and Fusionists who were strong in several of the outer boroughs. It was for this reason that more upright, semi-independent candidates began to appear on Tammany tickets after 1900—men such as Mayor Gaynor and Governor Sulzer, who were harder to control than their predecessors had been and who owed their nominations to Charles Murphy's grudging recognition that old-style machine politicians could no longer be sure of finding favor with the New York electorate. If something was not done, the sachems on Fourteenth Street recognized, a city in which hundreds of thousands of voters had no direct relationship with their local Tammany organizer—a place made cynical by the shocking revelations of the Lexow investigation—would no longer be safe for democracy.

While Big Tim Sullivan was alive to direct affairs, Tammany's organizers coped with the changing times relatively well. As early as

---

*On losing office, Mitchel immediately volunteered for military service and was sent to train as a pilot. On July 6, 1918, while completing his course of instruction in Louisiana, the former mayor fell out of his plane at five hundred feet and plunged to the ground, dying instantly at the age of only thirty-eight. It was thought he had forgotten to fasten his seat belt.

1895, a firm base among the Irish and German communities of lower Manhattan was no longer enough to guarantee electoral success, particularly when many established Democratic voters began to migrate north, driven out of their old tenements by the incoming floods of new Americans. But Sullivan took special pains to court the millions of Eastern European Jews pouring into the Lower East Side who threatened to wipe out Tammany's old power bases. It was during Big Tim's reign, as George Washington Plunkitt explained, that a Tammany block leader learned to eat "corned beef and kosher meat with equal nonchalance, and it's all the same to him whether he takes his hat off in the church or pulls it down over his ears in the synagogue."*

Tammany's dominance remained under threat even so. Many of the new generation of immigrants were socialists or anarchists who stubbornly refused to vote the Democratic ticket, and the self-sufficiency of the Jewish community—which ran many of its own social services—meant that Sullivan's tested strategy of supplying constituents with free socks and shoes and clambakes in exchange for votes could no longer be relied on. To make matters worse, a stringent new election law, pushed through by Mayor McClellan in 1908, required citizens to sign when registering to vote, and then again on polling day. This regulation made it far more difficult for district leaders to manipulate the ballot and fatally undermined many of Tammany's long-standing electoral malpractices.

In these changing times, the Becker scandal—with its revelations of corruption and its echoes of Lexow—had obvious potential to wreak havoc on the Hall. The lengths to which the Sullivans went to keep Big Tim's name out of the case suggest that Tammany was well aware of this. But down on Fourteenth Street the farsighted Boss Murphy was thinking further ahead than were his district leaders, whose concerns

---

*Big Tim's vote-winning adaptability was still in evidence before his final illness struck. The members of an Irish gang were caught harassing Orthodox Jews in his cousin Florrie's district. When word of this reached Sullivan, he spoke with the police; the toughs' clubhouse was raided, their landlord threw them out, and Tim promptly rented the rooms himself and had them turned into a synagogue.

seem to have extended no further than their own prospects and reputations. Long before Becker even came to trial, Murphy had realized that
Tammany could afford no more bad publicity. That meant finding new
ways to channel graft to the machine.

Murphy had learned the lesson of the scandals of the 1890s. "When
I was an Assembly district leader," he explained in a rare moment of
candor, "it was borne in on me that Tammany's evil repute came from its
association with the police." Less brutality and more discretion were
required; Becker was to be the last in a long line of New York policemen, extending back through Bill Devery at least as far as Clubber
Williams, to control a significant portion of Manhattan's graft. The new
middlemen would be gamblers themselves.

The most important point of contact between Tammany and New
York's gaming lords was now Arnold Rothstein. Even before Rosenthal was shot, the Big Bankroll had made a name for himself in his
field; more important, he was known to be sober, intelligent, shrewd,
and discreet. He was the obvious choice to become Murphy's "man
between."

Rothstein had always made money as a fixer, but after Becker's
arrest, when New York politicians were running scared from associating with gangsters, gamblers, and criminals, he took to arranging
loans and permissions. He was also clever enough to realize that the
lieutenant's well-publicized downfall meant the end of the era of
expensively accoutered Manhattan gaming clubs, places whose existence was an open secret. It was Rothstein, gambling lore insists, who
responded by inventing and perfecting the "floating game"—action
that moved from place to place and week to week. The floating game
was safer, less conspicuous, and yet it still appealed to the high rollers.
There was nothing, after all, to say that gentlemen gamblers of discretion should have to play in dirty, locked back rooms; some of the
biggest games flitted for years between New York's best hotels.
Swope—with Florenz Ziegfeld, the impresario, and a dozen or so
others—became a member of a Rothstein game known as the
Partridge Club, which rotated among the Astor, the Knickerbocker,

the Ritz-Carlton, and the Imperial hotels. Partridge Club members could get themselves dealt in for a mere $30, a fee that generally included a high-class dinner. But playing cost considerably more. Single bets were sometimes of the order of $100 to $1,000.

In the course of the next decade and a half, Rothstein expanded his operations incrementally and without apparent conscience. He moved into labor racketeering and narcotics, opened several new clubs in the suburbs, loaned nearly $2 million to the Communist Party at a high rate of interest, and reinvested some of his profits in theater shows and racing. It has been widely accepted, if never conclusively proved, that it was he who fixed the crooked World Series of 1919, in which the underdog Cincinnati Reds downed the apparently unstoppable Chicago White Sox. Certainly he became heavily involved in organized crime as it emerged during Prohibition.

Rothstein began the 1920s by importing cargoes of whiskey and progressed to advancing funds to gangsters such as Meyer Lansky, "Lucky" Luciano, and "Legs" Diamond. The uncouth, self-made Luciano was particularly in awe of his sophisticated mentor, anxiously soliciting lessons in etiquette such as "how to behave when I met classy broads":

> He taught me how to dress, how not to wear loud things, but
> to have good taste; he taught me how to use knives and forks,
> and things like that at the dinner table, about holdin' a door
> open for a girl, or helpin' her sit down by holdin' the chair. . . .
> Rothstein gimme a whole new image, and it had a lotta influ-
> ence on me.

Mixing in such company was dangerous, of course, but Arnold Rothstein prospered nonetheless for much of the decade. His luck finally ran out on November 5, 1928, when he was shot in a hotel room on West Fifty-sixth Street—part of a gamblers' feud. He staggered out into the street but died less than a day later, refusing until the end to name his assailant. By then his bankroll totaled somewhere between $2 and $3 million.

* * *

Rothstein's old friend Herbert Bayard Swope was given a pay raise for his work on the Becker case. His new salary, a highly satisfactory $125 a week, was further boosted by the lineage payments he received for his coverage of the policeman's trial. At space rates, Swope picked up an additional $645.29 from the *World* for a mere eleven days in John Goff's court.

Swope's role in the Rosenthal affair made him famous throughout New York. His paper awarded him a byline—still a rare honor at that time—and, during the First World War, sent him to Europe on two occasions to report on the fighting. *Inside the German Empire*, a collection of Swope's dispatches from Imperial Germany, won the inaugural Pulitzer Prize for journalism in 1917,* and by the early 1920s he was probably the most celebrated reporter in the United States. In the course of the next three decades, that fame spread throughout the world. When the old newsman died in 1958, the Columbia School of Journalism dedicated a room in his name.

Swope took full advantage of his new position. He became renowned as a host, and between the wars he got to know, apparently, everyone worth knowing in America and much of Western Europe. Among his more intimate acquaintances were Harpo Marx, Noël Coward, and John Barrymore; he was also on first-name terms with Howard Hughes, Woodrow Wilson, Al Smith, Adlai Stevenson, Joseph Kennedy, Franklin Roosevelt, and Winston Churchill. Humphrey Bogart once played an impromptu game of football in Swope's front hall; Douglas Fairbanks Jr. met his second wife there. None of these friendships—Swope himself was fond of saying— would ever have been possible had it not been for Charley Becker.

---

*Swope was the first writer to use the word "Inside" in the title of a book to denote exclusive or privileged access—a device that has been widely copied since. He had always been an innovator. In his youth he was the only newspaperman in St. Louis to wear spats. In New York, in 1928, he became the first man to affect midnight blue evening dress; within a short while it had become an accepted substitute for black. Swope is also stated to have been the first man brave enough to wear zippered bathing trunks in public.

* * *

While Swope's star rose, the Sullivans' sank swiftly. The family lost most of its power after Big Tim's death and had, in truth, been in decline for years. Florrie had died a lunatic in the summer of 1909, and Sullivan's cousin and trusted adviser Little Tim went the same way that same year, expiring from an undiagnosed "psychopathic trouble." Christy Sullivan fought on but gambled away virtually all of his personal fortune, also that same year, in a failed attempt to win election as sheriff of New York; he retired from Manhattan politics in 1915. At about the same time, Paddy Sullivan, Tim's brother, quarreled with the Tammany boss who ran the city's Third Assembly District and could never be sure of his support within the Hall thereafter.

For a while Paddy did keep up the old Sullivan tradition of hosting a free Christmas dinner for the poor of the Bowery, but the practice was eventually abandoned around 1918. "Now indeed," lamented Alvin Harlow, the chronicler of the famous street, "the giants were all departed, and nothing left but petty gangsters and ragamuffins." Even the Occidental faded away. The vast erotic fresco over the bar began to flake and crack not long after Becker's execution, and—stripped of Sullivan's prestige—the name of the place was changed and it became the dull and desperate Commercial, "just another cheap wayfarers' hotel." By 1931, Harlow observed, it was slipping into deserved obscurity. The oldest hotel in the whole of New York, and Big Tim's headquarters and home for many years, now differed little, except in size, "from the other forty- and fifty-cent upstairs hotels of the Bowery—a small, tile-floored office, shower baths, and a faint odor of disinfectant."

Charles Whitman, who had built a career on New York's disgust with Tammany and police corruption, never became president. He served two terms as governor of New York State, from 1914 to 1918, but his administration was widely viewed as undistinguished, even at the time, and historians have proved no less critical. Very little in the way of useful legislation was enacted, and much of Whitman's time and energy was devoted to courting popularity in preparation for his expected bid for the White House. As late as 1917, he left Albany for several weeks to drum up more support on a whistlestop tour of the United States.

Whitman's conviction that he might one day go to Washington was certainly not mere vanity. During his first days as governor, when memory of his stewardship of the Becker case remained strong everywhere, "Whitman for President" clubs sprang up around the country, and Woodrow Wilson himself was heard to say that the former DA was his most likely opponent in 1916. But Whitman's advantage gradually dissipated as his political ineffectiveness became obvious. He failed to secure the Republican nomination for the presidency, losing out to Charles Evans Hughes, and found himself facing stiff competition in his attempt to secure reelection in New York's gubernatorial contest. His Democratic opponent was none other than Samuel Seabury, who fought the election with the unlooked-for help of Thomas Mott Osborne. Osborne resigned his post as warden of Sing Sing in order to campaign against Whitman, citing Becker's execution as "the vilest of crimes." In one open letter, Osborne regretted that he could do nothing to change the past. "But," he went on,

> I do desire to influence the future . . . to the end that no man so weak as yourself—so shifty, so selfish, so false, so cruel—may be entrusted with further power.

Many of those who had followed the former DA's career felt that Osborne had a point. "Whitman isn't a great Governor," opined the *New York Call*, "not even a fairly decent Governor—he's just a temporizing, fence-fixing little politician." Even the sober *Times* had grown disillusioned by now, suggesting that Whitman's "entire political standing is based upon the convictions in the Rosenthal murder case," and for a long time the election seemed finely balanced. In the end the governor won, thanks largely to the final collapse of Theodore Roosevelt's Progressive Party, which had split the Republicans for several years. Thousands of Progressives returned to the conservative fold in time for the ballot, and when the ballots were counted, Whitman had secured reelection by 154,000 votes.

The governor was still haunted, nonetheless, by wraiths from his past. Jack Rose turned up in Albany in 1914, seeking a favor on behalf of a friend sentenced to Sing Sing for attempted murder. Whitman signed a pardon for the man. Jacob Luban, who had been on the DA's payroll for months in 1912, found himself back in prison serving twenty years for forgery. The governor saw to it that his sentence was commuted. Becker's remaining partisans were not alone in wondering if their old nemesis was buying the silence of men who could still seriously embarrass him, but the lieutenant had long vanished from the front pages by this time, and no one of importance made any real attempt to learn the truth.

Whitman's second term in Albany was in any case overshadowed by his escalating dependence on alcohol. Despite courting the religious vote by hinting that he would come out in favor of Prohibition, he appeared drunk in public on several occasions, prompting one sardonic reporter to observe that "some of the Governor's new friends don't seem to realize that when he says he favors a dry Manhattan, he doesn't mean what they mean by it." New York gossip attributed Whitman's drinking to "a desire to escape the huge accusing ghost of Becker, the dead policeman, which, according to rumor, could be seen tramping its beat night after night along the stone battlements of the old Albany State House." It came as no surprise when the governor failed to win a third term in office in 1918. The man who beat him was Al Smith, a large and popular Irishman and a Tammany loyalist through and through, who was widely regarded as Tim Sullivan's political heir.

Whitman did bid once more for high office. In 1922 he sought the Republican nomination for the presidency but lost to Herbert Hoover. He returned to New York, where he was humiliatingly defeated in a bid to regain his old job as district attorney, winning fewer than one-third of the votes. After that embarrassment he retired to private practice. He died in 1947 at the age of seventy-eight.

Many of the other men associated with Becker's prosecution served out distinguished careers.

John Goff completed his term on the New York Supreme Court bench, retiring at the beginning of 1919 only because he had reached the upper age limit for judges in the city and returning to his farmhouse and his fancy herons. He died toward the end of 1924, a month or so shy of his seventy-seventh birthday.

Samuel Seabury's public profile benefited considerably from his stewardship of Becker's second trial. He went to the court of appeals in 1915, dabbled in high politics with Roosevelt's Progressives, ran against Whitman, and was even talked of at one point as a possible presidential candidate. He continued to oppose Tammany Hall, and when, in 1931, another investigation into corruption in New York was ordered, Seabury was chosen to lead it. The evidence he uncovered showed that under the long succession of Democratic mayors who had ruled the city in the twenties, the NYPD had slipped back into some of its old ways. A stool pigeon named Chile Acuna ("The Human Spittoona") testified that he was paid $150 a week to help frame prostitutes swept up in vice raids. Several police officers explained that the vast and unexplained sums found in their bank accounts were "racetrack winnings" or the generous gifts of dead relatives; Officer Robert Morris claimed to have been handed forty thousand-dollar bills on the street in Coney Island by a wonderful "Uncle George" who conveniently dropped dead a week or two later in California. In time the investigation reached the upper echelons of the city's government, and Tammany's Jimmy Walker—a three-term mayor best known as the author of the sentimental ballad "Will You Love Me in December As You Do in May?"—was forced to testify. Walker was charged with accepting more than a million dollars' worth of bribes, and in September 1932 he resigned. This time there was no way back for Tammany Hall. The scandal of the Seabury hearings finally damaged it beyond repair.

Of the lawyers involved in the Becker case, James Sullivan, Jack Rose's attorney, became U.S. ambassador to the Dominican Republic, thanks in part to the enthusiastic endorsement of Charles Whitman. He was removed from the post a few months later after a special hearing into his "scandalously corrupt" behavior. The *New York World*, of all newspapers, led the anti-Sullivan campaign, revealing that within a few days of his arrival the attorney had telegraphed friends at home in New York to advise them to join him: "The pickings are fine."

Bourke Cockran, the most distinguished member of Becker's defense team, continued to display a willingness to take on unpopular causes. He represented Tom Mooney, the principal suspect in an infamous San Francisco anarchist bombing in 1916; Mooney, although found guilty and sentenced to be hanged, was eventually reprieved and pardoned. At about the same time, Cockran abandoned the Progressives to return to the Democratic Party and to Tammany. He nominated Al Smith as a possible Democratic presidential candidate in 1920 and opposed the introduction of Prohibition before dying of a brain hemorrhage in 1923. John McIntyre joined his old adversary Goff on the New York Supreme Court bench in 1916. Frank Moss continued to serve as assistant DA until Mayor Mitchel came in, then wrote an impenetrable book entitled *America's Mission to Serve Humanity*, which was published in 1919. He died soon afterward, aged sixty-one. Lloyd Stryker, who had worked on McIntyre's team and never wavered in his belief in Becker's innocence, became perhaps the most celebrated defense attorney in New York. "Preying" Manton, however, became the leading disgrace of the legal profession. While serving as senior judge of the U.S. Court of Appeals in 1939, he was caught taking backhanders and convicted of "running a mill for the sale of justice." In the end Becker's old counsel went to prison for two years. At his trial it emerged that in the eleven months following his appointment to the court—a period in which his official pay was less than $10,000—he had contrived to wipe out debts of $710,000 and banked an additional $750,000 in graft. "Presumably," one reporter noted, "he looked back on his most famous client as a piker."

Most of the policemen caught up in the case enjoyed less dramatic careers than Martin Manton. Rhinelander Waldo never held another job of consequence after his dismissal as police commissioner at the end of 1913; he died in 1927 at the age of only fifty. John Becker, Charley's brother, who had supported him throughout both trials, retired soon after the execution and went back to live in Sullivan County. He never married, and boarded with friends in Callicoon Center until his death in 1938. Max Schmittberger, Becker's old opponent, did better; he was promoted to chief inspector, but although he consistently professed his honesty, he never quite shook off suspicions that he returned quietly to his grafting ways each time the reformers were thrown out.

Lincoln Steffens, the muckraking journalist who had saved Schmittberger's job after the Lexow hearings, believed implicitly in the policeman's honor and became his firm supporter. But even Steffens—who once watched Schmittberger merrily cracking the heads of striking workers with his nightstick—had to admit that his protégé, "like all converts, was worse than the accustomed righteous [and] cared nothing for the technicalities of the law. 'To hell with the Constitution!' he shouted once at some Reds who cited that sacred instrument as a guaranty of their rights. He was still a policeman, in this and in other ways."

The other police chief who had shaped Becker's career died in the same year as Schmittberger, 1917. Clubber Williams lived rather quietly in his final years, having squandered virtually all of the spectacular wealth he had amassed in nearly three decades of service; when he died, the newspapers were shocked to discover that his estate totaled a mere $14. But Winfield Sheehan, Waldo's gnomic, strangely affluent assistant—the man often suspected of membership in Tim Sullivan's gambling commission—did pretty well for someone who had started out as a cub reporter on the *World*. He moved out to California during the war, found an opening in the film business, and by the early 1930s had emerged as head of the Fox studio, winning an Oscar there for *Cavalcade* in 1933. Today Sheehan's fame, such as it is, rests chiefly on the part he played in the discovery of Rita Hayworth, whom he spotted dancing in a nightclub. But a year or two earlier, the old New Yorker had also arranged a Hollywood screen test for a prop boy whom the veteran director Raoul Walsh had told him might make it as a cowboy star.

The two men watched the test together. "He'll do," Sheehan concluded. "What did you say his name was?" "Morrison," replied

Walsh. "Marion Morrison." It was Sheehan who renamed the youth John Wayne.

Thomas Mott Osborne's career as a reformer was very nearly destroyed not long after Becker's execution, when a committee appointed to investigate conditions at Sing Sing discovered that homosexuality was rife throughout the prison. One inmate admitted that he had sold himself to nearly two dozen fellow prisoners in a mere three months, and the recriminations that followed soon spiraled out of control. In the last days of 1915, Osborne found himself indicted on six counts. The allegations against him ranged from neglect of duty to the charge that he himself had sodomized men placed in his charge.

It cost the warden the better part of $75,000 in legal fees and payments to the famed private detective Val O'Farrell to get the charges dropped; even then their taint lingered for the rest of his career. Few were surprised when Osborne left Sing Sing in the autumn of 1916 and went to Portsmouth, New Hampshire, to be commander of the naval prison there. He retired not long afterward, retreating to his home in Auburn.

Osborne met with a bizarre end, dropping dead, aged sixty-eight, on his way to a masquerade party. When the police found the blue-blood reformer's body sprawled in the street, he was wearing false whiskers, a suit several sizes too small for him, and a set of slip-on goofy teeth.

The surviving members of the group that had secured Becker's conviction went their separate ways after the lieutenant's trials, falling out among themselves so utterly that they seldom agreed on anything again.

William Shapiro's career as a chauffeur was ended by the Becker affair. He had his driver's license revoked, and the infamous gray Packard had to be sold. His partner Louis Libby, deprived of his main source of income, turned to pimping instead, making a living for a while off the earnings of his wife. The oily and egotistical Sam Schepps tried his hand at the antique-furniture business, to which his talents as small-time con man undoubtedly suited him. His taste for cigarettes and good living did him in eventually, however; he died in 1936. Harry Vallon flitted from job to job on the Lower East Side—at one time giving his occupation as "chandelier salesman"—before vanishing entirely; no one knows what became of him. James Marshall, the tap-dancing perjurer whose evidence had secured Becker's second conviction and effectively condemned him to death, also disappeared for many years. But he returned in the end to his old stomping grounds uptown, just a block or two from the spot where the fateful Harlem Conference was said to have occurred, and was to be found running dice games in the district as late as 1947. Bridgey Webber, on the other hand, secured himself a comfortable position at a factory owned by his brother-in-law. The one-time dognapper and poker magnate spent the remainder of his life making cardboard boxes in Passaic, New Jersey.

Bald Jack Rose bought himself a wig. Thus disguised, he abandoned the Satan's Circus card rooms and turned his hand to setting up a company called Humanology Motion Pictures. The idea, supposedly, was to make moralistic shorts. When the necessary funds were not forthcoming, Rose instead forged himself an improbable evangelical career, dressing in black from head to toe and drawing church congregations numbering in the hundreds to his addresses on "Life in the Underworld." He pursued this line of work for several years, albeit with diminishing returns. By the time Becker stood trial for a second time, Rose had been reduced to lecturing in YMCA halls, and during the First World War he sometimes made appearances at army camps.

Eventually tiring of the religious circuit, Bald Jack went into catering, it is said with considerable success. During the Roaring Twenties, he sold rotisseries in Connecticut and on Long Island. For many years his name was preserved in the form of a "Jack Rose" cocktail, served in Broadway bars and consisting of applejack, grenadine, and lemon juice.* He died in October 1947 at the age of seventy-two.

---

*Combine two ounces of applejack, the potent New Jersey cider brandy, with the juice of half a lemon and a scant half ounce of grenadine. Shake well with cracked ice and strain into a chilled cocktail glass. As one drinks writer points out, the name pretty much suggested itself. "The cocktail is based on apple*jack* and it's *rose*-pink. Play on words."

* * *

Not every associate of Becker's went straight. Chicago May, the lieutenant's old acquaintance from the Stephen Crane affair, continued her criminal career into the 1920s, working variously as a pickpocket, a blackmailer, and a whore. She married twice and lived for shorter periods with a long succession of crooks, the most notable of whom was the famed Chicago safecracker Eddie Guerin.

In 1901 May and Guerin traveled to Paris, where they joined two men planning to rob the American Express office in the city. The group successfully blew the safe and got away with $250,000, a huge fortune in that day, but they were arrested before they had the chance to spend the money. The leader of the gang confessed, and the trial was a formality. May received a sentence of five years' hard labor, serving three; Guerin got life imprisonment in the infamous penal colony of Devil's Island, from which, a few years later, he contrived to make a spectacular escape.* The couple was reunited in London, where they promptly fell out, and, in 1907, Chicago May and her latest lover waylaid Guerin and opened fire on him with a revolver. Sadly for them, Guerin survived to identify his assailants. May spent the next ten years of her life sequestered in a women's prison in Aylesbury, Buckinghamshire.

Released in 1917 with her good looks largely gone, the onetime Queen of the Badger Game made her way back to New York to find herself queen of nothing much at all. She returned to a life of prostitution, robbing and blackmailing clients when she could, rising eventually to the rank of madam. After 1925—too old by now to earn much of a living from her trade—she made sporadic attempts to abandon her criminal career, at one point even penning a self-serving autobiography filled with reminiscences about her old days in Satan's Circus sipping champagne with Charley Becker.

When money became tight again, May returned to the streets. She was by now in her early fifties, blowsy and grown rather

---

*The safecracker got away in a canoe made from a hollowed-out tree accompanied by four other prisoners, none of whom lived to reach freedom. According to underworld legend, Guerin ate them.

stout, and America was teetering on the brink of the Great Depression. The fabled Chicago May died, utterly used up, in Philadelphia in 1929.

Letitia Stenson, Becker's second wife, headed westward to Nevada after her divorce, taking with her the policeman's only son. By the summer of 1912, she was living in Reno, where Paul Becker later acquired an interest in a blacksmith's shop. Letitia had virtually no contact with her former husband by this time—merely an envelope containing the monthly child-support payment—and she spoke only reluctantly to a reporter from the *New York World* who tracked her down to her new home in the last days of July. "It wrings my heart to speak of these things now," she said.

By 1915 Letitia had moved on again, to the little settlement of Winnemucca in the northern reaches of the state. There all trace of her is lost. She was no longer living in the town when the census was taken in 1920, and there is no way of saying where she went or when she died. Her son with Charley Becker, Howard, returned east a few years later, though enrolling at the University of Chicago to major in sociology. Chicago, in the 1920s, was perhaps the most important center for the study of this new and fashionable subject, and Becker excelled at it, eventually completing a postgraduate degree. He became a professor of sociology at the University of Wisconsin and built a distinguished academic career. He was the author of *Man in Reciprocity* and *Modern Sociological Theory in Continuity and Change*. When he died, on June 8, 1960, he had just been elected president of the American Sociological Association.

A number of the Beckers had reputations for being "difficult people to get along with," as one member of the family put it, but Howard was without doubt more difficult than most. He was particularly renowned for his heavy, quashing sarcasm, which many colleagues and former students still vividly recall today. He deployed this weapon freely against a namesake, Howard S. Becker, who became a sociologist during the 1940s. The two men were not related, but the elder Becker grew irritated whenever colleagues inadvertently confused them.

"I would get copies of letters he sent to people who made that mistake," the younger man recalled,

> heavily ironic letters saying it was kind of them to ask if he was interested in being an assistant professor in their department but he was already a full professor at Wisconsin. Things like that.
>
> I'm sorry to speak ill of him, but I have to tell you that he was widely hated by his colleagues at Wisconsin and by people who had been graduate students there. After he died, a number of people came up to me at the next big sociology convention to offer condolences, and, when I told them we were not related, said some version of, "Oh, you weren't? Well, he was a mean son of a bitch."

It would take a psychologist, or perhaps a sociologist, to trace the roots of Howard Becker's antipathetic personality. But it does not seem too much to suggest that the distressing memory of Charley Becker played its part in the son's development. Howard was, of course, just old enough to have had recollections of the father who had left when he was five, but he evidently found the knowledge of his relationship to so notorious a man quite shameful. His own children (there were three, two girls and a boy) were brought up to believe that Paul Becker was their grandfather and remained in utter ignorance of their infamous relative until the late 1980s, when a cousin who had been researching family history uncovered the truth. Charley's grandson, Christopher—a historian and renowned chess-problem setter by then in his late fifties—"really was astounded" by the news, another of the Beckers wrote, but quickly became fascinated by the Rosenthal murder and its aftermath. He assembled a large collection of material on the affair and, when he died, was interred in the old cemetery at Callicoon Center. His tombstone lies between the grave of Henry Becker and that of Charley's father, Conrad.

And finally, the widows of the Rosenthal affair.

Henrietta Young, Jack Zelig's girl, was last heard of on January 6,

1913, sitting in a box in the Arlington dance hall on St. Mark's Place with a little sack of money in her lap. She was gathering tribute from the gaggle of prostitutes, pimps, opium addicts, and policemen assembled to pay their respects to her husband's memory at a benefit arranged on her behalf.

Occasionally one of the Zelig's old acquaintances would leave the tables clustered around the dance floor, make his way upstairs, and thrust a fistful of dollars into the grieving widow's hands. "Humpty" Jackson, the hunchbacked leader of Spanish Louis's old gang, purchased sixteen quarts of champagne for the members of his party and left a few dollars more at the box office. But the dance was not much of a success. Zelig's power had dissipated so utterly after his death that the event was only sparsely attended, and few of those who showed themselves had much time for his wife. The whores up on Fourteenth Street had sent word that they would not attend. "Who is Mrs. Zelig?" one spit in disgust. "Let her go out and sell it the same as we do."

Every man admitted to the dance wore a button badge emblazoned with Zelig's broadly grinning face—the image of him snapped when he was arraigned on charges cooked up by Becker's Special Squad. But there was little joy, no laughter, and scarcely any dancing in the hall. Whenever she heard voices raised, Mrs. Zelig would send word down to the meager crowd "to be quiet for her husband's sake." And when the last guest had departed and the expenses had been paid, it was found that only $46 remained. "If the boys knew this would have occurred," Abe Shoenfeld wrote sadly, "they would have chipped in some money and given it to her, sooner than run a ball for $46 with two or three couples dancing on the floor."

The two other women robbed of their husbands by the case also found life difficult thereafter. Lillian Rosenthal, the murdered man's second wife, subsisted for a while on the charity of midtown Manhattan gamblers. But she lost money investing in a movie house and a failed dressmaking business and eventually alienated the men who had supported her by attempting to enlist them in a fresh campaign against Tammany graft. She died in considerable poverty, "a broken and fanatically embittered woman," in September 1928.

Helen Becker, meanwhile, long outlived her former rival. She saw nothing of the fortune her husband was supposed to have hidden away during a long career of grafting. The cash was eaten up in legal fees, and in fact she found herself liable for debts of several thousand dollars, which she paid off over several years from her skimpy teacher's salary. After that she was able to put aside enough to make several attempts to clear her husband's name, but nothing came of any of them. Her teaching career flourished moderately, however, and by the time of her retirement in the early 1940s she was assistant principal of an elementary school in the northern reaches of Manhattan.

Helen never remarried and never had another child, though she received a number of proposals and lived on until 1962. "I prefer," she always said to those who asked,

> to remain a widow in memory of a man who was put to death by the great state of New York for a crime he did not commit.
>
> He was not an angel; he never made a pretense of being one. He was just an ordinary human being, and that is why I loved him so.

NOTES

Abbreviations Used in the Notes

Klein   Henry Klein, *Sacrificed: The Story of Police Lieut. Charles Becker.* Privately published, 1927.

Levine   Jerald Levine, *Police, Parties and Polity: The Bureaucratization, Unionization, and Professionalization of the New York City Police, 1870–1917.* Ph.D. thesis, University of Wisconsin, 1971.

Lexow   New York State Senate, *Report and Proceedings of the Senate Committee Appointed to Investigate the Police Department of the City of New York.* 5 vols., 1895.

Logan   Andy Logan, *Against the Evidence: The Becker-Rosenthal Affair, A Great American Scandal.* London, Weidenfeld & Nicholson, 1970.

MBC   Mary Becker collection.

A Note on Citation

In order to keep the length of these notes to a reasonable minimum, I have referred to books consulted only in their short form. Full citations can be found in the Bibliography.

Notes on the Sources

PRIMARY SOURCES

Though none of the main participants in the Becker-Rosenthal affair left personal papers, manuscript material relating to the case does survive in the Municipal Archives, New York. The files of the district attorney's office, in particular, form the largest and most complete collection of records relating to crime extant in any city; notionally, at least, every criminal indicted in Manhattan between the eighteenth century and the mid-twentieth has a file of his or her own, and the DA's papers also include closed-case reports and even scrapbooks of newspaper clippings relating to significant prosecutions. Though disappointingly unrevealing in the Becker-Rosenthal case, they deserve to be better known.

In Becker's case, these records are supplemented by the New York *Reports*—printed summaries, designed to serve as records for the legal profession, of all the cases heard in the city—and by two smaller but unique collections, the Mary Becker and the Thomas Mott Osborne Papers. Mary Becker's papers, which remain in private hands, consist of a handful of Charles Becker's letters to relatives together with family histories and family trees assembled in the course of genealogical research carried out in the 1980s and 1990s. Although not so extensive as an historian might wish, they offer an invaluable insight into Becker's background and describe his thoughts as he faced execution. Thomas Mott Osborne's papers, at Syracuse University, contain several mentioning the Becker-Rosenthal affair amid much material relating to conditions at Sing Sing and prison reform.

Newspaper coverage of the Becker case was extraordinarily extensive, and the reporters of the day not only covered the two trials and multiple appeals in considerable detail, but made a point of informing their readers about the backgrounds and opinions of the main characters in the drama. Some of their stories need to be read with a certain caution; competition between titles was fierce and many journalists of the day were not above embellishing their reports, or even inventing material outright. So many dailies covered the Becker story, though, that a consensus of sorts can almost always be formed by the comparative study of coverage in different titles and by an awareness of the biases of the newspapers' publishers, editors, and readers.

Of New York's papers, the *American* and the *World* were richer and had more resources than their rivals. They pursued developments in the Becker case most vigorously and regularly broke new developments and tracked down witnesses ahead of the police. Their coverage was more complete and detailed than that of any of their rivals and their use of photographs and illustrations more usefully comprehensive. The *Sun*, though no longer the paper it had been in its nineteenth-century heyday (by 1912 it was the only major title that still lacked the technology to print photographs), was also comprehensive and provided more sober coverage. The *New York Times*, on the other hand, has the inestimable benefit of being fully archived and indexed. In the last couple of years, the old printed indexes—which are, inevitably, far from complete—have been supplemented by the appearance of the *Times* digital archive, an utterly invaluable repository (available online on a pay-per-article basis) that offers full-text searches of the complete run of the paper. Careful interrogation of this archive has led to the exhumation of several hitherto-unknown aspects of Becker's police career that would almost certainly never have been discovered through old-fashioned research, in particular his central involvement in the "Cops' Revolt" of 1902. Issues of the *Brooklyn Daily Eagle* have also been digitized and are available online free of charge, though to date the digitization project has reached only 1902.

A large proportion of what we reliably know about Jack Zelig and the Jewish gangsters of the Lower East Side comes from the voluminous and colorful reports compiled by Abe Shoenfeld, a private investigator retained by the Bureau of Social Morals, established by a wealthy group of concerned Jewish leaders to produce intelligence on Jewish criminal activities. The group's chief purpose in commissioning these reports was to provide intelligence on Jewish gangs, extortion rackets, and prostitution rings to the NYPD and so help clean up what was regarded as the shameful prevalence of crime within the Eastern European immigrant community. Shoenfeld responded by producing a long series of profiles on notable Jewish criminals of the period—among them most of the principals in the Becker-Rosenthal affair—together with monthly "Vice Reports" summarizing the day-to-day activities of his primary suspects. Because he was himself Jewish, Shoenfeld was able to penetrate the East Side underworld and mine a rich seam of anecdotal and generally unverifiable information, which paints an intricately detailed picture of New York's Jewish underworld in the years 1912–17. The nineteen hundred reports that Shoenfeld completed found their way into the papers of Rabbi Judah Magnes, and thence to Israel, where they are currently preserved in the Central Archives for the History of the Jewish People in Jerusalem.

One other "eyewitness" account of the events of 1912 exists in the form of *The Becker Scandal: A Time Remembered*, by Viña Delmar. The case itself forms only the backdrop to what is essentially a family memoir, but Delmar's account is of considerable interest because her father was a close friend of Herman Rosenthal's. The reliability of the author's recollections is debatable; Delmar was only nine years old at the time of the gambler's murder, compiled her memoir more than half a century after the fact, and used her skills as a novelist to tell the story, including the interpolation of large swaths of reported speech. The author's own view on the trustworthiness of her recollections is clearly stated, nonetheless: "I do not expect anyone to believe that I am repeating every word of every conversation with the precision of a tape recorder. However, I am convinced that all that was said, all that was done, is more vividly remembered than had I been thirty at the time. A child has the advantage of an uncluttered mind, and I had a unique observation post from which to view the lives around me."

SECONDARY SOURCES

Two detailed studies of the case stand out amid the secondary sources. The first, *Sacrificed: The Story of Police Lieut.Charles Becker*, is of special interest because its author, Henry Klein, was hired as chief investigator of a citizens' committee organized in August 1912 to investigate "police conditions" in the wake of the Rosenthal murder. Klein began his investigations convinced of Becker's guilt and ended them just as certain of his innocence. His detailed knowledge of the Rosenthal affair was augmented during the Great War by a stint serving as an auditor in the district attorney's office—a position that gave him the remarkable opportunity to illicitly search District Attorney Whitman's financial records for 1912 and turn up the first firm evidence of the methods used by the DA to assemble the bizarre collection of informants and ne'er-do-wells who testified at the two Becker trials. Receipts, examined by Klein, demonstrated that the majority had been retained, for long periods, at public cost in order to ensure Becker's conviction. Klein's book—privately published in 1927 and rather rare today—is an invaluable repository of all sorts of additional information as well; it incorporates statements from several of the surviving principals in the case, including revealing affidavits from Tim Sullivan's private secretary, and contains transcripts of large portions of the trial evidence. The author remained convinced until his death that Becker's conviction was a miscarriage of justice, and engaged in letter-column disputes with Herbert Bayard Swope over the policeman's guilt or innocence as late as 1951.

The second major contribution to the subject is Isabel Ann "Andy" Logan's *Against the Evidence: The Becker-Rosenthal Affair*, published in 1970. Logan was a well-known New York journalist who reported for years on affairs at City Hall for the *New Yorker* magazine and was renowned as "a diminutive figure in black with an encyclopedic knowledge of the city's social and political history."

She hated politicians' cant and was far from beloved by a succession of New York mayors; according to legend, Ed Koch was riding downtown one day when an aide looked up and saw the sixty-year-old Logan crossing across the street ahead of their limousine. "Look!" the aide exclaimed. "There's Andy Logan." "Hit her!" Koch ordered his driver.

Against the Evidence remains by far the densest and most detailed account of the Becker case. Like Klein, Logan became convinced of the policeman's innocence. Her book—heavily researched in the newspapers of the time—intelligently lays out the vast number of discrepancies in the prosecution case; it is a veritable gold mine of information, extremely thought-provoking and generally reliable. Its defects are a confused chronology and a complete lack of bibliography and footnotes. Fortunately, the Andy Logan Papers, held in the New York Public Library, contain a dozen boxes relating to the research Logan undertook before writing her book, and these papers have been used to verify and source a number of statements that I was otherwise unable to track down in the newspapers of the time.

A third book on the Becker case—the second published—proved less useful than Klein's and Logan's works. Jonathan Root's *The Life and Bad Times of Charlie Becker* is patchily researched and contains several instances of outright invention. I have used it only very occasionally, and then with caution.

When it comes to researching the story of New York itself, the historian is spoiled for choice. Virtually every aspect of the city's political, social, and economic life has been well illuminated by recent studies, from the highest of high society down to and including the everyday existences of boardinghouse lodgers and Bowery bums. Luc Sante's intoxicatingly anecdotal *Low Life*, while perhaps understandably distrusted by academic historians, is based on wide reading and remains a vivid introduction to the realities of life in a great city. I must also mention *Gotham*, by Edwin Burrows and Mike Wallace, a masterful, inclusive, and wonderfully readable study of the whole of New York's history up to 1898; at the established pace, Wallace's much-anticipated follow-up volume—covering the period from 1898 to the present day—is due in a little over a decade, and I will be waiting for my copy. No author, though, has taught me more about the thoughts, the sounds, and the rhythms of New York in the first half of the last century than has Joseph Mitchell, the renowned *New Yorker* correspondent, several of whose incomparable essays touch, if only tangentially, on my own subject. My respect for him grows all the time.

Notes on the Text

PREFACE

"ONLY ONE HAS BEEN EXECUTED FOR MURDER" At the time of writing, two other police officers sit on death row, awaiting execution for murders committed in 1995. One, Antoinette Frank of the New Orleans Police Department, was found guilty of the cold-blooded killing of two employees of a Vietnamese restaurant she had been hired to protect in her off-duty hours, together with the murder of a member of her own department who had the misfortune to be on the premises when she arrived after closing time intent on robbery. The other, Jack Ray Hudson Jr., shot and killed two fellow policemen who had caught him attempting to steal money, guns, and drugs from an evidence lockup in Yuma, Arizona. In New York, meanwhile, two retired police officers—Louis Eppolito and Stephen Caracappa—found guilty of working as hit men for the Mafia received life sentences that were subsequently overturned on the grounds that the statute of limitations had expired. Their trial revived memories of the Becker case in the New York press.

It is possible that other cases have occurred; indeed it surprises me that Charles Becker has retained his dubious distinction for as long as he has. But I have never, despite several searches, found any reference to the execution of another American police officer convicted for crimes committed while in uniform. The only reference work I have found on the subject, Michael Newton's *Killer Cops: An Encyclopedia of Lawless Lawmen* (Port Townsend, WA: Loompanics Unlimited, 1997), mentions only Becker, Frank, and Hudson.

"CROOKEDEST COP" Luc Sante, *Low Life*, p. 249.

1. WIDE-OPEN

BROADWAY GARDEN Richard O'Connor, *Hell's Kitchen*, p. 93; Lloyd Morris, *Incredible New York*, p. 259; Robert Stallman, *Stephen Crane*, p. 220.

THE YOUNG MAN DESCRIBED *New York Sun*, Sept. 17, and *Journal*, Oct. 17, 1896.

THE YOUNG MAN AND THE CHORUS GIRLS *New York Sun*, Sept. 17, and *Journal*, Sept. 20, 1896; Stallman, op. cit., p. 220.

DESCRIPTION OF THE REDHEAD *New York Journal*, Sept. 17, and Crane's testimony and pictures in the same paper, Sept. 20, 1896.

Shirtwaist Leon Stein, of the Ladies' International Garment Workers' Union, describes the shirtwaist, in his history of *The Triangle Fire*, p. 160, as "a cool and efficient bodice garment, generally worn with a tailored skirt," which conveyed the image of "a bright-eyed, fast-moving young lady, her long tresses knotted in a bun atop her proud head, ready to challenge the male in sport, drawing room, and, if properly equipped with paper cuff covers, even in the office. . . . The secret of its perennial popularity was in its lines. . . . The *bouffant* quality of the fabric enhanced the figure it enfolded."

Becker *New York Sun*, Sept. 17 and Oct. 16; *Journal*, Sept. 20 and Oct. 17, 1896; Stallman, op. cit., p. 220; Christopher Benfey, *The Double Life of Stephen Crane*, p. 175.

Germans in the NYPD Levine, p. 42; Cornelius Willemse, *A Cop Remembers*, p. 82; Lardner and Reppetto, *NYPD*, p. 61.

"Markedly intelligent" For standards prevalent in the NYPD of 1896, see Levine. Becker's unusual intelligence was mentioned by a number of contemporaries. Thomas Mott Osborne, warden of Sing Sing prison, for example, doubted that Becker was guilty of the crime he would eventually be charged with on the grounds that "if such a man had set his mind on murder, he would have made a better job of it." Rudolph Chamberlain, *There Is No Truce: A Life of Thomas Mott Osborne*, p. 308. From this perspective it is also noteworthy that Becker's son became a professor at the University of Wisconsin, that his grandson was a doctor of history, and that his great-granddaughter was at one time one of the leading female chess masters in the United States. Private information on the Becker family from Mary Becker, wife of the policeman's great-grandnephew, Todson Becker.

The encounter with Becker My descriptions of the participants' thoughts and actions are taken from Stephen Crane's third-person account, written almost immediately after the event. *New York Journal*, Sept. 20, 1896. For the location of the nearest transport links to Broadway Garden, see Eric Homberger, *The Historical Atlas of New York City*, pp. 106–7.

Satan's Circus Edwin Burrows and Mike Wallace, *Gotham*, pp. 955–9, 1068; Timothy Gilfoyle, *City of Eros*, pp. 204–5. Definitions of the district's boundaries vary from source to source, and the district itself shifted subtly from year to year. According to Luc Sante, however, the neighborhood comprised a sixteen-block strip of the West Side, stretching between Twenty-fourth and Fortieth Streets and from Fifth Avenue across to Seventh. Sante, *Low Life*, p. 185.

PROSTITUTION IN SATAN'S CIRCUS Gilfoyle, op. cit., pp. 58, 205–8; Sante, op. cit., p. 188.

"UNNATURAL PRACTICES" Gilfoyle, op. cit., p. 165.

BECKER'S REPONSE *New York Sun*, Sept. 19, and *Journal*, Sept. 20, 1896.

"TWO-THIRDS IRISH" During the 1850s one officer in every four had been born either in Ireland or to Irish parents; by 1888 the figure was six in every ten; and by 1910, three-quarters of the entire New York Police Department was Irish. Levine, pp. 23–25, 42–43.

AT THE STATION HOUSE Olov Fryckstedt, "Stephen Crane in the Tenderloin," pp. 141–42, 145.

"DORA CLARK" *New York Sun*, Sept. 16, and *Journal*, Sept. 17 and 20, 1896; Stallman, op. cit., p. 229. For her real name, see the *Sun* of Oct. 16, 1896.

RUBY YOUNG'S PROFESSION *New York World*, Oct. 16, 1896. Stallman, Crane's biographer, (op. cit., p. 229) asserts that Young was a "kept woman," the "mistress of a wealthy man living at the Waldorf." This seems to be incorrect. Young had indeed had an assignation with one of the Waldorf's guests on the night in question. But she had taken him to her own room on East Eighty-first Street, which argues against any long-term relationship. And, had she really been a rich man's mistress, there would have been no need for her to work as a streetwalker, as she evidently did; Becker later testified that he had known her for about two years. *Sun*, Oct. 16, 1896. For the prostitute's "drift," see the eloquent comments of Sante, op. cit., pp. 179–80.

THE YOUNG MAN AND THE SERGEANT *New York Journal*, Sept. 20, 1896.

"WHAT HE WAS THINKING WAS . . ." Ibid.

"BOHEMIAN IN THE BEST SENSE" *New York Journal*, Oct. 17, 1896.

CRANE'S SUBJECTS Keith Gandal, *The Spectacle of the Poor*, pp. 90, 126. For the details of the author's experiences in the slums, see also Burrows and Wallace, op. cit., p. 1186, 1189. Crane's experiences as a beggar were based on a night spent in line at the yeast manufacturer Louis Fleischmann's Model Vienna Bakery, next to Grace Church, which during the day sold sweet rolls and coffee and after midnight distributed a third of a loaf free to each of the local indigents who lined up to take advantage of this charity—thus popularizing the term "breadline."

"QUEER" Fryckstedt, op. cit., p. 140.

CRANE, OPIUM, AND THE *NEW YORK JOURNAL* Ibid., pp. 140–1; *Journal*, Sept. 20, 1896; Benfey, op. cit., p. 174; Logan, p. 109; Stallman, op. cit., pp. 219–20.

CRANE'S THOUGHTS *New York Journal*, Sept. 20, 1896.

CRANE'S "PLOT" For the *Boston Traveler*, see Frykstedt, op. cit., p. 151. The vast majority of Stephen Crane's biographers have chosen to accept his own version of these events, portraying him as an innocent, even chivalric, figure in this case. My account of the reporter's aims and motives follows the reinterpretation offered by Benfey, op. cit., pp. 171–81, which I find more thoughtful and considerably more persuasive. "It seems," Benfey writes, "highly likely that Crane knew precisely who Dora [Clark] was. It should be remembered that he set out to 'study the police court victims in their haunts,' and Dora was such a victim. . . . The coincidences are less glaring if we assume that Crane was cruising for a crisis, and that the chorus girls flagged down Dora Clark as someone who might help spark one. . . . It's probably closer to the truth to say that the target for entrapment was Officer Charles Becker himself, and that Dora Clark was the bait."

DOUBTERS *New York Journal*, Sept. 20, 1896; Stallman, op. cit., pp. 219, 221.

AT THE POLICE COURT *New York Sun, Tribune*, and *Journal*, Sept. 17, 1896; Frykstedt, op. cit., pp. 135–36; Stallman and Hagemann, *Sketches*, pp. 219–21, 261–62; Stallman, op. cit., pp. 222–25, 233–34; Benfey, op. cit., pp. 171–74.

BECKER DESCRIBED Pictures of Becker were published in the *New York Journal* of Sept. 19 and Oct. 17, alongside a description in the former case. See also Logan, p. 3.

ROSENBERG There were in fact no black officers in the New York Police Department at this time. The first, Samuel Battle, was not appointed until the summer of 1911, and he faced considerable hostility from his brother officers, all of whom refused to patrol with him. *New York Times*, June 29, July 28, and Sept. 26, 1911.

CRANE'S STATEMENT TO THE PRESS *New York Journal*, Sept. 19 and 20, 1896. On Crane's typescript—an early draft of a piece for the *Journal*, now in the Barrett Crane Collection—see Stallman, op. cit., p. 586. All this made first-rate copy for New York papers. Most of the court reporters were inclined to favor Crane—he was, after all, a fellow journalist, and in any case they did not like the police—and many of the accounts that appeared the next day took the obvious line, comparing Crane to the hero of his famous novel. "The red badge of courage," concluded an admiring column in the city's biggest daily, "flamed with a new brightness as Mr. Crane walked away." Still, not every paper published on September 19 agreed. Association with "women in scarlet," the *Chicago Dispatch* wrote, was hardly proof of courage of any description.

AFTERMATH *New York Tribune*, Sept. 29; *Journal*, Oct. 8, 11, and 17; *Times*, Nov. 2, 1896; Stallman, op. cit., pp. 221, 225–26, 228–29; Frykstedt, op. cit., p. 152. Chicago May, whose real name was May Sharpe, was using the alias "May Kane" at this time. At the beginning of November, she and Young fought a second battle in the New York streets. Both were again arrested. *New York Times*, Nov. 2, 1896. The combative May also got into a fight with one of the witnesses at Becker's police trial. As the people in the courtroom filed out at the end of the hearing, she was set upon by one of Crane's friends, Miss Effie Ward, who "made an energetic attempt to tear out all her hair." May responded "by trying to scratch out Miss Ward's eyes." *New York Sun*, Oct. 17, 1896.

FREQUENCY OF POLICE TRIALS Lexow, p. 54. The incidence of charges brought against members of the police peaked at an astonishing 4,000 in 1875. On average, the rate generally ran at 1,500 to 1,700 charges per year; Augustine Costello, *Our Police Protectors*, p. 560.

AT THE POLICE TRIAL *New York World*, Oct. 16; *Sun* and *Journal*, Oct. 17 and 18, 1896; Fryckstedt, op. cit., pp. 153–61; Logan, pp. 110–11; Hamlin Garland, *Roadside Meetings*, pp. 203–4; Stallman, op. cit., pp. 227–30. The charges against Becker were formally dropped a week before Christmas. According to the *Middletown Daily Argus* (NY), Dec. 17, 1894, "the only evidence against the officer was given by Mr. Crane, and the Police Commissioner seems to have reached the conclusion that he has dealt so much with fiction that he does not know where the truth ends and fiction begins."

POLICE HARASS CRANE James Richardson, *New York Police*, p. 262.

2. KING OF THE BOWERY

BECKER'S BIRTH The date of Becker's birth remains in some doubt. The birth of a child named Charles Becker on the date given is recorded in the nearest village, Callicoon Center, but the Becker family's genealogical research has revealed another record for the birth of a child with the same name dated exactly three years later. Records of the Callicoon Center Evangelical Church and birth registers kept in the Sullivan County Record Office, copies in MBC. Given the coincidence of both name and date, it seems one of the two records may be a misdated copy of the other. The best evidence favoring the earlier date is Becker's statement, on his conviction for murder, that his age was then forty-two; *New York Sun*, Oct. 25, 1912. Oddly enough, Becker's birthplace was not much more than twenty miles from Port Jervis, the childhood home of Stephen Crane; the two men, who were practically identical in age, thus grew up together as near neighbors.

DISTANCE FROM NEW YORK This is the distance between Callicoon and New York as the crow flies. The distance by rail, in Becker's day, was closer to 140 miles.

"NO ONE CAN MAKE MORE THAN A BASE LIVING . . ." Becker to Mary Weyrauch, Nov. 14, 1913, MBC.

HEINRICH BECKER AND HIS FARM Heinrich Becker appears to have dropped the German form of his given name on his arrival in New York and was known as Henry to his neighbors in Sullivan County. The German version of the name, however, appears on his tombstone, still clearly visible in the little cemetery at Callicoon Center. For the locale, see James Quinlan, *History of Sullivan County*, pp. 167–68; it is indicative of the low level of the early population of the county that Quinlan can devote nearly a page of this work to the story of the Becker family, down to recounting the results of a specific hunting expedition. For other accounts of the family's history, see the *Sullivan County Democrat*, Aug. 6, 1912, and family genealogies in MBC, based for these generations of the family on correspondence with the church authorities in Bebra, Hesse-Kassel, and extracts from the records of Callicoon and Sullivan County mentioned above.

CALLICOON DEPOT J. S. Graham, *The Callicoon Historian*, pp. 40, 54–55. Today its name has contracted to a simple "Callicoon"—a word that, incidentally, comes from the Dutch "Kollikoon," which is said to have derived from the call made by the wild turkeys that once abounded in the district.

"VARIOUSLY AS A BROKER . . ." Mary Becker, personal communication, Nov. 28, 2004, author's files.

BECKER'S YOUTH IN CALLICOON CENTER For the testimony of Philip Huff and Baltazer Hauser (both of whose names are incorrectly given by the source), see the *New York Herald* of Aug. 2, 1912. For the correct spellings of the witnesses' names, see Quinlan, op. cit., p. 168, and *Sullivan County Democrat*, Aug. 6, 1912. For the date of Becker's departure to New York, see the *Sullivan County Record*, Aug. 8, 1915.

THE NEW YORK OF 1890 Edwin Burrows and Mike Wallace, *Gotham*, pp. 943–44, 1040–88, 1116–17, 1228; Luc Sante, *Low Life*, pp. 23–45; John Kouwenhoven, *Historical Portrait of New York*, pp. 381, 393; Ric Burns and James Sanders with Lisa Ades, *New York*, pp. 182–215, 236, 262; Eric Homburger, *The Historical Atlas of New York City*, pp. 110–11, 126–28, 136–37; Albert Fried, *The Rise and Fall of the Jewish Gangster in America*, pp. 16–17; Daniel Czitrom, "Underworlds and Underdogs: Big Tim Sullivan and Metropolitan Politics in New York, 1889–1913," *Journal of American History* 78 (1991), p. 542; Marc Eliott, *Down 42nd Street*, p. 77.

Ice Trust *New York World*, Apr. 4, 1900; Oliver Allen, *The Tiger*, pp. vii–ix.

"Dense cat's cradles . . ." Overground telephone wires were already on the way out by 1890; the great blizzard of 1888 had demonstrated the vulnerability of such utilities—two-thirds of Manhattan's telephone and electricity poles were brought down by the worst storm of the century, which deposited drifts of snow as much as thirty feet deep in places—and the city had begun a major program of burying its millions of cables belowground. The speed of change accelerated further after October 1889, when thousands of New Yorkers were distressed at the sight of a Western Union lineman who had been electrocuted while making repairs to an overhead cable in the busiest part of the business district. The unfortunate electrician hung, caught in the still-live wires, for more than an hour before the power was turned off, with blue flames spitting from his mouth. Burrows and Wallace, op. cit., p. 1068; Burns, Sanders, and Ades, op. cit., p. 200.

Horse-cars As well as being slow, the horse-cars were inconvenient. Vicious competition between the various companies holding monopolies on various routes made it almost impossible to travel from place to place without a number of inconvenient and expensive changes. Traversing the length of Fourteenth Street, for example, meant making three changes and paying four fares. Burrows and Wallace, op. cit., p. 1057.

"Once a motorman . . ." Ibid., p. 1058.

"Wall Street supplied . . ." Ibid., p. xviii.

Tenements Jacob Riis, *How the Other Half Lives*, pp. 6–7, 17, 26–27, 30, 51, 71, 82, 124, 141, 143, 177, 185, 194; Owen Kildare, *My Mamie Rose*, pp. 15, 19; Sante, op. cit., pp. 23–34.

Boardinghouses Riis, op. cit., pp. 66–72; Rachel Bernstein, *Boarding-House Keepers and Brothel Keepers in New York City, 1880–1910*, pp. 30, 79, 87, 96–97; Burrows and Wallace, op. cit., p. 970.

Becker's jobs Becker's employment at Cowperthwait's is noted by the *Sullivan County Record*, Aug. 8, 1915; for more on the store, see Alvin Harlow, *Old Bowery Days*, p. 538. On clerking, see Burrows and Wallace, op. cit., p. 970. For Becker's work as a baker, a salesman, and a bouncer in saloons—unreferenced but likely, given the career paths generally followed by the New York police of the day—see Logan, p. 105.

SUICIDE HALL Sante, op. cit., pp. 119–20.

"ONLY A FEW YEARS LATER . . ." Cornelius Willemse, a New Yorker who applied to join the force in 1896, when Theodore Roosevelt's reform administration was in power (see chapter 4), had his initial application rejected on the grounds that he had once worked in the liquor business. Willemse, *Behind the Green Lights*, p. 20.

INFLUENCE OF SALOONKEEPERS Burrows and Wallace, op. cit., p. 823; Warren Sloat, *A Battle for the Soul of New York*, p. 14; Barlow, op. cit., p. 440; Sante, op. cit., p. 217. Several sources state that while Silver Dollar Smith's saloon was frequently visited by customers covertly armed with chisels, no one ever succeeded in removing one of the coins embedded in his floor. This is not correct; according to Smith's obituary in the *New York Herald* of January 1, 1900, one man successfully made off with fifty-two of them in a single night. Smith nonetheless proved singularly successful in getting out the vote for Tammany, which was, of course, the secret of his invulnerability. "Once," a contemporary named Abraham Cahan wrote, "I saw him making a campaign speech from the rear of a wagon parked diagonally across from his saloon. After talking for about five minutes, he growled, 'Boys, you know I deliver a better speech in my place than out here in the street. Let's go, boys!' The entire crowd followed him into his saloon. He set up drinks for everybody—on the house! That was the kind of speech he made." Fried, op. cit., p. 28.

TAMMANY HALL Gustavus Myers, *History of Tammany Hall*, pp. 73–74, 250–83; Oliver Allen, *The Tiger*, pp. 1–8, 21, 24–25, 46, 51, 60–61, 66–67, 70, 78, 80–169; Burrows and Wallace, op. cit., pp. 822–26. On the estimated extent of graft in the 1890s, see Jay Berman, *Police Administration and Progressive Reform*, p. 93.

RICHARD CROKER Even Tammany's sharpest brains found it hard to define exactly what made Boss Croker so formidable. Like many of the Hall's leaders, he was virtually uneducated and far from physically imposing. "All this homage," the journalist William Allen White observed toward the end of the boss's reign, in 1901,

all this boot-licking, to a mild-mannered, soft-voiced, sad-faced, green-eyed chunk of a man who talks slowly that he may peg in his "seens" and his "saws," his "dones" and his "dids" where they belong, who has a loggy wit, who cares neither for books, nor music, nor theatrical performances, nor good wine, nor a dinner, nor the society of his kind! And now he sits on a throne and dispenses a sort of jungle justice, while civilization knocks its knees together in stupid, terrified adulation!

Yet Croker did possess, another observer put it, "a pervasive, intangible quality which words can scarcely describe," but which made him a natural leader. So sure was the boss's grip on the Tammany machine that he was able to enjoy long leaves of absence, amounting in some cases to several years, without losing control of the organization. On several occasions during his long reign, he faced down angry district bosses and was never known to come off worst in such a confrontation. He was an effective politician, too, being personally responsible for managing the grotesque election fraud that saw Tammany to victory in the elections of 1886. Myers, op. cit., pp. 267–89; Theodore Stoddard, *Master of Manhattan*, pp. 174–77; Allen, op. cit., pp. 166–78, 192–93; Burrows and Wallace, op. cit., pp. 1108–10.

"AFFAIRS OF IMMIGRANTS" George Washington Plunkitt, for years the powerful boss of Hell's Kitchen, on the West Side, once talked a reporter through his working day. It typically began, he said, only two hours after he had retired to bed at midnight, with a knock on the door and a request to bail out a bartender arrested for violating the excise law. Having called at the police station, the boss was up again at 6:00 A.M., awakened by the noise of fire engines passing his house. Dressing quickly and following the engines—fires, Plunkitt explained, were great vote getters—he found several tenants who had been burned out, took them to a hotel, supplied them with food and clothing, and arranged temporary accommodation. By 8:30 he was in court, where he prevailed upon the magistrate to discharge four drunks and paid fines on behalf of another two. At 9:00 he was advancing the rent for a poor family so far in arrears they were about to be thrown into the street; at 11:00 he was at home, arranging jobs for four men who had called on him for help. At 3:00 in the afternoon, he attended the funeral of an Italian constituent, and in the early evening a Jewish ceremony at the synagogue. Around 7:00 P.M. he visited district headquarters to hear the reports of his captains; at 8:00 he was buying drinks for constituents at a church fair; at 9:00 he was listening to complaints from peddlers and buying tickets for a church excursion; and at 10:30 P.M. he looked in on a Jewish wedding, "having previously sent a handsome wedding present to the bride." At midnight he went back to bed, and the entire cycle began again. William Riordan, *Plunkitt of Tammany Hall*, pp. 91–93.

LIFE OF BIG TIM SULLIVAN Sullivan left no personal papers; nor did any of his relations or early colleagues. It is virtually impossible to say now how much of the picture he painted of his youth as "an honest Bowery boy" was true, how much embroidered, and how much outright invention. Daniel Czitrom, author of the only scholarly article on his life, writes that Tim's image was "at the core of [his] enormous personal popularity and political power," and posits that "Sullivan effectively cultivated a public persona, the character of Big Tim." This was undoubtedly true. Yet the recollections of Owen Kildare and others leave no doubt that Sullivan did possess a genuinely kindly, even altruistic streak, which need not preclude the supposition that least part of his behavior was an act. Every other Tammany leader, after all, had as much of a motive to pose as a friend of the poor and the dispossessed, yet Big Tim was undoubtedly the most popular and best-loved district boss of them all and could move an audience to a frenzy with the simplest of speeches. Alvin Harlow reports that one, given in support of the aldermanic candidacy of "Battery Dan" Finn, ran, in its entirety:

> Boys, I'm a Democrat [cheers]. I've been a Democrat all my life [loud cheers]. I have voted the Democratic ticket straight all my life [uproarious cheers]. I never scratched a ticket since I first cast my vote, and I never will [pandemonium].

Czitrom, op. cit., pp. 536–58; Kildare, op. cit., pp. 50–51; Alvin Harlow, op. cit., pp. 487–96, 505, 510–14; Sante, op. cit., p. 270.

SULLIVAN'S SALOONS A reporter from the *New York Times*, assigned in 1889 to track Tim down to another of his premises, in grubby Doyers Street, wrote wonderingly of the exotic experience of paying Sullivan a call: "It is safe to say that there are not a hundred people in this city who live above Canal street who know where Doyers Street is, and if they did they would avoid it like the plague. . . . It is narrow and dirty, and in the day time is repulsive enough to keep anybody from trying to penetrate its mysteries, but at night, in addition to its ugliness, it looks dangerous." Big Tim got out of the saloon business in 1893, selling what was by then a miniature empire of six establishments and moving into a new Democratic clubhouse close to the Bowery. Czitrom, op. cit., pp. 541–42.

THE OCCIDENTAL Known to its habitués as "The Ox." The identification of the celebrated fresco is conjectural. Commodore Dutch (below), who knew the place well, was probably typical of the Occidental's patrons in referring to this work of art as "one enormous painting of some dames giving themselves a bath." Joseph Mitchell, *McSorley's Wonderful Saloon*, p. 127.

RACKETS The notorious Jewish gangster "Dopey Benny" Fein, notes Jenna Joselit in *Our Gang: Jewish Crime and the New York Jewish Community, 1900–1940*, p. 27, "routinely walked down Grand Street 'plastering every storekeeper with two tickets for a ball or a dance. If they had a small store, they would have to buy a dollar's worth of tickets; if their business was larger, five dollars.' " The total raised by men of real influence often amounted to $4,000 per ball.

The dark side of Sullivan's and Croker's long reigns was, of course, equally considerable. Monstrous election frauds were perpetrated. In Boss Tweed's day, large sums (all stolen from the city) were allocated to buy elections, and considerable efforts were devoted to registering new voters. In the six weeks before one campaign, Tammany's block leaders distributed 105,000 registration forms and 69,000 blank certificates of naturalization and oversaw the registration of 41,112 new voters. False addresses were widely used (a later investigation revealed that no fewer than forty-two Democratic voters were registered at 70 Greene Street, the location of a well-known brothel), and false witnesses were employed to swear to the good character of the new citizens. Tame judges processed the applications at the rate of as many as 2,000 per judge per day. Meanwhile, Tammany hirelings registered to vote in as many as ten different wards under a variety of names. On Election Day, one repeater cast no fewer than twenty-eight votes and the polling clerks, one sachem said, smiling, "counted the ballots in bulk, or without counting them announced the result in bulk." All of these tactics became staples in Tammany's election armory, and though under Croker there was a decline in instances of Election Day coercion and violence—"Blood's news," one Tammany loyalist explained. "It gets into the papers"—outright fraud was as common as ever. Czitrom, op. cit., pp. 549, 546.

JOINING THE NYPD Levine, pp. 23, 173–74; Richardson, *The New York Police*, pp. 176–79; Willemse, op. cit., pp. 66–67, 156–58. The figure of $300 per appointment was neither widely known nor publicized but emerged during the 1894 Lexow hearings into police corruption in the city; see below.

CONVICTIONS FOR THEFT Levine, p. 104, notes that as many as three hundred to four hundred policemen with felony convictions served in the NYPD in the 1870s. Figures for later decades are not available, but even if the abuse stopped after Tweed's time, a good number of men recruited in the early 1870s were still serving on the force twenty years later.

COMMISSIONER MCCLAVE Becker's police contact is named as McClave by the *Sullivan County Record*, August 8, 1915, which must have had the information from a member of the Becker family. For the commissioner's background, see Costello, op. cit., p. 500. For "buffs," see Lewis Valentine, *Night Stick*, p. 24.

3. GRAFT

"IT WAS DARK . . ." Cornelius Willemse, *A Cop Remembers*, pp. 71–74, 101.

"ONE NIGHT I WOKE . . ." Ibid., p. 75.

INITIATION RITUALS Willemse, op. cit., pp. 72–73, 89; James Lardner and Thomas Reppetto, *NYPD*, p. 61.

EARLY HISTORY OF POLICING IN NEW YORK Levine, pp. 6, 23, 28; Richardson, pp. 16–17; Lardner and Reppetto, op. cit., pp. 4–10; Timothy Gilfoyle, *City of Eros*, pp. 92–98; Burrows and Wallace, op. cit., pp. 636–37. New Yorkers were well aware of the failings of the system—"While the city sleeps," the joke went, "the watchmen do, too." But, as many Londoners did in much the same period, they nonetheless opposed the creation of a more professional force because they feared the creation of what would amount to a standing army devoted to putting down any and all unrest in their city.

FORMATION AND EARLY YEARS OF THE NYPD Levine, pp. 20–22, 28, 94, 102, 117; Lardner and Reppetto, op. cit., pp. 20–23, 60; Luc Sante, *Low Life*, pp. 237–38, 240; Richardson, op. cit., pp. 21, 30–31, 32, 45, 49, 64–65, 68, 135–40, 144–45, 157, 158, 168–70, 204; Edmund Morris, *The Rise of Theodore Roosevelt*, p. 483; Burrows and Wallace, op. cit., p. 1061.

"NOT ONLY WILLING BUT EAGER TO PAY" McAdoo, *Guarding a Great City*, pp. 85–86.

PAYMENT FOR PROMOTIONS Lexow, p. 48; *New York Times*, Dec. 15, 1894; Levine, pp. 171–73; Lardner and Reppetto, op. cit., pp. 65, 97; Sante, op. cit., p. 238. Valentine, *Night Stick*, p. 31, estimates that the total cost of offices purchased throughout the department amounted at "a moderate estimate" to $7 million. The example of Timothy Creeden—the sergeant mentioned here—is particularly interesting because it illustrates the complex interplay between police, commissioners, and politicians. Creeden—a popular, decorated hero who had fought in twenty-six Civil War battles—had obtained promotion to the posts of roundsman and sergeant without paying, thanks largely to Commissioner-General William "Baldy" Smith's partiality to veterans. Expecting a lucrative promotion to captain free of charge was too much, however, and despite scoring 97.82 out of a hundred in his examination, he was told to borrow the necessary funds from friendly saloonkeepers and district leaders. When these supporters learned that Creeden's precinct was to be on Wall Street—where the graft was almost nonexistent—they backed off until he was promised a more profitable posting. The deal was consummated, but Creeden struggled to make enough in his relatively modest first precinct to repay his loans. His backers interceded with Tammany once again, and he was transferred for a second time, eventually winding up in a post where the graft was rich enough to repay his friends. The details of his case came out during his interrogation by the Lexow Committee. Lexow, pp. 4919–5057, 5524–55, 5569; the *New York World* of December 21, 1893, had already carried the story, without naming any names.

WEAK POSITION OF COMMISSIONERS Levine, p. 38; McAdoo, op. cit., pp. 2, 49–50; Astor, *The New York Cops*, op. cit., p. 109.

THE PARKHURST CRUSADE Warren Sloat, *A Battle for the Soul of New York*, pp. 5–59; James Lardner and Thomas Reppetto, *NYPD*, pp. 90–91, 99–101; Edwin Burrows and Mike Wallace, *Gotham*, pp. 1164–69; Sante, *Low Life*, pp. 111–12, 189–91, 281–87.

INSPECTOR BYRNES'S CORRUPTION Lexow, pp. 5711–27; Richardson, op. cit., pp. 209–10, 212; Steffens, pp. 221–30; Burrows and Wallace, op. cit., p. 1062; Edmund Morris, op. cit., p. 484; Larner and Reppetto, op. cit., pp. 82, 85; John Hickey, *Our Police Guardians*, pp. 69–71. Those who had believed in Byrnes found themselves discomfited when, after his enforced retirement, the number of arrests made by the Detective Bureau doubled within a year. Jay Berman, *Police Administration and Progressive Reform*, pp. 62–66.

CLUBBER WILLIAMS *New York Times*, Dec. 27, 28, and 29, 1894; Lexow, pp. 4524–31, 5242–5353; Richardson, op. cit., p. 205. Diligent investigation eventually showed that at least ten complaints had been lodged against Williams as early as 1879, but—thanks to his political connections—his total punishment amounted to three reprimands and the loss of two days' pay. *New York Sun*, March 16; *Tribune*, March 17, 18, and 19 and Nov. 19; *New York Times*, March 18 and 19,

NOTES

Nov. 19, 1879. Eventually even the Custom House gang could protect him no longer, however; Williams's ungovernable temper resulted in his transfer from Satan's Circus to a sinecure at the (extremely corrupt) Street Cleaning Bureau at the end of the year. *Tribune* and *World*, Dec. 16, 1879. For Williams's notorious career, see Levine, pp. 109–11; Costello, p. 558; Lardner and Reppetto, op. cit., pp. 64–65; Asbury, pp. 217–19; Richardson, op. cit., pp. 204–5; Sante, op. cit., pp. 247–49. Of course, not every senior policeman was a monster. Some, at least, remained essentially benign; among the most renowned was Tom Killilea, a muscular Galway man who ruled over Hell's Kitchen from the West Forty-seventh Street precinct for more than two decades. "A giant, with a walrus mustache and fists like sacks of sand, who disliked subtlety and lace-edged legalistic fumbling," Killilea dispensed rough justice to the neighborhood crooks until his retirement in 1892 but always remained, his wife averred, "a meek and gentle Christian." He expected his men to keep the peace with their bare hands, routinely banning them from carrying revolvers, and "would never have me look on him"—his wife recalled—"when he was splashed [with blood], so he worked out this plan: he would send one of his men before him to our house at Eighth Avenue and 52nd Street. 'Give my fondest to Mrs. K.,' he would tell him, 'and have her run a hot bath. She's not to come down till I call.'" This arrangement always seemed to work all right. Richard O'Connor, *Hell's Kitchen*, pp. 78–79; Meyer Berger, *The Eight Million: Journal of a New York Correspondent*, pp. 134–136.

Bill Devery Steffens, op. cit. I, pp. 327–37; Henry Collins Brown, *From Alley Pond to Rockefeller Center*, pp. 76–79; Richardson, op. cit., pp. 270–71; Richard O'Connor, *Courtroom Warrior*, p. 69; Herbert Asbury, *The Gangs of New York*, pp. 230–33; Sante, op. cit., pp. 248–49. Captain Herlihy's "crime," incidentally, was to raid gambling houses run by men with Tammany connections.

Threat of transfers Levine, pp. 38, 113, 138; Lardner and Reppetto, op. cit., pp. 63–64; McAdoo, op. cit., p. 89; Valentine, op. cit., p. 18.

Unsanitary station houses Willemse, *A Cop Remembers*, pp. 71, 101, 110. In 1906, during the commissionership of William McAdoo, an inspection identified no fewer than sixteen of the city's station houses as unsanitary. The list of complaints included old and run-down buildings, poisonous air and lack of ventilation, the lack of proper bathing facilities for men, fifty-year-old bedframes and dormitories "no better than prisons." The Nineteenth (Satan's Circus) Precinct, "the most important in New York, maybe in the United States," looked like "a second-class apartment house," McAdoo wrote, and, in general, "the police-man of New York spends his time at the station house in the vilest of surroundings, in constant discomfort, and at the risk of his health. Under such circumstances he has little incentive to read anything but sensational newspapers, and to swap stories and gossip about the department. The bad policeman gets the chance here to con-taminate the good one, and the whole arrangement makes for demoralization and hopelessness on the part of the rank and file." McAdoo, op. cit., pp. 134–37.

POLICE HOURS AND THE TWO-PLATOON SYSTEM To add to all the other discom-forts, precinct-house beds, Cornelius Willemse explained, were set no more than two feet apart, and when a group of patrolmen turned in after an evening at the saloon, "you could have all kinds of whiffs. If you got sick of Bass's Ale, you could turn over and might be fortunate enough to get *crème de menthe* or chartreuse. Flop houses and prisons would have been heaven in comparison to the hell holes the City of New York provided for what they proudly called 'The Finest.' " Willemse, p. 110; *New York Times*, Aug. 21, 1902; Richardson, op. cit., pp. 58, 172; Sante, op. cit., p. 244; McAdoo, op. cit., pp. 3, 134–37; Valentine, op. cit., pp. 16, 22, 23, 25. Even police headquarters was little better appointed than an ordinary station house. The old building on Mulberry Street, once the pride of the force, was "dingy, unattractive and not overclean" by Becker's day, the men within it alternately frozen or half baked, poisoned by coal gas and condemned to work in airless rooms in which the windows were nailed shut. Mulberry Street was finally abandoned in 1905, and the whole staff was transferred to new prem-ises a short way downtown on Centre Street.

TRAINING, ROUTINE PATROLS, ROUNDSMEN, AND SHOO FLIES Levine, p. 39; Willemse, *Behind the Green Lights*, pp. 96–99; Willemse, *A Cop Remembers*, p. 88; McAdoo, op. cit., pp. 24, 27; Sante, op. cit., pp. 241, 243.

UNIFORMS AND EQUIPMENT The cost of outfitting a new policeman was consider-able—$335 in 1882. Levine, p. 122.

LEVIES AND CONTRIBUTIONS Levine, pp. 137–41, 173–74; Willemse, pp. 124, 155–56; Richardson, op. cit., p. 68.

"COPS PICK UP AN EXTRA DOLLAR . . ." Willemse, p. 105.

HONEST AND DISHONEST GRAFT George Washington Plunkitt, the Tammany sage whose impromptu dissections of political realities were recorded by a reporter named William Riordan a few years later, drew clear and firm distinctions between the two. "Everybody is talkin' these days," he said, about Tammany men growin' rich on graft, but nobody thinks of drawin' the distinction between dishonest graft and clean graft. There's all the difference in the world between the two. Yes, many of our men have grown rich in politics. I have myself. I've made a big fortune out of the game, and I'm gettin' richer every day, but I've not gone in for dishonest graft—blackmailin' gamblers, saloon-keepers, disorderly people, etc.—and neither has any of the men who have made big fortunes in politics.

There's an honest graft, and I'm an example of how it works. I might sum up the whole thing by sayin': "I seen my opportunities and I took 'em."

Just let me explain by examples. My party's in power in the city, and it's goin' to undertake a lot of public improvements. I go to that place and I buy up all the land I can in the neighborhood. Then the board of this or that makes its plan public, and there is a rush to get my land, which nobody cared particular for before.

Ain't it perfectly honest to charge a good price and make a profit on my investment and foresight? Of course, it is. Well, that's honest graft.

William Riordan, *Plunkitt of Tammany Hall*, p. 3. On the subject of police graft, see Levine, p. 13; Willemse, op. cit., pp. 105, 152, 153; Lardner and Reppetto, op. cit., pp. 15, 137, 274; Sante, op. cit., pp. 237–38; Valentine, op. cit., p. 24. Costigan, wrote Commissioner McAdoo (op. cit., pp. 202–3), was "one of those rare men who are naturally, aggressively, and absolutely honest. He could have been made independently rich in a short time had he wished to do so. He was threatened and bullied and tempted in a thousand ways, and still remained an honest and, if anything, a better man than when he began his work. He was, withal a modest man, who never boasted, and talked little of himself."

"It will break you . . ." That the commissioner in question was Theodore Roosevelt and that Byrnes eventually proved correct in his assessment makes the quotation even more apposite, for Roosevelt was the bravest, straightest, and most self-confident politician of his day. Morris, op. cit., p. 491.

Becker's early career For Becker's first postings, see the *Sullivan County Record*, Aug. 8, 1915. For Dock Rats corruption, see Levine, p. 217; for the potential for graft, see Lardner and Reppetto, op. cit., p. 64, and Burrows and Wallace, op. cit., pp. 949–50.

"AMPLE OPPORTUNITY" Just how corrupt was the NYPD in 1893? According to Jerald Levine, who has studied the question more deeply than anyone, a significant proportion of the force, most of them the older "familymen" for whom police work was a way of life, probably were revolted by the prevalence of dirty graft and fastidiously refused to indulge in such practices themselves. But these same men—bound by the oaths of loyalty they had taken to their colleagues and all too conscious of the damage they could do to their careers—nevertheless ignored transgressions they knew of and so permitted excesses to persist. The remaining members of the NYPD, probably a quarter of the force at least, actively sought out dirty graft. The levels of these men's corruption varied, depending in part upon their postings, since there were many jobs and several precincts where graft was almost nonexistent. For those with the good fortune or connections to patrol the richest and most sinful districts of Manhattan, though, the opportunities to profit were considerable. Plainly, men serving in districts such as Satan's Circus had the best opportunities to extract graft from their districts. There was also a hierarchy of corruption within the department. Captains could channel far more in the way of illicit payments into their own pockets than could patrolmen and were consequently much more likely to be corrupt. No more than a handful of those serving in Manhattan in 1893 did not run their precincts as extortion rings for their personal benefit.

BECKER AND CHICAGO MAY May Sharpe, *Chicago May: Her Story*, pp. 48, 63–64, 76. "I knew big Chicago May," added reporter Bayard Veiller in his memoirs. "There were a great many distinguished things about [her]. At one time in her career she had been married to two men and lived with both of them at the same time—one working in the daytime and one at night, and May moving from one flat to the other. . . . She was a big Irish girl with fair hair—not bad looking. She had been married years before to a man named Churchill, so her real name was Churchill, and she always claimed that she was the divorced wife of Police Captain Churchill, to the intense rage of that very able officer. . . . She was husky, strong as a man, and [she once] picked this suitor up by the seat of his pants and the back of his neck, and threw him down two flights of stairs." Bayard Veiller, *The Fun I've Had*, pp. 39–40.

CREEP JOINTS AND PANEL HOUSES Willemse, *Behind the Green Lights*, pp. 71–72.

THE BADGER GAME There were many variations on the game; see Sante, op. cit., p. 186 for several.

Howe and Hummel Richard Rovere, *Howe & Hummel: Their True and Scandalous History*, pp. 19–37.

May and the jewelry theft The pursuit in this case was so fierce that eventually May reached an agreement to give herself up and return most of the jewels to the Jewish salesman she had taken them from: "The Jew got his jewelry, the lawyer was fixed, and the cops were fixed. The Jew said I was not the girl that robbed him, so I was not held, and I walked out." Sharpe, op. cit., p. 64.

"First appearance in the press" *New York Times*, Aug. 17, 1895.

"Had been unlawfully arrested" *New York Journal*, Sept. 17, 1896.

"A respectable New Jersey matron" *New York World*, July 17, and *American*, July 31, 1912.

Bail bond graft Willemse explains this form of graft in detail in *A Cop Remembers*, pp. 114–15.

Becker waylaid *Brooklyn Daily Eagle*, Sept. 4, 1896; *New York World*, July 17, 1912. Becker was fortunate to escape with his life on this occasion; one of the two women attacking him seized his gun from his pocket and attempted to discharge it in his face but was unable to pull the trigger.

Shooting of a burglar The shooting took place on West Thirty-fifth Street, close to Broadway. The policeman who fired the fatal bullet was named Robert Carey. *New York Journal*, Sept. 21 and 27; *Sun*, Sept. 21, 1896; *World*, July 17, 1912; *Sullivan County Record*, Aug. 8, 1915.

Nightsticks Levine, p. 107; Steffens, op. cit. I, p. 209; Lardner and Reppetto, op. cit., pp. 62, 70; Richardson, op. cit., p. 68; Sante, op. cit., pp. 241, 247.

Charged with beating up a boy Logan, p. 112. A few months later, Becker was in the news again, this time for arresting Satan's Circus prostitutes attempting to take clients into cheap hotels. On this occasion Becker had the full support of his superiors. "The law gives you no such authority," one girl's lawyer protested to Captain Chapman of the West Thirtieth Street station. "Then the law should be changed," Chapman shot back. "And, anyway, I don't care what the law says about it. My will is all the authority needed in this precinct." *New York Times*, June 14, 1897.

"King" Callahan H. Paul Jeffers, *Commissioner Roosevelt*, pp. 120–21.

Becker and Williams Logan, p. 112.

Intimately associated with the Tenderloin So much so, in fact, that it was he who, two decades earlier, was popularly assumed to have named the famous district. On derivation, see Benjamin Botkin, *New York City Folklore*, pp. 331–33.

The earliest reference known for the origin of the name comes from Clubber's testimony to the Lexow Committee, which went like this (Lexow, pp. 5569–70):

> Q. And in fact that the Tenderloin district is the most notorious district in New York; that is also a lie?
>
> A. No.
>
> Q. You gave it that name, the Tenderloin?
>
> A. No.
>
> Q. How did it originate?
>
> A. Through a newspaper reporter, a man that was on the *Sun* that used to call on me in the Fourth precinct; when I was transferred to the Twenty-ninth he came up there and asked me how I liked the change; I said, I will have been living on rump steak in the Fourth district, I will have some tenderloin now; he picked it up and it has been named that ever since. . . .
>
> Q. What did you mean by that?
>
> A. Well, I got a better living in the Twenty-ninth.

APPOINTMENT OF THE LEXOW COMMITTEE Lexow, pp. 4–15; Richardson, op. cit., pp. 238–39; Lardner and Reppetto, op. cit., p. 102; Gabriel Chin (ed.), *New York City Police Corruption Investigation Commissions, 1894–1994* I, p. 54; Robert Fogelson, *Big City Police*, pp. 3–4.

EARLY PROBES INTO NEW YORK CORRUPTION Very little is known about the 1840 investigation, which was held in camera; no report was ever published, and contemporary accounts are based almost entirely on hearsay, the newspapers of the day being reduced to seeking statements from witnesses and officials as they left the inquiry. David Johnson, *Policing the Urban Underworld*, pp. 23–25. For the 1875 investigation, see Theo Ferdinand, in his introduction to the 1972 edition of Augustine Costello's 1885 *Our Police Protectors*, p. xi; for 1884, see Morris, op. cit., pp. 235–36, 250–51; Berman, *Police Administration*, pp. 17–18. Roosevelt's Committee to Investigate the Local Government of the City and County of New York, Morris notes, heard a million words of testimony and published two weighty reports suggesting that blackmail, extortion, and lax accounting were still widespread in local government and that the police regularly collected "hush money."

JOHN GOFF Goff had made his name defending Charles Gardiner a few years earlier. For his early career and personality, see *Dictionary of American Biography* 7, pp. 359–60; Sloat, op. cit., pp. 127–42, 220–21. On his Irish nationalism—he had been a childhood friend of Charles Stewart Parnell—and Fenian activities, see Sloat, op. cit., pp. 249–50, and Peter Stevens, *The Voyage of the Catalpa*, pp. 170, 174.

LEXOW INVESTIGATIONS Lexow, pp. 16–54; Levine, pp. 210–39; Berman, op. cit., pp. 23–29.

McCLAVE QUESTIONED For the commissioner's disgrace, see Sloat, op. cit., pp. 249–65; *New York Times*, May 25 and July 17, 1894. The *Middletown Daily Argus*, in upstate New York, observed, "There can be no doubt but that Police Commissioner John McClave resigned because it was getting too warm for him. Charges of corruption were so strongly proved by internal evidence that he had no desire to remain longer on the board." *Argus*, July 20, 1894.

SCHMITTBERGER Captain Max's revelations concerning the protection enjoyed by several upmarket madams whose houses catered to men with real political influence proved to be equally shocking. These "high-toned" establishments were, Schmittberger pointed out, frequently above paying for protection, and it was easy for a man new to a precinct to make the mistake of trying to extort money from them. When Schmittberger had sent one of his men around to the house operated by a madam named Sadie West, he found himself hauled before Police Commissioner Martin that same day and ordered to apologize in person. Then there was Georgiana Hastings, "a very peculiar character" who ran an especially select establishment on Forty-fifth Street. "Some of the gentlemen who visit her house," Schmittberger offered, "probably would not like to see their names in print. . . . In fact she keeps a very quiet house, and I was given the tip, so to say, if I didn't want to burn my fingers, not to have anything to do with her, and I didn't; I never saw the woman and I wouldn't know her now if she stood before me." Costello, op. cit., p. 553; Lexow, pp. 5221, 5573; *New York Times*, Oct. 16, 1894; Richard O'Connor, *Hell's Kitchen*, pp. 127–29; Lardner and Reppetto, op. cit., pp. 103–4; Sloat, op. cit., pp. 361–62; Rachel Bernstein, *Boarding-House Keepers and Brothel Keepers in New York City, 1880–1910*, pp. 163–74.

WILLIAMS TESTIFIES *New York Times*, Dec. 27 and 28, 1894; Sante, op. cit., pp. 247–48; Lardner and Reppetto, op. cit., pp. 104–5; Richardson, op. cit., pp. 209–10.

"I GOT TO HAND IT TO YOU . . ." Logan, p. 115.

NEW YORK UNAWARE OF THE EXTENT OF THE SYSTEM Levine, pp. 214–15; Steffens, op. cit. I, p. 199.

THE ELECTIONS OF 1894 Sloat, op. cit., pp. 391–92, 411, 415–19.

THE NEW POLICE BOARD Morris, op. cit., p. 477; Lardner and Reppetto, op. cit., pp. 109–11; H. Paul Jeffers, *Commissioner Roosevelt*, pp. 58–74.

REMOVAL OF BYRNES AND WILLIAMS Morris, op. cit., pp. 491–92; Berman, op. cit., p. 51.

CONSEQUENCES OF THE LEXOW INQUIRY It was Tammany's misfortune that the 1894 elections fell right in the middle of the Lexow hearings. The Hall did its best to rally its shattered forces, sending its agents into the saloons to warn that no man would ever get a beer in New York if the reformers won, and—true to form—offering Goff the massive bribe of $300,000 to stand down as a Lexow counsel. But it was too late. Tammany's usual tactics were of no avail; Superintendent Byrnes—whether out of a genuine concern for fair play or, as likely, to ingratiate himself with the reformers—ordered the largest reassignment of men in the history of his department, packing half the force off to new precincts on Election Day to limit the prospects for sharp practice. Tammany was so demoralized that even the legendary Paddy Divver, leader of the Second Election District, was not in the city when the polling stations closed. Four years earlier Divver had worked miracles for the Democrats, "raising up the dead to vote." Now he spent Election Day alone on Long Island, drinking himself into oblivion while the last ballots were tallied and William Strong—who had run on what was called the Fusion ticket—was proclaimed mayor by the decisive margin of 43,000 votes. New York's Republicans, who generally counted themselves lucky to send three or four assemblymen to Albany, meanwhile triumphed in the state elections, more than quadrupling their representation. Berman, op. cit., pp. 62–91; Morris, op. cit., p. 488; Levine, pp. 239–87; Valentine, op. cit., p. 16.

"ROOSEVELT'S FIRST MONTHS IN CHARGE . . ." Roosevelt was, of course, only one of four police commissioners—two Democrats, two Republicans—all of whom were nominally equal. But he was elected chair of the board and proceeded to run the department as though he were its head. His fellow commissioners' disquiet at this state of affairs (Roosevelt encountered stubborn and protracted opposition from Andrew Parker, one of his Democratic colleagues) was in part responsible for the failure of his attempts at reform. Morris, op. cit., pp. 552–58, 561.

ROOSEVELT'S NOCTURNAL EXCURSIONS Not surprisingly, Roosevelt's encounters with the New York police featured prominently in many of the city's papers. On one occasion the commissioner discovered Patrolman William Rath taking an illicit supper in an oyster bar. Unfortunately for the policeman, he failed to recognize Roosevelt's distinctive features and angrily dismissed the man firing questions at him as a crank until his friend the bartender broke in, muttering, in a horrified whisper, "Shut up, Bill, it's his nibs, sure! Don't you see the teeth and glasses?" On another late-night excursion, Roosevelt and Avery Andrews chanced upon a patrolman named Meyers standing outside a bar in the very act of accepting a large schooner of lager from the owner. Roosevelt grabbed the policeman from behind, demanding, "Officer, give me that beer!" Instead Meyers leaped like a startled deer, tossed his schooner through the door of the saloon, and made off at full speed without bothering to find out who had accosted him. The commissioner gave chase, calling out, "Hi! Stop there, Officer, stop!" and was gaining on his quarry when the fleeing Meyers turned his head and caught a glimpse of spectacles and prominent teeth gleaming in the moonlight. "Roosevelt!" he squeaked. "Stop running, you fool!" gasped the winded commissioner, and Meyers pulled up, pleading implausibly that his drink had been a ginger ale. "That makes no difference," his pursuer retorted. "You come down to my office and see me in the morning." *New York Tribune*, May 20, 1896; Levine, pp. 246–48; Andrews, op. cit., pp. 119–20; Morris, op. cit., pp. 492–95; Jeffers, op. cit., pp. 105–10.

Excise law No Puritan himself, Roosevelt was personally sympathetic to the city's drinking men. But being stubborn, moralistic, and imbued with a sense of righteousness that at least matched Dr. Parkhurst's, he was convinced that he and his colleagues could not simply ignore statutes they did not believe in. Orders went out to the city's precincts: Henceforth the excise laws were to be scrupulously observed. Levine, pp. 252–68; Morris, op. cit., pp. 495–512, 529; Berman, op. cit., pp. 108–15; Lardner and Reppetto, op. cit., pp. 116–17; Allen Steinberg, "The 'Lawman' in New York," *University of Toledo Law Review* 34 (2003), p. 758–59; Sante, op. cit., pp. 134–35, 295. The law in force in 1895, incidentally, had been passed three years earlier by a Tammany administration. It had been voted through first to assuage the upstate religious vote, and second to provide the Hall with a useful weapon for blackmailing recalcitrant bar owners into supporting the Democrats.

Parkhurst's death Sloat, op. cit., p. 440.

"The people may not always like us . . . Tammany is not a wave . . ." Oliver Allen, *The Tiger*, p. 189.

TAMMANY TRIUMPHANT Ibid., pp. 190–205; Richard O'Connor, *Hell's Kitchen*, pp. 132–33.

BOSS MURPHY AND THE GRAFT Nancy Weiss, *Charles Francis Murphy*, pp. 59–62.

DEVERY AND THE CENTRALIZATION OF GRAFT Levine, pp. 294–96.

"THAT'S GOT TO STOP . . ." Brown, op. cit., pp. 76–79; Sloat, op. cit., p. 151, has a different version of the same story. See also Lardner and Reppetto, op. cit., pp. 120–23.

CHARLES BECKER'S PERSONAL LIFE *New York World*, July 30, 1912, and July 31, 1915; *Sullivan County Democrat*, Aug. 6, 1912; Sharpe, op. cit., p. 64; Logan pp. 31, 98, 314–16; Klein p. 395.

BECKER'S LEISURE TIME Helen Becker, "My Story," *McClure's Magazine*, Sept. 1914, pp. 33–34; *Sullivan County Record*, Aug. 8, 1915.

"LIKED BEING A POLICEMAN" Logan, pp. 105–102.

4. STUSS

THE HOUSE WITH THE BRONZE DOOR Herbert Asbury, *Sucker's Progress*, pp. 434, 451–54.

YANKEES Glenn Stout and Richard Johnson, *Yankees Century*, pp. 3–12, 14–15, 49. Farrell and Devery did not sell out until 1915, when their team was purchased by the noted brewer Jacob Ruppert and a construction millionaire named Tillinghast Hudson for a highly satisfactory $460,000.

"BY 1900 . . ." *New York Times*, March 9, 1900.

POOLROOMS, CARD SCHOOLS, ROULETTE William McAdoo, *Guarding a Great City*, pp. 206–8, 219; Luc Sante, *Low Life*, pp. 156–60, 166–68.

FARO AND STUSS Asbury, op. cit., pp. 3–19; Sante, op. cit., pp. 156–60.

"THE MEDIUM OF THE FIRST EXTENSIVE CHEATING . . ." Asbury, op. cit., p. 6.

DAN THE DUDE AND NEW YORK'S CON MEN Sante, op. cit., pp. 166–72; David Maurer, *The Big Con*, pp. 161, 163–64. For Dan the Dude's real name and involvement with Becker, see the *New York Herald*, July 24, 1915.

"AN INVESTIGATION" *New York Times*, March 9, 1900.

CANFIELD'S PROTECTION Henry Chafetz, *Play the Devil*, p. 331. Canfield, Chafetz adds, made $12.5 million in total from gambling before losing most of his fortune in the financial panic of 1907. He died in 1914 after fracturing his skull in a heavy fall in the New York subway. Ibid, p. 338.

TIM SULLIVAN AND GAMBLING Daniel Czitrom, "Underworlds and Underdogs: Big Tim Sullivan and Metropolitan Politics in New York, 1889–1913." *Journal of*

American History 78 (1991), pp. 547–48, 550–52; Logan p. 61; Chafetz, op. cit., pp. 348.

SULLIVAN'S HESPER CLUB LETTER *New York Sun*, July 17, 1912.

SULLIVAN'S "GAMBLING COMMISSION" *New York Times*, March 9; *World* and *Herald*, March 10, 1900; Logan, p. 59; Chafetz, op. cit., pp. 341, 348; Sante, op. cit., pp. 172–73. Czitrom, op. cit., pp. 547–48, doubts the existence of the "Syndicate," at least in the neat terms alleged by the *Times*. According to Jerald Levine, however, the commission was real enough but was more broadly based than suggested in the press: "Only about eight of the thirty to forty district leaders in Tammany Hall were members of the gambling combine. This clique was a closed corporation and ran things to suit themselves." Levine, p. 305.

SAM PAUL *New York Evening Post*, July 17, 1912; Logan, p. 69.

ARNOLD ROTHSTEIN Donald Henderson Clarke, *In the Reign of Rothstein*, pp. 19–20, 25; David Pietrusza, *Rothstein*, pp. 2–4, 16, 28, 31–33, 55. Rothstein is generally accepted to have been the model for Nathan Detroit in Damon Runyon's *Guys and Dolls*, and he was certainly caricatured as Meyer Wolfsheim in *The Great Gatsby*.

ROSENTHAL'S ANTECENDENTS AND YOUTH *New York Sun* and *American*, July 17, and *New York Times*, Aug. 17, 1912; Logan, p. 20, 53; Chafetz, op. cit., p. 398; Viña Delmar, *The Becker Scandal*, pp. 40–42.

ROSENTHAL THE PIMP An affidavit detailing Rosenthal's exploitation of his first wife, sworn by Dora herself and solicited by three gamblers at Becker's behest, was published in the *New York Morning Telegraph*, July 16, 1912. "I never liked him," Dora added to a reporter from the *World* the next day, "and when I married to him I was very young. He wasn't good to me, that is all." *World*, July 17, 1912. According to Sam Schepps, another East Side lowlife, Herman was notorious for trying to pry other prostitutes away from their pimps. "You know we fellows all have lots of girls and they are put out in districts and do the best they can," he told the *American* of August 12, 1912. "Rosenthal was always a guy to grab other fellows' girls, instead of working in his own field. . . . Rosenthal wouldn't let the other fellows' girls alone, but would try to take them for himself." For more on this phase of Herman's career, see also Klein, pp. 20 and 377.

HISTORY OF PROSTITUTION IN SATAN'S CIRCUS Brothel owners paid heavily for police protection, and shakedowns and raids were regular and merciless. Only the most popular houses were highly profitable. On top of the fees paid on opening and each time a new captain arrived in the precinct (see chapter 3), the weekly demand for graft could run as high as $150. Once all these costs were taken into account, the average madam held on to little more than 15 percent of her gross income. Rachel Bernstein, *Boarding-House Keepers and Brothel Keepers in New York City, 1880–1910*, pp. 121, 124, 135, 167; Timothy Gilfoyle, *City of Eros*, pp. 203–5, 207–8, 241, 254, 267, 291, 295; Ruth Rosen, *The Lost Sisterhood*, pp. 5, 92–93.

DORA AND THE BOARDINGHOUSE *New York Morning Telegraph*, July 16, and *American*, July 20, 1912.

ROSENTHAL'S APOGEE AND DECLINE *New York Journal* and *World*, July 17, and *Tageblat*, July 28 and 30, 1912; Logan, pp. 63–64; Arthur Goren, *New York Jews and the Quest for Community*, pp. 25–43, 134.

"FLASHY, GREEDY, LOUDMOUTHED BRAGGART" Lately Thomas, *The Mayor Who Mastered New York*, p. 411; Delmar, op. cit., p. 4.

SULLIVAN'S TROUBLES Thomas Henderson, *Tammany Hall and the New Immigrants*, pp. 4–5, 9–15, 42–46, 93, 99, 115–19, 121.

"TOUCHINGLY GENEROUS" This story was related by Viña Delmar's father, Charles. Delmar, op. cit., pp. 44–45.

WILLIAM TRAVERS JEROME Richard O'Connor, *Courtroom Warrior*, pp. 70–71; Allen Steinberg, "The 'Lawman' in New York," *University of Toledo Law Review* 34 (2003), pp. 753–80; Oliver Allen, *The Tiger*, pp. 203–4; Asbury, op. cit., pp. 454–55, 458–64.

ROSENTHAL RAIDED "These raids," noted the *Times*, "were the first that [Jerome] has undertaken in several years, and were suggestive of his old-time performances." *New York Times*, March 21 and Apr. 16, 1909, and *Sun* and *Morning Telegraph*, July 16, 1912.

THE DECLINE AND FALL OF THE HESPER CLUB *New York Times*, Apr. 20, 1911; Thomas Pitkin, *The Black Hand*, p. 157.

BRIDGEY WEBBER Shoenfeld story #123, Oct. 21, 1912, Magnes Papers P3/1782, Central Archives for the History of the Jewish People, Jerusalem; *New York World* and *Evening Post*, July 17, 1912; Klein, pp. 18–21; Logan, pp. 11–12; Sante, op. cit., pp. 127–29. The spellings "Bridgey" and "Bridgie" were used interchangeably by the newspapers of the day; I have preferred the former, the version used by both the *World* and the *Times*. By the 1930s, apparently, Webber had taken to calling himself William; see his obituary in the *New York Times*, July 31, 1936.

SPANISH LOUIS *New York Times*, June 9, 1912; Logan, p. 25; Patrick Downey, *Gangster City*, pp. 52–53. Louis's picture appears in the *Times*. According to Asbury (a heroically industrious collector of gangland gossip, some of it mostly accurate, the rest much exaggerated), Louis worked for the independent gang leader Humpty Jackson, whose headquarters was an old graveyard on Thirteenth Street. Asbury, *The Gangs of New York*, pp. 246–47. Downey disputes Asbury's account of Louis's origins, accepting his claim to have been born in South America and stating that he had been an active gangster from about the year 1900.

TOUGH TONY Klein, p. 190.

WEBBER'S CAMPAIGN Bridgey was a Tammany district captain for some years and had close connections with several other members of the Sullivan clan—notably Larry Mulligan and Paddy Sullivan—as well as Little Tim. The exact dates of the majority of the incidents noted in this section are not known; they occurred in the period 1909–11. Shoenfeld story #123, Oct. 21, 1912, Magnes Papers P3/1782; *New York Evening Post*, July 17, 1912; Klein, p. 20; Czitrom, op. cit., p. 555. For "Henry Williams," see *The Report of the Special Committee of the Board of Aldermen of the City of New York Appointed August 5, 1912, to Investigate the Police Department* [Curran committee], pp. 13–14.

SPANISH LOUIS'S STICKY END The murder took place on April 1, 1910; Downey, op. cit., p. 53. For the circumstances, see *New York American*, July 18, 1912. Other sources suggest other reasons for it. The killing may possibly have been a consequence of one of New York's gang wars, but Downey says the attack was ordered by Bridgey Webber in retaliation for the beating Louis had administered to him, which seems most plausible. According to Abe Shoenfeld, an East Side detective with a close knowledge of the criminals of the day, however, the gunman was Louis Rosenzweig, alias Lefty Louie, who "did the job" on the corner of Thirteenth Street and Second Avenue at none other than Rosenthal's behest. Louie would later be convicted as one of the murderers of Herman Rosenthal; see chapters 8 and 12. Shoenfeld story #124, Oct. 19, 1912, Magnes Papers P3/1782.

5. STRONG ARM SQUAD

"KILL A MAN WITH A PUNCH" Logan, p. 31.

OVERDUE PROMOTION Ibid., 112, 114; Lardner and Reppetto, op. cit., p. 65; *Sullivan County Record*, Aug. 8, 1915.

POLICE AGITATION AND THE TWO-PLATOON SYSTEM In fact, the problem with promotions was worse, and more complicated, than suggested here, since New York's police commissioners continued to favor certain candidates for elevation and deliberately marked down other, apparently better-qualified men. Sergeant Jacob Brown placed top in the written examination and was rated "excellent" by his captain, and in seventeen years' service had never been reprimanded or fined, but the commissioners graded him only "fair." Says Jerald Levine, "The police commissioners graded those they wished to promote 100 per cent while candidates they did not know were uniformly and intentionally marked 60 per cent." *New York World* and *Tribune*, Apr. 13, 1901, *New York Times*, Apr. 6, and Aug. 21, 1902; Levine, pp. 311–54; James Richardson, *The New York Police*, p. 282; Lardner and Reppetto, op. cit., pp. 120–23.

"CAPTAINS AND SERGEANTS" Conversation between Becker and a reporter from the *New York Times*, reported in the *Times* of Aug. 21, 1902.

"COSTS INVOLVED" It was estimated that more than 1,600 additional officers would be required to run three platoons. Levine, pp. 337–38.

BECKER'S TRANSFERS *New York Times*, June 30, 1901, and Apr. 6, 1902; Logan, pp. 112, 119. "The high point of police demoralization," notes Levine, p. 311, "was reached when Tammany began to extort money from policemen for transfers. Beginning in 1900, the officers had to pay $15 to $25 to secure a change of precinct. Policemen desired transfers because they disliked their posts or their commanding officers, or because they wanted to be nearer their homes. Some policemen were transferred frequently, while others were sent from one end of the city to the other, miles from their families. These men, naturally, were willing to pay to be transferred back. Although the rank and file complained often, they did not do so for public consumption."

BECKER'S PROMOTIONS Levine, pp. 40–41, 47–48; Logan pp. 114–15; *Sullivan County Record*, Aug. 8, 1915.

BECKER, SCHMITTBERGER, AND SCHMITTBERGER'S POST-LEXOW CAREER "With Jews and other Lower East Siders," observe Lardner and Reppetto of this Solomonic phase of Schmittberger's career, "[he] developed into a kind of judge or godfather. Men and women would run after him, gesticulating wildly as they scrambled for an opportunity to seek his advice, secure his protection, or gain official forgiveness for petty offenses." *New York Times*, June 30, 1901; *World*, July 17, and

American, 31, July 1912; William McAdoo, *Guarding a Great City*, pp. 158–59; Lincoln Steffens, *The Autobiography of Lincoln Steffens* I, pp. 266–68, 277–79; Logan, p. 112; Lardner and Reppetto, op. cit., pp. 112, 125–26. 134, 139.

BECKER ASSIGNED TO "GET" SCHMITTBERGER *New York Times*, Feb. 8 and March 21, 1903; *Sullivan County Record*, Aug. 8, 1915.

BECKER'S RESCUE The circumstances surrounding Butler's rescue remained controversial for years. A few months later, the supposed sufferer from epilepsy popped up in the New York press, having signed an affidavit to the effect that Becker had paid him $15 to stage the drama before an appreciative audience. The policeman, Butler added nastily, had struggled so badly in the water that he had been forced to help his "rescuer" ashore.

The notion that Becker faked the entire incident is certainly worth considering. Dubious river rescues became so commonplace in the early twentieth century that in 1911 a score of patrolmen were taken out onto the water and required to explain, in detail, how they had effected the rescues they claimed to have made. But in Becker's case the victim, Butler, withdrew his statement as soon as it was made. The next day he assured anyone interested that the incident had occurred just as the policeman had said, and Becker was able to produce three separate statements from Butler confirming that the rescue had taken place as described. He had been drunk when he signed the affidavit, the victim added, and he had been promised $200 for his signature. And who had paid him such a sum of money? None other than Martin Littleton, apparently, surely not coincidentally Max Schmittberger's legal representative. *New York Times*, Sept. 22, 1906; Feb. 9, 1911; and July 30, 1912; *Sullivan County Democrat*, Aug. 10, 1915; Logan, p. 113.

SCHMITTBERGER'S PROMOTION TO INSPECTOR *New York Times*, March 3 and 4, 1903.

BECKER'S INVESTIGATION OF SCHMITTBERGER IN 1906 *New York Times*, June 30, July 24, and 28, Aug. 15, and Sept. 22, 1906; Logan, p. 113.

BECKER'S SERVICE IN 1900s *New York Times*, March 19, 1906, and Jan. 5, 1907; *Sullivan County Record*, Aug. 8, 1915; Logan, p. 115.

BECKER'S DIVORCE Paul and Letitia Becker's marriage certificate from MBC; for Letitia's comments, see *New York World*, July 30, 1912; Logan, p. 98; information regarding family tradition from Mary Becker, personal communication Nov. 20, 2004, author's files. The *World* incorrectly named the Beckers' son as "Harold," an error picked up by other writers that has prevented his identification until now (see Epilogue).

HELEN LYNCH "My Story, by Mrs. Charles Becker," *McClure's Magazine*, Sept. 1914, pp. 33–44.

MRS. BECKER'S CAREER Helen completed high school and graduated from the normal college. Teaching was, nonetheless, neither prestigious nor well paid; education, indeed, was scarcely recognized as a profession at all. There were no universally accepted standards or qualifications, and conditions were all too often terrible. "A young woman with 56 pupils before her in her classroom," said Charles Eliot, the president of Harvard, "has a task before her which no ordinary mortal can perform." Matters were not helped by the fact that New York's public-school system itself had only come into existence in 1896, and that although Superintendent John Jasper "was famous for his ability to recognize each of the system's four thousand employees on sight, he never made a major policy recommendation." Tammany took a hand in many appointments, and the turnover of staff was high. "Tenures were often short— men usually taught only until they found a better-paying job, and women until they married." David Hammack, *Power and Society*, pp. 259–303.

BECKER'S CIRCUMSTANCES Becker paid Letitia Stenson alimony from their divorce in 1906 until her remarriage three years later. *New York World*, July 30; *American*, July 31, 1912. For circumstances in the Becker household, see *McClure's Magazine*, Sept. 1914, p. 36. For Becker's salary, see the *New York World*, Aug. 28, 1912.

MAYOR GAYNOR Lately Thomas, "Tammany picked an honest man," *American Heritage*, Feb. 1967, and *The Mayor Who Mastered New York*, pp. 14, 21, 120, 134, 162, 170, 200, 202–26, 260, 290–91, 294–95, 314; Oliver Allen, *The Tiger*, pp. 217–20; Christopher Thale, *Civilizing New York: Police Patrol, 1880–1935*, pp. 890–91; David Nasaw, *The Chief*, pp. 223–24; Allen Steinberg, "Narratives of Crime, Historical Interpretation and the Course of Human Events: The Becker Case and American Progressivism," in Amy Gilman Srebnick and René Lévy (eds.), *Crime and Culture*, p. 72. For Gaynor's long-term distrust of the New York police, see William Gaynor, "The Lawlessness of the Police of New York," *North American Review* 176 (1903), pp. 16–19.

"FOUR SQUARE BEHIND THE BILL OF RIGHTS" Gaynor, observed the *Globe and Mail*, "was a primitive American and really believed in the Bill of Rights. These things did not represent sentimental nonsense to him, nor did he regard them as impractical abstractions." Cited by Logan, p. 88.

ANECDOTE OF CHARLES CHAPIN Ibid., 24; James McGrath Morris, *The Rose Man of Sing Sing*, p. 202.

"AS SOON AS I BECAME MAYOR . . ." Gaynor to the editor of the *Daily Record*, Long Branch, New Jersey, n.d. (1911–12), cited by Thomas, op. cit., pp. 428–29.

"THE WAY IT WORKED . . ." Ibid., pp. 262, 411.

NARROWING POINTS OF CONTACT Ibid., pp. 429–30.

WALDO REPLACES CROPSEY Waldo's wealth came from his wife, who was the widow of the coal magnate John Heckscher. *New York Times*, May 24, 1911; Thomas, op. cit., p. 353; Logan, pp. 22–24, 116.

NEW SQUADS *New York World*, March 23, 24, 25, and 28, and *Times*, March 24, 26, and 27 and June 8 and July 9, 1911; Lardner and Reppetto, op. cit., p. 159.

HISTORY OF SQUADS AND RAIDING McAdoo, pp. 86–87, 202; Herbert Asbury, *The Gangs of New York*, pp. 95–96; Lardner and Reppetto, op. cit., p. 131; Logan, p. 116; Allen Steinberg, "The 'Lawman' in New York," *University of Toledo Law Review* 34 (2003), pp. 766–69.

SPECIAL SQUAD *New York Times*, Aug. 13, 1911; for details of the Car Barn Gang, see Asbury, op. cit., pp. 324–25.

ACTIVITIES OF THE SPECIAL SQUAD *New York Times*, Aug. 13, 1911.

RAIDS AND AMBITION Becker's career as a raider ran from October 5, 1911, to the middle of July 1912. *New York Times*, Feb. 10 and 15, and May 9, 1912; Klein, p. 404; Logan, pp. 45–46, 68–69, 116–18.

COMSTOCK'S RAID Steinberg, op. cit., pp. 758–59.

NEW ACQUAINTANCES For Hawley and Terry, see *New York Sun* and *American*, July 17, 1912; Klein, p. 33; Logan, pp. 29–30; for Masterson, see Robert DeArment, *Bat Masterson*, pp. 1–3, 373–97. There is, DeArment points out, no firm evidence that Masterson ever killed anybody, though he was certainly involved in a number of fights and led a generally exciting life.

POOR PUBLICITY, COMPLAINTS *New York Times*, Feb. 15, 1912; Logan, pp. 116–17.

EXTENT OF BECKER'S GRAFTING Details of the allegations against Becker—most of which were made by his former collector, Jack Rose (see chapter 7)—and of his hidden bank accounts appeared in the *New York World*, July 18 and 31, and Aug. 28, 1912; *New York Times*, March 9, 1900, Aug. 1 and 14, 1912, and Oct. 9, 1947; *Sun*, July 31, 1912; Klein, p. 428. Details of the bank accounts emerged after searches conducted on the orders of senior banking officials across the city; according to Klein, p. 57, some of the money banked by Becker consisted of "withdrawls from banks whose totals had already been included in the district attorney's calculation." Becker put the total at $23,000, which he insisted came from savings and bequests. The protection Becker was able to offer apparently extended to disrupting the work of the other two Strong Arm Squads; the *World* of July 26, 1912, published a statement by Dan Costigan explaining the circumstances in which Becker had contrived to ruin one of his planned raids. For Honest John Kelly, see Herbert Asbury, *Sucker's Progress*, pp. 432–34.

BECKER'S HOUSE This property, the newspapers of the day reported, extended over no fewer than four lots. *New York World*, July 20, and *American*, July 21, 1912.

WARNING SIGNS Anon., *The Report of the Special Committee of the Board of Aldermen of the City of New York Appointed August 5, 1912, to Investigate the Police Department* [Curran committee], pp. 13–14.

"JUST A LITTLE LIEUTENANT" Logan, p. 50.

ROSENTHAL'S DECLINE *New York World*, July 16 and 17; *Post*, July 16, 1912; *New York Times*, July 31, 1915; Logan, pp. 22, 63–67. For the total borrowed from Big Tim, see the affidavit of Sullivan's assistant, Harry Applebaum, in Klein, p. 410. According to Becker's statement of July 1915, Sullivan's interest in the club actually totaled $12,500. Klein, p. 366.

THE SECOND MRS. ROSENTHAL *New York World*, July 17, 1912; Viña Delmar, *The Becker Scandal*, p. 4.

BECKER AND ROSENTHAL Rosenthal's affidavits regarding this relationship—the details of which Becker naturally challenged—appeared in the *New York World* of July 13, 14, and 17, 1912; see also Klein, pp. 9–12. Logan, p. 43, points out the improbability that Becker had kissed Rosenthal, as was alleged: "The Elks' Club ball had been a crowded public affair. At the table where Rosenthal and Becker sat were some two dozen other revelers, and all the tables were jammed close together in the big ball room. The drunken kissing scene Rosenthal described would have had hundreds of possible witnesses. . . . Rosenthal's affidavit described Becker, a conspicuous man, as 'waving to the crowd' while he stood embracing his new friend. This would have been particularly reckless since the guests at the Elks' Club that night included George Dougherty, deputy police commissioner and head of the department's detective bureau, who undoubtedly would have caused immediate trouble for any member of the force making a spectacle of himself with a cop-baiting gambler. Yet no casual Elks' Club customer apparently saw the painful scene." Becker did not deny being at the same dinner as Rosenthal but said the pair had not sat closely together. It is certainly likely that any business conversation between the two took place away from the ball itself.

BECKER'S FALLING-OUT WITH ROSENTHAL At the time it was reported—and later authors have generally agreed—that Becker's falling-out with Rosenthal was occasioned by the actions of his press agent, Charles Plitt, who attended a Special Squad raid on March 14, 1912, presumably with the intention of gathering material for the press, and somehow contrived to shoot and kill the janitor of the house in question. See, e.g., *New York American*, July 18, 1912; Logan, pp. 263–65. When Plitt was arraigned and charged with manslaughter, Becker supposedly made a collection to raise money for his defense, forcing all of the businesses under his protection to pay $500 apiece toward the fund. It was allegedly Rosenthal's refusal to pay this additional sum that led to the falling-out between the two. The story is not implausible; at least Rosenthal would have been in no position to pay such a sum. But there is no evidence that any defense fund was actually raised for Plitt and, as Klein, pp. 280–89, points out, the press agent was represented at his trial not by an expensive private lawyer but by a public attorney.

RAID ON ROSENTHAL *New York World*, July 14, and *Sun*, July 24, 1912; Klein, pp. 10–11.

6. LEFTY, WHITEY, DAGO, GYP

ROSENTHAL'S PREMISES STAND EMPTY Viña Delmar, *The Becker Scandal*, pp. 4–5.

ROSENTHAL, SULLIVAN, AND WALDO'S BRIBE Klein, pp. 410–11; Logan, p. 231.

POLICE IN THE HOUSE *New York Evening Post*, July 16, 1912; Logan, pp. 8–9.

ROSENTHAL SQUEALS *New York Morning Telegraph*, July 16, and *American*, July 17, 1912; Lately Thomas, *The Mayor Who Mastered New York*, pp. 411–12; Logan, pp. 10, 63–64, 69, 203–4.

"NO HONORABLE MAN . . ." Louis Heaton Pink, *Gaynor*, p. 192.

THE NEW YORK PRESS John Stevens, *Sensationalism and the New York Press*, pp. 96–103; David Nasaw, *The Chief*, pp. 96–103.

"HEARST'S AMERICAN" This was the new title Hearst gave to the old *Journal* when a burst of patriotism was urgently required in the wake of President McKinley's 1901 assassination. The murder had been committed by a deranged anarchist inflamed (Hearst's rivals wasted no time in alleging) by the *Journal*'s rabble-rousing, left-wing editorials.

JACK SULLIVAN Klein, pp. 181–82; Logan, pp. 203–4.

THE WORLD The newspaper had begun life in 1860 as a religious daily and during the 1880s had been owned by the notorious financier Jay Gould, who treated it as a plaything and took it close to bankruptcy. It began to decline during the 1920s and closed in 1931. For the newspaper in Swope's day, see E. J. Kahn, *The World of Swope*, pp. 126–30; Donald Henderson Clarke, *Man of the World: Recollections of an Irreverent Reporter*, p. 81; my quotations regarding the paper's style are drawn from Edwin Burrows and Mike Wallace, *Gotham*, pp. 1151–54.

HERBERT BAYARD SWOPE Clarke, op. cit., pp. 207–8; Kahn, op.cit., pp. 8, 22–23, 109, 115, 117–18, 138, 142–43; Allan Lewis, *Man of the World*, pp. 4, 6–7, 19–20, 24–25, 27–28. Swope's apparently individual dress sense, incidentally, was aped; he copied it from Richard Harding Davis, who was previously the most celebrated newsman in the city, and who worked extensively for Pulitzer's rival, Hearst.

SWOPE AND ROTHSTEIN Leo Katcher, *The Big Bankroll*, p. 45; David Pietrusza, *Rothstein*, pp. 47–51. Donald Henderson Clarke, in *In the Reign of Rothstein*, p. 21, observes that "Arnold Rothstein loved to associate with newspapermen, who like to call themselves trained observers. He could always excel these trained observers. With him the power of observation was not a game—it was a matter of life and death."

"BEING JUST A LITTLE SMARTER . . ." Pietrusza, op. cit., p. 47.

"ROSENTHAL'S RUINING EVERYTHING" Logan, p. 67. Dave Busteed owned a large gambling house on West Forty-fourth Street; Klein, p. 362.

"THE TROUBLE WITH HERMAN . . ." *New York Evening Post*, July 15, 1912.

SOME OF THE GAMBLER'S GROWING RANKS OF ENEMIES According to the testimony of several attendees, the possibility of physically harming Rosenthal was one of the principal topics of conversation at a picnic organized by the Sam Paul Association late in the first half of July 1912. Logan, pp. 69–70.

ROTHSTEIN MEETS ROSENTHAL This is one of the murkiest and least well substantiated episodes of the Becker-Rosenthal affair. The story does not appear in contemporary press reports, and the earliest account of Rothstein's involvement in the Becker case comes in a passing mention by Clarke, op. cit., pp. 30–31, a contemporary who nonetheless wrote seventeen years after the fact. Even then Clarke merely records that while his subject kept his name out of newspapers and the public eye throughout the period 1910–17, in common "with other gambling house owners, his name was mentioned in connection with the shooting of Herman Rosenthal." The first detailed descriptions of Rothstein's meetings with Rosenthal are those cited here, given by Katcher, op. cit., pp. 80–84, and dating from the early 1950s. Katcher was, however, active in the late 1920s, when Rothstein was still alive, knew many of the gambler's acquaintances, and probably picked up the tale that way. His account is based on interviews with Swope, with Rothstein's widow, and with Nicky Arnstein, the Bankroll's longtime right-hand man, but it is undermined to an extent by the attribution of the moniker "Beansy" to Rosenthal ("Beansey" was actually the gambler Sigmund Rosenfeld's nickname; this error, first made by Herbert Asbury, has since appeared in many books). Clearly the dialogue is, at best, approximate. Nonetheless I think it likely, given Rothstein's known determination to keep Satan's Circus gaming running smoothly, that something of the sort must have taken place. Pietrusza, op. cit., pp. 74–75, gives a version of the story based on Katcher and makes the same error with nicknames, suggesting he has no new source of information. Abe Shoenfeld, the private detective, writing only a few weeks after the incident, heard that Rosenthal had been summoned to see Tim Sullivan, not Rothstein, which is also possible. Shoenfeld story #14, p. 7, Oct. 5, 1912, Magnes Papers P3/1780, Central Archives for the History of the Jewish People, Jerusalem.

BALD JACK ROSE *New York American*, July 20, 1912; Shoenfeld story #122, Oct. 21, 1912, Magnes Papers P3/1782; Klein, pp.18, 20, 31; Henry Chafetz, *Play the Devil*, p. 401; Logan, pp. 41–42, 46, 75–76, 192, 204; Pietrusza, op. cit., p. 398 n72.

"FINEST POKER PLAYER" *New York Sun*, Oct. 13, 1912.

HATTIE ROSE Mrs. Rose, detective Abe Shoenfeld recorded, was "a very beautiful woman" who had "conned a sucker" into believing the child she and her husband had was his. This man paid Hattie $200 a month in child support, Shoenfeld added: "He would visit her and oftimes ROSE would be sleeping in one room while MRS. ROSE and the 'sucker' would be discussing politics in the other. So it is that ROSE always has an income." Shoenfeld story #122, October. 21, 1912.

"VAMPIRIC" Indeed, some of the less flattering photographs and drawings of Rose in the newspapers of the period make him look alarmingly like Nosferatu, the famous vampire in the 1922 silent movie of that name, as played by Max Schreck. See particularly the *New York Sun* for October 13, 1912.

STOOL PIGEON In police custody Rose would indignantly deny he was any such thing. He was not believed. Klein, p. 32.

ROSE AND BECKER This passage is based on Rose's confession to the police, dated August 6, and Becker's statement of July 1915 concerning his relationship with

Rosenthal and Rose; *New York World*, Aug. 15, 1912; Klein, pp. 32, 59–62, 361–70. It is noteworthy that Rose's account places the start of his relationship with Becker at a time when the lieutenant's squad was engaged in anti-gang, not anti-gambling, work.

Dollar John Shoenfeld story #57, Sept. 28, 1912, Magnes Papers P3/1781.

Origins of New York's gangland Michael Kaplan, *The World of the B'hoys*, pp. 1–146; Tyler Anbinder, *Five Points*, pp. 156, 269–71, 284–89; T. J. English, *Paddy Whacked*, pp. 18–19. Virtually every author writing on the subject of organized crime in New York has followed the work of Herbert Asbury, whose *The Gangs of New York*, originally published in 1928, was the first great collection of oral traditions, newspaper reports, and gossip on the subject, but it is important to note that specialists in various areas have shown Asbury to be tendentious or plain wrong. The most recent guide, based in part on archival research but lacking references, is Patrick Dempsey, *Gangster City*, pp. 1–73. It goes without saying that virtually all accounts of crime and criminals in this period are anecdotal and likely to be inaccurate in important ways, hence my reliance, in this passage, on the more heavily researched and analytical treatments of Kaplan and Anbinder.

"A bullet-shaped head . . ." Sante, op. cit., p. 221.

"Just a lot of little wars . . ." *New York Times*, June 9, 1912. This story crops up in several crime books discussing the period, but is usually misattributed to 1917, when Eastman joined the U.S. Army.

Successors Downey, op. cit., pp. 11–12, 49–51. Asbury, Downey's narrative suggests, was wrong to state that Sirocco and Tricker were partisans of Eastman's. He was also incorrect to speculate that Zelig's rise to eminence began as early as 1908; according to detective Abe Shoenfeld, his name was rarely heard, even on the East Side, before 1910. Shoenfeld story #14, Oct. 5, 1912, Magnes Papers P3/1780.

Jack Zelig *New York Sun* and *World*, July 20, and *American*, Aug. 21, Oct. 6 and 7, 1912; Shoenfeld story #14, Oct. 5, 1912, Magnes Papers P3/1780; Downey, op. cit., pp. 51–59.

Selig Harry Lefkowitz Previous writers on the Becker case have almost always followed Herbert Asbury, who in *Gangs of New York*, p. 305, states, "Big Jack Zelig's name was William Alberts. He was born on Norfolk Street in 1882 of respectable Jewish parents, and began his criminal career at the age of 14. . . ." The author probably took his information from a contemporary newspaper, perhaps the extensive coverage of the *American* of Oct. 7, 1912, which reports many of the statements regarding Zelig's career that later appeared in Asbury's book. In fact, Zelig was born on Broome Street a full six years later than Asbury believed, on May 13, 1888, and was thus no more than twenty-four years old when he died in October 1912, as other newspapers of the time record (cf. *World*, Oct. 8, 1912). According to Patrick Downey, op. cit., p. 51, his parents adopted the name of Alberts, and detective Abe Shoenfeld's report on Zelig confirms that the gangster called himself "William Albert" occasionally in business, probably because—like other Jewish men who mixed with those from different backgrounds—he saw advantage in the possession of a gentile name. Zelig's background is discussed by Downey, op. cit., pp. 51–52, and his real name and correct dates are given on his tall and distinctively shaped gravestone, with inscriptions in Hebrew and English, which stands at Section 4, Post 396, Row 3, Grave 4, in New York's most crowded Jewish graveyard, the Washington Cemetery in Brooklyn.

ABE SHOENFELD Arthur Goren, *New York Jews and the Quest for Community*, pp. 79–80, 162–63, 169–72; Jenna Joselit, *Our Gang*, pp. 9–10, 25; Albert Fried, *The Rise and Fall of the Jewish Gangster in America*, pp. 1–7. Shoenfeld's reports began in August 1912, immediately after Zelig's murder (see chapter 9).

THE RISE OF THE JEWISH GANGSTER Goren, op. cit., pp. 3–4, 13–14, 25, 142, 145, 159, 161, 180–85; Joselit, op. cit., pp. 2–4, 30–34; Fried, op. cit., pp. 1–43; Rich Cohen, *Tough Jews*, p. 45; Robert Rockaway, *But He Was Good to His Mother*, pp. 101–12.

ZELIG'S POWER Zelig's power has been consistently overestimated in earlier accounts, most of which are based on Herbert Asbury's telling of his story. For Asbury, Zelig was the principal gang leader in New York between the jailing of Monk Eastman in 1904 and his own death eight years later. In fact, Zelig was only sixteen years old when Eastman went to jail, features not at all in the New York press until the last twelve months of his life, was permanently short of money, and frequently resorted to picking pockets for a living—scarcely the actions of a powerful gang lord. Shoenfeld's report on Zelig, compiled very shortly after his subject's death, is my source for the statement that Zelig graduated from petty crime to the role of gang leader only in 1910. Shoenfeld Story #14, Oct. 5, 1912, Magnes Papers P3/1780.

MRS. ZELIG *New York World*, Oct. 8, 1912.

ZELIG'S CAREER Shoenfeld Story #14, Oct. 5, 1912, pp. 1–12. *New York Times*, June 9, and *Evening Post*, July 16, and *Journal*, July 17, and *New York World*, Aug. 17, 1912; Asbury, op. cit., pp. 305–12; Logan, pp. 170–71, 197; Downey, op. cit., pp. 52–59.

INTERNATIONAL CAFÉ Shoenfeld story #6, Magnes Papers P3/1780. Thanks in part to the information supplied in Shoenfeld's report, the International Café actually was raided on November 19, 1912. It closed down in August 1913 on the death of its owner, Louis Segal.

ZELIG'S ALLEGIANCES For allegiance to Eastman, see Asbury, op. cit., p. 306.

"CUT-PRICE OPERATION" Compare, for example, the "rate card" that Asbury, op. cit., p. 211, reports was discovered on the Whyo gangster Piker Ryan in the 1880s—which, while antedating Zelig's by some three decades, nonetheless quotes higher prices for most "jobs":

Punching	$2
Both eyes blacked	$4
Nose and jaw broke	$10
Jacked out [knocked out with a blackjack]	$15
Ear chawed off	$15
Leg or arm broke	$19
Shot in leg	$25
Stab	$25
Doing the big job	$100 and up

LEFTY, WHITEY, DAGO, GYP One of the most peculiar contributions to the stock of information we possess concerning Zelig's confederates comes from "Datas," a noted British vaudeville performer whose act revolved around displays of startling feats of memory. Datas (born W. J. M. Bottle) was an otherwise-ordinary man ("He has little more education than the average laborer [and] is scarcely more articulate," one journalist who knew him wrote) possessed of a freakishly retentive memory for facts, figures, and dates. He had been working music halls on both sides of the Atlantic since 1901—when, according to the biographical sketch penned by Ricky Jay in *Learned Pigs & Fireproof Women* (New York: Farrar, Straus & Giroux, 1986), pp. 98–101, he "went to work as usual, stoking the furnace at the Crystal Palace Gas Works, and that evening, without so much as a thought of embracing show business, he walked onto the stage of the Standard Music Hall, Victoria. He was a legitimate overnight sensation." According to his autobiography, published two decades later, Datas was in New York around the beginning of 1912 and carrying $2,000 earned during his most recent engagement in the city. He was, he writes, in the habit of visiting Considine's infamous saloon (see chapter 8):

> One night I noticed a particularly tough lot of customers around the place. Presently old Jem Mace slithered across to me and said: "Don't look round, Datas, but I want to give you the tip. Have you got that dough on you still?"
>
> "Yes," I replied. "Why? What's the trouble?"
>
> "Keep your eyes peeled," said Jem; "there are some of the boys about, and I've heard something. If I were you I'd slope as quickly as you can. It don't look healthy to me." I was a young, and by this time fairly strong, fellow. Alas, I was rather intrigued. "What do you know?" I asked, and then he told me all about it.
>
> "You see those two sallow-faced fellows—one of 'em is 'Gyp the Blood' and the other is 'Leftie Louie.' They are two of the hottest things with guns you have ever seen. The other buck over there is 'Dago Frank,' and the one behind him is 'Whitey Lewis'; and they can all handle a gun like it was their own hand. They may not start any trouble to-night because Becker is here." Becker, I learned afterwards was Lieutenant Becker of the police. But Jem went on to say that he had heard the gangster saying that they were going to "bump me off" and also that I had been insured for $20,000, and it might be as well if my body could be found floating in New York Harbour.
>
> "They're after your $2,000," he assured me quite solemnly, "and they won't stick at nothing, so if I were you I'd get." As a matter of fact, I had booked my berth on board the *Teutonic*, which was to sail three days later, having finished my engagement, and although I felt that there was something wrong about the information, I decided that I would go aboard the next day. In the meantime I regarded the men who had been pointed out to me with more interest. I did not make my observation too conspicuous, but I could not help noticing that there seemed to be quite a friendly

atmosphere between Becker of the police and the gangsters. Had I but known it, they were all to perish in the electric chair for one of the foulest murders ever committed—the shooting down of Herman Rosenthal, a gambling-saloon keeper who accused Becker of corruption and graft. Becker was the instigator of the murder, and the rest, together with some others, were all parties to it in return for the blind eye of Becker and his minions on their own activities.

I did not know this, however. And I was rapidly becoming lulled into a sense of security when an incident happened which caused me to change my mind. I had ordered a bottle of ginger beer and it had just been set down on my table when suddenly—Bang, and off went the top of it. Gyp the Blood had simply pulled a gun and shot it from a distance of about seven yards. It was a wonderful shot, and everyone started up in alarm, but I guess there was nobody more alarmed than I was. But I take credit that I did not show it. Instead I laughed, and just poured out my drink and took a good draught.

A few moments later Jem slid over to me again. "Cut it, son," he whispered. "Get out right now. That was done to try and rattle you into making a fight, and if you had they would have said you started a rough house and got shot in the scrap which followed."

This time I decided that it might be discreetly valiant to make a dignified departure. I did not hurry, but took the opportunity when nobody was looking to slip out, and away. I did not go back to my hotel, but made straight for the docks. I went aboard the *Teutonic*, where I explained to the captain what had happened. I learned afterwards that the moment I was missed from the saloon, "Leftie Louie" had made off to intercept me on my way to the hotel. So it is just as well that I did not go there. (*Datas, The Memory Man, By Himself* [London: Wright & Brown, n.d. (1932)], pp. 22–29.)

This is a wildly improbable tale—even the prosecution at Becker's murder trial advanced no evidence that he had ever met the gunmen; Gyp's dangerous but barely remarked-on gunplay in a crowded saloon scarcely rings true; and the difficulties New York gangsters would experience in insuring and collecting on the suspicious death of a British citizen would surely be legion—but the use Datas makes of the case is, if nothing else, indicative of the grip that Becker's story exerted on the public as late as the 1930s, when his book was published. There is no reason to doubt that the performer was in New York around the date stated, though, nor that he knew a good deal about Becker. According to Jay, "Datas had a peculiar penchant for morbid trivia and his passions, both private and public, were murders, hangings and disasters. When he traveled to a new town on his music hall tours, he would start each day at the police station to learn of crimes and accidents, and then spend a few hours at churches, museums, etc., which was all he needed to make his act topical."

CHARLES WHITMAN Biographical details from *Dictionary of American Biography* supplement 4 (1946–50), pp. 884–85; Logan, pp. 31–32, 47–49.

FIRST ATTEMPTED MURDER *New York Journal*, July 17, and *Sun* and *New York Times*, Aug. 1, 1912; Kahn, op. cit., p. 146; Klein, pp. 118–19, points out that the four gunmen, when tried, denied that this incident had ever taken place.

ROSENTHAL'S AFFIDAVIT *New York World*, July 13, 1912.

SWOPE AND WHITMAN *New York Sun*, July 15, 1912; Kahn, op. cit., pp. 146–47; Logan, pp. 48–49; Lewis, op. cit., p. 29.

ROSENTHAL'S SECOND ENCOUNTER WITH ROTHSTEIN *New York American*, July 16, 1912; Katcher, op. cit., pp. 83–84.

"ALL QUITTERS" *New York Tribune*, July 13, 1912.

WHITMAN'S STATEMENT OF JULY 15 This statement appeared in the first editions of most New York papers of July 16, 1912. For reasons that will soon be clear, it was no longer news by the time later editions were printed.

"IT WAS IN THE AIR . . ." Chafetz, op. cit., p. 403.

"YOU'LL FIND ME DEAD . . ." Meyer Berger, *The Eight Million: Journal of a New York Correspondent*, p. 139.

"YOU MAY LAUGH . . ." Logan, p. 52.

"BETTER MEN THAN I AM . . ." *New York Journal*, July 16, 1912.

MEETING AT SEVEN *New York American*, July 17, 1912. Whitman would later allege that Rosenthal was due to appear before a grand jury on the morning he was murdered; this appears to be a post hoc statement designed to avert questions regarding his own hostility to the gambler before his death. Whitman to Waldo, July 18, 1912, in *New York World*, July 19, 1912.

7. "Good-bye, Herman"

THE METROPOLE HOTEL This was the hotel immortalized in Cole Porter's song "Ace in the Hole." James Morton, *Gangland: The Early Years*, p. 114.

ROSENTHAL AT THE METROPOLE *New York American, Sun, World*, and *Journal*, July 17, 1912; Logan, pp. 5–15. Newspaper accounts differ considerably in the small details of events at the hotel. Only a few of the discrepancies are material, however. They will be discussed later.

ROSENTHAL'S INTENTIONS Klein, pp. 419, 425, 427. According to a statement Rosenthal gave to the *World*—which was not published until the day after the murder—"There is only one man in the world who can call me off, that is the big fellow, Big Tim Sullivan, and he is as honest as the day is long and I know he is in sympathy with me. He don't want to see anybody hurt. My fight is with the police. It is purely personal with me. I am making no crusade and my friends know all about it. I am not going to hurt anyone else, and if I can't go through with this without bringing anyone else in, I'll quit." *New York World*, July 17, 1912.

THE CONSIDINES May Sharpe, *Chicago May*, p. 47; Leo Katcher, *The Big Bankroll*, pp. 25, 109; David Pietrusza, *Rothstein*, p. 93.

ROSENTHAL'S COMPANIONS The identity of Rosenthal's companions is uncertain. The *American* of July 17, 1912, identifies them as gamblers by the names of "Big Judge" Crowley, Sandy Clemons, and "MacMahon." Logan, p. 7, says the three were "Fat Moe" Brown, "Butch" Kitte, and "Boob" Walker, the last named of whom was a hoodlum who often worked as an enforcer for Bridgey Webber. Webber, in a statement to Deputy Police Commissioner Dougherty, said there were actually four men at Herman's table and named them as "Boob Walker, Hickey, Butch and Moe Brown." Klein, p. 19.

MURDER SCENE *New York Times* and *World*, July 17, 1912; Klein, p. 130; Logan, pp. 13–14.

TAXI STAND CLEARED *New York World*, July 22 and 28, 1912. At Becker's trial that October, the prosecution would imply that one of the mysterious men employed in clearing the line was none other than Charles Becker. This was plainly not the case; several people could give the lieutenant an alibi for about this time. Klein, p. 184.

ROSENTHAL'S MURDER AND AFTERMATH An interview with the New York coroner regarding Rosenthal's autopsy, in the *New York American*, July 18, contradicts numerous earlier reports that the gambler had been shot five times, which have been accepted by earlier writers on the case. Several of the dead man's wounds had in fact been caused by fragments of the two bullets that did hit him. For the details of the murder itself and its aftermath, see *New York Times* and *World*, July 16 and 17; *Evening Post* and *Sun*, July 16; *Journal*, July 17, 1912; Klein, pp. 7–8, 315; Logan, pp. 14, 16, 20; Jonathan Root, *The Life and Bad Times of Charlie Becker*, p. 15.

ALEXANDER WOOLLCOTT Alexander Woollcott, *While Rome Burns*, p. 212.

WEBBER LEAVES THE SCENE Klein, p. 28–30.

POLICE RESPONSE *New York World*, July 16; *American*, July 17; *Journal*, July 20, 1912.

NUMBER PLATES *New York Sun*, July 16 and 17; *World*, July 17; *American*, July 18, 1912.

MURDERERS' DESCRIPTION AND THE POLICE BLOTTER The Sixteenth Precinct blotters were kept in the station house basement at West Forty-seventh Street for years; they were mined by Meyer Berger for an article published in his *The Eight Million*, pp. 138–39.

CHARLES GALLAGHER *New York World*, July 17; *American*, July 18, 1912.

WORD OF THE MURDER SPREADS *New York Times, World, Sun, American*, and *Tribune* July 17, 1912; Allan Lewis, *Man of the World*, p. 30; E. J. Kahn, *The World of Swope*, p. 148; Berger, op. cit.; Klein, pp. 14–17; Logan, pp. 22–24, 28–33.

LIFTS HOME Becker had the use of the car loaned to him by Colonel Sternberger of the Twenty-two second Regiment. His companions were Deacon Terry, the *American* reporter, and Jacob Reich (Jack Sullivan), the newspaper distributors of whom more below. *New York American* and *Sun*, July 18, 1912.

MRS. ROSENTHAL *New York American*, July 16 and 17, 1912. According to the *American*, Mrs. Rosenthal alleged that her husband had gone to the Metropole to keep an appointment with Charles Becker. This allegation did not appear elsewhere and was never picked up by the district attorney or used in Becker's trials. It was almost certainly a fabrication. But, if true, the allegation would be a vital piece of evidence in favor of the lieutenant's guilt.

HAWLEY AND BECKER Klein, p. 180, 242.

ARREST OF LIBBY *New York American*, July 18, 1912. The *Post* of July 16 suggests that Libby was arrested as he was leaving the garage.

BECKER, THE BODY, AND WHITMAN'S STATEMENT *New York World*, July 17, 1912; Logan, pp. 36–38.

EVENTS OF JULY 16 *New York Post* and *Sun*, July 16; *New York World, American, Journal*, and *Times*, July 17 and 18, 1912.

"I WAS CERTAINLY SURPRISED . . ." *New York American*, July 18, 1912.

Who drove the car Libby and Shapiro, it transpired, worked alternate shifts as drivers of the taxi. Libby took the daylight hours and Shapiro the night. Libby, rather than Shapiro, had returned the car to the garage after the shooting simply because Shapiro was so apprehensive about his role in the murder that he drove directly to Stuyvesant Square to tell his partner what had happened. He then begged Libby to return the vehicle to the garage for him. Ibid.

Only give a statement to the DA No doubt the two chauffeurs also wanted to make sure they were not seen to be betraying Rosenthal's murderers. "We don't want to queer anybody else," Shapiro emphasized in a statement given to the *New York American* (July 17, 1912). "We'll get out of this trouble all right. Nobody has squealed."

"Murdered in cold blood . . ." *New York World* editorial, July 17, 1912.

"I accuse . . ." *New York Journal* and *World*, July 17, 1912.

8. Red Queen

Rosenthal's funeral *New York World*, July 19, 1912; Horace Green, *The Log of a Noncombatant*, p. 49; Viña Delmar, *The Becker Scandal*, pp. 64–65.

Number plate not concealed According to the *World* of July 18, 1912, the plate had indeed been pushed partly behind the Packard's rear lamp, partly obscuring the number. The fact that two witnesses did correctly identify its number shows that this attempt at concealment—if it was made at all—was ineffective.

"Never in their history . . ." Logan, pp. 121–22, who gives these statistics, adds that "someone once calculated that the *World* devoted more space to the testimony of one witness [Jack Rose] at Becker's first trial . . . than it had to the sinking of the *Titanic* the previous April."

"A challenge to our very civilization" Ibid.

Editorials and cartoons *New York World*, July 17, and *American*, July 19, 1912.

Swope's story E. J. Kahn, *The World of Swope*, p. 144. Although never acknowledged, the reporter's motives in becoming so involved in the Rosenthal affair may have included a desire to avenge one of Becker's raids, conducted on a club on West Forty-fifth Street operated by Arnold Rothstein and frequented by Swope. See Allen Steinberg, "The Becker Case and American Progressivism," in Amy Gilman Srebnick and René Lévy (eds.), *Crime and Culture*, p. 76.

Whitman's ambition "The consequences of the Becker case were legion," the legal historian Allen Steinberg observes. "It made Charles Whitman the oftcopied model of what an ambitious prosecutor in New York can achieve." Steinberg, "The Becker-Rosenthal Murder Case: The Cop and the Gambler," in Frankie Bailey and Steven Chermak (eds.), *Famous American Crimes and Trials*, p. 263. From this perspective, at least, the DA's successors certainly include Rudolph Giuliani, a onetime U.S. Attorney and later New York mayor.

SCHIEFFELIN'S COMMITTEE Logan, pp. 93–94.

WALDO'S CONFERENCE Ibid., p. 77.

CONFLICTING TESTIMONY *New York World*, July 16, 18, and 21, *American*, *Sun*, *Journal*, and *Herald*, July 16, 1912; Logan, pp. 70, 93.

SHAPIRO'S CONFESSION *New York Journal*, July 17, *Sun*, July 18, *World*, July 18 and 20, and *American*, July 19, 1912; Klein, p. 18.

HARRY VALLON Shoenfeld story #126, Oct. 21, 1912, Magnes Papers P3/1782; Logan, pp. 94–95.

SAM SCHEPPS Born in Austria, a known gambler and a messenger for Rose, Schepps—reported Abe Shoenfeld—"traveled a great deal and smokes so heavily he is known as 'the cigarette fiend.'" Shoenfeld story #125, Oct. 21, 1912, Magnes Papers P3/1782.

GAMBLERS CONVENE AT BATHS *New York American*, July 24 and 25, 1912.

WHITMAN AND WALDO *New York World*, July 18, and *American*, July 18 and 20, 1912.

WEBBER QUESTIONED *New York World* and *Evening Post*, July 17, 1912; Klein, pp. 18–19.

ROSE AT HEADQUARTERS *New York Evening Post*, July 18, and *World*, *Tribune*, and *American*, July 19, 1912; Klein, pp. 20–22; Logan, pp. 75–76.

ROSE AND BECKER IN DOUGHERTY'S OFFICE *New York World*, Aug. 4, 1912; Klein, pp. 52–55.

BECKER'S INTIMATIONS REGARDING ROSE Rose, too, had drawn some dangerous conclusions from his encounter with Becker at headquarters. According to the gambler's own account, the lieutenant had sworn that no harm would come to any of the men who disposed of Rosenthal. The "awful look" that Becker had shot at him convinced Bald Jack that that guarantee was void and he was "to be jobbed and made to stand for the whole thing." Whether or not there was any truth in this, Rose plainly saw that there was now little to be gained by staying silent. "I knew I would get a 'square deal' from Whitman," he continued, "so I waited until things shaped up right and then told him." Klein, p. 55.

"DO YOU WANT ME TO ARREST LIEUTENANT BECKER?" Logan, p. 92.

Paul, Vallon and Sullivan arrested *New York World*, July 23, 1912; Klein, pp. 23–25.

"Brought into court" This was a hearing before the New York coroner, Feinberg, who in this case acted as a magistrate. *New York Herald, World,* and *Tribune,* July 23, 24, and 25, 1912; Klein, pp. 28–32.

"I'll be out in five minutes" *New York World*, July 22, 1912.

"A symphony in brown" *New York World*, July 23, 1912. Rose, the *Sun* had predicted as early as July 18, would have a significant advantage over his fellow prisoners, possessing as he did the "gift of language."

Gamblers questioned *New York World*, July 24 and 25, and *American*, July 25, 1912; Delmar, op. cit., p. 70.

Shapiro's new confession *New York World*, July 26, 1912; Klein, pp. 26–27.

"Everybody knows" Logan, p. 77.

Exposure of the costs of Becker's home *New York World*, July 20 and 21, *American*, July 21, and *Times*, July 30, 1912. It is possible that these revelations were in some way connected to the mysterious ransacking of the offices of Becker's lawyer shortly beforehand. Numerous documents relating to the lieutenant's affairs went missing as a result of this burglary. *American*, July 21, 1912.

Exposure of Becker's grafting *New York World*, Aug. 9, 10, 11, 13, 14, and 28, 1912.

Becker's claims regarding the source of his wealth *New York Times*, July 30, 1912.

Sums raised for Tammany It would appear that under normal circumstances Tammany received 50 or 60 percent of the total extorted from the vice trade, the balance being retained by the police. Becker seems to have raised a total of at least $900,000 between October 1911 and the Rosenthal murder. Rose's calculation was that the total was far higher—as much as $2.5 million. Klein, pp. 52–53.

Senator Fitzgerald Logan, p. 79.

Waldo's backing *New York World*, July 20, 1912.

Mayor Gaynor's views Lately Thomas, *The Mayor Who Mastered New York*, pp. 415, 421; Logan, p. 95.

"Swaggering . . . very lightly" *New York American*, July 20, 1912.

Signs of trouble ahead Ibid. and *Sun*, July 27, 1912; Logan, pp. 92–93.

Becker and Tim Sullivan One of the revelations in Klein's book was that Sullivan had summoned Becker to a meeting on the day before Rosenthal was murdered and promised the lieutenant that he would use his influence to keep the gambler quiet. In return, Becker agreed not to drag Tim's name into the affair—a vow he kept long after the Boss's death and through two trials for murder. In fact, Sullivan's name was never mentioned by a single witness in either of the murder trials, a silent testimony to the influence even a failing Big Tim wielded at that time. Becker finally acknowledged his meeting with Sullivan in an affidavit made only a few days before his execution in July 1915. Klein, pp. 408–20 for Sullivan's decline. Daniel Czitrom, "Underworlds and Underdogs: Big Tim Sullivan and Metropolitan Politics in New York, 1889–1913." *Journal of American History* 78 (1991), pp. 556–58; Alvin Harlow, *Old Bowery Days*, pp. 519–20.

"To let Becker bear the brunt of things . . ." Logan, p. 80.

Strong Arm Squad broken up *New York American*, July 20, 1912.

"Stern lines in his face . . ." Ibid.

Supposed suicide Logan, p. 78.

Advised not to testify *New York Sun*, July 26, 1912.

Red Queen *New York Tribune*, July 19, 1912.

New precinct *New York World*, July 23, 1912.

"Roundsman's work" *New York American*, July 23, 1912.

Dougherty discusses charges *New York Sun*, July 21, and *American*, July 29, 1912.

Costigan testifies *New York World* and *Globe and Mail*, July 26, 1912.

Shapiro's memory improves *New York World* and *Sun*, July 20, 22, and 26, 1912.

"Big fish, small fish" *New York World*, July 26, 1912; Klein, pp. 38–39.

Frame up discussed *New York World*, July 30, 1912; Klein, pp. 182–83, citing Becker trial transcript (evidence of Jack Sullivan); Logan, p. 205. According to Logan, the chief witness to the conversation of the imprisoned gamblers was Bridgey Webber's attorney, Harford Marshall, who resigned from the case in consequence. In Marshall's later recollection, Webber's comment had been, "If what he wants is Becker, we'll give him to him on a platter." Logan, pp. 125–26.

Sleeping in the suite *New York Times*, July 30, 1912.

Becker completes work on his house "My Story, by Mrs. Charles Becker," *McClure's Magazine*, Sept. 1914, pp. 34, 36.

"Pounding one against the other . . ." *New York Sun*, July 30, 1912.

Grand jury assembled *New York American* and *World*, July 30, 1912.

Gambler's testimony Rather unusually, given Whitman's avid courting of publicity, the gamblers' statements to the grand jury were made in a closed session and the DA refused to divulge the details of their testimony. Reporters for the various dailies experienced little difficulty in reconstructing what was said, however. *New York Times, World,* and *Sun,* July 30, 1912.

SAM PAUL RELEASED Paul would play no further part in Becker's story or the coming trials, although, as Andy Logan pointed out after a long study of all the depositions in the case, "he had taken part in the last minute planning in Bridgey Webber's poker rooms and probably had delivered three of the gunmen [Gyp the Blood, Lefty Louie, and Whitey Lewis] there." Logan, p. 125.

BECKER ARRESTED *New York Times, World, American,* and *Sun,* July 30, 1912.

WEATHER CONDITIONS AT THE CRIMINAL COURT *New York Times,* July 30, 1912.

BECKER ARRAIGNED FOR MURDER Ibid. and *World* and *Herald,* July 30, and *American,* July 30 and 31, 1912.

9 . TOMBS

DESCRIPTION OF THE TOMBS The original Tombs building, with its Egyptian columns, was torn down in 1897 and replaced by an equally forbidding structure. Meyer Berger, *The Eight Million,* pp. 23–35, 51–53, 57; Logan pp. 100–101, 104. Problems with settling, endemic to both prisons, were not solved until well after Becker's time, when a third structure was erected on the site and concrete caissons, extending to bedrock 140 feet below the ground, were let into the foundations.

HELEN BECKER AND THE TOMBS "My Story, by Mrs. Charles Becker," *McClure's Magazine,* Sept. 1914, pp. 34–36.

BECKER'S VIEW OF THE TOMBS Logan, p. 138.

POLICE SHOCKED *New York American* and *Times,* July 30, 1912.

WALDO AND DOUGHERTY HEAR THE NEWS *New York Tribune,* July 30 and 31, 1912; Logan, p. 128.

DAGO FRANK CAPTURED *New York Sun* and *World,* July 26, 1912. This arrest took place on July 25, four days before Becker's arraignment. According to the *Sun,* the police had been following Rose Harris since the night of the murder. The *Times* and other papers agreed that the arrest was the result of a tip. Cirofici's brother and another man were also in the room and were both detained as material witnesses.

MURDER OF VERELLA *New York Times,* July 31, 1912.

CAPTURE OF WHITEY LEWIS *New York World*, Aug. 2, 3, and 4, 1912. According to Lewis's improbable tale, he was actually waiting at the railway station for a New York train so he could return to the city and give himself up.

"WHEN THAT EXTRA . . ." Viña Delmar, *The Becker Scandal*, p. 76.

THE HUNT FOR GYP THE BLOOD AND LEFTY LOUIE *New York World*, Aug. 2, 4, 10, and 17, and *Times*, Aug. 25, 1912; Logan, pp. 132, 163.

CAPTURE OF GYP AND LOUIE *New York World* and *Sun*, Sept. 15, 1912; Patrick Downey, *Gangster City*, pp. 60–61.

WHITMAN ACCUSES Klein, p. 82.

ZELIG TRACED *New York Times*, Aug. 20 and 21, 1912.

ZELIG BEFORE THE GRAND JURY *New York Sun*, Aug. 21, 1912; Klein, pp. 82–85; Logan, pp. 136–37.

LEAKS Klein, p. 93–94.

THREATS Klein, p. 57–58. Both men firmly believed that the threats against them had originated with Becker, though the lieutenant's partisans argued that they could just as easily have come from other gamblers.

BALD JACK'S CONFESSION *New York World*, Aug. 4, 11, and 15, 1912; Klein, pp. 59–71.

CORROBORATING WITNESSES Allen Steinberg, "The Becker Case and American Progressivism," in Amy Gilman Srebnick and René Lévy (eds.), *Crime and Culture*, pp. 79–80.

SAM SCHEPPS *New York American*, Aug. 12, and *World*, Aug. 13 and 14, 1912; Shoenfeld story #125, Oct. 21, 1912, Magnes Papers P3/1782; Klein, pp. 72–79.

"MURDER PAYMASTER" Logan, pp. 156, 161.

IN THE WEST SIDE PRISON *New York American*, July 31, Aug. 1, and Nov. 21, 1912; Klein, pp. 86–87; Logan, pp. 129, 155, 218.

JAMES L. SULLIVAN AND MAX STEUER *New York World*, July 30, 1912; Klein, p. 79. Steuer had won an acquittal for the owners of the notorious Triangle Shirtwaist factory when they were tried for causing the deaths of so many of their workers in the dreadful fire of 1911 (thus proving, as Andy Logan tartly observed, "that the deaths of 145 young garment workers were all their own fault." Logan, pp. 124–25). The district attorney at the time, of course, was Whitman.

"GREATEST CRIMINAL LAWYER OF HIS TIMES" *New York Times*, Aug. 22, 1940.

BECKER'S LAWYERS *New York World* and *American*, Aug. 6, 1912; Lloyd Stryker, *The Art of Advocacy*, pp. 40–41, 163; Logan, pp. 156–57.

Helen Becker helps her husband *New York World*, Aug. 28, 1912; "My Story, by Mrs. Charles Becker," *McClures Magazine*, Sept. 1914, p. 36; Viña Delmar, *The Becker Scandal*, pp. 96–98, 111–12; Logan, p. 118. Helen Becker, Delmar added, contrasted vividly in her mind with Lillian Rosenthal, whom her father liked to defend ("There are women who are not given the chance to fight for their husbands. Who knows what Lillian would have done for Herman?"). "My private opinion," she wrote, "was that Lillian would have wept and fainted and been totally inept at the desperate business of trying to save Herman's life."

"They have no one to testify . . ." Testimony of James Hallen in Becker's first trial. Hallen, a convicted swindler, added that Becker continued: "After this sensation is passed over, they will give me a pension for killing that damn crook Rosenthal." Whatever Hallen's believability, the comments he attributed to Becker regarding the unreliability of criminals' evidence reflect the lieutenant's known opinion. That Becker would have gone on to openly confess to a murder he had just pleaded not guilty to, while sitting in prison, within earshot of numerous other prisoners, strikes me as considerably less likely. Hallen's reliability as a witness was certainly undermined by the manner in which he gave his evidence, reading notes he said he jotted down at the time on a sheet of yellow legal paper. Under cross-examination, Hallen—a disbarred lawyer by then serving a four-year sentence for forgery—said he could not remember how he had come by such a pad. The judges in the court of appeals were especially scathing about his testimony. Klein, pp. 173–74.

Murder by proxy, twice removed This was one of the chief criticisms of the appeals court judges who looked at Becker's original conviction; see 210 NY 274. Frank Moss Steinberg, op. cit., p. 78.

Goff's probe of the Becker letters; other committees Logan, p. 163; Anon (ed.), "Report of the Citizens' Committee Appointed at the Cooper Union Meeting, August 12, 1912," pp. 1–34.

Curran committee Henry Curran, *Pillar to Post*, pp. 152–54, 162–74; Steinberg, op. cit., p. 79.

Goff appointed to try the case *New York Times*, Aug. 16, 1912; Logan, p. 159.

Life and reputation of John Goff *New York Times*, Nov. 10, 1924; *Dictionary of American Biography* 7, 359–60; Stryker, op. cit., pp. 66–70; Logan, pp. 157–60; Steinberg, op. cit., p. 78.

"The most odious vice . . ." Stryker, op. cit., p. 67. The phrase is from Macaulay.

<small>Early trial date</small> *New York Times*, Sept. 6, 1912; Klein, pp. 92–93.

"<small>Probably the shortest</small> . . ." Logan, p. 160.

<small>Viña Delmar's family</small> Delmar, op. cit., pp. 96–99, 112–13.

<small>Coupe and Masterson</small> Logan, pp. 160–63.

<small>Zelig's anticipated testimony</small> *New York Times*, *American*, *World*, and *Sun*, Oct. 7 and 8, 1912; Logan, pp. 171–73. Whitman later conceded that he had been "misquoted" in claiming Zelig as his witness. He had meant—he said—to imply he expected to obtain useful evidence from the gangster on cross-examination, if he appeared for the defense. Whether a man in Zelig's peculiar position was really likely to give honest testimony regarding his ability and willingness to hire out gunmen to commit murder was not mentioned by the advocates on either side.

<small>Zelig's death, Davidson's gun</small> The gangster survived the shooting for a few minutes and actually died in an ambulance on his way to the hospital. *New York American*, *Times*, *World*, and *Sun*, Oct. 6, 1912; Shoenfeld story #14, Oct. 5, 1912, pp. 14–15, Magnes Papers P3/1780; Downey, op. cit., pp. 61–64.

<small>Contents of Zelig's pockets</small> *New York Sun*, Oct. 6, and *Times*, Oct. 8, 1912.

<small>Horse poisoner</small> Jenna Joselit, *Our Gang*, p. 36; Albert Fried, *The Rise and Fall of the Jewish Gangster in America*, p. 35.

<small>Zelig's funeral</small> Shoenfeld story #14, Oct. 5, 1912, pp. 16–17, Magnes Papers P3/1780; *New York Times*, Oct. 8, 1912; Delmar, op. cit., p. 113. Delmar is the source for "forty coaches"; Shoenfeld lists details of the hirers of thirty-five of them.

<small>Davidson's sentence</small> *New York American*, Oct. 31, 1912.

10. Five Minutes to Midnight

<small>Whitman's opening statement</small> *New York Evening Post*, Oct. 10, and *Times* and *World*, Oct. 11, 1912; Logan, p. 178.

<small>Description of the courthouse</small> Frances Nevins, "Mr. Tutt's Jurisprudential Journey: The Stories of Arthur Train," in *Legal Studies Forum* 19 (1995), p. 59. The quotation is an extract from one of the "Ephraim Tutt" short stories Train turned to writing after a career as an assistant district attorney in the first decade of the twentieth century.

<small>Newspaper coverage</small> Allen Steinberg, "The Becker-Rosenthal Murder Case: The Cop and the Gambler," in Frankie Bailey and Steven Chermak (eds.), *Famous American Crimes and Trials*, p. 257.

Becker on the morning of the trial Jonathan Root, *The Life and Bad Times of Charlie Becker*, p. 127.

Becker's views on jury selection *New York Sun*, Oct. 8, 1912.

Jury selection Ibid. and *World*, Oct. 8, 1912.

"A reputation for being willing . . ." Logan, p. 176.

Goff urges speed Lloyd Stryker, *The Art of Advocacy*, p. 68; Nevins, op. cit., p. 60.

Evening questioning *New York Sun* and *Evening Post*, Oct. 13, 1912; Klein, pp. 134–41; Logan, pp. 191–94.

Temperature, fans *New York Times*, *World*, and *Sun*, Oct. 13, 1912.

"Have the shades drawn low" Stryker, op. cit., p. 66.

"Saint-like son of a bitch" Logan, p. 173.

"Buzz, buzz, buzz" Ibid.

Goff biography For Goff's character and career, see *New York Evening Post*, Feb. 1, 1913, and *Times*, Nov. 10, 1924; *Dictionary of American Biography* pp. 7, 359–60.

"A sufferer from ulcers . . ." Logan, p. 184.

"Mr. McIntyre was many times over-ruled" *New York Sun*, Oct. 8, 1912.

Threatened with arrest Ibid.

Becker's appearance Ibid. and *New York American*, Oct. 8, 1912.

"Small, charmingly feminine and cheery" *New York Tribune* and *World*, Oct. 11, 1912.

Helen moved "My Story, by Mrs. Charles Becker," *McClure's Magazine*, Sept. 1914, p. 36.

First witnesses *New York Times*, Oct. 11, 1912; Klein, p. 97–99. "The writer," Klein adds, speaking of himself, "met Krause many times after Becker's second trial . . . and wouldn't believe him under oath."

Paid $2,5000 *New York Times* and *American*, Oct. 12, 1912.

Becker not mentioned *New York Sun*, Oct. 12, 1912.

The four gunmen paraded Logan, pp. 181–82. Jack Sullivan was also included in this parade; Klein, pp. 98, 101.

"Wild animal" *New York World*, Oct. 12, 1912.

"This is a court of justice . . ." Klein, p. 221.

Morris Luban *New York American*, *Globe and Mail*, and *Herald*, Oct. 12, 1912; Klein, pp. 101–11. Whitman proved better able to accommodate the Luban brothers than had McIntyre and Becker. The pair were released from prison after the trial concluded and saw the charges against them dropped. Years later, in the 1960s,

Andy Logan tracked down the junior member of Whitman's staff who had been sent over to the Essex County Jail to interview the Luban brothers. "They were the very worst looking men I ever saw," the man—by then in his eighties—told Logan. "They were abominable. They told me their awful stories, and I believed every word of them. How could I have believed such things? I went back and told Whitman. He was older and I think now he should have known better, but he seemed to have believed them, too. Looking back on it now, it all seems incredible." Logan, pp. 182–83.

ROSE IN COURT *New York World*, Oct. 13, 1912; Logan, p. 186.

"SHAVEN TO THE BLOOD" *New York Times*, Oct. 13, 1912.

"DO YOU MEAN THAT YOU WANT SOMEONE CROAKED?" Klein, p. 118.

"THE FELLOW IS GETTING DANGEROUS . . ." Ibid., pp. 119, 121, 124.

FEATURES OF ROSE'S EVIDENCE Ibid., pp. 118–19, 120, 123.

HARLEM CONFERENCE Ibid. pp. 125–26.

"HALF ON HIS FEET" Logan, p. 187.

"LIKE THAT IN WHICH MACBETH . . ." Stryker, op. cit., p. 69.

MURRAY HILL BATHS This piece of evidence is especially problematic, as Andy Logan points out, because the timings Rose gave for the meeting in court cannot be reconciled with those the gambler gave in his evidence before the grand jury some weeks earlier. In his grand-jury testimony, Rose said Becker had met him at the Murray Hill Baths before going to the station house at West Forty-seventh Street. In Goff's courtroom he amended this statement and said Becker had gone to the station house first. Logan, pp. 190–91.

"DON'T WORRY, JACK . . ." Klein, p. 131.

BECKER'S EXHORTATIONS Ibid., pp. 120, 124.

"GLOATING OVER THE BODY . . ." *New York Times*, Oct. 13, 1912.

"NEARLY EVERY MAN AND WOMAN . . ." *New York Sun*, Oct. 13, 1912.

"EVERY FEW MOMENTS . . ." Logan, p. 187.

"AT HALF–PAST TWO . . ." Stryker, op. cit., pp. 68–70.

ROSE'S OBSTRUCTIVENESS Logan, pp. 192–93.

"BALD-HEADED PIMP" Klein, p. 135.

"THE JUDGE LEANED DOWN . . ." Logan, p. 191.

"VISIBLY BEGAN TO LOSE HIS TRAIN OF THOUGHT" "Mr. McIntyre's questions," the reporter from the *Sun* observed, "began apparently to drift back over much-covered ground. *New York Sun*, Oct. 13, 1912.

"I AM TOTTERING . . ." Ibid.

"DIDN'T YOU GO DOWN . . ." *New York Times*, *World*, and *American*, Oct. 13, 1912; Klein, pp. 138–39.

"ONE OF JUSTICE GOFF'S CURIOUS ATTRIBUTES . . ." Logan, p. 193.

"COLD, CALCULATED, DELIBERATE OPPRESSION" Stryker, op. cit., p. 70.

"YOUR HONOR . . ." *New York Sun*, Oct. 13, 1912.

"NO GOOD REASON . . ." Stryker, op. cit., p. 70. McIntyre, added Swope, who watched proceedings from the press box, "was almost a wreck. . . . It was physically impossible for the lawyer to continue." *New York World*, Oct. 13, 1912.

GOFF ENDS LUBAN'S CROSS-EXAMINATION *New York Herald*, Oct. 12, 1912; Klein, p. 100.

ROSE STANDS DOWN Most of the assembled press believed that the gambler had passed his test. "Jack Rose," wrote the *New York Sun* (Oct. 13, 1912), "told his whole story on the witness stand yesterday and last night and the defense failed to catch him in a lie. Without hesitating, without stopping to weigh his words, without the slightest emotion, he swore that Becker ordered and contrived the murder of Herman Rosenthal."

GOFF'S BIAS Klein, pp. 220–32; Stryker, op. cit., p. 69; Logan, pp. 174, 204–5. The strictures cited in the text are drawn from the criticisms of the court of appeals in *People* v. *Becker*, 210 NY, p. 289.

FRANK MOSS ASKS MCINTYRE'S QUESTIONS FOR HIM Klein, pp. 193–94; Logan, p. 205.

"WEBBER'S STORY WAS AS COLD . . ." *New York Sun*, Oct. 15, 1912.

WEBBER TESTIFIES Klein, pp. 142–49.

VALLON TESTIFIES *New York Times*, Oct. 15, 1912; Klein, pp. 149–51.

SCHEPPS'S APPEARANCE *New York Sun*, Oct. 16, 1912.

"PROSPEROUS DEPARTMENT STORE AUDITOR" Logan, p. 196.

"DODGING DETECTIVES IN THE CATSKILLS" *New York Sun*, Oct. 16, 1912.

"MORE AND MORE PUGNACIOUS" Ibid.

"FAVORITE CHICK OF A WITNESS" Ibid.

"CAREFULLY EXCLUDED HIMSELF" Ibid.

"WHISPERED IN EACH OTHER'S EARS" Klein, p. 169.

SCHEPPS AND BECKER Ibid., pp. 164–65; Logan, p. 197.

"FROM LUNCHTIME UNTIL EVENING . . ." Klein, p. 162.

"WHAT HAD THE GAMBLERS DISCUSSED . . .?" Logan, pp. 196–97.

"HERMAN'S AT THE METROPOLE" Ibid.

"CORNER OF THE MOUTH SMILE" *New York Sun*, Oct. 16, 1912.

"SOME HEAVY KICKS . . ." Klein, p. 164.

"TRY AND THINK AGAIN, MR. SCHEPPS" Ibid., p. 168.

TIME TAKEN IN CROSS-EXAMINATION *New York Sun*, Oct. 16, 1912.

JEROME'S AND WALDO'S TESTIMONY *New York World* and *American*, Oct. 19, 1912; Klein, p. 179; Logan, pp. 200–1.

HAWLEY'S TESTIMONY Klein, pp. 180–81; Logan, pp. 201–2.

SULLIVAN'S TESTIMONY *New York Times* and *Evening Post*, Oct. 19, 1912; Klein, pp. 181–84; Logan, pp. 203–4.

"ONE WITNESS FROM HOT SPRINGS" His name was Michael Becholtz, and the conversation, he recalled (Klein, p. 190), had run as follows:

> BECHOLTZ: For God's sake, why did you have Herman Rosenthal killed?
> SCHEPPS: Why, Mike, you have no idea what a dirty dog he turned out to be afterwards.

It was scarcely the stuff courtroom sensations were made of.

SULLIVAN AFTERMATH Logan, pp. 206–7.

SHAPIRO'S EVIDENCE *New York Sun*, Oct. 23, 1912.

"FIVE FORMAL IMMUNITY AGREEMENTS" Logan, p. 207.

MCINTYRE'S SUMMATION *New York Times*, Oct. 23, 1912; Klein, pp. 196–202.

"BECKER BECAME MANIFESTLY NERVOUS" *New York Evening Post*, Oct. 22, 1912.

"AT LEAST ONE NEWSPAPER" *New York Sun*, Oct. 23, 1912.

MOSS'S SUMMATION Klein, pp. 203–8.

STATE OF THE CASE *New York Sun*, and *Times*, Oct. 24 and 25, 1912; Logan, pp. 210–11.

GOFF'S CHARGE Klein, pp. 209–19; Logan, pp. 208–9.

VIRTUALLY ORDERED TO FIND BECKER GUILTY *New York American*, Oct. 25, 1912.

THE WAIT *New York World*, *American*, *Sun*, and *Tribune*, Oct. 25, 1912; Logan, pp. 210–11.

THE VERDICT *New York Times*, *World*, and *Sun*, Oct. 25, 1912; "My Story," pp. 36, 38; Logan, pp. 210–11. The *Sun* revealed that the long delay in arriving at a verdict had had nothing to do with disputes over Becker's innocence or guilt—all twelve jurors were certain from the start that he was guilty. The debate was rather over the issue of whether the verdict should be murder in the first or second degree. Two jurors held out for a considerable time for the lesser verdict.

11. RETRIAL

"WELL," SAID EMORY BUCKNER ... *New York World*, Oct. 25, 1915. In 1912 Buckner was counsel to the Curran Committee; later, in the 1920s, he became one of the two highest-paid trial lawyers in the country.

WHITMAN'S POST-TRIAL CAREER For Swope, see *New York World*, Oct. 26, 1912; for political aspirations, see *Dictionary of American Biography*, supplement 4 (1946–50), p. 886; for Borah, the *Evening Post*, and the Committee of Fourteen, see Logan, pp. 219–21; for enhancement, Allen Steinberg, "The Becker–Rosenthal Murder Case: The Cop and the Gambler," in Frankie Bailey and Steven Chermak (eds.), *Famous American Crimes and Trials*, p. 260.

"THE MAN OF THE HOUR ..." Viña Delmar, *The Becker Scandal*, p. 124.

"A GREAT TRIAL"; SOCIETY WOMEN Logan, pp. 213–15; Steinberg, op. cit., p. 261.

BECKER AFTER THE VERDICT *New York World* and *Sun*, Oct. 26, 1912.

"HAVE YOU EVER BEEN CONVICTED. . . .?" Logan, p. 212.

TOO DISCOURAGED TO TALK "My Story, by Mrs. Charles Becker," *McClure's Magazine*, Sept. 1914, p. 38.

"EVERYBODY WAS CRYING BUT US TWO" Ibid.

SING SING *New York Sun* and *American*, Oct. 30, 1912; Lewis Laws, *20,000 Years in Sing Sing*, pp. 24–25, 78, 80; Logan, pp. 216, 221–22, 235–36; Scott Christianson, *Condemned*, pp. 4, 43.

A MEASURE OF REDEMPTION Logan, pp. 235–36.

SHORTAGE OF FUNDS *New York Times*, Oct. 27, 1912.

NEW LAWYERS Logan, pp. 212–13; Klein, p. 240.

HELEN BECKER'S TRAVAILS *New York Times*, Dec. 13, 1913; "My Story," p. 36.

CHARLOTTE BECKER For the name "Ruth," see "My Story," p. 39; quotations from Logan, pp. 223–24. The girl is referred to as "Charlotte," however, in a letter Becker wrote to his niece Mary Weyrauch on April 3, 1913, soon after her burial. MBC.

"I KNOW MAMA PICTURED HELEN ..." Viña Delmar, *The Becker Scandal*, p. 131.

GUNMEN'S TRIAL So promptly did the twelve jurors reach a verdict that they did not even request that sandwiches be sent into the jury room, and, according to the *New York Sun*, their decision would have been announced even more swiftly had it not been for a certain sense of propriety—not to mention concern that they be seen to be doing their job conscientiously. *New York Sun, World, Times*, and *American*, Nov. 20, 1912; Logan, p. 217.

LEWIS'S PROTESTATIONS On Whitey's atrocious marksmanship, see Shoenfeld story #127, Oct. 21, 1912, Magnes Papers P3/1782, Central Archives for the History of the Jewish People, Jerusalem. For his final statement, see *New York American*, Apr. 14, 1914.

"GETTING ENTANGLED WITH THE DISTRICT'S STREET GANGS" "I had the best father and mother a boy ever had," Louie wrote, "but I was not a good son to them. I went the wrong way. Tell all the boys on the East side, the boys I know—there are hundreds of them—tell them about the mistakes I made, which I could have avoided if I had done the right thing. Let them know that the synagogue is their best home and God is their best friend. . . . We were supposed, the other three boys and I, to have as many friends as any fellows on the East side, but when it came to a showdown, it was only the synagogue that stood by us, outside of our parents." *New York American*, Apr. 12 and 13, 1914.

DAGO FRANK'S CONFESSION *New York American*, Apr. 14, 1914.

EXECUTION OF THE FOUR GUNMEN The execution was a dramatic one, not least for the discovery, the day before the date set for the electrocution, that the chair had been sabotaged by another prisoner; the dynamo had been damaged so badly that it would not have delivered any current. *New York American*, Apr. 13, 1914. As the bodies of the four gunmen were prepared for burial, thousands of curiosity seekers flooded into the streets. The crowds appeared so menacing that Lefty Louie's body had to be hidden in order to deter them from laying siege to the undertakers'. No such precautions were taken in the case of Gyp the Blood, whose remains were laid out at Samuel Rothschild's undertaking establishment on Lenox Avenue. A mob of some four thousand people quickly surrounded the premises, anxious for sight of the coffin, causing such severe traffic congestion that the police decided to disperse the crowd by the stratagem of loading a dummy coffin onto a hearse. The horses pulling the carriage were lashed and set off toward a nearby cemetery at a gallop, most of the spectators streaming after it as best they could on foot. *New York World*, Apr. 14, 1914.

Gyp was buried the day after his execution. He was interred alongside Whitey Lewis in Mount Zion Cemetery, Maspeth. The cortege succeeded in outdistancing the crowd of gawkers still thronging the streets outside Rothschild's, and the funeral itself was attended by only twenty people, seven of whom were members of the dead man's immediate family. "There were no flowers and not a word was spoken until the last shovel of dirt had been thrown upon the mound," reported the *New York World* on April 15, 1914. "Then Horowitz's father fell over the grave, crying: 'My heart is broken. He was a good boy and a good son.'"

Lefty Louie was buried in Mount Hebron Cemetery, Flushing, that same day. His interment was as disorderly as that of Gyp the Blood. The dead man's wife fainted on her arrival at the undertaker's and then lapsed into hysterics, delaying the cortege by twenty minutes.

Dago Frank Cirofici, meanwhile, was interred on April 15. Anxious to avoid the scenes of chaos that had marred the funerals of Rosenberg and Horowitz, his family abandoned plans for a public funeral and held a simple service in their home instead. That did not stop an unruly crowd from assembling outside the family's "little frame dwelling" on East 187th Street, and when a neighbor's porch collapsed under the weight of sightseers, "a panic was only narrowly averted." Five carriages were required to carry flowers to the cemetery. *World*, Apr. 16, 1914.

RELEASE OF THE FOUR GAMBLERS Accounts of the release of the gamblers differ; several newspapers state that Vallon left separately through a side door and the other two men slunk off in taxis with the blinds drawn low. *New York World*, *American*, and *Sun*, Nov. 22, 1912; Klein, pp. 243–45; my quotation comes from Logan, p. 218.

GAMBLERS ON BROADWAY Klein, pp. 430–31.

HELEN'S MEETING WITH SCHEPPS Logan, pp. 299–300.

MARTIN MANTON *New York Herald* and *Globe and Mail*, May 14, 1914; *Dictionary of American Biography* supplement 13.

"MAINLY AN OFFICE-SHARING ARRANGEMENT" Logan, p. 253.

WILLIAM SULZER Klein, pp. 431–32; Jacob Friedman, *The Impeachment of Governor William Sulzer*, pp. 15–72.

BECKER'S DEMEANOR *New York Herald*, Feb. 29, 1913; Logan, pp. 224–25.

IMPEACHMENT OF SULZER Friedman, op. cit., pp. 148–90.

MANTON'S NEW EVIDENCE *New York Herald*, Dec. 13, 1913.

BECKER "BRIBES" WITNESSES; POLICE RAISE DEFENSE FUND Logan, p. 255.

DECLINE AND FALL OF BIG TIM SULLIVAN *New York Times*, Sept. 14, 15, and 30, and *Sun* and *World*, Sept. 16, 1913; Klein, p. 340; Daniel Czitrom, "Underworlds and Underdogs: Big Tim Sullivan and Metropolitan Politics in New York, 1889–1913," *Journal of American History* 78 (1991), p. 558.

COMMODORE DUTCH Joseph Mitchell, *McSorley's Wonderful Saloon*, pp. 131–32.

COURT OF APPEALS DECISION 210 NY, pp. 289–366; *New York Times*, Feb. 25, and *World*, Feb. 25 and 27, 1914; Klein, pp. 220–46; Logan, pp. 234–47.

"FROM A HUNDRED SLITTED WINDOWS . . ." *New York World*, Feb. 27, 1914.

RETRIAL *New York Times*, *World*, and *American*, May 5, 12, 14, and 19, 1914; *Sun*, May 19 and 23, 1914; Herbert Mitgang, *The Man Who Rode the Tiger*, pp. 102–105; Klein, pp. 247–332; Logan, pp. 254–76.

MARSHALL'S EVIDENCE *New York Times*, *Herald*, and *World*, May 19, 1914; Klein, pp. 290–314.

12. DEATH-HOUSE

RETRIALS AND MISTRIALS *New York Sun*, May 23, 1914.

POSSIBLE VERDICTS Ibid.

MOB; DEATH-HOUSE CELL "My Story, by Mrs. Charles Becker," *McClure's Magazine*, Sept. 1914, p. 43; Logan, p. 275.

THOMAS MOTT OSBORNE Rudolph Chamberlain, *There Is No Truce*, pp. 28, 34, 149, 181, 193–94, 213, 229, 235–36, 241–60, 264–74, 284, 294–95, 298, 327.

OSBORNE AND BECKER Ibid., pp. 304–6.

RELIGIOUS CONVERSION The date of the conversion is not certain, but Andy Logan puts it during the summer of 1913. Becker gave his religion as "Catholic" after his second trial a few months later (*New York Sun*, May 23, 1914). As for his influences, Becker's mother was a member of the Roman church, and his wife was nominally an Irish Catholic but in practice was not religious and was not a churchgoer. Helen's experiences during her husband's trials and failed appeals made her if anything an atheist, leaving Father Cashin—and Becker's own terminal predicament—as the most likely reasons for the policeman's embracing of the Catholic faith. "My Story," pp. 43–44; Logan, pp. 222–23, 235–36.

READING MATTER Among the effects disposed of by Becker just before his execution were copies of Theodore Roosevelt's *Through the Brazilian Wilderness* and a book on the Panama Canal. *New York Times*, July 29, 1915.

LETTERS Becker to Gus Neuberger, Dec. 8, 1912; Becker to Mary Weyrauch, Apr. 3, 1913, both MBC; "My Story," p. 43.

BECKER'S MOTHER Her condition was reported in the *Sullivan County Record*, Oct., 31, 1912.

"QUEEN OF MY HEART . . ." Letter dated June 19, 1914, reprinted in "My Story," p. 37. "I TRY . . ." Ibid p. 43.

OLINVILLE AVENUE Ibid., p. 36; Logan, p. 276.

"ANOTHER BAD TIME" "My Story," p. 42.

WHITMAN'S POLITICAL CAREER For Whitman's gubernatorial campaign and presidential ambitions, see *Dictionary of American Biography* supplement 4 (1946–50), pp. 885–86; Logan, pp. 278–80; Allen Steinberg, "The Becker Case and American Progressivism" in Amy Gilman Srebnick and René Lévy (eds.), *Crime and Culture*, p. 81.

WHITMAN'S DRINKING Logan pp. 316, 336; *Dictionary of American Biography* supplement 4 (1946–50), pp. 885–86.

MARSHALL'S RETRACTION *Philadelphia Evening Ledger*, Feb. 13, 1915; New York *Reports*, 215 NY, pp. 159–60; Klein, pp. 293–314. Klein notes in conclusion that when, in 1919, Marshall was arrested once again, on a charge of extortion, the lawyer who represented him was Frederick Groehl.

BECKER'S SECOND APPEAL Klein, pp. 332–33. Logan, pp. 283–89, advances a detailed analysis of the voting patterns of the court of appeals and uses her knowledge of state politics to convincingly explain them.

"FRANTIC AND FUTILE ANGER" Logan, p. 285.

BRIDGEY WEBBER'S VIEWS *New York Globe and Mail*, May 18, 1915.

BECKER'S ACCOUNT AND APPLEBAUM'S CORROBORATION Klein, pp. 342–87, 408–15; Logan, pp. 299–306. Klein adds that Applebaum told him that he was at the Capitol in Albany a few days before Becker's execution and passed on the details of these conversations then to Whitman, who unsurprisingly failed to act on them.

"APPLEBAUM HAD FELT UNABLE . . ." In fact, Applebaum said, he had had a conference with Lieutenant John Becker, the condemned man's brother, shortly before the second trial, expressed a willingness to testify, and even suggested that Becker retain a lawyer friend of his as his trial attorney. For some unknown reason, this offer was never taken up. Klein, pp. 414–15.

LAST LEGAL EFFORTS Klein, pp. 333–41; Logan, p. 307.

"DENIED, DENIED" *New York Sun*, July 29, 1912.

"Die like a man" *New York Times*, July 29, 1915.

Leo Frank case Robert Seitz Frey and Nancy Thompson, *The Silent and the Damned*, pp. 85–89.

Helen Becker's appeal *New York Herald*, July 30, 1915; Logan, pp. 310, 316–17.

Sing Sing prepares *New York Times*, July 19, 1915; Logan, pp. 308, 320.

Statements of press and lawyers *New York Times*, July 29 and 31, and *American* and *World*, July 31, 1915; Logan, pp. 317–18.

Becker prepared for death *New York Times*, *World*, and *Sun*, July 29, 1915.

Last letters Klein, pp. 388–95, 399.

Relatives; "Rock of Ages" *New York Times*, July 30, 1915.

Helen Becker's journey Ibid. and *Sun* and *World*, July 30, 1915.

History of electrocution John Laurence, *A History of Capital Punishment*, pp. 64–68.

The execution *New York World, Sun Times*, and *American*, July 31, 1915. The executioner's name was John Hilbert; he remained in the job until 1926 but became progressively more morose and depressed by it, finally resigning unexpectedly on the night before two more men were due to go to the chair. Hilbert was subsequently found dead, a suicide who had shot himself in the head.

Becker's autopsy *New York Sun, American*, and *Journal*, July 31, 1915; Logan, p. 323.

Epilogue

Rothstein at Jack's There is no contemporary authority for this oft-told story. It first appeared in Donald Henderson Clarke's *In the Reign of Rothstein*, p. 31. Clarke knew Rothstein and had the story from several of the men present at the time, however, so it may be accepted as probably accurate. Jack's stood on the corner of West Forty-third Street and Sixth Avenue and was—adds Herbert Asbury in *Gangs of New York*, p. 312—"famous for its Irish bacon and its flying wedge of waiters who ejected obstreperous customers with a minimum of motion and a maximum of efficiency."

Body brought back to New York The hearse's journey to and from Ossining had been fraught. The vehicle broke down five times on the way up from New York City—"tire trouble" was blamed—and once on the way back, taking a total of eleven hours to complete the round-trip. Becker's body made the journey in a cheap, black-painted wooden coffin provided by the state. *New York Journal*, July 30; *Tribune* and *World*, July 31, 1915.

VISITORS *New York Sun*, Aug. 1, 1915; Logan, pp. 325–26.

MRS. BECKER AND THE SILVER PLATE As the papers of the time noted, there was a precedent for this. When, more than two decades earlier, a prisoner named Carlyle Harris was executed for the murder of his wife, his mother had a plate inscribed with the words "Murdered by New York State" screwed to his coffin. In Harris's case the plate remained on the coffin and he was buried with it. *New York Times*, Aug. 2; *World*, Aug. 1 and 2; *American*, Aug. 2 and 3; *New York Sun*, Aug. 2, 1915.

BECKER'S FUNERAL An estimated eight-tenths of the vast crowd were women, the *World* reported, noting, too, that Becker was buried with the photograph of his wife that he had worn to his execution tucked into an inside pocket of his suit. *New York American* and *Sun*, Aug. 2; *New York World*, Aug. 2 and 3; *Sullivan County Record*, Aug. 8, 1915; Logan, pp. 326–27.

A SECOND SPASM OF REFORM It would be misleading to attribute all these changes solely to reaction to the Becker case. The impeachment of Governor Sulzer certainly aroused a statewide fury that turned more voters against the Democratic candidates for office than the murky uncertainties of the Rosenthal affair could ever do. But within the confines of New York City, the impact of Becker's arrest, trials, and conviction was considerable. Levine, p. 14; Oliver Allen, *The Tiger*, pp. 223–27; Lately Thomas, *The Mayor Who Mastered New York*, pp. 484, 491; Gustavus Myers, *The History of Tammany Hall*, pp. 387–91.

COMMISSIONER WOODS Woods was a former *New York Sun* reporter and an English instructor who had once taught Roosevelt's children. He was first appointed a deputy commissioner of police by Theodore Bingham in 1907. A few years later, he cemented his position and considerably enhanced his social status by marrying J. P. Morgan's granddaughter. Levine, pp. 373–81; James Lardner and Thomas Reppetto, *NYPD*, p. 143; Gabriel Chin, *New York City Police Corruption Investigation Commissions, 1894–1994* II, p. x; Lewis Valentine, *Night Stick*, pp. 34–35; Edwin Lewison, *John Purroy Mitchel*, pp. 117–21.

"YOU HAVE SHOWN US . . ." Cited in Levine, p. 380.

CURRAN COMMITTEE See *The Report of the Special Committee of the Board of Aldermen of the City of New York Appointed August 5, 1912, to Investigate the Police Department*, pp. 1–5; Henry Curran, *Pillar to Post*, pp. 162–70, 173–74.

MITCHEL VOTED OUT Though the mayor was criticized for his personal conduct—unlike his predecessor, Gaynor, he enjoyed the New York social scene—the principal issue in the campaign was education. Mitchel had backed a new program of vocational education, which Tammany used to accuse him of denying immigrants the right to the best schooling. He lost overwhelmingly.

CONFIDENTIAL SQUAD SHUT DOWN The fate of the squad's officers was all too predictable. Transferred to Brooklyn and given unpleasant desk duty, Lewis Valentine spent the next eight years in internal exile, suffering incessant hazing from his colleagues. Valentine, op. cit., p. 37.

THE DECLINE OF TAMMANY HALL Thomas Henderson, *Tammany Hall and the New Immigrants*, pp. 4–5, 9–15, 42–46, 93, 99, 115–19, 121.

TAMMANY AND GRAFT Ibid., pp. 97–98; Nancy Weiss, *Charles Francis Murphy, 1858–1924*, p. 59; Allen, op. cit., pp. 212–13.

ROTHSTEIN David Pietrusza, *Rothstein*, pp. 4, 91–100, 147–92, 195–203; Leo Katcher, *The Big Bankroll*, pp. 91–101, 349. Rothstein's murder, incidentally, occurred within the boundaries policed by the same West Forty-seventh Street precinct house where Herman Rosenthal's body had been brought sixteen years earlier and was recorded in the same police blotter. Meyer Berger, *The Eight Million*, pp. 140–41.

SWOPE Allan Lewis, *Man of the World: Herbert Bayard Swope*, pp. ix–x, 43, 223, 287; E. J. Kahn, *The World of Swope*, pp. 20, 25, 26, 149, 152–53, 331, 378, 475.

DECLINE OF THE SULLIVANS *New York Times*, Dec. 26, 1913; Alvin Harlow, *Old Bowery Days*, pp. 517–22, 535–36. It is true that Christy Sullivan went on to serve a lengthy stint in Congress on behalf of his old constituency, returning in 1937 to become the chief of Tammany Hall. But he accomplished little or nothing in either role. Allen, op. cit., p. 257.

THE OCCIDENTAL The hotel is still there and still in use, though nowadays it is known as the Sohotel Privilege—a low-budget place with a varied clientele and plenty of activity in the lobby after dark.

WHITMAN'S TERM AS GOVERNOR AND LATER LIFE No study devoted to Whitman's administration exists. My passage is based on the entry for Whitman (by Andy Logan) in the *Dictionary of American Biography*, supplement 4 (1946–50), pp. 884–86; Klein, p. 423; Herbert Mitgang, *The Man Who Rode the Tiger*, pp. 117–22; Logan, pp. 333–38; Rudolph Chamberlain, *There Is No Truce*, p. 347; and Whitman's *New York Times* obituary, March 30, 1947.

"EVEN THE SOBER TIMES . . ." *New York Times*, July 24, 1915.

JACOB LUBAN "This," Luban wrote to a friend, "is the biggest commutation ever handed down in this State, or in any other State. . . . Now you understand that during my thirteen months [in jail] I have used my friends all I possibly could." Luban's letter was discovered by Henry Klein when he searched through the district attorney's files relating to the Becker case. Klein, p. 115.

JOHN GOFF See the *Dictionary of American Biography* p. 7, pp. 359–60.

SAMUEL SEABURY Mitgang, op. cit., pp. 107–8, 181–82, 188, 203–300, 363–66; Allen, op. cit., pp. 242–59.

SULLIVAN, COCKRAN, MCINTYRE, MOSS, STRYKER, AND MANTON James McCurrin, *Bourke Cockran*, pp. 292–302, 321–22; Logan, pp. 281–82, 332–33; *Dictionary of American Biography* supplement 13, pp. 279–80; Lloyd Stryker, *The Art of Advocacy*, pp. 285–96.

RHINELANDER WALDO *New York Times*, Aug. 14, 1927.

JOHN BECKER Mary Becker, personal communication, Nov. 28, 2004, author's files.

MAX SCHMITTBERGER AND CLUBBER WILLIAMS Previous writers on the Becker case have never agreed on Williams's financial position or the date of his death, some stating that he died a millionaire as early as 1910. In fact, Clubber died on March 31, 1917; a report on the appraisal of his estate, revealing his poverty and giving this as the date of his death, appeared in the *New York Times*, Jan. 30, 1918. For Schmittberger's career and later life, see the *Times* of March 14, 1909; Lincoln Steffens, *The Autobiography of Lincoln Steffens* I, 278, 284; Augustine Costello, *Our Police Protectors*, p. 558; Logan, p. 330.

WINFIELD SHEEHAN Logan, pp. 59, 319, 330.

THOMAS MOTT OSBORNE Chamberlain, op. cit., pp. 328, 362, 367, 404, 412.

LIBBY AND SHAPIRO Shoenfeld Story #121, Magnes Papers P3/1782, Central Archives for the History of the Jewish People, Jerusalem.

"INFAMOUS GRAY PACKARD" The Rosenthal "death car" was purchased from Libby and Shapiro by a company that used it to chauffeur tourists around the main sites made famous by the Becker case. Logan, p. 220.

VALLON, SCHEPPS, MARSHALL, WEBBER, AND ROSE *New York Times*, June 17, 1913, and Nov. 26, 1941; Meyer Berger, "The Becker Case: View of 'The

System,' " *New York Times Magazine*, Nov. 11, 1951, pp. 65–66; Klein, pp. 430–31; Logan, pp. 225–28, 248, 266, 286, 299, 333; Jonathan Root, *The Life and Bad Times of Charlie Becker*, pp. 227, 231. Bridgey Webber died, of complications resulting from a burst appendix, on the twenty-first anniversary of Becker's execution: July 30, 1936; *New York Times*, July 31, 1936. Rose died in Roosevelt Hospital, Manhattan, on October 4, 1947; a short obituary appeared in the *New York Times*, Oct. 9, 1947.

CHICAGO MAY May Sharpe, *Chicago May: Her Story*, pp. 56, 135–41, 336; Eddie Guerin, *Crime*, pp. 158–279; James Morton, *Gangland: The Early Years*, pp. 211–12, 217 and n, 221. Guerin's escape, incidentally, was from the French prison camp at Moroni, on the mainland of French Guinea, not from Devil's Island itself.

LETITIA, PAUL, HOWARD, AND CHRISTOPHER BECKER *New York World*, July 30, 1912; *Sullivan County Record*, Aug. 8, 1915; Humboldt and Washoe County censuses, Nevada, for 1920; *American Sociological Review*, Dec. 1960. Details of Howard's personality and the "difficulty" of other members of the family are from Howard S. Becker to Mary Becker, e-mail, undated, and Mary Becker to Howard S. Becker, e-mail, undated, MBC; details of Christopher Becker's interment are from the author's visit to the cemetery at Callicoon Center, October 2004. Christopher Becker died in a house fire in March 1994, and it would appear that his collection of Becker material was destroyed in the same blaze.

MRS. ZELIG'S BENEFIT Shoenfeld story #272, Jan. 6, 1913, Magnes Papers P3/1786. Henrietta Young seems to have left New York for Boston soon afterward. At the end of February 1913, a bail bondsman named Henry Friedman was jailed in that city for the theft of $600 from her. This implies she must have been arrested there. *Fitchburg Daily Sentinel* [MA], Feb. 28, 1913.

HUMPTY JACKSON Luc Sante, *Low Life*, pp. 218–19.

LATER LIFE OF LILLIAN ROSENTHAL Berger, op. cit., p. 65.

LATER LIFE OF HELEN BECKER Ibid., p. 66; Logan, p. 331; Klein, p. 407. She was buried—under her maiden name—in the same grave as her husband; grave photos in MBC.

"I PREFER TO REMAIN A WIDOW" Root, op. cit., p. 285.

"HE WAS NOT AN ANGEL . . ." *New York Herald*, July 31, 1915; Logan, p. 325.

BIBLIOGRAPHY

---

1. Archival sources

[A] Mary Becker collection (MBC)
Charles Becker letters and Becker family histories in a private archive
[B] New York Public Library
Andy Logan papers
[C] Central Archives for the History of the Jewish People, Jerusalem
Judah Leib Magnes Papers

2. Official papers

New York State Senate. *Report and Proceedings of the Senate Committee Appointed to Investigate the Police Department of the City of New York* [Lexow Committee]. In *Documents of the Senate of the State of New York*, vols. 9–13. Albany: James B. Lyon, 1895.

Special Committee of the Board of Aldermen. *The Report of the Special Committee of the Board of Aldermen of the City of New York Appointed August 5, 1912, to Investigate the Police Department* [Curran committee]. New York: n.p., 1913.

New York *Reports*, vols. 210, 215.

3. Unpublished theses

Bernstein, Rachel. *Boarding-House Keepers and Brothel Keepers in New York City, 1880–1910*. Ph.D. thesis, Rutgers University, 1984.

Gandal, Keith. *The Spectacle of the Poor: Jacob Riis, Stephen Crane and the Representation of Slum Life*. Ph.D. thesis, University of California at Berkeley, 1990.

Kaplan, Michael. *The World of the B'hoys: Urban Violence and the Political Culture of Antebellum New York City, 1825–1860*. Ph.D. thesis, New York University, 1996.

Levine, Jerald. *Police, Parties and Polity: The Bureaucratization, Unionization, and Professionalization of the New York City Police, 1870–1917*. Ph.D. thesis, University of Wisconsin, 1971.

Thale, Christopher. *Civilizing New York: Police Patrol, 1880–1935*. Ph.D. thesis, University of Chicago, 1995.

4. NEWSPAPERS AND PERIODICALS
(all published in New York City unless otherwise stated)

American
Brooklyn Daily Eagle
Daily Argus (Middletown, NY)
Daily Sentinel (Fitchburg, MA)
Evening Ledger (Philadelphia, PA)
Evening Post
Globe and Mail
Herald
Journal
McClure's Magazine
Morning Telegraph
Sullivan County Democrat (Callicoon, NY)
Sullivan County Record (Jeffersonville, NY)
Sun
Tageblat
Times
Tribune
World

5. PUBLISHED WORKS

Allen, Oliver. *The Tiger: The Rise and Fall of Tammany Hall*. Reading [MA]: Addison-Wesley, 1993.

Anbinder, Tyler. *Five Points: The 19th Century New York City Neighborhood that Invented Tap Dance, Stole Elections, and Became the World's Most Notorious Slum*. New York: The Free Press, 2001.

Anon. (ed.). *Report of the Citizen's Committee Appointed at the Cooper Union Meeting, August 12, 1912*. New York: n.p., 1913.

Asbury, Herbert. *Sucker's Progress: An Informal History of Gambling in America from the Colonies to Canfield.* New York: Dodd Mead, 1938.

————. *The Gangs of New York: An Informal History of the Underworld.* New York: Thunder's Mouth Press, 1998.

Astor, Gerald. *The New York Cops: An Informal History.* New York: Charles Scribner's Sons, 1971.

Benfey, Christopher. *The Double Life of Stephen Crane.* London: Andre Deutsch, 1992.

Berger, Meyer. *The Eight Million: Journal of a New York Correspondent.* New York: Columbia University Press, 1983.

Berman, Jay S. *Police Administration and Progressive Reform: Theodore Roosevelt as Police Commissioner of New York.* Greenwood [CT]: Greenwood Press, 1987.

Botkin, Benjamin (ed.). *New York City Folklore.* New York: Random House, 1956.

Brown, Henry Collins, *From Alley Pond to Rockefeller Center.* New York: E. P. Dutton, 1936.

Burns, Ric, and James Sanders, with Lisa Ades. *New York: An Illustrated History.* New York: Alfred A. Knopf, 1999.

Burrows, Edwin, and Mike Wallace. *Gotham: A History of New York City to 1898.* New York: Oxford University Press, 1999.

Chafetz, Henry. *Play the Devil: A History of Gambling in the United States from 1492 to 1950.* New York: Clarkson N. Potter, 1960.

Chamberlain, Rudolph. *There Is No Truce: A Life of Thomas Mott Osborne.* New York: Macmillan, 1935.

Chin, Gabriel (ed.). *New York City Police Corruption Investigation Commissions, 1894–1994,* 6 vols. Buffalo: W. S. Hein, 1997.

Christianson, Scott. *Condemned: Inside the Sing Sing Death House.* New York: New York University Press, 2000.

Clarke, Donald Henderson. *In the Reign of Rothstein.* New York: Grosset & Dunlap, 1929.

————. *Man of the World: Recollections of an Irreverent Reporter.* New York: Vanguard Press, 1950.

Cohen, Rich. *Tough Jews: Fathers, Sons, and Gangster Dreams.* New York: Simon & Schuster, 1998.

Costello, Augustine. *Our Police Protectors: A History of the New York Police.* Montclair [NJ]: Patterson Smith, 1972.

Crane, Milton (ed.). *Sins of New York*. New York: Bantam Books, 1950.

Curran, Henry. *Pillar to Post*. New York: Charles Scribner's Sons, 1941.

Czitrom, Daniel. "Underworlds and Underdogs: Big Tim Sullivan and Metropolitan Politics in New York, 1889–1913." *Journal of American History* 78 (1991).

DeArment, Robert. *Bat Masterson: The Man and the Legend*. Norman [OK]: University of Oklahoma Press, 1989.

Delmar, Viña. *The Becker Scandal: A Time Remembered*. New York: Harcourt, Brace & World, 1968.

Downey, Patrick. *Gangster City: The History of the New York Underworld 1900–1935*. Fort Lee [NJ]: Barricade Books, 2004.

Eliot, Marc. *Down 42nd Street: Sex, Money, Culture, and Politics at the Crossroads of the World*. New York: Warner Books, 2001.

English, T. J. *Paddy Whacked: The Untold Story of the Irish-American Gangster*. New York: Regan Books, 2005.

Fogelson, Robert. *Big City Police*. Cambridge [MA]: Harvard University Press, 1977.

Frey, Robert Seitz, and Nancy Thompson. *The Silent and the Dammed: The Murder of Mary Phogan and the Lynching of Leo Frank*. New York: Cooper Square Press, 2002.

Fried, Albert. *The Rise and Fall of the Jewish Gangster in America*. New York: Columbia University Press, 1993.

Friedman, Jacob. *The Impeachment of Governor William Sulzer*. London: P. S. King & Son, 1939.

Fryckstedt, Olov. "Stephen Crane in the Tenderloin." *Studia Neophilologica* 34 (1962).

Garland, Hamlin. *Roadside Meetings*. London: John Lane, 1931.

Gilfoyle, Timothy. *City of Eros: New York City, Prostitution, and the Commercialization of Sex, 1790–1920*. New York: W. W. Norton, 1992.

Goren, Arthur. *New York Jews and the Quest for Community: The Kehillah Experiment, 1908–1922*. New York: Columbia University Press, 1970.

Graham, J. S. *The Callicoon Historian: A Narrative of Leading Events in the History of the Delaware Valley, from the Earliest Times to the Present Day*. Hancock [NY]: Herald Press, 1892.

Green, Horace. *The Log of a Noncombatant*. New York: Houghton Mifflin, 1915.

Guerin, Eddie. *Crime: The Autobiography of a Crook.* London: John Murray, 1928.

Hammack, David. *Power and Society: Greater New York at the Turn of the Century.* New York: Columbia University Press, 1999.

Harlow, Alvin. *Old Bowery Days: The Chronicles of a Famous Street.* New York: D. Appleton, 1931.

Henderson, Thomas. *Tammany Hall and the New Immigrants: The Progressive Years.* New York: Arno Press, 1976.

Hickey, John. *Our Police Guardians: History of the Police Department of the City of New-York* . . . New York: n.p., c. 1925.

Homberger, Eric. *The Historical Atlas of New York City.* New York: Owl Books, 1998.

Jeffers, H. Paul. *Commissioner Roosevelt: The Story of Theodore Roosevelt and the New York City Police, 1895–1897.* New York: John Wiley & Sons, 1994.

Joselit, Jenna. *Our Gang: Jewish Crime and the New York Jewish Community, 1900–1940.* Bloomington: Indiana University Press, 1983.

Kahn, E. J. *The World of Swope.* New York: Simon & Schuster, 1965.

Katcher, Leo. *The Big Bankroll: the Life and Times of Arnold Rothstein.* New York: Harper, 1959.

Kildare, Owen. *My Mamie Rose: The Story of My Regeneration.* New York: Baker & Taylor Company, 1903.

Klein, Henry. *Sacrificed: The Story of Police Lieut. Charles Becker.* New York: privately published, 1927.

Kouwenhoven, John. *Historical Portrait of New York: An Essay in Graphic History.* Garden City [NY]: Doubleday, 1953.

Lardner, James, and Thomas Reppetto. *NYPD: A City and Its Police.* New York: Henry Holt, 2000.

Laurence, John. *A History of Capitol Punishment.* New York: Citadel Press, 1960.

Lewis, Alfred. *Man of the World. Herbert Bayard Swope: A Charmed Life of Pulitzer Prizes, Poker and Politics.* Indianapolis: Bobbs-Merrill, 1978.

Lewison, Edwin. *John Purroy Mitchel: The Boy Mayor of New York.* New York: Astra Books, 1965.

Logan, Andy. *Against the Evidence: The Becker-Rosenthal Affair.* London: Weidenfeld & Nicholson, 1971.

McAdoo, William. *Guarding a Great City.* New York: Harper and Brothers, 1906.

430 BIBLIOGRAPHY

McCurrin, James. *Bourke Cockran: A Freelance in American Politics*. New York: Charles Scribner's Sons, 1948.

Maurer, David. *The Big Con: The Story of the Confidence Men*. New York: Anchor Books, 1999.

Mitchell, Joseph. *McSorley's Wonderful Saloon*. New York: Duell, Sloan & Pearce, n.d. (1943).

Mitgang, Herbert. *The Man Who Rode the Tiger: The Life and Times of Judge Samuel Seabury*. Philadelphia: J. B. Lippincott, 1963.

Morris, Edmund. *The Rise of Theodore Roosevelt*. London: William Collins, Sons & Co., 1979.

Morris, James McGrath. *The Rose Man of Sing Sing: A True Tale of Life, Murder and Redemption in the Age of Yellow Journalism*. New York: Fordham University Press, 2003.

Morris, Lloyd. *Incredible New York: High Life and Low Life of the Last 100 Years*. New York: Random House, 1951.

Morton, James. *Gangland: The Early Years*. London: Time Warner, 2004.

Myers, Gustavus. *The History of Tammany Hall*. New York: Boni & Liveright, 1917.

Nasaw, David. *The Chief: The Life of William Randolph Hearst*. London: Gibson Square Books, 2002.

Nevins, Frances. "Mr. Tutt's Jurisprudential Journey: The Stories of Arthur Train." In *Legal Studies Forum* 19 (1995).

O'Connor, Richard. *Hell's Kitchen: The Roaring Days of New York's Wild West Side*. Philadelphia: J. B. Lippincott, 1958.

———. *Courtroom Warrior: The Combative Career of William Travers Jerome*. Boston: Little, Brown, 1963.

Pietrusza, David. *Rothstein: The Life, Times and Murder of the Criminal Genius Who Fixed the 1919 World Series*. New York: Carroll & Graf, 2003.

Pink, Louis Heaton. *Gaynor: The Tammany Mayor Who Swallowed the Tiger; Lawyer, Judge, Philosopher*. New York: International Press, 1931.

Pitkin, Thomas. *The Black Hand: A Chapter in Ethnic Crime*. Totowa [NJ]: Littlefield, Adams & Co., 1977.

Quinlan, James. *History of Sullivan County*. Liberty [NY]: W. T. Morgans & Co., 1873.

Richardson, James. *The New York Police: Colonial Times to 1901*. New York: Oxford University Press, 1970.

Riis, Jacob. *How the Other Half Lives: Studies Among the Tenements of New York.* New York: Penguin, 1997.

Riordan, William. *Plunkitt of Tammany Hall: A Series of Very Plain Talks on Very Practical Politics.* Mattituck [NY]: Amereon House, 1982.

Rockaway, Robert. *But He Was Good to His Mother: The Lives and Crimes of Jewish Gangsters.* Jerusalem: Gefen Publishing House, 2000.

Root, Jonathan. *The Life and Bad Times of Charlie Becker: The True Story of a Famous American Murder Trial.* London: Secker & Warburg, 1961.

Rosen, Ruth. *The Lost Sisterhood: Prostitution in America, 1900–1918.* Baltimore: Johns Hopkins University Press, 1982.

Rovere, Richard. *Howe & Hummel: Their True and Scandalous History.* London: Michael Joseph, 1948.

Sante, Luc. *Low Life: Lures and Snares of Old New York.* London: Granta Books, 1998.

Sharpe, May. *Chicago May: Her Story.* New York: Macaulay Company, 1928.

Sloat, Warren. *A Battle for the Soul of New York: Tammany Hall, Police Corruption, Vice and the Reverend Charles Parkhurst's Crusade Against Them, 1892–1895.* Lanham [MD]: Cooper Square Press, 2002.

Stallman, Robert. *Stephen Crane: A Biography.* New York: George Brazillier, 1968.

———, and E. R. Hagemann (eds.). *The New York City Sketches of Stephen Crane, and Related Pieces.* New York: New York University Press, 1966.

Steffens, Lincoln. *The Autobiography of Lincoln Steffens,* 2 vols. New York: Harcourt, Brace & Company, 1931.

Stein, Leon. *The Triangle Fire.* Ithaca [NY]: ILR Press, 2001.

Steinberg, Allen. "The 'Lawman' in New York: William Travers Jerome and the Origins of the Modern District Attorney in Turn-of-the-Century New York." *University of Toledo Law Review* 34 (2003).

———. "The Becker-Rosenthal Murder Case: The Cop and the Gambler." In Frankie Bailey and Steven Chermak (eds.), *Famous American Crimes and Trials.* Westport [CT]: Praeger, 2004.

———. "The Becker Case and American Progressivism." In Amy Gilman Srebnick and René Lévy (eds.), *Crime and Culture: An Historical Perspective.* Aldershot [England]: Ashgate, 2005.

Stevens, John. *Sensationalism and the New York Press.* New York: Columbia University Press, 1991.

Stoddard, Theodore Lothrop. *Master of Manhattan: The Life of Richard Croker.* New York: Longman's Green, 1931.

Stout, Glenn, and Richard Johnson, *Yankees Century: 100 Years of New York Yankees Baseball.* New York: Houghton Mifflin, 2002.

Stryker, Lloyd. *The Art of Advocacy.* New York: Cornerstone Library, 1965.

Thomas, Lately. *The Mayor Who Mastered New York: The Life and Opinions of William J. Gaynor.* New York: William Morrow, 1969.

Valentine, Lewis. *Night Stick: The Autobiography of Lewis J. Valentine, Former Police Commissioner of New York.* New York: Dial Press, 1947.

Veiller, Bayard. *The Fun I've Had.* New York: Reynal & Hitchcock, 1941.

Weiss, Nancy. *Charles Francis Murphy, 1858–1924: Respectability and Responsibility in Tammany Hall Politics.* Northampton [MA]: Smith College, 1968.

Werner, M. K. *Tammany Hall.* Garden City [NY]: Doubleday, Doran, 1928.

Willemse, Cornelius. *Behind the Green Lights.* New York: Alfred A. Knopf, 1931.

———. *A Cop Remembers.* New York: E. P. Dutton, 1933.

Woollcott, Alexander. *While Rome Burns.* New York: Viking Press, 1934.

ACKNOWLEDGMENTS

Research conducted in various archives in New York City and Sullivan County was partly funded by a generous travel grant made by the Society of Authors, to whom I tender grateful thanks.

Satan's Circus would have been a much poorer book without the unstinting help I received from a number of people along the way. In Canada, Mary Becker of Kingston, Ontario—wife of Charley Becker's grandnephew, the late Todson Harvey Becker Jr.—made her private collection of letters, papers, and family histories freely available to me. In the United States, John Conway, historian of Sullivan County, kindly read and criticized the sections concerning Becker's youth in upstate New York, and Sandra Vossler of Humboldt County, Nevada, researched the later life of Becker's second wife, Letitia, on my behalf. I would also like to thank Diane Hess of the *Sullivan County Democrat*, Howard S. Becker, Susan J. Becker, and Rachel Kahan. In Jerusalem, Hadassah Assouline arranged access to Abe Shoenfeld's reports on Lower East Side criminals, archived among the Judah Magnes Papers. In New York and London, Sean Desmond, my vigorous new editor at Crown; Sara Holloway, my valued editor at Granta; and Patrick Walsh and Emma Parry, my agents—all strong supporters of the project—proffered invaluable advice and support. At home, Penny and Ffion made writing the book not merely possible but pleasurable. I can never properly express my gratitude for the sacrifice both have made on my behalf.

INDEX